【英汉对照全译本】

AN INQUIRY INTO THE NATURE AND CAUSES OF THE WEALTH OF NATIONS

## 国民财富的性质与原理

[英]亚当·斯密 著

赵东旭 丁 毅 译

(六)

中国社会科学出版社

# CONCLUSION

<small>The expence of defence and of maintaining the dignity of the sovereign should be paid by general contribution.</small>  The expence of defending the society, and that of supporting the dignity of the chief magistrate, are both laid out for the general benefit of the whole society. It is reasonable, therefore, that they should be defrayed by the general contribution of the whole society, all the different members contributing, as nearly as possible, in proportion to their respective abilities.

<small>But the expense of justice may be defrayed by fees of court,</small>  The expence of the administration of justice too, may, no doubt, be considered as laid out for the benefit of the whole society. There is no impropriety, therefore, in its being defrayed by the general contribution of the whole society. The persons, however, who give occasion to this expence are those who, by their injustice in one way or another, make it necessary to seek redress or protection from the courts of justice. The persons again most immediately benefited by this expence, are those whom the courts of justice either restore to their rights, or maintain in their rights. The expence of the administration of justice, therefore, may very properly be defrayed by the particular contribution of one or other, or both of those two different sets of persons, according as different occasions may require, that is, by the fees of court. It cannot be necessary to have recourse to the general contribution of the whole society, except for the conviction of those criminals who have not themselves any estate or fund sufficient for paying those fees.

<small>and expenses of local benefit ought to be defrayed by local revenue.</small>  Those local or provincial expences of which the benefit is local or provincial (what is laid out, for example, upon the police of a particular town or district) ought to be defrayed by a local or provincial revenue, and ought to be no burden upon the general revenue of the society. It is unjust that the whole society should contribute towards an expence of which the benefit is confined to a part of the society.

The expence of maintaining good roads and communications is,

# 结　论

　　社会的国防费用和维持一国元首的费用,都是为社会的一般利益而支出的。因此,按照推理,这两者应当由全社会一般的收入来开支,而社会所有个人的资助又必须尽可能地与他们各自的能力相称。

　　司法行政费用无疑是为全社会的一般利益而支出的。这种费用由全社会一般的收入来开支,就其本身来说并不不当之处。然而,国家之所以有必要进行这项费用支出,社会有些人多行不义,使得人们有必要向法院寻求补偿和保护;而最直接受益于法院的人又是那些由法院恢复其权利或维持其权利的人。因此,根据不同情况所要求的,司法行政费用由他们双方或其中一方支付,即由法院手续费来开支是很恰当的。除非罪犯自己没有足够财产或资金来支付这项手续费,否则,这项费用是不用社会全体来进行负担的。

　　为一个地方或一个省受益所发生的地方费用或省级费用(例如,为某个城市或某一地区所支出的警察费),应当由地方收入或省级收入来开支,而不应该由全社会的一般收入来开支。要社会全体承担由于社会局部利益而发生的开支,这样做是个公正的。

　　良好道路和交通设施无疑是有利于全体社会的,所以,其费

# 国民财富的性质与原理

The expense of roads may not unjustly be defrayed by general contribution, but better by tolls.

no doubt, beneficial to the whole society, and may, therefore, without any injustice, be defrayed by the general contribution of the whole society. This expence, however, is most immediately and directly beneficial to those who travel or carry goods from one place to another, and to those who consume such goods. The turnpike tolls in England, and the duties called peages in other countries, lay it altogether upon those two different sets of people, and thereby discharge the general revenue of the society from a very considerable burden.

The expense of education and religious instruction may also be defrayed by general contribution, but better by fees and voluntary contribution.

The expence of the institutions for education and religious instruction, is likewise, no doubt, beneficial to the whole society, and may, therefore, without injustice, be defrayed by the general contribution of the whole society. This expence, however, might perhaps with equal propriety, and even with some advantage, be defrayed altogether by those who receive the immediate benefit of such education and instruction, or by the voluntary contribution of those who think they have occasion for either the one or the other.

Any deficiencies in the revenue of institutions beneficial to the whole society must be made up by general contribution.

When the institutions or public works which are beneficial to the whole society, either cannot be maintained altogether, or are not maintained altogether by the contribution of such particular members of the society as are most immediately benefited by them, the deficiency must in most cases be made up by the general contribution of the whole society. The general revenue of the society, over and above defraying the expence of defending the society, and of supporting the dignity of the chief magistrate, must make up for the deficiency of many particular branches of revenue. The sources of this general or public revenue, I shall endeavour to explain in the following chapter.

# 结论

用由全社会的一般收入来开支,并无不当之处。不过,最直接地受益于这些费用的人,乃是往来于各地运输货物的商人和购买货物的消费者。所以,英格兰的道路交通规费和欧洲其他各国所称呼的路桥捐,完全是由这两种人负担;这样一来,社会一般人的负担就要减轻许多。

一国的教育设施和宗教设施肯定一样对整个社会来说是有益的,其费用由社会的一般收入来开支并无不妥之处。然而,这些费用如果由那些直接受到教育利益和宗教利益的人来支付,或者由那些自以为有受教育利益或宗教利益的必要的人自愿捐资来开支,大概也是一种妥当办法,甚至还会有一些好处。

凡是有利于全社会的各种公共设施或土木工程,如果不能全部由那些最直接受益的人来维护,或不是全部由他们来维护,那么,在大多数情况下,不足的数量就必须由全社会的一般收入来弥补。因此,社会的一般收入,除了国防费和君主供养费开支以外,还必须补充许多特殊收入部门的不足。一般收入或公共收入的源泉,我将在下一章再详细说明。

# CHAPTER II
# Of The Sources Of The General Or Public Revenue Of The Society

<small>All revenue comes from one of two sources: (1) property belonging to the sovereign; (2) the revenue of the people.</small>

The revenue which must defray, not only the expence of defending the society and of supporting the dignity of the chief magistrate, but all the other necessary expences of government, for which the constitution of the state has not provided any particular revenue, may be drawn, either, first, from some fund which peculiarly belongs to the sovereign or commonwealth, and which is independent of the revenue of the people; or, secondly, from the revenue of the people.

## Part I  Of The Funds Or Sources Of Revenue Which May Peculiarly Belong To The Sovereign Or Commonwealth

<small>The property may be in stock or land.</small>

The funds or sources of revenue which may peculiarly belong to the sovereign or commonwealth must consist, either in stock, or in land.

<small>Revenue from stock may be profit or interest.</small>

The sovereign, like any other owner of stock, may derive a revenue from it, either by employing it himself, or by lending it. His revenue is in the one case profit, in the other interest.

The revenue of a Tartar or Arabian chief consists in profit. It arises principally from the milk and increase of his own herds and flocks, of which he himself superintends the management, and is the

<small>Tartar and Arabian chiefs make profit from herds and flocks.</small>

principal shepherd or herdsman of his own horde or tribe. It is, however, in this earliest and rudest state of civil government only that profit has ever made the principal part of the public revenue of a monarchical state.

Small republics have sometimes derived a considerable revenue

# 第二章　论社会一般收入或公共收入的来源

一个社会的收入不仅要支付保卫社会和维持元首尊严的费用,还要为那些宪法中没有规定任何特殊收入来源的一切政府必要支出进行支付。这些社会收入可以来自于两方面。首先,来自于某些专属于君主或国家而与人民收入无关的资金;第二,来自于人民的收入。

> 所有的收入来自于两方面:(1)属于君主的财产;(2)人民的收入。

## 第一节　专属于君主或国家的资金或收入来源

那些专属君主或国家的资金或收入源泉,要么由资本、要么由土地构成。

> 财产可以是资本或者土地。

像所有的其他资产所有人一样,君主可以从使用他的资本或者贷出他的资本中获得收入。前者情况下他的收入为利润,后者情况下为利息。

> 来自于资本的收入可以是利润或者利息。

鞑靼或阿拉伯酋长的收入由利润构成。这种利润主要来自于牛羊的奶和增殖,他们自己监督管理牲畜,是本部落主要的牧羊人或者牧牛人。不过,这种利润构成王国公共收入的主要部分的现象只在最早、最原始的政府状态下才会发生。

> 鞑靼或阿拉伯酋长来自于羊

小共和国有时可以从商业经营的利润中获得相当可观的收

国民财富的性质与原理

Hamburg from a wine cellar and apothecary's shop, and many states from banks

from the profit of mercantile projects. The republic of Hamburgh is said to do so from the profits of a public wine cellar and apothecary's shop. ① The state cannot be very great of which the sovereign has leisure to carry on the trade of a wine merchant or apothecary. The profit of a public bank has been a source of revenue to more considerable states. It has been so not only to Hamburgh, but to Venice and Amsterdam. A revenue of this kind has even by some people been thought not below the attention of so great an empire as that of Great Britain. Reckoning the ordinary dividend of the bank of England at five and a half per cent. and its capital at ten millions seven hundred and eighty thousand pounds, the neat annual profit, after paying the expence of management, must amount, it is said, to five hundred and ninety-two thousand nine hundred pounds. Government, it is pretended, could borrow this capital at three per cent. interest, and by taking the management of the bank into its own hands, might make a clear profit of two hundred and sixty-nine thousand five hundred pounds a year. The orderly, vigilant, and parsimonious administration of such aristocracies as those of Venice and Amsterdam, is extremely proper, it appears from experience, for the management of a mercantile project of this kind. But whether such a government as that of England; which, whatever may be its virtues, has never been famous for good economy; which, in time of peace, has generally conducted itself with the slothful and negligent profusion that is perhaps natural to monarchies; and in time of war has constantly acted with all the thoughtless extravagance that democracies are apt to fall into; could be safely trusted with the management of such a project, must at least be a good deal more doubtful.

and post offices.

The post office is properly a mercantile project. The government advances the expence of establishing the different offices, and of buying or hiring the necessary horses or carriages, and is repaid with a large profit by the duties upon what is carried. It is perhaps the only

---

① See Memoires concernant les Droits & Impositions en Europe: tome i. page 73. This work was compiled by the order of the court for the use of a commission employed for some years past in considering the proper means for reforming the finances of France. The account of the French taxes, which takes up three volumes in quarto, may be regarded as perfectly authentic. That of those of other European nations was compiled from such informations as the French ministers at the different courts could procure. It is much shorter, and probably not quite so exact as that of the French taxes. [ The book is by Moreau de Beaumont, Paris, 1768-1769, 4 vols. , 4 to. The correct title of vol. i. is *Mémoires concernant les Impositions et Droits en Europe* ; vols. *ii – iv*, are *Mémoires concernant les Impositions et Droits*, 2de. Ptie. , *Impositions et Droits en France*. Smith obtained his copy through Turgot, and attached great value to it, believing it to be very rare. See Bonar, *Catalogue*, p. 10. ]

入。据说,汉堡共和国的收入就是来自于公共葡萄酒窖和药店①。而一个君主有空从事葡萄酒和药的买卖的国家,当然不会是很大的。对于更大的国家来说,公立银行的利润才是一种收入的来源。不仅汉堡是如此,威尼斯和阿姆斯特丹也都是如此。有些人认为,就连大不列颠这样大的帝国,也不能忽视这种收入。按照英格兰银行的普通股息为5.5%,资本金1078万镑计算,在支付管理费用后,据说每年剩余的纯利润还有592900镑。有人主张政府可以用3%的利息将这笔资本借来,自己经营这家银行,那么每年可以得到269500镑的纯利润。经验表明,要想经营这种商业项目,只有像威尼斯和阿姆斯特丹那种贵族政治下的有序、谨慎、节约的政府才最为适宜;而像英格兰这样的政府,尽管其优点很多,却从未以善于理财著称。它平时的行为,总是流于怠惰和疏忽造成的浪费,这或许是君主国家天生的吧。而在战时又常常流于一切民主国家所易犯的毫无打算的浪费。把这种事业让这样的国家来管理,它是否能胜任至少是一个很大的疑问。

邮局是一种合适的商业项目。政府事先垫付了建立各地邮局并购买或租赁必要马匹车辆的费用,进而从所运邮费中得到补偿获得巨大的利润。我相信,这或许是各种政府所能经营成功

---

① 参见《欧洲法律与赋税的记录》,第1卷,第73页。法国为了进行财政改革采取了一些适当的手段。这本书就是几年前宫廷命令编纂的以便成立的一个委员会使用的。这里面关于法国赋税的记录占了四开本的三卷,可以看作是完全可信地。关于欧洲其他国家是根据法国驻各国大使所得到的资料编纂的。它篇幅较短,可能不及法国赋税那样记录详细。该书作者为摩瑞欧,波芒,巴黎,1768~1769年。斯密从杜尔阁那里得到了这本书,极为重视它,认为这相当稀缺。参见波拿《书目》第10页。

国民财富的性质与原理

mercantile project which has been successfully managed by, I believe, every sort of government. The capital to be advanced is not very considerable. There is no mystery in the business. The returns are not only certain, but immediate.

<small>But generally princes are unsuccessful as traders.</small>   Princes, however, have frequently engaged in many other mercantile projects, and have been willing, like private persons, to mend their fortunes by becoming adventurers in the common branches of trade. They have scarce ever succeeded. The profusion with which the affairs of princes are always managed, renders it almost impossible that they should. The agents of a prince regard the wealth of their master as inexhaustible; are careless at what price they buy; are careless at what price they sell; are careless at what expence they transport his goods from one place to another. Those agents frequently live with the profusion of princes, and sometimes too, in spite of that profusion, and by a proper method of making up their accounts, acquire the fortunes of princes. It was thus, as we are told by Machiavel, that the agents of Lorenzo of Medicis, not a prince of mean abilities, carried on his trade. The republic of Florence was several times obliged to pay the debt into which their extravagance had involved him. He found it convenient, accordingly, to give up the business of merchant, the business to which his family had originally owed their fortune, and in the latter part of his life to employ both what remained of that fortune, and the revenue of the state of which he had the disposal, in projects and expences more suitable to his station. ①

<small>The two characters are inconsistent.</small>   No two characters seem more inconsistent than those of trader and sovereign. If the trading spirit of the English East India company renders them very bad sovereigns; the spirit of sovereignty seems to have rendered them equally bad traders. While they were traders only, they

---

① [ *Hist. of Florence*, bk. viii. , *ad fin.* ]

的唯一的商业项目了。进行垫付的资金并不多,也不存在商业秘密。资本的回报不仅是确定的,而且是立即就可以得到。

然而,君主们也常常从事许多其他的商业企业,他们也期望同别的个人一样,能够通过投资那些普通的商业部门来改善他们的财产状态。可是他们很少能够成功。君主经营管理事务中常常出现的浪费,就使得他们几乎不可能成功。君主的代理人常常以为自己的主人有无尽的财富,他们不关心以什么样的价格购入货物,以什么样的价格卖出产品,由一个地方运往别的地方的费用多少。他们通常过着与君主一样的奢侈浪费的生活;有时尽管浪费了,他们还能以适当的方法来弥补他们的账目,获得君主那样大的财产。因此据马基雅弗利说,麦迪斯的洛伦佐,并不是一个无能的君主,但他的代理人经营他的商业时情况就是如此。佛罗伦萨共和国[1]不得不几次偿还因他的代理人的浪费而负下的债务。因此,他发现放弃他的家族最初赖以发家的商业事业是更为适宜的选择。在其后半生,他把剩下的财产和他所能支配的国家收入,用在了更适合于其地位的事业和用途上。①

看来没有比商人与君主性格那样更加不相兼容了。如果说英格兰东印度公司的商人精神使其成为了非常差的君主,那么君主的精神,似乎也使他们成为了同样差的商人。当他们仅仅是商

---

① 《佛罗伦萨史》第八篇至最后。

[1] 佛罗伦萨(Florence),意大利中部一城市,位于比萨城东的阿尔诺河畔。最初为一片埃特鲁斯坎人的拓居地,后成为罗马的一个城镇,在意大利文艺复兴时期是一座在梅迪契家族统治下的强大城邦,并涌现出了以乔托、米开朗琪罗、列奥那多·达·芬奇、但丁和拉斐尔为代表的一批杰出艺术家。

国民财富的性质与原理

managed their trade successfully, and were able to pay from their profits a moderate dividend to the proprietors of their stock. Since they became sovereigns, with a revenue which, it is said, was originally more than three millions sterling, they have been obliged to beg the extraordinary assistance of government in order to avoid immediate bankruptcy. ① In their former situation, their servants in India considered themselves as the clerks of merchants: in their present situation, those servants consider themselves as the ministers of sovereigns.

<small>Treasure may be lent to subjects or foreign states.</small>

A state may sometimes derive some part of its public revenue from the interest of money, as well as from the profits of stock. If it has amassed a treasure, it may lend a part of that treasure, either to foreign states, or to its own subjects.

The canton of Berne derives a considerable revenue by lending a part of its treasure to foreign states; that is, by placing it in the public funds of the different indebted nations of Europe, chiefly in those of

<small>Berne lends to foreign states,</small>

France and England. The security of this revenue must depend, first, upon the security of the funds in which it is placed, or upon the good faith of the government which has the management of them; and, secondly, upon the certainty or probability of the continuance of peace with the debtor nation. In the case of a war, the very first act of hostility, on the part of the debtor nation, might be the forfeiture of the funds of its creditor. This policy of lending money to foreign states is, so far as I know, peculiar to the canton of Berne.

<small>Hamburg has a pawn-shop,</small>

The city of Hamburgh has established a sort of public pawn-shop, which lends money to the subjects of the state upon pledges at six per cent. interest. This pawn-shop or Lombard, as it is called, affords a revenue, it is pretended, to the state of a hundred and fifty thousand crowns, which, at four-and-sixpence the crown, amounts to 33, 750*l*. sterling.

The government of Pensylvania, without amassing any treasure, invented a method of lending, not money indeed, but what is equiva-

---

① [ Details are given above, but that is in a passage which appears first in ed. 3]

人时，他们经营商业是非常成功的，而且可以能从利润中给资本所有人支付适当的股息。但自从他们成为了君主，据说最初有了300万镑以上的收入，却不得不向政府请求额外援助，以避免将要发生的破产。① 在前种情况下，该公司在印度的人员，把自己看作商人的职员；而在现在的地位，这些职员却把自己看作了郡主的钦差。

一个国家有时会从货币的利息中得到公共收入的一部分，正如从资本中得到利润一样。如果国家积蓄了一笔财富，就可以将一部分财富，贷给外国或者贷给自己的子民。

> 可以给外国或子民。

伯尔尼郡在将一部分财富贷给外国中获得了巨大的收入，即通过将财富投资于欧洲各债务国主要是法国、英国的公债中获得收入。这种收入的安全性取决于：第一，所投资的公债安全与否，或者说管理这种公债的政府的信用如何；第二，与债务国继续保持和平的确定性和可能性如何。在战争状态时，债务国第一采取的敌对行为恐怕就是没收债权国的公债。据我所知将货币贷给外国是伯尔尼郡所特有的政策。

> 伯尔尼郡贷款给外国。

汉堡市设立有一种公家当铺[1]，当铺给有抵押品的人民提供贷款，利息为6%。这种当铺或者所谓的放债者可以给国家带来15万克朗的收入，按照每克朗4先令6便士来算，则合33750英镑。

> 汉堡有一种当铺。

宾夕法尼亚政府没有积累什么财富，但它发明了一种向人民贷款的方式，它不是借贷货币，而是借贷货币等价物。在向私人

---

① 详情上面已经给出，但这首先出现于版本三中的一段。
[1] 参见《欧洲法律与赋税的记录》，第1卷，第3页。

## 国民财富的性质与原理

<small>Pennsylvania lent paper money on land security.</small> lent to money, to its subjects. By advancing to private people, at interest, and upon land security to double the value, paper bills of credit to be redeemed fifteen years after their date, and in the mean time made transferrable from hand to hand like bank notes, and declared by act of assembly to be a legal tender in all payments from one inhabitant of the province to another, it raised a moderate revenue, which went a considerable way towards defraying an annual expence of about 4,500 *l*. the whole ordinary expence of that frugal and orderly government. The success of an expedient of this kind must have depended upon three different circumstances; first, upon the demand for some other instrument of commerce, besides gold and silver money; or upon the demand for such a quantity of consumable stock, as could not be had without sending abroad the greater part of their gold and silver money, in order to purchase it; secondly, upon the good credit of the government which made use of this expedient; and, thirdly, upon the moderation with which it was used, the whole value of the paper bills of credit never exceeding that of the gold and silver money which would have been necessary for carrying on their circulation, had there been no paper bills of credit. The same expedient was upon different occasions adopted by several other American colonies: but, from want of this moderation, it produced, in the greater part of them, much more disorder than conveniency.

<small>No great revenue can be derived from such a source.</small> The unstable and perishable nature of stock and credit, however, render them unfit to be trusted to, as the principal funds of that sure, steady and permanent revenue, which can alone give security and dignity to government. The government of no great nation, that was advanced beyond the shepherd state, seems ever to have derived the greater part of its public revenue from such sources.

<small>Revenue from land is much more important,</small> Land is a fund of a more stable and permanent nature; and the rent of public lands, accordingly, has been the principal source of the public revenue of many a great nation that was much advanced beyond the shepherd state. From the produce or rent of the public lands, the ancient republics of Greece and Italy derived, for a long time, the greater part of that revenue which defrayed the necessary expences of the commonwealth. The rent of the crown lands constituted for a long time the greater part of the revenue of the ancient sovereigns of Europe.

War and the preparation for war, are the two circumstances

贷款时，贷款人需要支付利息，并且以两倍价值的土地作担保。此证券规定15年偿还，在偿还期满以前，可以像银行钞票一样在市面流通，而且通过议会法律宣布成为本州流通的法定货币。对于像宾夕法尼亚政府这样一个节俭而有秩序的政府，政府从这个贷款中所得到的并不太多的收入，就可以支付其每年约4500英镑开支的大部分了。这种办法的成功要依三种不同的情况而定：第一，取决于对金银货币以外的其他交易媒介的需要，换言之，即取决于对必须要用金银货币向国外购买才能买到的消费品的需要；第二，取决于利用这种方法的政府的信用如何；第三，取决于运用这个方法的恰当程度。这种信用证券的全部价值，不能超过在没有这种证券时市场流通所需要的全部金银币的价值。同样的政策应用于几个美洲殖民地的不同的情形下，但由于分寸把握不好，大多数情况下结果是混乱多于便利。

不过，由于资本和信用的不稳定和不经久的本性，使得它们不能成为政府的主要收入来源。而只有那种确定的、稳定的、持久的收入，才能维持政府的安全与尊严。所以任何超过游牧阶段的大国政府，从来都不是通过这种来源来获得其大部分公共收入的。

土地是一种更加稳定和持久的资源。所以公共土地的地租就成了许多超过了游牧阶段的大国的主要公共收入来源。古代希腊和意大利各共和国长期以来就是从公有土地的产物或者地租中获取收入，其中的大部分都用于支付国家必要的开支。而对于古欧洲君主们来说，很长一段时间内，他们的大部分收入也是由王室土地的地租得来。

在现代社会中，对于所有的大国来说战争和战争的准备都是

国民财富的性质与原理

*especially when war cost little, as in ancient Greece and Italy,* which in modern times occasion the greater part of the necessary expence of all great states. But in the ancient republics of Greece and Italy every citizen was a soldier, who both served and prepared himself for service at his own expence. Neither of those two circumstances, therefore, could occasion any very considerable expence to the state. The rent of a very moderate landed estate might be fully sufficient for defraying all the other necessary expences of government.

*and in feudal times, when all expenses were small.* In the ancient monarchies of Europe, the manners and customs of the times sufficiently prepared the great body of the people for war; and when they took the field, they were, by the condition of their feudal tenures, to be maintained, either at their own expence, or at that of their immediate lords, without bringing any new charge upon the sovereign. The other expences of government were, the greater part of them, very moderate. The administration of justice, it has been shown, instead of being a cause of expence, was a source of revenue. The labour of the country people, for three days before and for three days after harvest, was thought a fund sufficient for making and maintaining all the bridges, highways, and other public works which the commerce of the country was supposed to require. In those days the principal expence of the sovereign seems to have consisted in the maintenance of his own family and houshold. The officers of his houshold, accordingly, were then the great officers of state. The lord treasurer received his rents. The lord steward and lord chamberlain looked after the expence of his family. The care of his stables was committed to the lord constable and the lord marshal. His houses were all built in the form of castles, and seem to have been the principal fortresses which he possessed. The keepers of those houses or castles might be considered as a sort of military governors. They seem to have been the only military officers whom it was necessary to maintain in time of peace. In these circumstances the rent of a great landed estate might, upon ordinary occasions, very well defray all the necessary expences of government.

In the present state of the greater part of the civilized monarchies of Europe, the rent of all the lands in the country, managed as they probably would be if they all belonged to one proprietor, would scarce perhaps amount to the ordinary revenue which they levy upon the people even in peaceable times. The ordinary revenue of Great Britain, for example, including not only what is necessary for defraying the current expence of the year, but for paying the interest of the public

第五篇 第二章

造成大部分必要开支的两种情况。但在古代的希腊和意大利各共和国,每个市民都是兵士,无论是服役还是准备服役,费用都要由自己来出。因此,这两种情况都不会给国家带来非常巨大的开支。一份不太大的地产的地租,就可能足以支付政府一切别的必要开支了。

其是意大利那样,战争耗费很少尤其像希腊和

在欧洲古代君主国家中,当时的风俗习惯使得大多数人民都对战争有充分的准备;一旦参加了战争,他们依据封建的土地使用权的条件,或者由他们自己负责生活费用,或者由直属领主出资维持,而无须给君主带来新的负担。政府的其他费用,它们大部分都非常有限。前面已经说过,司法行政不仅不会造成开支,而且还是收入的来源。乡村的劳动人民每年在收割以前和收割以后,都各提供三天的劳动。这种资源就足以建造维修一切桥梁、大道和其他国家商业所必需的公共建设。在当时君主的主要费用似乎就是他自身家庭及宫廷的维持费用。因此,他宫廷的官吏也即国家的大官。财政大臣为他收取地租,宫内大臣和内务大臣负责掌管他的家庭费用。君主的厩舍,则委任给治安大臣和典礼官来管理。君主所有的房舍,也都是修建为城堡的形式,似乎也就是他所拥有的主要要塞。这些房舍或者城堡的守护者,则可以被看作卫戍总督。他们似乎是唯一的在和平时期必须出资维持的军官。在这些情况下,一个大的地产的地租通常就可能完全可以支付所有必须的政府开支了。

在封建时期,所有的开支都很小

在目前欧洲大部分的文明君主国家里,即便全国所有的土地管理就像是全都属于一个人所有,其地租恐怕也达不到和平时期向人民征收的普通收入那样多。例如,大不列颠的普通收入,不仅要支付每年所必须支付的经常费用,还要支付公债利息,以及

— 1717 —

<small>The present rent of all the land in the country would not suffice for the ordinary expenditure</small> debts, and for sinking a part of the capital of those debts, amounts to upwards of ten millions a year. But the land tax, at four shillings in the pound, falls short of two millions a year. This land tax, as it is called, however, is supposed to be one-fifth, not only of the rent of all the land, but of that of all the houses, and of the interest of all the capital stock of Great Britain, that part of it only excepted which is either lent to the public, or employed as farming stock in the cultivation of land. A very considerable part of the produce of this tax arises from the rent of houses, and the interest of capital stock. The land-tax of the city of London, for example, at four shillings in the pound, amounts to 123,399 *l*. 6*s*. 7 *d*. That of the city of Westminster, to 63,092 *l*. 1 *s*. 5 *d*. That of the palaces of Whitehall and St. James's, to 30,754*l*. 6 *s*. 3 *d*. ① A certain proportion of the land-tax is in the same manner assessed upon all the other cities and towns corporate in the kingdom, and arises almost altogether, either from the rent of houses, or from what is supposed to be the interest of trading and capital stock. According to the estimation, therefore, by which Great Britain is rated to the land-tax, the whole mass of revenue arising from the rent of all the lands, from that of all the houses, and from the interest of all the capital stock, that part of it only excepted which is either lent to the public, or employed in the cultivation of land, does not exceed ten millions sterling a year, the ordinary revenue which government levies upon the people even in peaceable times. The estimation by which Great Britain is rated to the land-tax is, no doubt, taking the whole kingdom at an average, very much below the real value; though in several particular counties and districts it is said to be nearly equal to that value. The rent of the lands alone, exclusive of that of houses, and of the interest of stock, has by many people been estimated at twenty millions, an estimation made

---

① [ The figures are those of the Land Tax Acts. ]

清偿一部分公债等，每年达到1000万镑以上。然而所收的土地税，按每镑征收4先令来算，一年还不到200万镑。然而按照设想，这个所谓的土地税，征收的比例定为1/5。即不仅征收一切土地地租的1/5，而且征收一切房租、大不列颠所有资本利息的1/5，只有借贷给国家或者用于土地耕种的农业资本的那一部分资本才可以免征土地税。这个税收的很大部分是来自于房租和资本利息。例如，按每镑征收4先令来算，伦敦市的土地税，可以达到133399镑6先令7便士；威斯敏斯特市[1]的土地税为63092镑1先令6便士；怀特霍尔宫和圣詹姆斯两座宫殿的土地税为30754镑6先令3便士①。土地税的一定数额，是按照统一方式向王国所有其他的城市城镇征收的，它们几乎全都来自于房租以及商业资本和借贷资本的利息。因此根据这个估计，大不列颠所征收的土地税，即从所有土地的地租、所有房屋的租金、扣除贷给国家或者用于耕种土地的那部分资本以外的所有资本的利息中所征收的土地税收入，每年不超过1000万镑，也就是说甚至不超过英国在和平时期向人民征收的普通收入。毫无疑问，按照全国平均来看，大不列颠为征收土地税对各种收入所作的估计远远低于其实际价值，尽管据说在几个州和几个区，这个估计和实际价值非常接近。单是土地地租，还不计房租和资本利息，就有许多人估计每年总额应该为2000万镑。他们的估计在很大程度上是非常随

现在国内所有土地都浪费式地管理下，租费模式会很少，但国有土地如果置于普通地租支付不足以付通国家所有的支出，

---

① 这些数据源于《土地税法》。
[1] 威斯敏斯特(Westminster)，英格兰东南部大伦敦的一个市区，位于泰晤士河岸。它包括英国政府的主要官邸，尤其是沿着怀特霍尔街与唐宁街的官邸，以及如威斯敏斯特教堂和白金汉宫等有名的建筑物。

## 国民财富的性质与原理

<small>but if the whole of the country were under the extravagant management of the state, the rent would be much reduced,</small> in a great measure at random, and which, I apprehend, is as likely to be above as below the truth. ① But if the lands of Great Britain, in the present state of their cultivation, do not afford a rent of more than twenty millions a year, they could not well afford the half, most probably not the fourth part of that rent, if they all belonged to a single proprietor, and were put under the negligent, expensive, and oppressive management of his factors and agents. The crown lands of Great Britain do not at present afford the fourth part of the rent, which could probably be drawn from them if they were the property of private persons. If the crown lands were more extensive, it is probable they would be still worse managed.

<small>and the revenue of the people would be reduced by a still greater amount.</small> The revenue which the great body of the people derives from land is in proportion, not to the rent, but to the produce of the land. The whole annual produce of the land of every country, if we except what is reserved for seed, is either annually consumed by the great body of the people, or exchanged for something else that is consumed by them. Whatever keeps down the produce of the land below what it would otherwise rise to, keeps down the revenue of the great body of the people, still more than it does that of the proprietors of land. The rent of land, that portion of the produce which belongs to the proprietors, is scarce anywhere in Great Britain supposed to be more than a third part of the whole produce. If the land, which in one state of cultivation affords a rent of ten millions sterling a year, would in another afford a rent of twenty millions; the rent being, in both cases, supposed a third part of the produce; the revenue of the proprietors would be less than it otherwise might be by ten millions a year only; but the revenue of the great body of the people would be less than it otherwise might be by thirty millions a year, deducting only what would be necessary for seed. The population of the country would be less by the number of people which thirty millions a year, deducting always the seed, could maintain, according to the particular mode of living and expence which might take place in the different ranks of men among whom the remainder was distributed.

---

① [See on these estimates Sir Robert Giffen, *Growth of Capital*, 1889, pp. 89, 90.]

便的,我认为正如前者估计过低一样,这个又很可能估计的过高了①。但是,如果在目前的耕种状态下大不列颠所有的土地所提供的地租,还不超过 2000 万镑。那么,如果这些土地全都归一个人所有,而且他的代办人和代理人又管理的非常怠慢、浪费和专横,那么这些土地所提供的地租,不要说会不到 2000 万镑的 1/20,恐怕连 1/4 也无法提供。目前大不列颠王室领地所提供的地租,恐怕还不及如果这些属于私人的情况下所能提供的地租数额的 1/4。如果王室的土地更为广阔,恐怕他们的管理会更加糟糕。

　　大部分人民从土地上获取的收入,不是与土地的地租成比例,而是与土地的产物成比例。扣除留作种子之用的产物,一国每年所有的土地产物,都是由这些人民所消费,或者用来交换他们所消费的其他物品。凡是使土地产物降低到其本来可能达到的程度以下的东西,都会让人民大众的收入减少,而且他们减少的程度,要大于地主们收入减少的程度。大不列颠土地的地租,即生产物中属于地主的那部分产物,几乎没有一个地方会超过土地产物的 1/3。假设土地在一种耕种状态下一年可以提供 1000 万镑的地租,而在另一种耕种状态下一年可以提供 2000 万镑的地租。再假设这两种情况,地租都为年产物的 1/3,那么,地主的收入在前者要只比在后者每年少 1000 万镑,而人民大众的收入还扣除必须留作种子的以外,相比于后者一年却要少 3000 万镑。国家的人口也将随之减少,其人口减少的数目就是按照这 3000 万镑扣除种子后所能维持的人数,余额根据不同阶层人民特定的

<small>而人民收入减少的数目将会更大。</small>

---

① 这些估计参见罗伯特·吉芬爵士《资本的增长》,1889 年,第 89、90 页。

*The sale of crown lands would benefit both sovereign and people.*

Though there is not at present, in Europe, any civilized state of any kind which derives the greater part of its public revenue from the rent of lands which are the property of the state; yet, in all the great monarchies of Europe, there are still many large tracts of land which belong to the crown. They are generally forest; and sometimes forest where, after travelling several miles, you will scarce find a single tree; a mere waste and loss of country in respect both of produce and population. In every great monarchy of Europe the sale of the crown lands would produce a very large sum of money, which, if applied to the payment of the public debts, would deliver from mortgage a much greater revenue than any which those lands have ever afforded to the crown. In countries where lands, improved and cultivated very highly, and yielding at the time of sale as great a rent as can easily be got from them, commonly sell at thirty years purchase; the unimproved, uncultivated, and low-rented crown lands might well be expected to sell at forty, fifty, or sixty years purchase. The crown might immediately enjoy the revenue which this great price would redeem from mortgage. In the course of a few years it would probably enjoy another revenue. When the crown lands had become private property, they would, in the course of a few years, become well-improved and well-cultivated. The increase of their produce would increase the population of the country, by augmenting the revenue and consumption of the people. But the revenue which the crown derives from the duties of customs and excise, would necessarily increase with the revenue and consumption of the people.

*The revenue from crown lands costs the people more than any other.*

The revenue which, in any civilized monarchy, the crown derives from the crown lands, though it appears to cost nothing to individuals, in reality costs more to the society than perhaps any other equal revenue which the crown enjoys. It would, in all cases, be for the interest of the society to replace this revenue to the crown by some other equal revenue, and to divide the lands among the people, which could not well be done better, perhaps, than by exposing them to public sale.

生活方式和消费方式进行分配。

尽管在欧洲所有类型的现代文明国家中,没有一个是从国家拥有的土地的地租中得到大部分的公共收入;但在所有的大君主国家里,王室仍然拥有大片的土地。王室的领地主要都是森林,然而当你在这个林地走了几英里,也不一定能发现一棵树木。这种土地,从产物和人口方面而言,只能说是纯粹的浪费和国家的损失。如果这些欧洲大的君主国出售其皇室领地的话,就可以赚到相当可观的货币;如果用之以清偿国债,不仅可以收回担保品,而且由此所得的收入,也要比这种土地过去任何时候为皇室提供的收入多得多。在那些土地改良、耕种得极好,出售时可以得到丰厚的地租的国家,普遍来说是按 30 倍年租的价格来出售土地。而那些土地没有经过改良耕种,地租较低的国家,其土地可以按照 40 倍、50 倍或者 60 倍的年租出售。按照这个价格出售土地,君主可以赎回国债担保品,立即可以享受所带来的收入。而且在几年之中,还可以享有其他收入。原因在于,皇室领地一旦成为私人财产,在几年之内就会得到很好的改良和耕种。这样生产物的增加,人民的收入将会增加和消费将会扩大,国家的人口也将随之增加。而人民收入的增加和消费的扩大,君主从关税和消费税中得到的收入也必将增加。

出售皇室的领地既对君主有利,也对人民有利。

在所有文明的君主国家,皇室由其领地所获得的收入,看起来并不消耗人民的钱,但实际上,社会所付出的代价要远远比君主所享受到的其他任何同等收入所付出的代价大得多。所以为了社会的利益,不如用某些其他的收入去代替皇室的这种收入,而将皇室领地分配给人民,最好的方式可能莫过于公开出售了。

从皇室领地得到的收入比任何人出让付出的收入更多的代价。

|国民财富的性质与原理

Public parks etc., are the only lands which should belong to the sovereign.
　　　　Lands, for the purposes of pleasure and magnificence, parks, gardens, public walks, &c. possessions which are every where considered as causes of expence, not as sources of revenue, seem to be the only lands which, in a great and civilized monarchy, ought to belong to the crown.

The greater part of the sovereign's expense must be defrayed by taxes.
　　　　Public stock and public lands, therefore, the two sources of revenue which may peculiarly belong to the sovereign or commonwealth, being both improper and insufficient funds for defraying the necessary expence of any great and civilized state; it remains that this expence must, the greater part of it, be defrayed by taxes of one kind or another; the people contributing a part of their own private revenue in order to make up a public revenue to the sovereign or commonwealth.

## Part II  *Of Taxes*

Taxes may be intended to fall on rent, profit, or wages, or upon all three sorts of revenue.
　　　　The private revenue of individuals, it has been shewn in the first book of this Inquiry, arises ultimately from three different sources; Rent, Profit, and Wages. Every tax must finally be paid from some one or other of those three different sorts of revenue, or from all of them indifferently. I shall endeavour to give the best account I can, first, of those taxes which, it is intended, should fall upon rent; secondly, of those which, it is intended, should fall upon profit; thirdly, of those which, it is intended, should fall upon wages; and, fourthly, of those which, it is intended, should fall indifferently upon all those three different sources of private revenue. The particular consideration of each of these four different sorts of taxes will divide the second part of the present chapter into four articles, three of which will require several other subdivisions. Many of those taxes, it will appear from the following review, are not finally paid from the fund, or source of revenue, upon which it was intended they should fall.

There are four maxims with regard to taxes in general.
　　　　Before I enter upon the examination of particular taxes, it is necessary to premise the four following maxims with regard to taxes in general.
　　　　I. The subjects of every state ought to contribute towards the support of the government, as nearly as possible, in proportion to their respective abilities; that is, in proportion to the revenue which

那些为了供游乐与观赏之用的土地，如公园、花园和散步场所等，它们在各地都被认为会带来支出，而不会带来收入。这些似乎是在大的文明君主国家里应当属于皇室的唯一土地。

因此，公共资本和公共土地作为专属于君主或者国家的两种收入来源，是不适宜也不足以支付一个文明大国的必要费用的。必要费用的大部分，必须要靠这种或者那种赋税来保障。人民将自己的一部分私人收入，贡献出来作为君主或者国家的公共收入。

## 第二节　论赋税

本书第一篇已经表明，个人的私人收入，最终来自于三种不同的来源：地租、利润与工资。每种赋税最终必定是由这三种收入来源的这种或那种支付，或者无差异地由它们共同支付。我将尽我可能的对以下各点做最好的说明：第一，打算加于地租的赋税；第二，打算加于利润上的赋税；第三，打算加于工资上的赋税；第四，打算无差异地加于私人收入所有这三项收入来源的赋税。本章第二节将分为四项，分别对这四种赋税进行专门的考察，其中三项还要细分为若干细则。在后面的评论中将会看到，许多赋税开始打算是加在某项资金或者收入来源，但最后却不是由这项资金或者收入来源来支付。

在我着手考察每个特定赋税以前，必须预先论述有关一般赋税的下面四项原则。

第一，每个国家的国民应该尽可能的按照他们各自能力的比例为维持政府做出自己的贡献；也就是说要按照各自在国家保护下获

(1) equality, they respectively enjoy under the protection of the state. The expence of government to the individuals of a great nation, is like the expence of management to the joint tenants of a great estate, who are all obliged to contribute in proportion to their respective interests in the estate. In the observation or neglect of this maxim consists, what is called the equality or inequality of taxation. Every tax, it must be observed-once for all, which falls finally upon one only of the three sorts of revenue above mentioned, is necessarily unequal, in so far as it does not affect the other two. In the following examination of different taxes I shall seldom take much further notice of this sort of inequality, but shall, in most cases, confine my observations to that inequality which is occasioned by a particular tax falling unequally even upon that particular sort of private revenue which is affected by it.

(2) certainty, II. The tax which each individual is bound to pay ought to be certain, and not arbitrary. The time of payment, the manner of payment, the quantity to be paid, ought all to be clear and plain to the contributor, and to every other person. Where it is otherwise, every person subject to the tax is put more or less in the power of the taxgatherer, who can either aggravate the tax upon any obnoxious contributor, or extort, by the terror of such aggravation, some present or perquisite to himself. The uncertainty of taxation encourages the insolence and favours the corruption of an order of men who are naturally unpopular, even where they are neither insolent nor corrupt. The certainty of what each individual ought to pay is, in taxation, a matter of so great importance, that a very considerable degree of inequality, it appears, I believe, from the experience of all nations, is not near so great an evil as a very small degree of uncertainty.

(3) convenience of payment, III. Every tax ought to be levied at the time, or in the manner, in which it is most likely to be convenient for the contributor to pay it. A tax upon the rent of land or of houses, payable at the same term at which such rents are usually paid, is levied at the time when it is most likely to be convenient for the contributor to pay; or, when he is most likely to have wherewithal to pay. Taxes upon such consumable goods as are articles of luxury, are all finally paid by the consumer, and generally in a manner that is very convenient for him. He pays them by little and little, as he has occasion to buy the goods. As he is at liberty too, either to buy, or not to buy, as he pleases, it must be his own fault if he ever suffers any considerable inconveniency from such taxes.

得的收入的比例缴纳赋税维持政府。一个大国的支出对于该国的个人而言,就像是一宗大地产的管理费用对于该地产的所有佃户一样,佃户们应须按照各自在该地产上获得利益的比例来支付各自的管理费用。所谓赋税平等、不平等,就要看是否遵守这项原则。必须彻底地注意的是,如果任一赋税仅仅加在上面提到的三种收入之一的上面,而不影响其他两种收入的话,这种赋税必然是不平等的。在下面研究不同的赋税时,我将很少再更多地谈论这种不平等。在多数情况下,我将只讨论由于某特种赋税不平等地落在它所影响的特定私人收入上而引起的那种不平等。[1] 平等,

第二,每个人应当缴纳的赋税应当是确定的,而不是随意性的。缴纳的日期,缴纳的方法,缴纳的数额,都应当被所有的纳税人和其他的人了解得清清楚楚。如若不然,每个纳税人都多少会被征税者的权力所左右;对于他所讨厌的纳税人,征税者可能会加重赋税,或者以加税来恐吓征税者以勒索礼物或贿赂。赋税的不确定性,就会让这些本来就不受欢迎的人变得更为骄横、腐化,即便他们原本既不骄横、又不腐化。从所有国家的经验来看,我认为,在课税时每个人应当缴纳赋税的确定性是一件极为重要的事。一点点的不确定的危害也要远胜于很大程度的不平等的危害。[2] 确定性,

第三,所有赋税缴纳的时间和缴纳的方法,应该以纳税人最方便为原则去征收。征收地租税和房租税的时间,应通常在缴纳房租、地租的同一个时期去征收,这个时候对纳税人来说最为方便,或者说,在这时期他最容易有钱来缴税。对奢侈品这一类的消费品的赋税,最终要出消费者来支付,一般来说征收的方法对他也非常方便。当他购物时,就缴纳了相应的一点赋税。他有买东西或者不买东西的自由;如果因为他对这种赋税感到相当的不便,那[3] 缴纳赋税的方便性,

and (4) economy in collection,

IV. Every tax ought to be so contrived as both to take out and to keep out of the pockets of the people as little as possible, over and above what it brings into the public treasury of the state. A tax may either take out or keep out of the pockets of the people a great deal more than it brings into the public treasury, in the four following ways. First, the levying of it may require a great number of officers, whose salaries may eat up the greater part of the produce of the tax, and whose perquisites may impose another additional tax upon the people. Secondly, it may obstruct the industry of the people, and discourage them from applying to certain branches of business which might give maintenance and employment to great multitudes. While it obliges the people to pay, it may thus diminish, or perhaps destroy, some of the funds which might enable them more easily to do so. Thirdly, by the forfeitures and other penalties which those unfortunate individuals incur who attempt unsuccessfully to evade the tax, it may frequently ruin them, and thereby put an end to the benefit which the community might have received from the employment of their capitals. An injudicious tax offers a great temptation to smuggling. But the penalties of smuggling must rise in proportion to the temptation. The law, contrary to all the ordinary principles of justice, first creates the temptation, and then punishes those who yield to it; and it commonly enhances the punishment too in proportion to the very circumstance which ought certainly to alleviate it, the temptation to commit the crime. ① Fourthly, by subjecting the people to the frequent visits and the odious examination of the tax-gatherers, it may expose them to much unnecessary trouble, vexation, and oppression; and though vexation is not, strictly speaking, expence, it is certainly equivalent to the expence at which every man would be willing to redeem himself

---

① See *Sketches of the History of Man* [ 1774, by Henry Home, Lord Kames, vol. i. ] page 474 & seq. [ This author at the place quoted gives six 'general rules' as to taxation :
　1. 'That wherever there is an opportunity of smuggling taxes ought to be moderate. '
　2. 'That taxes expensive in the levying ought to be avoided. '
　3. 'To avoid arbitrary taxes. '
　4. 'To remedy' inequality of riches ' as much as possible, by relieving the poor and burdening the rich. '
　5. 'That every tax which tends to impoverish the nation ought to be rejected with indignation. '
　6. 'To avoid taxes that require the oath of party. ' ]

就是他自己的问题了。

第四，在设计所有赋税的征收时，应该是从人民那里取来的赋税应尽可能地与进入国库的收入相一致而不会超出太多。有四种情况可能使得一种赋税从人民那得来的要多于进入国库的：第一，征收赋税可能需要大量的官吏，他们的工资可能耗掉赋税的大部分，而且他们额外的津贴也是对人民的另一种额外负担。第二，赋税可能妨碍了人民的勤劳，使他们放弃从事那些可以给许多人提供生计和就业的事业。当逼迫民众去纳税时，就可能导致一些使人们易于去从事上述事业的基金缩减乃至于消亡。第三，对那些不幸运的逃税未遂者没收财物和其他惩罚措施往往会使其破产，因而社会也就失去了原本使用他们的资本所能带来的利益。不合理的赋税是对走私的巨大引诱。而逃税的惩罚又必然会与诱惑的程度成正比。这样的法律完全违反所有公平的一般原则，首先造成了逃税的诱因，然后又用严刑来惩罚逃税的人，并常常按照诱惑的大小来定刑罚的轻重，原本这种情况下应该减轻处罚的①。第四，征税者频繁的造访和烦人的稽查，会使得纳税人受到许多不必要的麻烦、困扰和压迫。尽管严格意义上讲，这种烦扰不会造成多少金钱上的损失，但肯定它是一种花费，因为人人都想设法来摆脱这种烦扰。正是由于这四种情况中的一种或者

（4）征收的经济性，

---

① 参见《人类历史纲要》，1774年，亨利·霍姆（凯姆斯勋爵），第1卷第474页及以下。霍姆在引证处给出了关于赋税的六项"一般原则"。即：1. 在有机会进行走私的地方，赋税应该是适度的。2. 应该避免征收费用高昂的赋税。3. 避免随意性的赋税。4. 通过减轻穷人的赋税，加重富人的赋税，来纠正富人愈富的不平等。5. 应该坚决地拒绝那些让国家变得贫困的所有赋税。6. 应当避免要求当事人宣誓的赋税。

from it. It is in some one or other of these four different ways that taxes are frequently so much more burdensome to the people than they are beneficial to the sovereign.

<small>which have recommended themselves to all nations.</small>   The evident justice and utility of the foregoing maxims have recommended them more or less to the attention of all nations. All nations have endeavoured, to the best of their judgment, to render their taxes as equal as they could contrive; as certain, as convenient to the contributor, both in the time and in the mode of payment, and in proportion to the revenue which they brought to the prince, as little burdensome to the people. The following short review of some of the principal taxes which have taken place in different ages and countries will show, that the endeavours of all nations have not in this respect been equally successful.

## Article I  Taxes Upon Rent.
## Taxes Upon The Rent Of Land

<small>A tax on the rent of land may be on a constant or variable valuation.</small>   A tax upon the rent of land may either be imposed according to a certain canon, every district being valued at a certain rent, which valuation is not afterwards to be altered; or it may be imposed in such a manner as to vary with every variation in the real rent of the land, and to rise or fall with the improvement or declension of its cultivation.

<small>If on a constant valuation it becomes unequal, like the British land tax.</small>   A land-tax which, like that of Great Britain, is assessed upon each district according to a certain invariable canon, though it should be equal at the time of its first establishment, necessarily becomes unequal in process of time, according to the unequal degrees of improvement or neglect in the cultivation of the different parts of the country. In England, the valuation according to which the different counties and parishes were assessed to the land-tax by the 4th of William and Mary was very unequal even at its first establishment. This tax, therefore, so far offends against the first of the four maxims above-mentioned. It is perfectly agreeable to the other three. It is perfectly certain. The time of payment for the tax, being the same as that for the rent, is as convenient as it can be to the contributor. Though the landlord is in all cases the real contributor, the tax is

另一种,使得赋税常常对人民更多的是种负担,这种负担远远超过了给君主带来的好处。

上述四项原则明显的公正性和实用性,使得它们或多或少地受到所有国家的关注。他们都尽其所知,让他们的赋税设计的尽量公平。尽可能地让纳税时间、纳税方式对纳税人更为确定和方便。让赋税与送交给君主的收入成比例,尽量减少人民的负担。但下面对于不同的年代和不同的国家的几种主要赋税的简短评述,将表明各国在这方面的努力并没有取得同样的成功。

<sub>这些原则已经受到所有国家重视的</sub>

## 第一项 地租税,即加在土地地租上的赋税

加在土地地租上的赋税可以按照一定的标准去征收,即要么对每个地区评定一定数额的地租,一旦确定后就不再更改;要么可以按照征税税额随着土地实际地租的变动而变动的方式征收,这种情况下随着土地耕种情况的改善或恶化赋税也相应地增加或减少。

<sub>地租的可以按照评定或者变动的去征收</sub>

像在英国那样征收的土地税,每个区就是基于一定的不变的标准来制定的税额。这种赋税赋,尽管在刚开始设立之初是公平的,但因为整个国家内各个地方对土地耕种的改良或者忽视程度的不均等,随着时间的推移必然会变得不平等。在英格兰,不同郡和不同教区的土地税是根据威廉和玛利四年法令评估设定的,在设立之初就是非常不公平的。所以,这种赋税违反上述四项原则的第一项原则,但它却是完全符合其他三项原则的。它是十分确定的,缴税的时间就是缴租的时间,这对于纳税人来说十分的便利。尽管在所有的场合,地主都是真正的纳税者,但税款通常

<sub>大颠地就像一如照的来税不样果征那等列土税,按定,评那不</sub>

commonly advanced by the tenant, to whom the landlord is obliged to allow it in the payment of the rent. This tax is levied by a much smaller number of officers than any other which affords nearly the same revenue. As the tax upon each district does not rise with the rise of the rent, the sovereign does not share in the profits of the landlord's improvements. Those improvements sometimes contribute, indeed, to the discharge of the other landlords of the district. But the aggravation of the tax, which this may sometimes occasion upon a particular estate, is always so very small, that it never can discourage those improvements, nor keep down the produce of the land below what it would otherwise rise to. As it has no tendency to diminish the quantity, it can have none to raise the price of that produce. It does not obstruct the industry of the people. It subjects the landlord to no other inconveniency besides the unavoidable one of paying the tax.

<small>Circumstances have made the constant valuation favourable to the British landlords, the country having prospered and rents risen,</small>  The advantage, however, which the landlord has derived from the invariable constancy of the valuation by which all the lands of Great Britain are rated to the land-tax, has been principally owing to some circumstances altogether extraneous to the nature of the tax.

It has been owing in part to the great prosperity of almost every part of the country, the rents of almost all the estates of Great Britain having, since the time when this valuation was first established, been continually rising, and scarce any of them having fallen. The landlords, therefore, have almost all gained the difference between the tax which they would have paid, according to the present rent of their estates, and that which they actually pay according to the ancient valuation. Had the state of the country been different, had rents been gradually falling in consequence of the declension of cultivation, the landlords would almost all have lost this difference. In the state of things which has happened to take place since the revolution, the constancy of the valuation has been advantageous to the landlord and hurtful to the sovereign. In a different state of things it might have been advantageous to the sovereign and hurtful to the landlord.

As the tax is made payable in money, so the valuation of the land is expressed in money. Since the establishment of this valuation the value of silver has been pretty uniform, and there has been no alteration in the standard of the coin either as to weight or fineness.

都是由佃户垫付的。只是地主在收取租金时允许在地租中扣除。与别的可以提供近似收入的赋税相比,这种赋税的征收只需要很少数量的官吏。由于各地区的税赋不会随着地租的增加而增加,所以君主无法分享到由于地主改良土地而产生的利润。的确有时这些改良会导致同地区内的其他地主的破产者。但由此所可能造成的某宗特定地产赋税的增加的程度是非常有限的,并不会阻碍土地的改良,也不会使土地的产量低于其应有的产量。因为土地产量没有减少的趋势,产品的价格也就没有了抬高的趋势,从而也就不会影响人民的勤劳。除了必须缴纳赋税外,并不会给地主带来任何别的不便。

不过,由于大不列颠所有的土地按照不变的评定缴纳土地税,地主们从这种恒久性得到的好处却主要归功于一些外部情况,而与赋税本身的性质无关。

这部分地归功于基本上大不列颠所有的县郡都是繁荣昌盛的,自从这种评定首次确定以来,几乎所有地产的租金都在持续上涨,鲜有跌落。这样,在按照目前地产的租金他们应付的赋税和按过去评定的他们实际支付的赋税之间,就产生了一种差额。地主们几乎都获得了这个差额的利益。如果国家的状况与此不同,由于耕种的恶化地租也在逐渐下降,那么地主们将几乎全部失去这份差额。自从革命以后,英国的状况就使得土地税的不变性有利于而不利于君主。如果情况不同,也可能会有利于君主,而不利于地主。

由于赋税是以货币支付的,所以土地的评定也是用货币来表示的。自从这种评定确定以来,银的价格就变得相当的稳定;铸币的标准在重量上或者成色上也没有什么改变。假如像美洲银

*and the value of money and silver remained uniform.*

Had silver risen considerably in its value, as it seems to have done in the course of the two centuries which preceded the discovery of the mines of America, the constancy of the valuation might have proved very oppressive to the landlord. Had silver fallen considerably in its value, as it certainly did for about a century at least after the discovery of those mines, the same constancy of valuation would have reduced very much this branch of the revenue of the sovereign. Had any considerable alteration been made in the standard of the money, either by sinking the same quantity of silver to a lower denomination, or by raising it to a higher; had an ounce of silver, for example, instead of being coined into five shillings and two-pence, been coined, either into pieces which bore so low a denomination as two shillings and seven-pence, or into pieces which bore so high a one as ten shillings and four-pence, it would in the one case have hurt the revenue of the proprietor, in the other that of the sovereign.

*The constancy of valuation might have been very inconvenient to one or other of the parties.*

In circumstances, therefore, somewhat different from those which have actually taken place, this constancy of valuation might have been a very great inconveniency, either to the contributors, or to the commonwealth. In the course of ages such circumstances, however, must, at some time or other, happen. But though empires, like all the other works of men, have all hitherto proved mortal, yet every empire aims at immortality. Every constitution, therefore, which it is meant should be as permanent as the empire itself, ought to be convenient, not in certain circumstances only, but in all circumstances; or ought to be suited, not to those circumstances which are transitory, occasional, or accidental, but to those which are necessary and therefore always the same.

*The French economists recommend a tax varying with the rent.*

A tax upon the rent of land which varies with every variation of the rent, or which rises and falls according to the improvement or neglect of cultivation, is recommended by that sect of men of letters in France, who call themselves the economists, as the most equitable of all taxes. All taxes, they pretend, fall ultimately upon the rent of land, and ought therefore to be imposed equally upon the fund which must finally pay them. That all taxes ought to fall as equally as possible upon the fund which must finally pay them, is certainly true. But without entering into the disagreeable discussion of the metaphysical arguments by which they support their very ingenious theory, it will sufficiently appear, from the following review, what are the taxes which fall finally upon the rent of the land, and what are those which fall finally upon some other fund.

矿发现以前的两个世纪那样，银的价格大幅上升，那么这种评定的不变性就可能会对地主产生很大的压力。而如果像在美洲银矿发现后的一个世纪里那样，银的价格明显跌落，那么同样的评定的不变性就会导致君主这一部分收入大大减少。还有，如果货币的标准发生了重大改变，同样数量银的面值降低或面值升高，例如，一盎司的银不是铸成5先令2便士，而是铸成2先令7便士或者10先令4便士，那么前者情况下将会损害地主的收益，而在后者情况下则会损害君主的利益。

货币的价值和白银的价值保持稳定。

可见，如果情况与实际正在发生的事情略有不同的话，这种评定的不变性，就可能会对纳税人或国家产生极大的不便。可是，在岁月的长河中，这种情况必然有发生的一天。尽管所有的帝国都与所有别的人为的事物一样，他们都试图能够千秋万代永存不朽，但迄今为止证明都是要消亡的。所以每种期望与帝国一样永久的制度，都应该力求不仅在某些特定情况下是便利的，而且应当在所有的情况下都是便利的。即制度不是为了去适应那些暂时的、偶然的或意外的情况，而是为了去适应那些必然的因而总是不变的情况。

评定的不变性可能会对当事人一方或另一方不利。

法国有一派自称为经济学家的学者，他们认为所有赋税中最公平的征税方式莫过于土地税随着地租的变化而变化，即随着耕种的改良或者荒废赋税也随之升降。他们宣称，由于所有的赋税最终都是落在土地的地租上，所以应该平等地对最后支付赋税的税源进行课税。所有的赋税应该尽可能平等地落在支付最终赋税的来源上，这点肯定是毫无争议的。但是他们用来支持他们这种非常微妙的学说却是形而上学的论证，我不打算就此做令人不悦地讨论。通过下面的评述，我们就会清楚地看到哪些赋税最终

法国经济学家建议采用随着地租的变化而变化的赋税。

# 国民财富的性质与原理

<small>In the Venetian territory rented lands are taxed 10 per cent. and lands cultivated by the proprietor 8 per cent.</small>

In the Venetian territory all the arable lands which are given in lease to farmers are taxed at a tenth of the rent. ① The leases are recorded in a public register which is kept by the officers of revenue in each province or district. When the proprietor cultivates his own lands, they are valued according to an equitable estimation, and he is allowed a deduction of one-fifth of the tax, so that for such lands he pays only eight instead of ten per cent. of the supposed rent.

<small>Such a land tax is more equal but is not so certain, and is more troublesome and expensive than the British.</small>

A land-tax of this kind is certainly more equal than the land-tax of England. It might not, perhaps, be altogether so certain, and the assessment of the tax might frequently occasion a good deal more trouble to the landlord. It might too be a good deal more expensive in the levying.

Such a system of administration, however, might perhaps be contrived as would, in a great measure, both prevent this uncertainty and moderate this expence.

<small>The uncertainty and expense could be diminished.</small>

The landlord and tenant, for example, might jointly be obliged to record their lease in a public register. Proper penalties might be enacted against concealing or misrepresenting any of the conditions; and if part of those penalties were to be paid to either of the two parties who informed against and convicted the other of such concealment or misrepresentation, it would effectually deter them from combining together in order to defraud the public revenue. All the conditions of the lease might be sufficiently known from such a record.

<small>Leases should be registered,</small>

<small>fines taxed higher than rent,</small>

Some landlords, instead of raising the rent, take a fine for the renewal of the lease. This practice is in most cases the expedient of a spendthrift, who for a sum of ready money sells a future revenue of much greater value. It is in most cases, therefore, hurtful to the landlord. It is frequently hurtful to the tenant, and it is always hurtful to the community. It frequently takes from the tenant so great a part of his capital, and thereby diminishes so much his ability to cultivate the

---

① *Memoires concernant les Droits*, [tom. i. ] pp. 240, 241.

落到土地地租上,哪些赋税最终落到其他资金上。

在威尼斯境内,所有租给农场主的可耕地都是按照 1/10 的地租征税的①。租约都登记在公共登记簿上,由每个郡县或者地区的税收官员保管。如果土地所有者耕种自己的土地,其土地会被公平的估价,所有者的赋税可以享受税收 1/5 的折扣。所以这样土地所有者为这种土地所缴纳的赋税仅仅是估定的地租的 8%, 而不是 10%。

这种类型的土地税当然要比英国的土地税公平。也许,它也没有完全肯定。税额的估定上可能常常给地主带来大量的麻烦,在征收上花费的费用可能也要大得多。

然而,或许可以设计一种管理制度,既能在很大程度上防止这种不确定性,又能在很大程度上减轻这种花费。

例如,可以命令地主和佃户都必须在公共登记簿上登记他们的租约。对于有隐瞒、虚报者,要处以适当的处罚。如果将罚金的一部分给予两者中揭发或者控告另一方存在隐瞒、虚报行为的话,就可以有效地防止他们联合起来诈取公共收入。这样从登记的记录中就可以清楚地了解到所有有关租约的条件了。

有些地主在续签租约时,不要求抬高租金,而是从续签租约中收取续租金。在大多数情况下,这是一种爱挥霍的人的行为,他们为了一点现金而出卖价值要大得多的未来收入。所以说在大多数情况下,这是有害于地主自身的。它也常常有害于佃户,总是有害于社会。由于佃户经常需要拿出他很大一部分资金,所以他用于耕种土地的能力也相应大大减少了。他发现由于较低

---

① 《欧洲的法律和赋税的记录》,第 1 卷,第 240、241 页。

land, that he finds it more difficult to pay a small rent than it would otherwise have been to pay a great one. Whatever diminishes his ability to cultivate, necessarily keeps down, below what it would otherwise have been, the most important part of the revenue of the community. By rendering the tax upon such fines a good deal heavier than upon the ordinary rent, this hurtful practice might be discouraged, to the no small advantage of all the different parties concerned, of the landlord, of the tenant, of the sovereign, and of the whole community.

conditions of cultivation should be discouraged by high valuation,

Some leases prescribe to the tenant a certain mode of cultivation, and a certain succession of crops during the whole continuance of the lease. This condition, which is generally the effect of the landlord's conceit of his own superior knowledge (a conceit in most cases very ill founded), ought always to be considered as an additional rent; as a rent in service instead of a rent in money. In order to discourage the practice, which is generally a foolish one, this species of rent might be valued rather high, and consequently taxed somewhat higher than common money rents.

rents payable in kind should be valued high,

Some landlords, instead of a rent in money, require a rent in kind, in corn, cattle, poultry, wine, oil, &c. others again require a rent in service. Such rents are always more hurtful to the tenant than beneficial to the landlord. They either take more or keep more out of the pocket of the former, than they put into that of the latter. In every country where they take place, the tenants are poor and beggarly, pretty much according to the degree in which they take place. By valuing, in the same manner, such rents rather high, and consequently taxing them somewhat higher than common money rents, a practice which is hurtful to the whole community might perhaps be sufficiently discouraged.

and an abatement given to landlords cultivating a certain extent of their land.

When the landlord chose to occupy himself a part of his own lands, the rent might be valued according to an equitable arbitration of the farmers and landlords in the neighbourhood, and a moderate abatement of the tax might be granted to him, in the same manner as in the Venetian territory; provided the rent of the lands which he occupied did not exceed a certain sum. It is of importance that the landlord should be encouraged to cultivate a part of his own land. His capital is generally greater than that of the tenant, and with less skill

的租金需要提供续租金，这样支付较低的租金反而比支付较高的租金还要困难。无论什么导致了佃户耕种能力的降低，都会使作为社会收入的最重要部分的地租税降低到它原本应有的水平以下。如果对这种续租金课以比普通地租重得多的赋税，就可能会阻止这种有害的做法，所有相关的当事人——地主、佃户、君主和整个社会也都将受益匪浅。

有的租约规定了在整个租约期佃户应该以何种耕种方式和何种轮种谷物来耕种。这个情况，一般是由于地主自负他有超众的知识的结果，然而在大多数情况下这种自负是毫无根据的。这种条件就应被视为额外的地租，一种不是以货币支付而是以劳务支付的地租。为了阻止这种通常情况下都是愚蠢的行为，应该对这种地租评定高点，从而课以比普通的货币地租更高的赋税。<sub>应该用较高的评定阻止规定耕种条件的租约。</sub>

有些地主不是收取货币地租，而是要求以类似谷物、牲畜、家禽、葡萄酒、油等实物来缴纳地租，还有的地主要求用劳务支付地租。这些地租对佃户的害处总是多于对地主的好处。佃户所付出的地租，总是要多于进入地主口袋的收入。凡是存在这些地租的国家，佃户都是一贫如洗，而且实行得越严重，贫困也越严重。同样的方式，对这种的地租要评定高点，从而对它们课以比普通的货币地租较高的赋税，或许可以完全地阻止这种对整个社会有害的行为。<sub>对实物地租应该评定高点。</sub>

当地主选择自己耕种其土地的一部分时，其地租可以由附近的农场主和地主做出公平的评价。如果他所耕种的地租没有超过一定数额的话，就可以像在威尼斯境内实行的方法一样，给予适当的减税优惠。鼓励地主自耕一部分土地是非常重要的。因为一般来说他的资本要多于佃户的资本，所以尽管他的耕种技术<sub>给予自耕一部分土地的地主优惠地税减惠。</sub>

he can frequently raise a greater produce. The landlord can afford to try experiments, and is generally disposed to do so. His unsuccessful experiments occasion only a moderate loss to himself. His successful ones contribute to the improvement and better cultivation of the whole country. It might be of importance, however, that the abatement of the tax should encourage him to cultivate to a certain extent only. If the landlords should, the greater part of them, be tempted to farm the whole of their own lands, the country (instead of sober and industrious tenants, who are bound by their own interest to cultivate as well as their capital and skill will allow them) would be filled with idle and profligate bailiffs, whose abusive management would soon degrade the cultivation, and reduce the annual produce of the land, to the diminution, not only of the revenue of their masters, but of the most important part of that of the whole society.

*Such a system would free the tax from inconvenient uncertainty and encourage improvement.* Such a system of administration might, perhaps, free a tax of this kind from any degree of uncertainty which could occasion either oppression or inconveniency to the contributor; and might at the same time serve to introduce into the common management of land such a plan or policy, as might contribute a good deal to the general improvement and good cultivation of the country.

*The extra expense of levying the tax would be inconsiderable.* The expence of levying a land-tax, which varied with every variation of the rent, would no doubt be somewhat greater than that of levying one which was always rated according to a fixed valuation. Some additional expence would necessarily be incurred both by the different register offices which it would be proper to establish in the different districts of the country, and by the different valuations which might occasionally be made of the lands which the proprietor chose to occupy himself. The expence of all this, however, might be very moderate, and much below what is incurred in the levying of many other taxes, which afford a very inconsiderable revenue in comparison of what might easily be drawn from a tax of this kind.

*The value of improvements should be for a fixed term exempt from taxation,* The discouragement which a variable land-tax of this kind might give to the improvement of land, seems to be the most important objection which can be made to it. The landlord would certainly be less disposed to improve, when the sovereign, who contributed nothing to the expence, was to share in the profit of the improvement. Even this objection might perhaps be obviated by allowing the landlord, before he began his improvement, to ascertain, in conjunction with the

要差点,通常也能提高土地的产量。他有能力进行这样的试验,而且一般是愿意进行这样的试验。试验失败对它自己的损失也非常有限。而一旦试验成功,就会有助于整个国家耕种的改良和优化。但是,重要的一点是,减税的做法只能鼓励耕种到一定的程度。如果大部分地主都被诱使去耕种自己所有的土地,那么整个国家将充满了游手好闲、肆意挥霍的地主管家(而不是那些朴素的、勤劳的佃户,他们受自身利益的驱动,会尽自己资本和技术的可能来耕种土地)。这些地主管家们胡乱的经营会很快使得耕种退化、土地减产。这样不仅会使得他们主人的收入减少,整个社会收入的最重要的一部分也会减少。

这样一种管理制度,也许可以免除这种赋税的不确定性所带给纳税人的压迫或不便;同时也可以给土地的一般经营,引进一种可以极大地促进全国土地的总体改善与优良耕种的计划或政策。

征收这种土地税随着地租变动而变动的费用,无疑要比征收总是按照固定评定的不变土地税的花费要多。因为实行这种制度时,就需要在全国不同的地区设立不同的登记处;由于地主要耕种自己的土地,也需要对这些土地进行重新的评定。这些都必然会造成额外的费用。不过,所有这些花费可能很少,远远小于其他提供比这种土地税少得多的收入的费用。

最重要的反对这种可变土地税的理由看来就是它会妨碍土地的改良。君主根本没有对改良支出做出任何贡献,却还要分享改良的利润,那么地主当然不愿意进行土地的改良了。然而即便是这种反对的理由也可以通过以下的方法解决,即允许地主在进行土地改良以前,会同税收税官员,由当事人双方共同选择若干

officers of revenue, the actual value of his lands, according to the equitable arbitration of a certain number of landlords and farmers in the neighbourhood, equally chosen by both parties; and by rating him according to this valuation for such a number of years, as might be fully sufficient for his complete indemnification. To draw the attention of the sovereign towards the improvement of the land, from a regard to the increase of his own revenue, is one of the principal advantages proposed by this species of land-tax. The term, therefore, allowed for the indemnification of the landlord, ought not to be a great deal longer than what was necessary for that purpose; lest the remoteness of the interest should discourage too much this attention. It had better, however, be somewhat too long than in any respect too short. No incitement to the attention of the sovereign can ever counterbalance the smallest discouragement to that of the landlord. The attention of the sovereign can be at best but a very general and vague consideration of what is likely to contribute to the better cultivation of the greater part of his dominions. The attention of the landlord is a particular and minute consideration of what is likely to be the most advantageous application of every inch of ground upon his estate. The principal attention of the sovereign ought to be to encourage, by every means in his power, the attention both of the landlord and of the farmer; by allowing both to pursue their own interest in their own way, and according to their own judgment; by giving to both the most perfect security that they shall enjoy the full recompence of their own industry; and by procuring to both the most extensive market for every part of their produce, in consequence of establishing the easiest and safest communications both by land and by water, through every part of his own dominions, as well as the most unbounded freedom of exportation to the dominions of all other princes.

and the tax would then be as little inconvenient as is possible.

If by such a system of administration a tax of this kind could be so managed as to give, not only no discouragement, but, on the contrary, some encouragement to the improvement of land, it does not appear likely to occasion any other inconveniency to the landlord, except always the unavoidable one of being obliged to pay the tax.

It would adjust itself to all changes.

In all the variations of the state of the society, in the improvement and in the declension of agriculture; in all the variations in the value of silver, and in all those in the standard of the coin, a tax of this kind would, of its own accord and without any attention of government, readily suit itself to the actual situation of things, and would be equally just and equitable in all those different changes. It would, therefore, be much more proper to be established as a perpetual and unalterable regulation, or as what is called a fundamental law of the commonwealth, than any tax which was always to be levied according to a certain valuation.

邻近的地主和农场主进行公平地评定,确定该地主土地的实际价值。然后在一定的年份里按照这个评定征税,使这个地主的改良费用能够得到完全的补偿。这种赋税的主要好处之一就在于,让君主从提高自己收入的角度出发而关注土地的改良。所以,允许对地主做出补偿的年限不应该远远超出达到此目的所必需的年限;以免由于地主享受这种年限太久,使君主失去改良土地的兴趣。然而无论如何,与其把期限定得太短,倒不如把时间定得长一些。因为没有任何让君主注重改良的激励能弥补抵消对地主改良的一点点打击。君主的注重至多只能从一般的、笼统的意义上,考虑如何能够促进他大部分领土的改良。而地主的注重,则会具体的从细节上考虑如何才能最有效的利用他地产的每一寸土地。君主应该主要关注于如何运用他所有的权力手段,去鼓励地主和农场主注重土地改良,允许他们按照自己的判断、依据自己的方式追求他们自己的利益,给予他们最安全的保障使他们能够充分地享受他们自己辛勤劳动的成果,通过在领土内建立最安全便利的水陆交通、保障所有国家间无限制的自由出口,使农场主与地主的所有生产物享有最广阔的市场。

<small>应该给改良价值以一个固定的免税期,</small>

如果这种类型赋税的管理制度,能够管理得不但不会阻碍土地的改良,而且还会对土地改良有所促进,那么除了要必须缴税外,看来不会给地主带来任何的不便。

<small>那么赋税带来的不便就可能尽的小了。</small>

无论社会状态如何变更,无论农业繁荣还是衰退,无论白银价值和铸币标准如何变动,这样一种赋税不需要政府的任何干预,都会自动地适应于事物的实际状态,而且会在所有的变动中都保持同样的公平合理。这种赋税更适宜作为一种永久不变的规章,成为所谓的国家基本法,而不是将其仅作为基于某种评定

<small>它会自动适应于一切变动。</small>

— 1743 —

| 国民财富的性质与原理

<small>Some states make a survey and valuation for the land tax,</small>   Some states, instead of the simple and obvious expedient of a register of leases, have had recourse to the laborious and expensive one of an actual survey and valuation of all the lands in the country. They have suspected, probably, that the lessor and lessee, in order to defraud the public revenue, might combine to conceal the real terms of the lease. Doomsday-book seems to have been the result of a very accurate survey of this kind.

<small>for example, Prussia, Silesia,</small>   In the ancient dominions of the king of Prussia, the land-tax is assessed according to an actual survey and valuation, which is reviewed and altered from time to time. ① According to that valuation, the lay proprietors pay from twenty to twenty-five per cent. of their revenue. Ecclesiastics from forty to forty-five per cent. The survey and valuation of Silesia was made by order of the present king; it is said with great accuracy. According to that valuation, the lands belonging to the bishop of Breslaw are taxed at twenty-five per cent. of their rent. The other revenues of the ecclesiastics of both religions, at

---

① *Memoires concernant les Droits*, &c. tome i. p. 114, 115, 116, &c.

课征的土地税。

有些国家不是采用这种简单明了的登记租约的方法,而是采用劳民伤财地对全国土地进行实际测量和评估的方法。之所以这样做或许是因为他们怀疑出租人和承租人为了诈取公共收入,会串通起来隐瞒租约的实际条件。所谓《末日裁判书》[1],似乎就是这种非常精确的测量的结果。

在古代普鲁士国王的领土内,土地税都是基于实际地测量和评估课征的,而且随着时间的推移进行审查和更正①。根据该评估,普通的土地所有者按照他们收入的20%~25%缴税,神职人员按照40%~45%缴税。对西里西亚[2]土地的测量与评估是按照当今国王的命令进行的,据说十分准确。根据这个评估,属于布勒斯洛主教的土地按照地租的25%缴税;新旧两个教会神职人员的其他收入则按照50%缴税。条顿骑士团和马尔他骑士团[3]

---

① 《欧洲法律和赋税的记录》,第1卷,第114、115、116页。
[1] 末日裁判书(Doomsday Book),英格兰人口土地清册,1086年英王威廉一世下令编造土地清册,传说铁面无私,犹如末日审判,故名。
[2] 西里西亚(Silesia),欧洲中部一地区,主要位于波兰西南部和捷克斯洛伐克北部。公元500年斯拉夫民族在此定居,长期以来各国和各公国都对该地区进行争夺。第一次世界大战以后,西里西亚被德国、波兰和捷克斯洛伐克分割。1938年慕尼黑条约签订以后,捷克斯洛伐克所占的那部分归入德国和波兰。1939年至1945年德国占领了波兰属西里西亚,第二次世界大战后波兰合并了大部分德属西里西亚。波兰南部的上西里西亚是一个重要的工业区。
[3] 骑士团是在十字军东征期间建立的军事修会组织,他们把中世纪欧洲的传统的骑士阶层和僧侣的纪律、节制相结合,称为"新型的骑士"。三大骑士团中最早成立的是圣约翰骑士团,通常被称为医院骑士团,它一直延续至今,称为马尔他骑士团(Malta Order)。第二个成立的是圣殿骑士团,它

fifty per cent. The commanderies of the Teutonic order, and of that of Malta, at forty per cent. Lands held by a noble tenure, at thirty-eight and one-third per cent. Lands held by a base tenure, at thirty-five and one-third per cent. ①

The survey and valuation of Bohemia is said to have been the work of more than a hundred years. It was not perfected till after the peace of 1748, by the orders of the present empress queen. ② The survey of the dutchy of Milan, which was begun in the time of Charles VI. , was not perfected till after 1760. It is esteemed one of the most accurate that has ever been made. The survey of Savoy and Piedmont was executed under the orders of the late king of Sardinia. ③

---

① *Memoires concernant les Droits*, &c. tome i. p. 83, 84[ and 79].
② [*Ibid.* , pp. 117~119. ]
③ Ibid. p. 280, &c. also p. 287, &c. to 316.

的封地按照40%缴税。贵族占有地按照 $38\frac{1}{3}\%$ 征税①,而平民占有地则按 $35\frac{1}{3}\%$ 征税。

据说对于波希米亚土地[1]的测量和评估工作进行了100年<sup>和波希米亚</sup>以上,直到1748年和平以后,才根据现在女王的命令完成了②。在查理六世时期就开始进行的米兰公国领土的测量,直到1760年后才完成。据估计这次测量是迄今为止最精确的一次测量。萨伏伊和皮埃蒙特的测量是根据已故撒丁尼亚国王的命令进行的③[2]。

---

是十字军东征期间最显赫、力量最强大的骑士团,不过下场也最惨。最后一个成立的是条顿骑士团(Teutonic Order),它的成员是清一色的德意志贵族。在耶路撒冷期间条顿骑士团并没有什么突出的表现,但它后来回到欧洲,在德意志东方殖民的历史上书写了重要的一页。

① 《欧洲法律和赋税的记录》,第117~119页。
② 同上,第83、84页,也包括第79页。
③ 《欧洲法律和赋税的记录》,第280页,第287~316页。
[1] 波希米亚(Bohemia),历史上的地区和王国,在今天的捷克斯洛伐克西部。在1世纪和5世纪之间,斯拉夫人的一支捷克人在此定居。在公元15世纪,其中主要部分独立出来,成立匈牙利,后来又变成哈布斯堡王朝。1918年,波希亚地区成为新成立的捷克斯洛伐克共和国的核心。
[2] 萨伏伊(Savoy),历史上的地区名,是法国东南、瑞士西部和意大利西北部以前的一个公国。此地在为裘力斯·恺撒征服以后几次易手,并在15世纪早期成为公国,1720年萨伏伊大公取得撒丁尼亚国王的头衔,1861年萨伏伊征服者伊曼纽尔二世登上新成立的意大利王国皇座,同时原萨伏伊的大部地区割让给了法国。
皮埃蒙特区(Piedmont),意大利西北的一个历史地区,与法国和瑞士接壤。公元前1世纪时,被罗马人占领,11世纪被萨伏伊王室统治,1814年后成为意大利复兴运动的中心。

# 国民财富的性质与原理

*Under the Prussian land tax the church lands are taxed higher than the rest; in some states they are taxed lower than the rest.*

In the dominions of the king of Prussia the revenue of the church is taxed much higher than that of lay proprietors. ① The revenue of the church is, the greater part of it, a burden upon the rent of land. It seldom happens that any part of it is applied towards the improvement of land; or is so employed as to contribute in any respect towards increasing the revenue of the great body of the people. His Prussian majesty had probably, upon that account, thought it reasonable, that it should contribute a good deal more towards relieving the exigencies of the state. In some countries the lands of the church are exempted from all taxes. In others they are taxed more lightly than other lands. In the dutchy of Milan, the lands which the church possessed before 1575, are rated to the tax at a third only of their value. ②

*Differences are often made between land held by noble and base tenures.*

In Silesia, lands held by a noble tenure are taxed three per cent. higher than those held by a base tenure. The honours and privileges of different kinds annexed to the former, his Prussian majesty had probably imagined, would sufficiency compensate to the proprietor a small aggravation of the tax; while at the same time the humiliating inferiority of the latter would be in some measure alleviated by being taxed somewhat more lightly. In other countries, the system of taxation, instead of alleviating, aggravates this inequality. In the dominions of the king of Sardinia, and in those provinces of France which are subject to what is called the real or predial taille, the tax falls altogether upon the lands held by a base tenure. Those held by a noble one are exempted.

*A land tax assessed according to a general survey and valuation soon becomes unequal,*

A land-tax assessed according to a general survey and valuation, how equal soever it may be at first, must, in the course of a very

---

① [As stated just above.]

② [*Mémoires*, tom. i. , p. 282.]

在普鲁士国王的领土内,对教会收入的课税要比普通土地所有者收入的课税高得多①。教会的大部分收入都是取自于地租,却很少用来改良土地或者用于在某方面促进大多数人民的收入。或许因为这个原因,普鲁士国王认为理应将教会的收入更多的用于解救国家急难。但在有些国家,教会的土地却完全免税;而在别的一些国家,相对于其他土地,教会的土地税要轻得多。在米兰公国,教会在1577年以前占有的土地,只是按照其实际价值的1/3征税①。

在西里西亚,对贵族占有地的赋税要比平民占有地的赋税高3%。这可能是因为普鲁士国王认为,前者享有的种种荣誉、特权,就足以弥补他略高的赋税;而同时,较轻的赋税也在某种程度上可以减轻后者屈辱低下的感觉。但在其他国家,赋税制度不仅没有减轻,反而加重了这种不平等。比如在撒丁尼亚国王的领地内,以及实行实物贡税或者土地贡税的法国各省里,赋税完全落在了平民占有地上,而贵族占有地则完全免税。

无论根据总的测量评估所确定的土地税刚开始是多么的公平,必然会在非常短的时间内就沦为不公平。为了防止这种变

---

撒丁尼亚(Sardinia),意大利地中海中的一个岛屿,位于科西嘉岛南面。在公元前6世纪前由腓尼基人、希腊人和迦太基人居住,该岛于公元前238年被罗马人占领,然后又分别被汪达尔人(公元5世纪)和拜占庭人(6世纪早期)占领该岛,于1720年归入萨瓦王朝统治下,成为撒丁王国的中心。

① 如前面所提及的。
② 《欧洲法律和赋税的记录》,第282页。

moderate period of time, become unequal. To prevent its becoming so would require the continual and painful attention of government to all the variations in the state and produce of every different farm in the country. The governments of Prussia, of Bohemia, of Sardinia, and of the dutchy of Milan, actually exert an attention of this kind; an attention so unsuitable to the nature of government, that it is not likely to be of long continuance, and which, if it is continued, will probably in the long-run occasion much more trouble and vexation than it can possibly bring relief to the contributors.

<small>as in Montauban.</small> In 1666, the generality of Montauban was assessed to the Real or predial taille according, it is said, to a very exact survey and valuation. ① By 1727, this assessment had become altogether unequal. In order to remedy this inconveniency, government has found no better expedient than to impose upon the whole generality an additional tax of a hundred and twenty thousand livres. This additional tax is rated upon all the different districts subject to the taille according to the old assessment. But it is levied only upon those which in the actual state of things are by that assessment under-taxed, and it is applied to the relief of those which by the same assessment are over-taxed. Two districts, for example, one of which ought in the actual state of things to be taxed at nine hundred, the other at eleven hundred livres, are by the old assessment both taxed at a thousand livres. Both these districts are by the additional tax rated at eleven hundred livres each. But this additional tax is levied only upon the district under-charged, and it is applied altogether to the relief of that over-charged, which consequently pays only nine hundred livres. The government neither gains nor loses by the additional tax, which is applied altogether to remedy the inequalities arising from the old assessment. The application is pretty much regulated according to the discretion of the intend-

---

① *Memoires concernant les Droits*, &c. tome ii. p. 139, &c. [pp. 145-147].

化，政府必须要不断地耐心地关注国内每个农场的状态和产物的所有变动。普鲁士、波希米亚、撒丁尼亚和米兰公国的政府，都的确进行了这种关注。然而这种关注却有悖于政府的天性，不可能持续长久；即便能够长久地关注，长期当中它所带给纳税人的麻烦与困扰可能也会多于给他们带来的救济。

据说1666年，蒙托邦[1]区所征收的实物贡税或土地贡税，是根据极其精确的测量和评估来确定的①。但到了1727年，这种评估已经变得完全的不公平了。为了纠正这种弊端，政府别无他法，只好对全区征收12万里弗的附加税。虽然按照旧的评估标准这项附加税要加在所有实行贡税的地区里，但实际上只对那些按照旧的估定税额实际缴税过少的地方进行征税，以减轻按照旧的标准缴税过多地区的负担。例如，有两个地区，其中一个地区按照实际情况应该征收900里弗，而另一个地区按照实际情况应该征收1100里弗，而按照旧的评估二者都应该缴纳1000里弗。根据征收的附加税两个地区都定为1100里弗。但这种附加税只对以前缴税过低的地区征收，完全用来救济以前缴税过高的地区，所以以前缴税过高的地区只需缴纳900里弗。附加税完全用来纠正由于过去旧的评估税额所引起的不公平，所以对政府来说无得也无失。不过这种方法相当程度上取决于税区行政长官的

如在蒙托邦。

---

① 《欧洲法律和赋税的记录》，第2卷，第139页、第145~147页。
〔1〕蒙托邦（Montauban），法国中南部城市，塔恩—加龙省（Tarn-et-Garonne）首府。地处阿基坦盆地东南部、加龙河支流塔恩河畔。

ant of the generality, and must, therefore, be in a great measure arbitrary.

## Taxes Which Are Proportioned, Not To The Rent, But To The Produce Of Land

<small>Taxes on the produce are finally paid by the landlord,</small>    Taxes upon the produce of land are in reality taxes upon the rent; and though they may be originally advanced by the farmer, are finally paid by the landlord. When a certain portion of the produce is to be paid away for a tax, the farmer computes, as well as he can, what the value of this portion is, one year with another, likely to amount to, and he makes a proportionable abatement in the rent which he agrees to pay to the landlord. There is no farmer who does not compute beforehand what the church tythe, which is a land-tax of this kind, is, one year with another, likely to amount to.

<small>and are very unequal taxes,</small>    The tythe, and every other land-tax of this kind, under the appearance of perfect equality, are very unequal taxes; a certain portion of the produce being, in different situations, equivalent to a very different portion of the rent. In some very rich lands the produce is so great, that the one half of it is fully sufficient to replace to the farmer his capital employed in cultivation, together with the ordinary profits of farming stock in the neighbourhood. The other half, or, what comes to the same thing, the value of the other half, he could afford to pay as rent to the landlord, if there was no tythe. But if a tenth of the produce is taken from him in the way of tythe, he must require an abatement of the fifth part of his rent, otherwise he cannot get back his capital with the ordinary profit. In this case the rent of the landlord, instead of amounting to a half, or five-tenths of the whole produce, will amount only to four-tenths of it. In poorer lands, on the contrary, the produce is sometimes so small, and the expence of cultivation so great, that it requires four-fifths of the whole produce to replace to the farmer his capital with the ordinary profit. In this case, though there was no tythe, the rent of the landlord could amount to no

裁决,所以必然在很大程度上是武断的。

## 不与地租成比例,而与土地生产物成比例的赋税

对土地生产物征收的赋税,其实质上是土地地租征收赋税。尽管最初它们可能有农场主垫付,但最终还是由地主支付。当要将一部分生产物支付赋税时,农场主必然会尽其可能地计算这部分生产物价值几何,这样逐年累积会达到怎样的数目?这样当他给地主支付地租时就会索取一定比例的折扣。教会的什一税就是这样一种土地税,当农场主在缴纳什一税时全都会预先计算一下这样一年一年这个税会达到什么样的数目。

对产物征收的赋税最终要由地主来支付,

什一税和其他这种类型的土地税,表面看起来相当的公平,实际上非常的不公平。在不同的情况下,一定部分的生产物,等于极不相同部分的地租。在一些非常肥沃的土地上,物产非常的丰富;这些生产物的一半就足以补偿农场主用于耕种的资本和附近地区农业资本的普通利润。另一半,或者说另一半价值,其实都是一回事,如果没有什一税的话,就可以支付地主的地租了。但如果生产物的1/10要被以什一税的形式取走,那么他要想还收回资本和普通利润,就必须要求减少支付1/5的地租。这种情况下,地主的地租就不会是所有生产物的一半或者5/10,而只剩4/10了。反之,在贫瘠的土地上,有时产物非常少,而耕种的支出又非常大,以至于需要全部生产物的4/5才能补偿他的资本和普通利润。在这种情况下即便没有什一税,地主得到的地租也不会

这是一种非常不公平的赋税,

more than one-fifth or two-tenths of the whole produce. But if the farmer pays one-tenth of the produce in the way of tythe, he must require an equal abatement of the rent of the landlord, which will thus be reduced to one-tenth only of the whole produce. Upon the rent of rich lands, the tythe may sometimes be a tax of no more than one-fifth part, or four shillings in the pound; whereas upon that of poorer lands, it may sometimes be a tax of one-half, or of ten shillings in the pound.

<small>which discourage both improvement and good cultivation.</small>

The tythe, as it is frequently a very unequal tax upon the rent, so it is always a great discouragement both to the improvements of the landlord and to the cultivation of the farmer. The one cannot venture to make the most important, which are generally the most expensive improvements; nor the other to raise the most valuable, which are generally too the most expensive crops; when the church, which lays out no part of the expence, is to share so very largely in the profit. The cultivation of madder was for a long time confined by the tythe to the United Provinces, which, being presbyterian countries, and upon that account exempted from this destructive tax, enjoyed a sort of monopoly of that useful dying drug against the rest of Europe. The late attempts to introduce the culture of this plant into England, have been made only in consequence of the statute which enacted that five shillings an acre should be received in lieu of all manner of tythe upon madder.

<small>They form the principal revenue of the state in many Asiatic countries,</small>

As through the greater part of Europe, the church, so in many different countries of Asia, the state, is principally supported by a land-tax, proportioned, not to the rent, but to the produce of the land. In China, the principal revenue of the sovereign consists in a tenth part of the produce of all the lands of the empire. This tenth part, however, is estimated so very moderately, that, in many provinces, it is said not to exceed a thirtieth part of the ordinary produce. The land-tax or land-rent which used to be paid to the Mahometan government of Bengal, before that country fell into the

超过所有生产物的 1/5 或者 2/10。但如果农场主又要将生产物的 1/10 用来支付什一税，它必然会从地租那里索取相等数额的折扣，这样地主就仅仅得到所有生产物的 1/10 了。对肥沃土地征收什一税，有时可能仅仅是不超过 1/5 地租的税负，即每镑 4 先令的税，而对贫瘠土地征收的什一税，有时税负则会达到 1/2 地租那样多，即每镑 10 先令。

由于什一税通常都是一种非常不公平的租金税，所以它总是阻碍地主改良土地、农场主耕种土地。教会不负担任何费用，却享受到这样巨大的利润，所以地主就不肯冒险进行最重要一般也是最费钱的土地改良，农场主也不肯冒险种植最有价值也是最费钱的作物。长期以来只有在荷兰联邦才有茜草[1]的种植，长期以来享受着这种有用染料的垄断利益。原因在于那里是长老教会国家，因而免征了这种破坏性的赋税。最近英格兰开始试图引进栽培这种植物，这就是因为议会制定了法令，规定所有种植茜草的土地每亩只征收 5 先令，以代替原来的什一税。

<small>这种赋税妨碍土地改良和良好耕种。</small>

正如欧洲大部分地区的教会主要由不与地租成比例而是与土地生产物成比例的土地税来维持，亚洲也有许多国家的政府靠这种土地税来维持。在中国，君主的主要收入由帝国所有土地生产物的 1/10 构成。不过这个 1/10 是从宽估计了，以至于在许多省份据说还没有超过普通生产物的 1/30。在孟加拉落入东印度公司之手以前，向该国伊斯兰政府所缴纳的土地税或者地租据说

<small>在许多亚洲国家这种赋税形成了政府的主要收入。</small>

---

[1] 茜草（Madder），亚洲西南部的多年生（茜草属，欧茜草）植物开有小黄花，生有卷状叶和红根。该植物的根，原为染料茜素的重要来源。

hands of the English East India company, is said to have amounted to about a fifth part of the produce. The land-tax of ancient Egypt is said likewise to have amounted to a fifth part.

<small>and are said to interest the sovereign in the improvement and cultivation of land there.</small>

In Asia, this sort of land-tax is said to interest the sovereign in the improvement and cultivation of land. The sovereigns of China, those of Bengal while under the Mahometan government, and those of ancient Egypt, are said accordingly to have been extremely attentive to the making and maintaining of good roads and navigable canals, in order to increase, as much as possible, both the quantity and value of every part of the produce of the land, by procuring to every part of it the most extensive market which their own dominions could afford. The tythe of the church is divided into such small portions, that no one of its proprietors can have any interest of this kind. The parson of a parish could never find his account in making a road or canal to a distant part of the country, in order to extend the market for the produce of his own particular parish. Such taxes, when destined for the maintenance of the state, have some advantages which may serve in some measure to balance their inconveniency. When destined for the maintenance of the church, they are attended with nothing but inconveniency.

<small>They may be in kind or in money</small>

Taxes upon the produce of land may be levied, either in kind; or, according to a certain valuation, in money.

The parson of a parish, or a gentleman of small fortune who lives upon his estate, may sometimes, perhaps, find some advantage in receiving, the one his tythe, and the other his rent, in kind. The quantity to be collected, and the district within which it is to be collected, <small>Collection in kind is quite unsuitable for public revenue.</small> are so small, that they both can oversee, with their own eyes, the collection and disposal of every part of what is due to them. A gentleman of great fortune, who lived in the capital, would be in danger of suffering much by the neglect, and more by the fraud of his factors and agents, if the rents of an estate in a distant province were to be paid to him in this manner. The loss of the sovereign, from the abuse and depredation of his tax-gatherers, would necessarily be much greater. The servants of the most careless private person are, perhaps, more under the eye of their master than those of the most careful prince; and a public revenue, which was paid in kind, would suffer so much from the mismanagement of the collectors, that a very small

已经大约占了土地生产物的1/5。古埃及的土地税据说也站到了土地生产物的1/5。

在亚洲,这种土地税据说促使君主们都关注于土地的改良和耕种。据说中国的国君们、伊斯兰统治下的孟加拉政府、古埃及君主们都极端地关注修建和维护良好的道路和通航运河,尽可能增加他们国内所有土地生产物的数量和价值,在国土范围内为各种产品提供尽可能广阔的市场。欧洲的什一税被分成许多数量细微的小份,所以没有任何土地所有者会像亚洲那样关注土地的改良与耕种。一个教区的牧师绝不会看到向国家的偏远地区修建道路或者运河以拓展本教区产物的市场对他有什么好处。所以这种赋税当用来维持国家时,其所带来的好处就可以在某种程度上抵消它们的不便;但如果用来维持教会时,除了不便就没有什么好处可言了。

对土地生产物的赋税,可以征收实物,或者按照某种评定征收货币。

教区牧师或者居住在自己地产上的小乡绅,有时会觉得以实物来收取什一税或者地租或许有好处。因为征收的数量很少,征收的地区很小,所以他们可以亲自监督、处理每一部分应收实物。但对于一个居住在首都的富绅,如果他在远处省份的地产也按照实物来缴纳,那么他就有遭受代办人或者代理人疏忽、更多是蒙骗的危险。那么君主因为征税人员的滥用职权和巧取豪夺肯定会遭到更大的损失。即便最粗心大意的个人对他的仆人们的监控或许也要比最小心谨慎的君主对他的仆人们的监控强得多。所以如果以实物来征收公共收入,由于收税者的管理不当,以至于从人民那里征收到的税收就只有很小的一部分进入了君主的

— 1757 —

part of what was levied upon the people would ever arrive at the treasury of the prince. Some part of the public revenue of China, however, is said to be paid in this manner. The Mandarins and other tax-gatherers will, no doubt, find their advantage in continuing the practice of a payment which is so much more liable to abuse than any payment in money.

<small>A money tax on produce may be always the same or may vary with the market price of produce.</small>

A tax upon the produce of land which is levied in money, may be levied either according to a valuation which varies with all the variations of the market price; or according to a fixed valuation, a bushel of wheat, for example, being always valued at one and the same money price, whatever may be the state of the market. The produce of a tax levied in the former way, will vary only according to the variations in the real produce of the land according to the improvement or neglect of cultivation. The produce of a tax levied in the latter way will vary, not only according to the variations in the produce of the land, but according to both those in the value of the precious metals, and those in the quantity of those metals which is at different times contained in coin of the same denomination. The produce of the former will always bear the same proportion to the value of the real produce of the land. The produce of the latter may, at different times, bear very different proportions to that value.

<small>When a certain sum of money is to be paid in compensation for the tax it becomes exactly like the English land tax.</small>

When, instead either of a certain portion of the produce of land, or of the price of a certain portion, a certain sum of money is to be paid in full compensation for all tax or tythe; the tax becomes, in this case, exactly of the same nature with the land-tax of England. It neither rises nor falls with the rent of the land. It neither encourages nor discourages improvement. The tythe in the greater part of those parishes which pay what is called a modus in lieu of all other tythe, is a tax of this kind. During the Mahometan government of Bengal, instead of the payment in kind of the fifth part of the produce, a modus, and, it is said, a very moderate one, was established in the greater part of the districts or zemindaries of the country. Some of the servants of the East India company, under pretence of restoring the public revenue to its proper value, have, in some provinces, exchanged this modus for a payment in kind. Under their management

国库。可是,中国的一部分公共收入据说就是以这种方式征收的。官员们和其他征税者毫无疑问都会发现继续保持这种征税方式对他们有好处,相比于征收货币,征收实物可以使他们更容易徇私舞弊。

对土地生产物以货币征收赋税,可以按照随市场价格变动而变动的评估来征收;或者按照一个固定的评估征收,例如无论市场状况如何变化,一蒲式耳小麦总是估作一个相同的货币价格。以前者征收方式征收的税额,只随着耕种的改良或荒废导致的实际土地生产物的变化而变化;而以后者征收方式征收的税额,不仅仅随着土地生产物的变化而变化,而且会随着贵金属价值的变化和不同时期同样面值铸币所包含的这些贵金属的分量的变化而变化。所以,前者的税额总是与土地的实际生产物价值保持相同的比例;而后者的税额则会在不同的时期,与土地的实际生产物价值有着差异很大的比例。

> 对产物征收的货币赋税,可以不随着或随着产物市场价格变化而变化。

如果不是按照土地生产物的一定部分或者一定部分的价格来征收,而是征收一定数额的货币来完全替代所有的赋税或者什一税。这种情况下这种赋税就变得和英格兰土地税的性质完全相同了。它既不会随着土地地租变化而涨落,也不会促进或打击土地的改良。在大多数用一定的货币负担来代替其他什一税的教区所征收的什一税,就是这种类型的赋税。在孟加拉伊斯兰统治时期,他们大部分的地区或领土内都不是以实物形式缴纳生产物的 1/5,而是据说以数量较少的货币缴纳土地税。东印度公司的某些雇员借口要将公共收入恢复到其应有的价值,在某些省份将货币支付赋税改为了实物支付赋税。在他们管理下,这种改变既阻碍了耕种,又造成征收公共收入方面新的徇私舞弊机会,所

> 一定额的货币赋税,就变得和英格兰土地税完全一样了。当用一定数额的货币支付赋税时,它得格地全了。

this change is likely both to discourage cultivation, and to give new opportunities for abuse in the collection of the public revenue, which .has fallen very much below what it was said to have been, when it first fell under the management of the company. The servants of the company may, perhaps, have profited by this change, but at the expence, it is probable, both of their masters and of the country.

## *Taxes Upon The Rent Of Houses*

House rent consists of two parts, building rent.

The rent of a house may be distinguished into two parts, of which the one may very properly be called the Building rent; the other is commonly called the Ground rent.

The building rent is the interest or profit of the capital expended in building the house. In order to put the trade of a builder upon a level with other trades, it is necessary that this rent should be sufficient, first, to pay him the same interest which he would have got for his capital if he had lent it upon good security; and, secondly, to keep the house in constant repair, or, what comes to the same thing, to replace, within a certain term of years, the capital which had been employed in building it. The building rent, or the ordinary profit of building, is, therefore, every where regulated by the ordinary interest of money. Where the market rate of interest is four per cent. the rent of a house which, over and above paying the ground rent, affords six, or six and a half per cent. upon the whole expence of building, may perhaps afford a sufficient profit to the builder. Where the market rate of interest is five per cent. , it may perhaps require seven or seven and a half per cent. If, in proportion to the interest of money, the trade of the builder affords at any time a much greater profit than this, it will soon draw so much capital from other trades as will reduce the profit to its proper level. If it affords at any time much less than this, other trades will soon draw so much capital from it as will again raise that profit.

Whatever part of the whole rent of a house is over and above what is sufficient for affording this reasonable profit, naturally goes to the ground-rent; and where the owner of the ground and the owner of the building are two different persons, is, in most cases, completely

以据说公共收入已经远远低于他们刚开始接管时的水平。从这个改变中,这个公司的雇员们可能得到了好处,但代价可能却是他们的主人和国家做出了牺牲。

## 房租税

房租可以分为两部分:一种可以非常恰当地称之为建筑物租金,另一种通常称之为地皮租金。<sub>房租包括两部分:</sub>

建筑物租金是用于建造房屋的资本的利息或利润。为了使建筑业与其他行业处于同等水平上,这个租金必须满足以下两个条件:第一,起码得到如果他把资本贷给具有良好担保信用的人所能得到的利息;第二,足以使他能经常地维修房屋,或者换句话说,他能在一定年限内收回用于建造房屋的资本。所以,建筑物租金即建筑物的普通利润,到处都受到货币的普通利息的调控。在市场利率为4%的地方,如果房屋的租金除了支付地皮租金外,还能提供全部建筑费用的6%或6.5%的收入,那么建筑者可能就由此得到了充足的利润。而在市场利率为5%的地方,可能需要提供全部建筑费用的7%或7.5%的收入建筑者才能得到充足的利润。利润是与利息成比例的,如果任何时候建筑行业的利润都要高于这个比例很多,那么很快就会吸引其他行业的许多资本来建筑行业投资,使利润降低到正当水平。与之相反,如果任何时候建筑行业的利润都要低于这个比例很多,建筑行业的资本就会很快转移到其他行业上,从而使利润提高上去。<sub>建筑物租金,</sub>

全部房屋租金中,凡是超过了足以提供合理利润的部分,都自然地归作地皮租。当地皮的主人与建筑物的主人是不同的人时,大多数情况下这种剩余都要完全归地皮的主人所有。这种剩

## 国民财富的性质与原理

and ground rent.
paid to the former. This surplus rent is the price which the inhabitant of the house pays for some real or supposed advantage of the situation. In country houses, at a distance from any great town, where there is plenty of ground to chuse upon, the ground rent is scarce any thing, or no more than what the ground which the house stands upon would pay if employed in agriculture. In country villas in the neighbourhood of some great town, it is sometimes a good deal higher; and the peculiar conveniency or beauty of situation is there frequently very well paid for. Ground rents are generally highest in the capital, and in those particular parts of it where there happens to be the greatest demand for houses, whatever be the reason of that demand, whether for trade and business, for pleasure and society, or for mere vanity and fashion.

A tax on house rent paid by the tenant falls partly on the inhabitant and partly on the owner of the ground,
A tax upon house-rent, payable by the tenant and proportioned to the whole rent of each house, could not, for any considerable time at least, affect the building rent. If the builder did not get his reasonable profit, he would be obliged to quit the trade; which, by raising the demand for building, would in a short time bring back his profit to its proper level with that of other trades. Neither would such a tax fall altogether upon the ground-rent; but it would divide itself in such a manner as to fall, partly upon the inhabitant of the house, and partly upon the owner of the ground.

as may be shown by an example.
Let us suppose, for example, that a particular person judges that he can afford for house-rent an expence of sixty pounds a year; and let us suppose too that a tax of four shillings in the pound, or of one-fifth, payable by the inhabitant, is laid upon house-rent. A house of sixty pounds rent will in this case cost him seventy-two pounds a year, which is twelve pounds more than he thinks he can afford. He will, therefore, content himself with a worse house, or a house of fifty pounds rent, which, with the additional ten pounds that he must pay for the tax, will make up the sum of sixty pounds a year, the expence which he judges he can afford; and in order to pay the tax he will give up a part of the additional conveniency which he might have had from a house of ten pounds a year more rent. He will give up, I say, a part of this additional conveniency; for he will seldom be obliged to give up the whole, but will, in consequence of the tax, get a better house for fifty pounds a year, than he could have got if there had been no

余租金,是房屋居住者为了房屋位置的某种真实的或者想象的利益而支付的价格。在离大都市很远的乡村,那里有充足的地皮可供选择,因此地皮租几乎为零,或者不超过当房屋的地皮用于农业时所能得到的数额。在大都市附近的郊区别墅,有时地皮租就要贵很多。那里特殊的便利或环境的优美常常可以卖到很好的价钱。地皮租最高的地方一般在首都,以及首都的那些对房屋有最大需要的特别地段,不管这种需要的理由是什么,是为了贸易、商业,为了娱乐、社交,还仅仅是为了虚荣和时髦。

和地皮租金。

如果由租客来支付对房屋租金课征的赋税,而且赋税与房屋的全部租金成比例,那么至少在相当长的时间内,赋税都不会影响建筑物的租金。如果建筑者无法得到他合理的利润,他就会被迫退出这个行业。这样建筑物的需求就提高了,很快他的利润又回到与其他行业一样的利润水平。这种赋税也不会全部落到地皮租上,而是会自行地以一部分落在住户头上、另一部分落在地皮所有者头上这种方式来划分。

由租客来支付对房屋租金的赋税,那部分会落在住户头上,部分会落在地皮所有者身上。

例如,假设有一个人他认为能支付每年 60 镑的房租,我们再假设,加在房租上由住户支出的税为每镑 4 先令,或者全部租金的 1/5。这种场合下,每年 60 镑的房屋租金就要耗掉他 72 镑,比他认为可以负担的金额超出了 12 镑。这样,他将愿意租个差点的房屋,即年租金 50 镑的房屋,再加上他必须缴纳的 10 镑的赋税,加起来每年 60 镑,等于他认为所能支付的数额。为了支付房租税,他要放弃房租贵了 10 镑的房屋所能提供的部分额外便利。我之所以说他将放弃部分的额外便利,原因在于他不会被迫放弃全部便利。因为房租税,他就可以以 50 镑租到在没有房租税时 50 镑所租不到的较好的房屋。这种赋税就把他这个竞争者排除

有一个例子可以说明。

国民财富的性质与原理

tax. For as a tax of this kind, by taking away this particular competitor, must diminish the competition for houses of sixty pounds rent, so it must likewise diminish it for those of fifty pounds rent, and in the same manner for those of all other rents, except the lowest rent, for which it would for some time increase the competition. But the rents of every class of houses for which the competition was diminished, would necessarily be more or less reduced. As no part of this reduction, however, could, for any considerable time at least, affect the building rent; the whole of it must in the long-run necessarily fall upon the ground-rent. The final payment of this tax, therefore, would fall, partly upon the inhabitant of the house, who, in order to pay his share, would be obliged to give up a part of his conveniency; and partly upon the owner of the ground, who, in order to pay his share, would be obliged to give up a part of his revenue. In what proportion this final payment would be divided between them, it is not perhaps very easy to ascertain. The division would probably be very different in different circumstances, and a tax of this kind might, according to those different circumstances, affect very unequally both the inhabitant of the house and the owner of the ground.

On the inhabitants it would be an unequal tax, falling heaviest on the rich.

The inequality with which a tax of this kind might fall upon the owners of different ground-rents, would arise altogether from the accidental inequality of this division. But the inequality with which it might fall upon the inhabitants of different houses would arise, not only from this, but from another cause. The proportion of the expence of house-rent to the whole expence of living, is different in the different degrees of fortune. It is perhaps highest in the highest degree, and it diminishes gradually through the inferior degrees, so as in general to be lowest in the lowest degree. The necessaries of life occasion the great expence of the poor. They find it difficult to get food, and the greater part of their little revenue is spent in getting it. The luxuries and vanities of life occasion the principal expence of the rich; and a magnificent house embellishes and sets off to the best advantage all the other luxuries and vanities which they possess. A tax upon house-rents, therefore, would in general fall heaviest upon the rich; and in this sort of inequality there would not, perhaps, be any thing very unreasonable. It is not very unreasonable that the rich should contribute to the public expence, not only in proportion to their revenue, but something more than in that proportion.

掉了,从而减少了年租金为60镑的房屋的竞争,同样也会减少年租金为50镑的房屋的竞争,这样除了租金最低以外所有其他租金房屋的竞争都会以同样方式减轻。而在一定的时期内,最低租金的房屋的竞争则会增加。但对各种租金房屋的竞争减少了,就必然会使得各类房屋的租金或多或少地下降一些。然而,由于至少在相当长的时间里,减少的任何一部分都不会影响建筑物租金,所以长期内必然全部要落在地皮租上。所以,房租税的最终支付,将部分地落在住户身上,他们为了支付他们的份额,不得不放弃部分便利;部分地落在地皮所有者身上,他们为了支付他们的份额,不得不放弃部分收入。或许也不是很容易确定他们之间最终支付分配的比例。在不同情况下,这种分配可能会差异很大,而且根据这些不同的情况,这种房租税可能会对房屋的住户和地皮的所有者产生非常不平等的影响。

　　落在不同地皮租所有者身上的这种赋税的不平等,完全是由于这种分配的偶然的不平等造成的。但落在不同的房屋住户身上的不平等,除了分配的原因外,还有别的原因。房租支出占全部生活支出的比例,随着财产大小程度的不同而不同。财产最多时,这种比例也最高;随着财产的减少,这种比例也逐渐减少;财产最少时,这种比例一般来说也是最低。生活必需品构成了穷人的大部分支出。他们发现吃饱饭就很不容易了,所以他们微薄收入的大部分都用于获取食物。生活奢侈品和虚饰品则构成了富人们的主要支出,而富丽堂皇的房屋又可以将他们占有的其他奢侈品和虚饰品装点衬托到极致。所以,这种房租税一般是对富人征收的最重。而且这种类型不平等,或许也没有什么不合理的。富者不仅仅应该与他们收入成比例地为国家公共支出做出贡献,

对于住户,这是一种非常不平等的赋税,它对富人征收最重。

# 国民财富的性质与原理

<small>It would be like a tax on any other consumable commodity, it would be very much in proportion to men's whole expense, and it would produce considerable revenue.</small>

The rent of houses, though it in some respects resembles the rent of land, is in one respect essentially different from it. The rent of land is paid for the use of a productive subject. The land which pays it produces it. The rent of houses is paid for the use of an unproductive subject. Neither the house nor the ground which it stands upon produce any thing. The person who pays the rent, therefore, must draw it from some other source of revenue, distinct from and independent of this subject. A tax upon the rent of houses, so far as it falls upon the inhabitants, must be drawn from the same source as the rent itself, and must be paid from their revenue, whether derived from the wages of labour, the profits of stock, or the rent of land. So far as it falls upon the inhabitants, it is one of those taxes which fall, not upon one only, but indifferently upon all the three different sources of revenue; and is in every respect of the same nature as a tax upon any other sort of consumable commodities. In general there is not, perhaps, any one article of expence or consumption by which the liberality or narrowness of a man's whole expence can be better judged of, than by his houserent. A proportional tax upon this particular article of expence might, perhaps, produce a more considerable revenue than any which has hitherto been drawn from it in any part of Europe. If the tax indeed was very high, the greater part of people would endeavour to evade it, as much as they could, by contenting themselves with smaller houses, and by turning the greater part of their expence into some other channel.

<small>The rent could be easily ascertained. Empty houses should be exempt, and houses occupied by their proprietor should be assessed at their letting value.</small>

The rent of houses might easily be ascertained with sufficient accuracy, by a policy of the same kind with that which would be necessary for ascertaining the ordinary rent of land. Houses not inhabited ought to pay no tax. A tax upon them would fall altogether upon the proprietor, who would thus be taxed for a subject which afforded him neither conveniency nor revenue. Houses inhabited by the proprietor ought to be rated, not according to the expence which they might have cost in building, but according to the rent which an equitable arbitration might judge them likely to bring, if leased to a tenant. If rated according to the expence which they may have cost in building, a tax of three or four shillings in the pound, joined with other taxes, would

而且还应该多贡献一点,这并没有什么非常不合理的。

尽管房租在某些方面与土地地租相似,但在一方面却与其有着本质的区别。支付土地地租是为了使用一种有生产力的东西。支付地租的土地,自己生产这种地租。而支付房租,却是为了使用一种没有生产力的东西。房屋和房屋所占的地皮都不生产任何东西。所以,支付房租的人必须要从区别独立于房屋的其他收入来源中提取地租。只要房租税落在住户身上,它就与房租本身有着一样的来源,必须都由他们的收入来支付,无论这些收入来自于劳动工资、资本利润还是来自于土地地租。只要房租税落在住户身上,它就不是仅仅落在一项收入来源、而是无差异地落在所有这三项收入来源的一种赋税。从各方面来说,房租税都与对其他消费品征收的赋税有着同样的性质。总的来说,可能没有别的支出或者消费比房租更能反映一个人全部消费的奢侈或节俭。对房租这种特殊支出征收的比例税所得的收入,或许比欧洲所有地区迄今为止任一其他税收的收入都要多得多。但如果这种赋税定得太高,大部分人又会尽其可能设法逃避它,满足于较小的房子,把他们的大部分支出移转到其他渠道。

所以房租像其他消费品一样,与人们的支出比例可以成全部收入,并带来观入。

通过确定普通地租所必须采用的相同的政策,就可以很容易十分精确地确定房租。无人居住的房屋应予免税。如果对这些房屋征税,那么赋税就会全部落在房屋所有者身上,让他为这些既不给他提供收入也不给他提供便利的东西缴税。如果房屋是所有者自己居住,他就不应按照建筑房屋时所可能的花费缴税,而应按照出租房屋时根据公平裁定所可能得到的租金来缴税。如果按照建筑房屋时所可能的花费缴税,那么每镑3先令或4先令的税负,再加上其他的税负,就几乎可以让国家所有的富人和

很容易确定空房,应予免税,所居住的房子应该按其出租价值评估。房租定给房租所有者自己出其税。

ruin almost all the rich and great families of this, and, I believe, of every other civilized country. Whoever will examine, with attention, the different town and country houses of some of the richest and greatest families in this country, will find that, at the rate of only six and a half, or seven per cent. upon the original expence of building, their house-rent is nearly equal to the whole neat rent of their estates. It is the accumulated expence of several successive generations, laid out upon objects of great beauty and magnificence, indeed; but, in proportion to what they cost, of very small exchangeable value. ①

Ground rent is a still more proper subject of taxation than building rent,

Ground-rents are a still more proper subject of taxation than the rent of houses. A tax upon ground-rents would not raise the rents of houses. It would fall altogether upon the owner of the ground-rent, who acts always as a monopolist, and exacts the greatest rent which can be got for the use of his ground. More or less can be got for it according as the competitors happen to be richer or poorer, or can afford to gratify their fancy for a particular spot of ground at a greater or smaller expence. In every country the greatest number of rich competitors is in the capital, and it is there accordingly that the highest ground-rents are always to be found. As the wealth of those competitors would in no respect be increased by a tax upon groundrents, they would not probably be disposed to pay more for the use of the ground. Whether the tax was to be advanced by the inhabitant, or by the owner of the ground, would be of little importance. The more the inhabitant was obliged to pay for the tax, the less he would incline to pay for the ground; so that the final payment of the tax would fall altogether upon the owner of the ground-rent. The groundrents of uninhabited houses ought to pay no tax.

---

① Since the first publication of this book, a tax nearly upon the abovementioned principles has been imposed. [ This note appears first in ed. 3. The tax was first imposed by 18 Geo. III. , c. 26, and was at the rate of 6d. in the pound on houses of £ 5 and under £ 50 annual value, and Is. in the pound on houses of higher value, but by 10 Geo. III. , c. 59, the rates were altered to 6d. in the pound on houses of £ 5 and under £ 20 annual value, 9d. on those of £ 20 and under £ 40, and Is. on those of £ 40 and upwards. ]

大家族破产。而且我相信这种情况在其他的文明国家也是一样。无论是谁,只要他用心考察一些最富最大的家族在不同城镇和乡村的房屋,就会发现如果按照最初建筑费用的 6.5% 或 7% 征收房租税,他们的房租几乎等于他们所有地产的净租金。虽然他们的房屋都是历经了几代人的积累,造就了今天美丽壮观的建筑,但与它们所耗去的费用相比,交换价值却很小①。

相比于房屋租金,地皮租金是一种更为适当的征税对象。对地皮租征税不会抬高房租价格,这种赋税将完全落在地皮所有者身上。地皮所有者总是扮演垄断者的角色,对使用他的地皮的人索以最大的租金。他获得租金的多少,取决于竞争其地皮的人的贫富,或者这些竞争者能为自己对某一特殊地点的偏好支出的多少。在所有的国家,竞争地皮的富人数目最多的地点就在首府,因此在那里也常常能发现最昂贵的地皮租金。由于这些竞争者的财富绝不会随着地皮税的增加而增加,所以他们也不可能愿意为使用这些地皮支付更高的租金。地皮租金税是由住户垫付、还是由地皮所有者垫付,是无关紧要的。住户被迫支付的地皮租金税越多,他所愿意支付的地皮租金就越少。所以最终地皮租金税的支付就会完全地落在地皮所有者身上。无人居住的房屋的地皮租不应缴税。

---

① 自从本书首次出版以来,已经征收了和上述原则几乎完全一致的赋税。本脚注首次出现实在第 3 版。这个赋税是根据乔治三世十八年第 26 号法令课征,对年房租为 5 镑到 50 镑之间的房屋每镑征税 6 便士,而对价值较高的房屋则每镑征税 1 先令。但根据乔治三世十九年第 59 号法令,改成了年租金介于 5 镑到 20 镑之间的房屋每镑征税 6 便士,介于 20 镑到 40 镑之间的房屋每镑征税 9 便士,年租金 40 镑及 40 镑以上的房屋每镑征税 1 先令。

| | |
|---|---|
| as no discouragement is given to industry by the taxation of the rent of land. | Both ground-rents and the ordinary rent of land are a species of revenue which the owner, in many cases, enjoys without any care or attention of his own. Though a part of this revenue should be taken from him in order to defray the expences of the state, no discouragement will thereby be given to any sort of industry. The annual produce of the land and labour of the society, the real wealth and revenue of the great body of the people, might be the same after such a tax as before. Ground-rents, and the ordinary rent of land, are, therefore, perhaps, the species of revenue which can best bear to have a peculiar tax imposed upon them. |
| Ground rents are even a more proper subject of taxation than ordinary land rents. | Ground-rents seem, in this respect, a more proper subject of peculiar taxation than even the ordinary rent of land. The ordinary rent of land is, in many cases, owing partly at least to the attention and good management of the landlord. A very heavy tax might discourage too much this attention and good management. Ground-rents, so far as they exceed the ordinary rent of land, are altogether owing to the good government of the sovereign, which, by protecting the industry either of the whole people, or of the inhabitants of some particular place, enables them to pay so much more than its real value for the ground which they build their houses upon; or to make to its owner so much more than compensation for the loss which he might sustain by this use of it. Nothing can be more reasonable than that a fund which owes its existence to the good government of the state, should be taxed peculiarly, or should contribute something more than the greater part of other funds, towards the support of that government. |
| Ground rents are nowhere separately taxed, but might be. | Though, in many different countries of Europe, taxes have been imposed upon the rent of houses, I do not know of any in which ground-rents have been considered as a separate subject of taxation. The contrivers of taxes have, probably, found some difficulty in ascertaining what part of the rent ought to be considered as ground-rent, and what part ought to be considered as building-rent. It should not, however, seem very difficult to distinguish those two parts of the rent from one another. |

In Great Britain the rent of houses is supposed to be taxed in the same proportion as the rent of land, by what is called the annual landtax. The valuation, according to which each different parish and district is assessed to this tax, is always the same. It was originally extremely

第五篇 第二章

在许多场合,地皮租金和普通土地地租都是一种所有者本人不需要关心或关注就可以享受到的收入。尽管这种收入的一部分会被用来支付国家开支,但并不会因此而对任何产业打击。社会的土地年产物和劳动年产物,是大部分国民真正的财富和收入,在征收地皮租金税后和以前并没什么两样。所以,地皮租和普通土地地租,或许是最适于被征收某种特定赋税的收入种类了。

> 对地皮租金课税不会对所有的产业有任何的打击。

在这方面,地皮租看来要比普通土地地租更适于作为特定税的对象。在许多场合,普通土地地租至少还部分地归功于地主的关注和良好的经营。太重的赋税可能就会严重地打击这种关注和良好的经营。只要地皮租超过了土地的普通地租,这就完全是由于君主的良好治理,保护了全体人民或者某特定地区的居民的产业,使他们能够为房屋所占的地皮支付远远超过其实际价值的租金,或者给地皮所有者提供了远远超出地皮被人使用所造受的损失的报酬。对因国家的良好治理而存在的资金征收特别税,或者使它比其他大部分资金对支援政府做出更大的贡献,这是最合理不过的事情了。

> 相比于普通土地地租,地皮租金是一种更当适征税对象。

尽管欧洲的各个国家都对房租征收赋税,但我没听说过有哪个国家曾经将地皮租当作一个单独的征税实体。这或许是因为税法设计者感到很难确定房租中哪些部分应被当作地皮租金,哪些部分应被当作建筑物租金。不过,要区分房租的这两部分看起来并非那么困难。

> 地皮租被单独课税,但完全是可以的。

在大不列颠,对房屋租金和土地租金以相同的税率课税,即所谓的年土地税。各个不同的教区和地区对于年土地税税率的估价都总是相同的。最初这就是非常的不公平,现在依然如此。

## 国民财富的性质与原理

<small>House rent is legally liable to the British land tax.</small> unequal, and it still continues to be so. Through the greater part of the kingdom this tax falls still more lightly upon the rent of houses than upon that of land. In some few districts only, which were originally rated high, and in which the rents of houses have fallen considerably, the land-tax of three or four shillings in the pound, is said to amount to an equal proportion of the real rent of houses. Untenanted houses, though by law subject to the tax, are, in most districts, exempted from it by the favour of the assessors; and this exemption sometimes occasions some little variation in the rate of particular houses, though that of the district is always the same. Improvements of rent, by new buildings, repairs, &c. ; go to the discharge of the district, which occasions still further variations in the rate of particular houses.

<small>In Holland there is a tax on the capital value of houses.</small> In the province of Holland ① every house is taxed at two and a half per cent. of its value, without any regard either to the rent which it actually pays, or to the circumstance of its being tenanted or untenanted. There seems to be a hardship in obliging the proprietor to pay a tax for an untenanted house, from which he can derive no revenue, especially so very heavy a tax. In Holland, where the market rate of interest does not exceed three per cent. two and a half per cent. upon the whole value of the house, must, in most cases, amount to more than a third of the building-rent, perhaps of the whole rent. The valuation, indeed, according to which the houses are rated, though very unequal, is said to be always below the real value. When a house is rebuilt, improved or enlarged, there is a new valuation, and the tax is rated accordingly.

<small>House taxes in England have not been proportioned to the rent.</small> The contrivers of the several taxes which in England have, at different times, been imposed upon houses, seem to have imagined that there was some great difficulty in ascertaining, with tolerable exactness, what was the real rent of every house. They have regulated their taxes, therefore, according to some more obvious circumstance, such as they had probably imagined would, in most cases, bear some proportion to the rent.

---

① *Memoires concernant les Droits*, &c. [ tom. i. ], p. 223.

在王国的大部分地区,年土地税仍然是落在房屋租金上的部分要比落在土地地租上的部分要轻些。只有几个地区最初对房屋租金课税较高,之后房屋租金已经跌了很多,据说每镑 3 先令或 4 先令的土地税才能使其与房屋真实租金相等的比例。尽管按照法律无人租用的房屋也要缴税,但在大多数地区都被税收评估人员开恩给免除了。虽然有时这种免除会让特定房屋的税率有小的变动,但整个地区的税率却总是相同的。由于新修建筑物、修缮等致使租金增加,但房租税却没有增加,这样就会使特定房屋的税率发生进一步的变动。在大不列颠,按照法律房屋租金应该缴纳土地税。

在霍兰德[1]省境内,不管实际支付的房租是多少,也不管有没有人租住,所有的房屋全都按其价值的 2.5% 征税①。强迫房屋所有者对没有出租从而没有得到收入的房屋缴税,而且税负还如此之重,未免也太苛刻了。荷兰的市场利率不超过 3%,对房屋征以全部价值的 2.5% 的赋税,在大多数情况下就会达到建筑物租金或者全部房屋租金的 1/3 以上。的确,尽管据以定税的评估非常不平等,但据说都总是低于实际价值。当再建房屋、改善或者扩建时,就要对房屋重新进行评估,而房租税也将按照这个新的评估征税。在荷兰,对房屋的资本价值征税。

在英格兰,不同年代几种房屋税的设计者,看来认为很难比较精确地确定每个房屋的实际租金。因此,他们根据一些比较明显的事实来规定赋税,他们可能认为在大多数情况下这种明显的事实与房租有一定的比例关系。英格兰房屋税是与租金成比例,

---

① 《欧洲法律和赋税的记录》,第 1 卷,第 223 页。
[1] 霍兰德(Holland),荷兰以前的一个省。

> but first to the number of hearths,

The first tax of this kind was hearth-money; or a tax of two shillings upon every hearth. In order to ascertain how many hearths were in the house, it was necessary that the tax-gatherer should enter every room in it. This odious visit rendered the tax odious. Soon after the revolution, therefore, it was abolished as a badge of slavery.

> and later to the number of windows.

The next tax of this kind was, a tax of two shillings upon every dwelling house inhabited. A house with ten windows to pay four shillings more. A house with twenty windows and upwards to pay eight shillings. This tax was afterwards so far altered, that houses with twenty windows, and with less than thirty, were ordered to pay ten shillings, and those with thirty windows and upwards to pay twenty shillings. The number of windows can, in most cases, be counted from the outside, and, in all cases, without entering every room in the house. The visit of the tax-gatherer, therefore, was less offensive in this tax than in the hearth-money.

> The present window tax augments gradually from 2d. per window to 2s.

This tax was afterwards repealed, and in the room of it was established the window-tax, which has undergone too several alterations and augmentations. The window-tax, as it stands at present (January, 1775), over and above the duty of three shillings upon every house in England, and of one shilling upon every house in Scotland, lays a duty upon every window, which, in England, augments gradually from two-pence, the lowest rate, upon houses with not more than seven windows; to two shillings, the highest rate, upon houses with twenty-five windows and upwards.

> Window taxes are objectionable, chiefly on the ground of inequality.

The principal objection to all such taxes is their inequality, an inequality of the worst kind, as they must frequently fall much heavier upon the poor than upon the rich. A house of ten pounds rent in a country town may sometimes have more windows than a house of five hundred pounds rent in London; and though the inhabitant of the former is likely to be a much poorer man than that of the latter, yet so far as his contribution is regulated by the window-tax, he must contribute more to the support of the state. Such taxes are, therefore, directly contrary to the first of the four maxims above mentioned. They do not seem to offend much against any of the other three.

第一种这样的赋税叫做炉捐,即每个壁炉征收 2 先令的税。为了确定一个房屋中有多少壁炉,征税人员必须进入每一个房间察看。这种令人讨厌的访问也使这种赋税变得可憎。所以革命后不久,它就当作奴隶制的标志予以废除了。

<small>首先是炉目比与壁炉的数成例,</small>

接下来的这种赋税,是对每栋有人居住的房屋征收 2 先令的赋税。有 10 个窗户的房屋加征 4 先令,有 20 个和 20 个以上窗户的房屋加征 8 先令。这个赋税后来修改了。窗户数大于等于 20 但少于 30 的房屋要缴纳 10 先令的税负,窗户数大于等于 30 的房屋缴纳 20 先令的税负。大多数情况下从外面就可以数出窗户数,无论如何都不用进入房屋的每间房子。所以对于这种赋税,征税人员的访问就没有炉捐那样令人生厌了。

<small>后来与窗户的数目成比例。</small>

后来这个赋税也被废除了,取而代之的是窗户税。窗户税也是经历了几次修改与补充,到目前(1775 年 1 月),除了英格兰的每栋房屋课征 3 先令的赋税、苏格兰的每栋房屋课征 1 先令的赋税外,每个窗户也要缴纳赋税。在英格兰,税率是逐渐上升的,最低的税率是对不超过 7 个窗户的房屋征收 2 便士税率的赋税,最高的税率是对不少于 25 个窗户的房屋征收 2 先令税率的赋税。

<small>目前的窗户税税率,是从每个窗士增便逐渐到每个窗户两先令。</small>

反对所有这些赋税的主要理由在于它们的不公平性,而且是最坏的一种不公平,因为这些赋税落在穷人身上的常常要比落在富人身上的重。一个乡村城镇 10 镑租金房屋的窗户数可能有时比伦敦 500 镑租金房屋的窗户数还要多。尽管前者的住户很可能比后者的住户穷得多,但由于他的贡献是受到窗户税的调控,他必须负担更多的国家费用。因此,这些赋税就直接与上面提到的四项原则的第一条原则相违背。但看来它们没有怎么违背其他三项原则。

<small>窗户税遭到反对的主要理由在于它的不平等性。</small>

> Taxes on houses lower rents.

The natural tendency of the window-tax, and of all other taxes upon houses, is to lower rents. The more a man pays for the tax, the less, it is evident, he can afford to pay for the rent. Since the imposition of the window-tax, however, the rents of houses have upon the whole risen, more or less, in almost every town and village of Great Britain, with which I am acquainted. Such has been almost every where the increase of the demand for houses, that it has raised the rents more than the window-tax could sink them; one of the many proofs of the great prosperity of the country, and of the increasing revenue of its inhabitants. Had it not been for the tax, rents would probably have risen still higher.

## ARTICLE II  *Taxes Upon Profit, Or Upon The Revenue Arising From Stock*

> Profit is divided into interest and surplus over interest.

The revenue or profit arising from stock naturally divides itself into two parts; that which pays the interest, and which belongs to the owner of the stock; and that surplus part which is over and above what is necessary for paying the interest.

> The surplus is not taxable.

This latter part of profit is evidently a subject not taxable directly. It is the compensation, and in most cases it is no more than a very moderate compensation, for the risk and trouble of employing the stock. The employer must have this compensation, otherwise he cannot, consistently with his own interest, continue the employment. If he was taxed directly, therefore, in proportion to the whole profit, he would be obliged either to raise the rate of his profit, or to charge the tax upon the interest of money; that is, to pay less interest. If he raised the rate of his profit in proportion to the tax, the whole tax, though it might be advanced by him, would be finally paid by one or other of two different sets of people, according to the different ways in which he might employ the stock of which he had the management. If he employed it as a farming stock in the cultivation of land, he could raise the rate of his profit only by retaining a greater portion, or, what comes to the same thing, the price of a greater portion of the produce of the land; and as this could be done only by a reduction of rent, the

窗户税和其他一切房屋税的自然趋势就是降低租金。很显然，一个人支付越多的赋税，他所能支付的租金也就越少。不过据我所知，自从实施窗户税以来，几乎大不列颠所有的城镇乡村的房屋租金大体上都或多或少地提高了。这是由于各地对房屋的需要都增长了，使房租增加的超过了窗户税使房租减少的，这可以作为国家的繁荣昌盛、人民收入水平的提高的许多佐证之一。如果没有窗户税，或许房租会升得更高。

房屋税会降低房租。

## 第二项　利润税，即加在资本收入上的赋税

由资本产生的收入或利润，会自然地分为两部分：第一，支付利息的部分，它属于资本所有者；第二，超过了须支付利息的那一部分后的剩余部分。

利润分为利息和超过利息的剩余。

显然，利润的后一部分是不能作为直接课税的对象的。它是对使用资本的风险和麻烦的补偿，而且大多数情况下，这个补偿都是非常微薄的。必须要给予资本使用者这个补偿，否则他就不会再做下去了，因为这样就无法与他的自身利益相符。所以，如果他被按照全部利润的比例直接征税，那么他要么就不得不提高利润率，要么就不得不把赋税转移到货币利息上去，即少支付利息。如果他按照赋税的比例提高利润率，那么尽管全部赋税可能由他垫付，但最终要依据他经营的资本的使用方法的不同而由以下两种人之一来支付。如果他将资本用作农业资本以栽种土地，他要想提高利润率，只能靠保留土地生产物的较大部分或土地生产物的较大部分的价格，二者是一回事。而这要行得通，只有减少地租，这样这种赋税的最终支付就落到了地主身上。如果他将

剩余部分是不能征税的。

final payment of the tax would fall upon the landlord. If he employed it as a mercantile or manufacturing stock, he could raise the rate of his profit only by raising the price of his goods; in which case the final payment of the tax would fall altogether upon the consumers of those goods. If he did not raise the rate of his profit, he would be obliged to charge the whole tax upon that part of it which was allotted for the interest of money. He could afford less interest for whatever stock he borrowed, and the whole weight of the tax would in this case fall ultimately upon the interest of money. So far as he could not relieve himself from the tax in the one way, he would be obliged to relieve himself in the other.

<small>interest at first sight seems as fit to be taxed as rent,</small>  The interest of money seems at first sight a subject equally capable of being taxed directly as the rent of land. Like the rent of land, it is a neat produce which remains after completely compensating the whole risk and trouble of employing the stock. As a tax upon the rent of land cannot raise rents; because the neat produce which remains after replacing the stock of the farmer, together with his reasonable profit, cannot be greater after the tax than before it: so, for the same reason, a tax upon the interest of money could not raise the rate of interest; the quantity of stock or money in the country, like the quantity of land, being supposed to remain the same after the tax as before it. The ordinary rate of profit, it has been shewn in the first book, is every where regulated by the quantity of stock to be employed in proportion to the quantity of the employment, or of the business which must be done by it. But the quantity of the employment, or of the business to be done by stock, could neither be increased nor diminished by any tax upon the interest of money. If the quantity of the stock to be employed therefore, was neither increased nor diminished by it, the ordinary rate of profit would necessarily remain the same. But the portion of this profit necessary for compensating the risk and trouble of the employer, would likewise remain the same; that risk and trouble being in no respect altered. The residue, therefore, that portion which belongs to the owner of the stock, and which pays the interest of money, would necessarily remain the same too. At first sight, therefore, the interest of money seems to be a subject as fit to be taxed directly as the rent of land.

<small>but it is not, since,</small>  There are, however, two different circumstances which render the interest of money a much less proper subject of direct taxation than the rent of land.

资本用作商业资本或者制造业资本,他要想提高利润率,只能靠提高商品的价格。在这种情况下,这种赋税的最终支付,就要完全落到这些商品的消费者身上。如果他没有提高利润率,他将不得不把全部赋税转移到利润中分配给货币利息的那一部分上。他只能给借入资本提供较少的利息,这种情况下全部赋税最终就落在货币利息上。只要他不能以某种方法减轻自己的税负,他就不得不采用另一种方法来减轻自己的税负。

乍看起来,货币的利息就像和土地地租一样,可以作为直接征税的对象。像土地地租一样,货币利息也是完全地补偿了使用资本的风险和麻烦后的净产物。对地租征收的赋税不会抬高地租,因为偿还了农场主资本和其合理利润后的净产物,不可能在征税后比在征税前还大。同样的道理,对货币利息征收的赋税,也不会抬高利息率。就像土地的数量一样,一个国家的资本量或货币量,肯定会在征税后和征税前保持相同。本书第一篇曾经讲过:普通的利润率,在各地都是受可供使用的资本量与使用的资本量或必须用资本来进行的营业量的比例的支配。但使用的资本量或使用资本进行的营业量,不会因为对利率征税而增加或减少。所以,如果可供使用的资本量没有增加也没有减少,那么,普通的利润率就必然会保持不变。但是,必要的用于报偿资本使用者的风险和麻烦的那部分利润,也同样会保持不变,因为风险和麻烦也根本没有改变。因此,残余部分,即属于资本所有者,用于支付货币利息的那部分,也必然会保持不变。所以,乍看起来货币利息似乎像土地地租一样适于作直接征税的对象。

但是,有两种情况导致了货币利息远远不能像土地地租那样成一种适当的直接征税对象。

| 国民财富的性质与原理

(1) the amount received by an individual cannot be readily and exactly ascertained,

First, the quantity and value of the land which any man possesses can never be a secret, and can always be ascertained with great exactness. But the whole amount of the capital stock which he possesses is almost always a secret, and can scarce ever be ascertained with tolerable exactness. It is liable, besides, to almost continual variations. A year seldom passes away, frequently not a month, sometimes scarce a single day, in which it does not rise or fall more or less. An inquisition into every man's private circumstances, and an inquisition which, in order to accommodate the tax to them, watched over all the fluctuations of his fortune, would be a source of such continual and endless vexation as no people could support.

and (2) stock may be removed from the country imposing the tax.

Secondly, land is a subject which cannot be removed, whereas stock easily may. The proprietor of land is necessarily a citizen of the particular country in which his estate lies. The proprietor of stock is properly a citizen of the world, and is not necessarily attached to any particular country. He would be apt to abandon the country in which he was exposed to a vexatious inquisition, in order to be assessed to a burdensome tax, and would remove his stock to some other country where he could either carry on his business, or enjoy his fortune more at his ease. By removing his stock he would put an end to all the industry which it had maintained in the country which he left. Stock cultivates land; stock employs labour. A tax which tended to drive away stock from any particular country, would so far tend to dry up every source of revenue, both to the sovereign and to the society. Not only the profits of stock, but the rent of land and the wages of labour, would necessarily be more or less diminished by its removal.

Where such a tax exists it is levied on a loose and very low valuation,

The nations, accordingly, who have attempted to tax the revenue arising from stock, instead of any severe inquisition of this kind, have been obliged to content themselves with some very loose, and, therefore, more or less arbitrary estimation. The extreme inequality and uncertainty of a tax assessed in this manner, can be compensated only by its extreme moderation, in consequence of which every man finds himself rated so very much below his real revenue, that he gives himself little disturbance though his neighbour should be rated somewhat lower.

By what is called the land-tax in England, it was intended that

第一,每一个人所拥有土地的数量和价值,不可能永远是个秘密,常常是可以准确地查明的。但一个人所拥有的资本总量,却几乎总是个秘密,几乎无法比较准确地查明。而且,个人所拥有的资本总量也总是在变化。一年之中,常常是一个月之中、有时甚至是一天之中,它都会或多或少地有所增减。为了使赋税与每个人的情况符合,要调查每个人的私人情况,监视个人财富的所有波动,这会给人们带来持续的无穷无尽的烦恼,没有人会支持这种调查。

<small>(1)个人获得的数量很难精确地查明,</small>

第二,土地不能够移动,但资本却可以很容易地流动。土地所有者必然是他的地产所在的特定国家的公民,而资本所有者却完全是个世界公民,他不必归属于任何特定国家。当他在一个国家受到麻烦的调查,以便对其征以重税,他就会离开这个国家,将他的资本移往别的一些国家,在那里他可以经营自己的事业,或者比较自在地享受他的财富。移出他的资本,就会结束在他所离开的国家里经营的所有产业。资本耕种土地,资本雇佣劳动。一种将资本驱赶出去的赋税,必然枯竭君主和社会的所有收入来源。不仅仅是资本利润,土地地租和劳动工资也都必然会随着资本的移出或多或少地减少。

<small>(2)征税的话,资本会出国,这个会。</small>

因此,打算对资本收入征税的国家,并非采用这种非常严格地调查方式,而是不得不满足于采用一些非常宽松的因而也多少有点武断的评估来征收赋税。为了弥补采用这种征税方式所带来的极端不公平和不确定,只能把税率定的相当低,结果每个人都发现自己缴纳的税额远远低于他的实际收入,以至于尽管他的邻居被征收的税负更低一些,他也感到没什么大不了的。

<small>在这种存在的地方,都按照非常宽松和非常低的评估来征税的。</small>

根据英格兰所谓的土地税,资本和土地应该征以同样的税

as under the English land tax.
stock should be taxed in the same proportion as land. When the tax upon land was at four shillings in the pound, or at one-fifth of the supposed rent, it was intended that stock should be taxed at one-fifth of the supposed interest. When the present annual land-tax was first imposed, the legal rate of interest was six per cent. Every hundred pounds stock, accordingly, was supposed to be taxed at twenty-four shillings, the fifth part of six pounds. Since the legal rate of interest has been reduced to five per cent. every hundred pounds stock is supposed to be taxed at twenty shillings only. The sum to be raised, by what is called the land-tax, was divided between the country and the principal towns. The greater part of it was laid upon the country; and of what was laid upon the towns, the greater part was assessed upon the houses. What remained to be assessed upon the stock or trade of the towns (for the stock upon the land was not meant to be taxed) was very much below the real value of that stock or trade. Whatever inequalities, therefore, there might be in the original assessment, gave little disturbance. Every parish and district still continues to be rated for its land, its houses, and its stock, according to the original assessment; and the almost universal prosperity of the country, which in most places has raised very much the value of all these, has rendered those inequalities of still less importance now. The rate too upon each district continuing always the same, the uncertainty of this tax, so far as it might be assessed upon the stock of any individual, has been very much diminished, as well as rendered of much less consequence. If the greater part of the lands of England are not rated to the land-tax at half their actual value, the greater part of the stock of England is, perhaps, scarce rated at the fiftieth part of its actual value. In some towns the whole land-tax is assessed upon houses; as in Westminster, where stock and trade are free. It is otherwise in London.

Inquisition is avoided.
In all countries a severe inquisition into the circumstances of private persons has been carefully avoided.

At Hamburgh ① every inhabitant is obliged to pay to the state, one-fourth per cent. of all that he possesses; and as the wealth of the people of Hamburgh consists principally in stock, this tax may be considered as a tax upon stock. Every man assesses himself, and, in

---

① *Memoires concernant les Droits*, tome i. p. 74.

率。当土地税为每镑4先令，或者1/5的推定地租时，对资本征收的赋税也应该为1/5的推定利息。当现行的土地税刚开始执行时，法定利率为6%。相应地，每100镑资本应该征收6镑的1/5，即24先令。自从法定利率降到5%后，每100镑资本只应该征收20先令的赋税。这种所谓的土地税的总额，要在乡村和主要城市间分摊。其中大部分税负落在乡村，而城市负担的那块，大部分则落在房屋上。剩下来对城市中的资本或商业（因为原本就不打算对用在土地上的资本征税）征收的赋税，则远远低于资本或商业的实际价值。所以，无论最初评估的税额有多么的不公平，都不会引起什么骚乱。所有的教区和地区仍然按照最初评估的税额对土地、房屋和资本征收赋税。而且由于国家整体的普遍繁荣，许多地方的土地、房屋和资本的价值已经提高了很多，使得这些不公平变得更加无关紧要。而且，各个地区的税率总是保持不变，就其对个人资本征税来说，这种赋税的不确定性已经大大减少了，同时也变得不那么重要了。如果英格兰大部分的土地没有按照其实际价值的一半评定税额，那么英格兰大部分的资本或许还没有按照其实际价值的1/50评定税额。例如在威斯敏斯特，那里的资本和商业都是免税。伦敦情况则不同。

在所有的国家，都非常谨慎地避免对私人情况进行严格地调查。

在汉堡[①]，每个居民必须给政府缴纳他所有财产0.25%的赋税。由于汉堡人民的财产主要由资本构成，所以这项赋税就可以看作对资本征收的赋税。每个人自行评估自己应该缴纳的税

---

① 《欧洲法律和赋税的记录》，第1卷，第74页。

| 国民财富的性质与原理

<small>At Hamburg each inhabitant privately assesses himself on oath.</small> the presence of the magistrate, puts annually into the public coffer a certain sum of money, which he declares upon oath to be one-fourth per cent. of all that he possesses, but without declaring what it amounts to, or being liable to any examination upon that subject. This tax is generally supposed to be paid with great fidelity. In a small republic, where the people have entire confidence in their magistrates, are convinced of the necessity of the tax for the support of the state, and believe that it will be faithfully applied to that purpose, such conscientious and voluntary payment may sometimes be expected. It is not peculiar to the people of Hamburgh.

<small>In some Swiss cantons each man assesses himself publicly,</small> The canton of Underwald in Switzerland is frequently ravaged by storms and inundations, and is thereby exposed to extraordinary expences. Upon such occasions the people assemble, and every one is said to declare with the greatest frankness what he is worth, in order to be taxed accordingly. At Zurich the law orders, that, in cases of necessity, every one should be taxed in proportion to his revenue; the amount of which, he is obliged to declare upon oath. They have no suspicion, it is said, that any of their fellow-citizens will deceive them. At Basil the principal revenue of the state arises from a small custom upon goods exported. All the citizens make oath that they will pay every three months all the taxes imposed by the law. All merchants and even all inn-keepers are trusted with keeping themselves the account of the goods which they sell either within or without the territory. At the end of every three months they send this account to the treasurer, with the amount of the tax computed at the bottom of it. It is not suspected that the revenue suffers by this confidence. ①

<small>which would be a hardship at Hamburg.</small> To oblige every citizen to declare publicly upon oath the amount of his fortune, must not, it seems, in those Swiss cantons, be reckoned a hardship. At Hamburgh it would be reckoned the greatest. Merchants engaged in the hazardous projects of trade, all tremble at

---

① *Memoires concernant les Droits*, tome i. p. 163, 166, 171. [The statements as to the confidence felt in these self-assessments are not taken from the *Mémoires*. ]

第五篇 第二章

额,每年在地方长官面前,将一定数额的货币放入公共金库,并宣誓这就是他所有财产总额的 0.25%。他不需要公布这个财产总额的具体数字,也不用接受任何的检查。一般来说,缴纳这种赋税都应该是非常诚实的。在一个小共和国里,人们完全信赖地方长官,都深信赋税是维持国家所必需的。他们相信他们缴纳的赋税会被忠实地用于维持国家,这种凭良心和自愿缴纳赋税的方法有时是可能的,它不是汉堡人民所特有的行为。

在瑞士的翁德沃尔德州,常常遭到暴风雪和洪水的破坏,因此常常需要超额的支出。遇到这种情况,人们就聚集在一起,都以最开诚布公的方式宣布他们的财产数额,以便相应地征税。在苏黎世,当遇到紧急情况时,法律规定每个人都要按照他收入的比例缴税。此时每个人必须宣誓并公布其收入的数额。据说从来没人怀疑他们的同胞会欺骗他们。在巴兹尔,政府的收入主要都来自于对出口商品所征收的小额关税。所有的公民都宣誓他们会每三个月缴付一次法律规定的所有赋税。所有的商人甚至所有的旅店老板,都被委托自行记录他们在国内或国外销售的商品。每到三个月末的时候,他们就在这个记录的底下计算出他们应该缴纳的税额,将纪录送到财务官员那里。没有人怀疑国家收入会因为这种信托而遭到损失[①]。

在瑞士的这些州郡,看来让每个公民都公开地宣誓并公布他的财产总额并非什么难事。但在汉堡,这恐怕就是非常困难的事情了。那些从事商业中冒险投机项目的商人,一想到要随时向公

---

① 《欧洲法律和赋税的记录》,第 1 卷,第 163、166、171 页。关于在这种自行估税的信任的陈述,不是根据《欧洲法律和赋税的记录》。

1785

the thoughts of being obliged at all times to expose the real state of their circumstances. The ruin of their credit and the miscarriage of their projects, they foresee, would too often be the consequence. A sober and parsimonious people, who are strangers to all such projects, do not feel that they have occasion for any such concealment.

<small>Holland once adopted the Hamburg practice.</small>
In Holland, soon after the exaltation of the late prince of Orange to the stadtholdership, a tax of two per cent. or the fiftieth penny, as it was called, was imposed upon the whole substance of every citizen. Every citizen assessed himself and paid his tax in the same manner as at Hamburgh; and it was in general supposed to have been paid with great fidelity. The people had at that time the greatest affection for their new government, which they had just established by a general insurrection. The tax was to be paid but once; in order to relieve the state in a particular exigency. It was, indeed, too heavy to be permanent. In a country where the market rate of interest seldom exceeds three per cent. , a tax of two per cent. amounts to thirteen shillings and fourpence in the pound upon the highest neat revenue which is commonly drawn from stock. It is a tax which very few people could pay without encroaching more or less upon their capitals. In a particular exigency the people may, from great public zeal, make a great effort, and give up even a part of their capital, in order to relieve the state. But it is impossible that they should continue to do so for any considerable time; and if they did, the tax would soon ruin them so completely as to render them altogether incapable of supporting the state.

<small>On that occasion the tax was meant to be a tax on the capital.</small>
The tax upon stock imposed by the land-tax bill in England, though it is proportioned to the capital, is not intended to diminish or take away any part of that capital. It is meant only to be a tax upon the interest of money proportioned to that upon the rent of land; so that when the latter is at four shillings in the pound, the former may be at four shillings in the pound too. The tax at Hamburgh, and the still more moderate taxes of Underwald and Zurich, are meant, in the same manner, to be taxes, not upon the capital, but upon the interest or neat revenue of stock. That of Holland was meant to be a tax upon the capital.

众公布他们经营财产的实际状况就要不寒而栗。他们可以预见，这样做十有八九的结果会是信用破产和项目流产。而对于那些不从事这种冒险投机项目的质朴节俭的人们，则不会觉得有什么需要隐瞒。

在荷兰，已故的奥林奇王子就任总督后不久，就对每个公民的全部财产征收了2%的赋税，即所谓五十便士取一的赋税。就像汉堡一样，每个公民自行评估自己的财产并缴纳税负。一般来说，缴纳这种赋税也都应该是非常诚实的。当时人们刚刚经历了全面暴动建立了自己的新政府，他们对这个政府有着深厚的感情。这种赋税是为了拯救国家特殊之需，而且只征收一次。当然，这个税负太重了，也不可能长久持续缴纳下去。当时荷兰的市场利率很少超过3%。征收2%的赋税，对于通常来自于资本的最高净收入，这种赋税每镑就要征去13先令4便士。这项赋税太重了，如果不或多或少地牺牲自己的一部分资本恐怕就没有几个人能缴得起了。当国家处于特殊的紧急关头，人民为了拯救国家，出于巨大的爱国热情，可能会做出巨大的努力，牺牲自己的一部分资本。但不可能任何时候他们都继续去做，因为如果他们长此这样做的话，这种赋税很快就会使他们破产，从而使他们无力再支持这个国家。

<small>荷兰曾经采用了汉堡的做法。</small>

在英格兰，尽管按照土地税法对资本征收的赋税与资本量成比例，但这个赋税并不打算减少或取走资本的任何部分。它只是打算按照与土地的地租税同样的税率，对货币利息征税。所以当地租税为每镑4先令时，货币利息税也是每镑4先令。汉堡、翁德沃尔德和苏黎世征收的赋税，都是为了以同样的方式对资本的利息或纯收入征税，而不是为了对资本征税。而荷兰则是为了对

<small>在这种情况下，赋税目的在于对资本征税。</small>

## *Taxes Upon The Profit Of Particular Employments*

Taxes are sometimes imposed on particular profits,

In some countries extraordinary taxes are imposed upon the profits of stock; sometimes when employed in particular branches of trade, and sometimes when employed in agriculture.

such as those on hawkers, pedlars, etc.

Of the former kind are in England the tax upon hawkers and pedlars, that upon hackney coaches and chairs, and that which the keepers of ale-houses pay for a licence to retail ale and spirituous liquors. During the late war, another tax of the same kind was proposed upon shops. ① The war having been undertaken, it was said, in defence of the trade of the country, the merchants, who were to profit by it, ought to contribute towards the support of it.

These fall not on the dealers but on the consumers of the goods,

A tax, however, upon the profits of stock employed in any particular branch of trade, can never fall finally upon the dealers (who must in all ordinary cases have their reasonable profit, and, where the competition is free, can seldom have more than that profit), but always upon the consumers, who must be obliged to pay in the price of the goods the tax which the dealer advances; and generally with some overcharge.

A tax of this kind when it is proportioned to the trade of the dealer, is finally paid by the consumer, and occasions no oppression to the dealer. When it is not so proportioned, but is the same upon all dealers, though in this case too it is finally paid by the consumer, yet it favours the great, and occasions some oppression to the small dealer. The tax of five shillings a week upon every hackney coach, and that of ten shillings a year upon every hackney chair, so far as it is

---

① [Proposed by Legge in 1759. See Dowell, *History of Taxation and Taxes in England*, 1884, vol. ii. , p. 137. ]

资本征税。

## 用于特殊用途的资本的利润税

有些国家对资本的利润征收特殊的赋税。有时这些资本是用在了特殊的商业部门,有时这些资本是用在了农业上。

<small>有时对特殊利润税,如对小贩征收的税等。</small>

在英格兰,属于前者这种赋税的有:对叫卖小贩所征收的赋税、对出租马车和轿子所征收的赋税和对酒店老板为得到淡色浓啤酒和烈性酒零售营业执照所征收的赋税。在最近战争中,另外又提出了要对店铺征以同样的赋税①。据说是因为战争是为了保护国家的商业,所以获利的商人应该为支持这场战争做出贡献。

不过,对于特殊商业部门的资本所征收的赋税,最终都不会落在商人身上(他们在通常情况下都要有合理的利润,而且在自由竞争的地方,他们的利润也很少会超过这个合理利润),而总是落在消费者身上。消费者必然要在购买的商品的价格中支付商人垫付的赋税,而且商人还总是会多要一些。

<small>这些税不是落在商人身上,而是落在商品的消费者身上。</small>

当这种赋税与商人的交易成比例时,它最终是由消费者来支付,不会对商人造成什么压力。但是当它不是与商人的交易成比例,而是同样地对所有的商人征税,尽管这种情况下最终也是由消费者来支付,但却会对大商人有利,而给小商人带来一些压力。每辆出租马车每周征收5先令的赋税,每辆出租轿子每周征收10

---

① 莱格在1759年提出,参见道尔《英格兰赋税和赋税史》,1884年,第2卷,第137页。

— 1789 —

advanced by the different keepers of such coaches and chairs, is exactly enough proportioned to the extent of their respective dealings. It neither favours the great, nor oppresses the smaller dealer. The tax of twenty shillings a year for a licence to sell ale; of forty shillings for a licence to sell spirituous liquors; and of forty shillings more for a licence to sell wine, being the same upon all retailers, must necessarily give some advantage to the great, and occasion some oppression to the small dealers. The former must find it more easy to get back the tax in the price of their goods than the latter. The moderation of the tax, however, renders this inequality of less importance, and it may to many people appear not improper to give some discouragement to the multiplication of little ale-houses. The tax upon shops, it was intended, should be the same upon all shops. It could not well have been otherwise. It would have been impossible to proportion with tolerable exactness the tax upon a shop to the extent of the trade carried on in it, without such an inquisition as would have been altogether insupportable in a free country. If the tax had been considerable, it would have oppressed the small, and forced almost the whole retail trade into the hands of the great dealers. The competition of the former being taken away, the latter would have enjoyed a monopoly of the trade; and like all other monopolists would soon have combined to raise their profits much beyond what was necessary for the payment of the tax. The final payment, instead of falling upon the shopkeeper, would have fallen upon the consumer, with a considerable over-charge to the profit of the shopkeeper. For these reasons, the project of a tax upon shops was laid aside, and in the room of it was substituted the subsidy 1759.

What in France is called the personal taille is, perhaps, the most important tax upon the profits of stock employed in agriculture that is levied in any part of Europe.

In the disorderly state of Europe during the prevalence of the feudal government, the sovereign was obliged to content himself with taxing those who were too weak to refuse to pay taxes. The great lords, though willing to assist him upon particular emergencies, refused to

# 第五篇 第二章

先令的赋税,由于这些赋税是由这些马车和轿子的所有者垫付的,所以赋税的多少就与他们的交易规模保持着准确的比例。按照这种赋税,它既不会有利于大商人,也不会给小商人带来压力。对销售淡色浓啤酒的营业执照每年征收20先令的赋税,对销售烈性酒的营业执照每年征收40先令的赋税,对销售葡萄酒的营业执照每年则征收80先令的赋税。由于这种赋税对所有的零售酒店都以同样的方式征税,所以必然会给大店主带来一些好处,而给小店主带来一些压力。前者肯定会发现要比后者更容易通过商品的销售回收到垫付的赋税。不过,因为这种赋税非常轻微,就使得这种不公平变得无关紧要。而且在许多人看来,给予这种数目不断增长的小酒店一些打击也未尝不可。对店铺征税,其本意也就是打算对所有的店铺一视同仁地征税,而且实际上也只能如此,别无他法。要想比较准确地依据店铺的交易量按比例征税,除非对它们实行那种在一个自由国家里完全无法接受的调查。如果这项赋税非常重,它就会挤压小商人,从而导致几乎所有的零售业都会落入大商人手中。既然没有了前者的竞争,后者就会享受该行业的垄断权。而且他们还会像其他所有的垄断者一样,很快就会联合起来抬高他们的利润,使其远远超过了必须支付的税额。这样店铺税的最终支付,就不是落在店主身上,而是以远远超出店主利润的数额落在消费者身上。因为以上原因,对店铺征税的方案就被搁置下来,取而代之的是1759年的补助税。

在法国被称之为个人贡税的赋税,或许是欧洲所有地区对农业资本利润征收的最重要的赋税。

在封建制度盛行,欧洲处于混乱状态的时期,君主不得不满足于仅对那些一般无力拒绝支付赋税的人民征税。尽管大领主们在特殊的紧要关头,也会愿意给君主提供帮助,但他们拒绝支

当不人易例这税,挤比而商税压小大有利易比较,赋小有利。

在法国对农业资本利润征收的个人贡税既不武断又不确定。

subject themselves to any constant tax, and he was not strong enough to force them. The occupiers of land all over Europe were, the greater part of them, originally bond-men. Through the greater part of Europe they were gradually emancipated. Some of them acquired the property of landed estates which they held by some base or ignoble tenure, sometimes under the king, and sometimes under some other great lord, like the ancient copy-holders of England. Others, without acquiring the property, obtained leases for terms of years, of the lands which they occupied under their lord, and thus became less dependent upon him. The great lords seem to have beheld the degree of prosperity and independency which this inferior order of men had thus come to enjoy, with a malignant and contemptuous indignation, and willingly consented that the sovereign should tax them. In some countries this tax was confined to the lands which were held in property by an ignoble tenure; and, in this case, the taille was said to be real. The land-tax established by the late king of Sardinia, and the taille in the provinces of Languedoc, Provence, Dauphine, and Brittany; in the generality of Montauban, and in the elections of Agen and Condom, as well as in some other districts of France, are taxes upon lands held in property by an ignoble tenure. In other countries

付永久的赋税。而君主又没有强大到足以迫使他们必须缴税。欧洲所有土地的占有者,最初大部分都是农奴。在欧洲的大部分地区,他们都逐渐地得到解放。其中一部分人,获得了地产的财产权,有时是在国王的下面,有时是在大领主的下面,他们以贱奴的条件保有地产,就像古代英格兰的不动产的所有人一样[1]。而其他没有获得财产权的人,则获得在他们领主占有土地一定年限的租地权,这样他们也变得不那么依赖于他们的领主了。对于这些下级人民即将享受的繁荣与独立,大领主们充满了恶意的轻蔑的敌意,因此乐于君主对他们征收赋税。在有些国家,这种赋税仅限于那些通过贱奴的条件保有财产权的土地,这种情况下,这种赋税就称为不动产的贡税。已故的撒丁尼亚国王设定的土地税,朗格多克、普罗旺斯、多菲那、布列塔尼半岛各州郡的贡税,对蒙托邦课税区、亚琛和康顿选举区,及法国其他某些地区所征收的赋税,都是对以贱奴的条件保有财产权的土地征收的赋税[2]。在其他国家,这种赋税是对所有拥有农场的人或租用他人土地的

---

[1] 不动产的所有人或者副本持有不动产的人(Free holder or Copy holder),英国法律名词。不动产的所有人指一个人可以占有无条件继承的不动产,指定继承人继承的不动产,或者终身占有的不动产;副本持有不动产的人就是指根据土地登录簿(公簿)的副本而持有土地的人。

[2] 朗格多克(Languedoc),历史上的一个地区和法国中南部的以前的一个省,位于罗讷河西部地中海海湾处。得名于当地居民所讲的罗曼语,它于8世纪被法兰克人所征服并于1271年并入法兰西王室统治范围。

普罗旺斯(Provence),法国历史上东南部的一个地区和以前法国的一个省,临近地中海大约公元前600年古希腊人开始在此定居,后来腓尼基商人也进入此地。公元前2世纪,普罗旺斯成为罗马殖民地公元933年它成为亚耳王国的一部分,后来又归金雀花王朝所有(1246年)1486年归入法国。

布列塔尼半岛(Brittany),历史上的一个地区,原法国西北部一省,位于英吉利海峡和比斯开湾之间的半岛上。公元500年,被盎格鲁-撒克逊人驱逐出家园的布立吞人定居于此。1532年该地区正式并入法国。

the tax was laid upon the supposed profits of all those who held in farm or lease lands belonging to other people, whatever might be the tenure by which the proprietor held them; and in this case the taille was said to be personal. In the greater part of those provinces of France, which are called the Countries of Elections, the taille is of this kind. The real taille, as it is imposed only upon a part of the lands of the country, is necessarily an unequal, but it is not always an arbitrary tax, though it is so upon some occasions. The personal taille, as it is intended to be proportioned to the profits of a certain class of people, which can only be guessed at, is necessarily both arbitrary and unequal.

The authority which assesses it is always ignorant of the real abilities of the contributors and often misled by friendship, party animosity and private resentment.

In France the personal taille at present (1775) annually imposed upon the twenty generalities, called the Countries of Elections, amounts to 40, 107, 239 livres, 16 sous. ① The proportion in which this sum is assessed upon those different provinces, varies from year to year, according to the reports which are made to the king's council concerning the goodness or badness of the crops, as well as other circumstances, which may either increase or diminish their respective abilities to pay. Each generality is divided into a certain number of elections, and the proportion in which the sum imposed upon the whole generality is divided among those different elections, varies likewise from year to year, according to the reports made to the council concerning their respective abilities. It seems impossible that the council, with the best intentions, can ever proportion with tolerable exactness, either of those two assessments to the real abilities of the province or district upon which they are respectively laid. Ignorance and misinformation must always, more or less, mislead the most upright council. The proportion which each parish ought to support of what is assessed upon the whole election, and that which each individual

---

① *Memoires concernant les Droits*, &c. tome ii. p. 17.

人所得到的推定利润征税,而不管保有这些土地的条件是什么。这种情况下,这种赋税就是所谓的个人的贡税。被称之为"选区"的法国大部分州郡,它们那里实行的贡税就是这种类型的贡税。由于不动产的贡税只是对国家的一部分土地征税,所以必然是不公平的。不过尽管它有时是不公平,但却不总是武断的赋税。而由于个人的贡税是打算以一定的比例对某一阶层人民的利润征税,但是这个利润又只能通过猜测推断得到,这样这种赋税必然是武断的,也是不公平的。

在法国,目前(1775年)每年对20个称之为"选区"的课税区征收个人贡税,共计达到40107239里弗16苏①。这个总额分配到各个州郡上的比例年年都不相同。这要取决于枢密院[2]所收到关于各个州郡作物丰歉状况及其他可能增加或减少它们各自支付赋税能力情况的报告。每个课税区又分成一定数量的小选区,对全区征收的税收总额又在这些小选区之间分配,分配的比例也是年年均不相同,这个比例也是取决于枢密院所收到关于它们各别支付赋税能力的报告。这样看来,即便枢密院有最好的愿望,也不可能相当准确地评估这些州郡、选区各自的实际支付能力。最正直的枢密院,也一定会受到无知与错误信息的误导。每个教区应该负担的整个选区赋税总额的比例,每个人应该负担的所属教区赋税总额的比例,也都是同样地年年都不相同,依环境

①《欧洲法律和赋税的记录》,第2卷,第17页。
〔2〕 枢密院(King's Council),原来是政府行政权力的源泉,给君主提供"私人"建议。它在历史上也称为国王议会。今天它的主要作用是礼节性的,如建议君主批准政府的法令。它的主要成员有400人左右,包括内阁阁员,下议院院长及英国、英联邦的高级政治家等。

国民财富的性质与原理

ought to support of what is assessed upon his particular parish, are both in the same manner varied, from year to year, according as circumstances are supposed to require. These circumstances are judged of, in the one case, by the officers of the election; in the other by those of the parish; and both the one and the other are, more or less, under the direction and influence of the intendant. Not only ignorance and misinformation, but friendship, party animosity, and private resentment, are said frequently to mislead such assessors. No man subject to such a tax, it is evident, can ever be certain, before he is assessed, of what he is to pay. He cannot even be certain after he is assessed. If any person has been taxed who ought to have been exempted; or if any person has been taxed beyond his proportion, though both must pay in the mean time, yet if they complain, and make good their complaints, the whole parish is reimposed next year in order to reimburse them. If any of the contributors become bankrupt or insolvent, the collector is obliged to advance his tax, and the whole parish is reimposed next year in order to reimburse the collector. If the collector himself should become bankrupt, the parish which elects him must answer for his conduct to the receivergeneral of the election. But, as it might be troublesome for the receiver to prosecute the whole parish, he takes at his choice five or six of the richest contributors, and obliges them to make good what had been lost by the insolvency of the collector. The parish is afterwards reimposed in order to reimburse those five or six. Such reimpositions are always over and above the taille of the particular year in which they are laid on.

Taxes on the profits of agriculture do not, like those on profits of other trades, fall on the consumer, but on the landlord.

When a tax is imposed upon the profits of stock in a particular branch of trade, the traders are all careful to bring no more goods to market than what they can sell at a price sufficient to reimburse them for advancing the tax. Some of them withdraw a part of their stocks from the trade, and the market is more sparingly supplied than before. The price of the goods rises, and the final payment of the tax falls upon the consumer. But when a tax is imposed upon the profits of stock employed in agriculture, it is not the interest of the farmers to withdraw any part of their stock from that employment. Each farmer occupies a certain quantity of land, for which he pays rent. For the proper cultivation of this land a certain quantity of stock is necessary;

要求而定。在前种场合,这些情况是由选区的官吏判定;在后种场合,这些情况是由教区的官吏判定。但这两种情况都会或多或少地受到州长的指导及影响。不仅仅是无知和错误信息,据说友谊、党派仇恨和私怨都经常会误导这些评估税额的人。很显然没有人在税额没有评定以前会确切地知道他应缴纳的税额,甚至在税额已经评定后他都不能够确切地知道。如果一个应该免税的人被征税了,或者一个人被征收的税额超出了他的比例,尽管他们当时必须要支付这些税额,但如果他们申诉,而且申诉的理由充分的话,那么整个教区来年就要追加征税以补偿他们。如果有纳税人破产或者没有支付能力了,那么征税员就必须代他垫付他的税负,而在来年整个教区要追加征税来补偿这个征税员。如果这个征税员自己也破产了,那么选举出这个征税员的教区就必须为他的行为向选区的总征税员负责。但对于总征税员来说,控诉一个教区可能会是件非常麻烦的事情,所以他就会选择五六个最富有的纳税人,强迫他们补偿由于那个征税员无力支付所带来的损失,而在以后再向这个教区追加征税来补偿这五六个人。这种追征税常常超过了该征税年份的贡税。

当对一特定的商业部门的资本利润征税时,商人们都会非常小心地控制上市的货物量,使它们出售的价格能足以弥补他们所垫付的税款。他们中的一些人就会从该行业中撤回一部分资本,从而使市场的供应比以前减少了。这样货物的价格就会上升,赋税的最终支付就落在了消费者身上。但是当对农业资本的利润征税时,对于农场主来说,从中撤回一部分资本是不符合他们自身利益的。每个农场主占有一定的他们支付了地租的土地,为了合理地耕种这些土地,就必须一定量的资本。如果从这一定量的

其业利润的征税会落在消费者身上那样,对资本利润的征税却会落在地身上。不像其他行业的利润的征税落在消费者身上,农业资本利润的征税却会落在土地身上。

and by withdrawing any part of this necessary quantity, the farmer is not likely to be more able to pay either the rent or the tax. In order to pay the tax, it can never be his interest to diminish the quantity of his produce, nor consequently to supply the market more sparingly than before. The tax, therefore, will never enable him to raise the price of his produce, so as to reimburse himself by throwing the final payment upon the consumer. The farmer, however, must have his reasonable profit as well as every other dealer, otherwise he must give up the trade. After the imposition of a tax of this kind, he can get this reasonable profit only by paying less rent to the landlord. The more he is obliged to pay in the way of tax, the less he can afford to pay in the way of rent. A tax of this kind imposed during the currency of a lease may, no doubt, distress or ruin the farmer. Upon the renewal of the lease it must always fall upon the landlord.

<small>The discouragement to good cultivation caused by the personal taille injures the public, the farmer and the landlord.</small>   In the countries where the personal taille takes place, the farmer is commonly assessed in proportion to the stock which he appears to employ in cultivation. He is, upon this account, frequently afraid to have a good team of horses or oxen, but endeavours to cultivate with the meanest and most wretched instruments of husbandry that he can. Such is his distrust in the justice of his assessors, that he counterfeits poverty, and wishes to appear scarce able to pay any thing for fear of being obliged to pay too much. By this miserable policy he does not, perhaps, always consult his own interest in the most effectual manner; and he probably loses more by the diminution of his produce than he saves by that of his tax. Though, in consequence of this wretched cultivation the market is, no doubt, somewhat worse supplied; yet the small rise of price which this may occasion, as it is not likely even to indemnify the farmer for the diminution of his produce, it is still less likely to enable him to pay more rent to the landlord. The public, the farmer, the landlord, all suffer more or less by this degraded cultivation. That the personal taille tends, in many different ways, to discourage cultivation, and consequently to dry up the principal source of the wealth of every great country, I have already had occasion to observe in the third book of this Inquiry.

What are called poll-taxes in the southern provinces of North Amer-

资本中撤回一部分资本，他就不可能更有能力支付地租或赋税了。为了缴税，为了他的利益他绝不会减少生产物的数量，这样也就不能使农产品市场的供应量比以前减少。因此，这种赋税就无法使他提高生产物的价格，从而无法使他通过将最终支付转移到消费者身上来回收自己的税款。然而，就像是其他商人一样，农场主也要有自己的合理利润，否则他就会放弃这个行业。在被征收这种赋税后，他要想获得合理的利润，只有给地主少支付地租。他必须缴纳的税负越多，他能支付的地租就越少。毫无疑问，当在租约有效期时，征收这种赋税就会使农场主陷于困境或者使其破产。但是当重订租约时，这个赋税就必然最终落在了地主身上。

在实行个人贡税的国家，农场主征收的税额通常与他表面上投入耕种的资本成比例。因此，他常常不敢保有一群好马或好牛，而是尽可能地使用最简陋、最寒酸的农具进行耕种。由于他不相信评估赋税人员的公正，担心被强迫支付赋税太多，所以假装贫穷，希望能够表现得几乎无力支付任何东西。采用这种可怜的手段，或许并没有以最有效的方式考虑他自己的利益。由于使用简陋农具所造成的生产物的减少，或许要比他所节省的赋税还要多呢。毫无疑问，尽管这种拙劣耕种会造成市场供应稍微减少，但由此可能引起的价格的小幅上涨甚至都无法补偿农场主生产物减少的损失，更不要提能使他多给地主支付地租了。这种耕种的退化，使得公众、农场主和地主都或多或少地蒙受损失。关于在很多方面，个人贡税都打击耕种，从而枯竭一个国家的财富主要来源。我在本书的第三篇中已经对此论述过了。

在北美南方各州和西印度群岛征收的所谓的人头税，即每年

<small>个人贡税对良好耕种的打击，伤害公众、农场主和地主。</small>

> **Per capita taxes on negro slaver fall on the landlords.**

ica, and in the West Indian islands, annual taxes of so much a head upon every negroe, are properly taxes upon the profits of a certain species of stock employed in agriculture. As the planters are, the greater part of them, both farmers and landlords, the final payment of the tax falls upon them in their quality of landlords without any retribution.

> **Poll taxes have been represented as badges of slavery, but, to the taxpayer every tax is a badge of liberty.**

Taxes of so much a head upon the bondmen employed in cultivation, seem anciently to have been common all over Europe. There subsists at present a tax of this kind in the empire of Russia. It is probably upon this account that poll-taxes of all kinds have often been represented as badges of slavery. Every tax, however, is to the person who pays it a badge, not of slavery, but of liberty. It denotes that he is subject to government, indeed, but that, as he has some property, he cannot himself be the property of a master. A poll-tax upon slaves is altogether different from a poll-tax upon freemen. The latter is paid by the persons upon whom it is imposed; the former by a different set of persons. The latter is either altogether arbitrary or altogether unequal, and in most cases is both the one and the other; the former, though in some respects unequal, different slaves being of different values, is in no respect arbitrary. Every master who knows the number of his own slaves, knows exactly what he has to pay. Those different taxes, however, being called by the same name, have been considered as of the same nature.

> **Taxes on menial servants are like taxes on consumable commodities.**

The taxes which in Holland are imposed upon men and maid servants, are taxes, not upon stock, but upon expence; and so far resemble the taxes upon consumable commodities. The tax of a guinea a head for every man servant, which has lately been imposed in Great Britain, is of the same kind. It falls heaviest upon the middling rank. A man of two hundred a year may keep a single man servant. A man of ten thousand a year will not keep fifty. It does not affect the poor.

对每一个黑人征收的赋税,就是真正地对投入到农业的特定资本的利润征收的赋税。由于大部分的耕种者既是农场主又是地主,所以作为地主这种赋税的最终支付就落在了他们身上,没有任何补偿。

对黑人头税落在了地主身上。

对耕种中使用的奴隶征收一定的赋税,看来自古在欧洲就比较普遍,迄今俄罗斯帝国仍有这种赋税。目前在俄罗斯还存在着这样一种赋税。可能因为这个原因,所有类型的人头税都经常被当作奴隶制的标志。可是,对于纳税人来说所有的赋税都不是奴隶制的标志,而是自由的标志。纳税意味着他是隶属于政府,所以既然他有一些财产,那么他自己就不可能是主人的财产。对奴隶征收的人头税与对自由人征收的人头税是截然不同的。后者是被征税的人自己支付的赋税,而前者则是由另外一类人支付的赋税。后者是完全武断的或者完全不公平的,而且在大多数情况下,既是完全武断的又是完全不公平的。而前者尽管在一些方面是不公平的,但因为不同的奴隶有不同的价值,所以在任何方面都不是武断的。每个主人都知道他自己奴隶的人数,所以也就准确地知道他应该缴纳多少赋税。不过,这些赋税都叫一样的名字,所以就被当作了同样性质的赋税。

人头税作为奴隶制的标志,但税来所有的赋税都是自由的标志。

在荷兰,对男仆和女仆征收的赋税,不是对资本的赋税,而是对支出的赋税,因此和对消费品课征的赋税非常类似。最近不列颠对每个男仆征收的一几尼的赋税,就是这种类型的赋税。它对中产阶级征收的税负最重。一个年收入 200 镑的人可能会雇用一个男仆,而一个年收入 10000 镑的人却不会雇用 50 个男仆。这种赋税不会影响穷人[1]。

对仆人的赋税与消费品征税类似。

---

[1] 乔治三世十七年第 39 号法令。

— 1801 —

**Taxes on particular profits cannot affect interest.**

Taxes upon the profits of stock in particular employments can never affect the interest of money. Nobody will lend his money for less interest to those who exercise the taxed, than to those who exercise the untaxed employments. Taxes upon the revenue arising from stock in all employments, where the government attempts to levy them with any degree of exactness, will, in many cases, fall upon the interest of money. The Vingtieme, or twentieth penny, in France, is a tax of the same kind with what is called the land-tax in England, and is assessed, in the same manner, upon the revenue arising from land, houses, and stock. So far as it affects stock it is assessed, though not with great rigour, yet with much more exactness than that part of the land-tax of England which is imposed upon the same fund. It, in many cases, falls altogether upon the interest of money. Money is frequently sunk in France upon what are called Contracts for the constitution of a rent; that is, perpetual annuities redeemable at any time by the debtor upon repayment of the sum originally advanced, but of which this redemption is not exigible by the creditor except in particular cases. The Vingtieme seems not to have raised the rate of those annuities, though it is exactly levied upon them all.

对用于特殊用途的资本的利润征收的赋税,永远不会影响货币利息。对于将资本用在要被征税的用途上的人和将资本用在不被征税的用途上的人,没有人会把钱借给前者,因为如果把钱借给前者的话,就会收到较低的利息。在那些政府打算比较准确地征税的地方,对各种用途的资本收入的赋税,在许多情况下都会落在货币利息上。法国的廿一税[1],即二十便士取一的税,就是与英格兰所谓的土地税性质相同的赋税,都是同样地对土地、房屋和资本的收入征税。就其影响资本而言,它对资本的评估虽然不是那么严格,但相比英格兰对同样的资本所征收的土地税,却要准确得多。在许多情况下,它都完全地落在货币利息上。在法国,钱经常被投在所谓的年金契约上,它是一种永久年金,如果债务人能够偿还他最初所借的金额,就可以随时赎回。而对于债权人,除了特殊场合外,不得随意赎回。这种二十取一的税,却好像没有提高这些年金率,尽管它是准确地按照这些年金征税的。

对某些利润征税不会影响利息。

----

[1] 廿一税(Vingtieme),1750年开征,课及不动产、商业、地租甚至封建租税收入,贵族采取少报、谎报财产、收入的方法逃税、漏税。

# Appendix To Articles I And II

## Taxes Upon The Capital Value Of Land, Houses, And Stock

Taxes on the transmission of property often necessarily take a part of the capital value.

While property remains in the possession of the same person, whatever permanent taxes may have been imposed upon it, they have never been intended to diminish or take away any part of its capital value, but only some part of the revenue arising from it. But when property changes hands, when it is transmitted either from the dead to the living, or from the living to the living, such taxes have frequently been imposed upon it as necessarily take away some part of its capital value.

Transfers from the dead to the living and all transfers of immovable property can be taxed directly; transfers by way of loan of money have been taxed by stamp duties or duties on registration.

The transference of all sorts of property from the dead to the living, and that of immoveable property, of lands and houses, from the living to the living, are transactions which are in their nature either public and notorious, or such as cannot be long concealed. Such transactions, therefore, may be taxed directly. The transference of stock or moveable property, from the living to the living, by the lending of money, is frequently a secret transaction, and may always be made so. It cannot easily, therefore, be taxed directly. It has been taxed indirectly in two different ways; first, by requiring that the deed, containing the obligation to repay, should be written upon paper or parchment which had paid a certain stamp-duty, otherwise not to be valid; secondly, by requiring, under the like penalty of invalidity, that it should be recorded either in a public or secret register, and by imposing certain duties upon such registration. Stamp-duties and duties of registration have frequently been imposed likewise upon the deeds transferring property of all kinds from the dead to the living, and upon those transferring immoveable property from the

# 第一项和第二项的附录

## 对土地、房屋和资财的资本价值征收的赋税

当财产保留在所有者手中时,无论对财产征收多么永久的赋税,这些赋税都不在于去减少其资本价值或者取走其一部分资本价值,而在于取走由财产产生的收入的一部分。但是当财产转手时,无论是由死者转移到生者,还是由生者转移到生者,这种对财产征收的赋税往往就必然会取走其资本价值的一部分。

所有从死者到生者的财产转移,以及像土地、房屋这样的不动产由生者到生者的转移,它们在本质上都是公开的、众人皆知的交易,所以不可能长期隐瞒。因此这样的交易就可以直接对其征税。而这种资本或者动产的转移,通过借贷从生者转移至生者,这种转移就常常是一种秘密的交易,而且经常可以这么做。因此这样的交易就不容易对其直接征税。对待这个问题有两种间接的征税方法:第一,要求必须将包含偿还义务的契约写在付过一定印花税的纸上或羊皮纸上,否则该契约将被视为无效;第二,要求这种契约必须登记在一个公开的或秘密的登记簿上,并对这种登记征收一定的赋税,否则同样将被视为无效。对于可能比较容易直接征税的所有类型的从死者到生者的财产转移和从

> 对财产转手征收的赋税,往往必然会带走其资本价值的一部分。

> 对于从死者到生者的和不动产所有权的转移,都可直接征税。对以借贷形式发生的转移,则以印花税或登记的方法征收赋税。

living to the living, transactions which might easily have been taxed directly.

<small>Transfers from the dead to the living were taxed by the Vicesima Hereditatum,</small>

The Vicesima Hereditatum, the twentieth penny of inheritances, imposed by Augustus upon the ancient Romans, was a tax upon the transference of property from the dead to the living. Dion Cassius, the author who writes concerning it the least indistinctly, says, that it was imposed upon all successions, legacies, and donations, in case of death, except upon those to the nearest relations, and to the poor.

<small>and the Dutch tax on successions.</small>

Of the same kind is the Dutch tax upon successions. ① Collateral successions are taxed, according to the degree of relation, from five to thirty per cent. upon the whole value of the succession. Testamentary donations, or legacies to collaterals, are subject to the like duties. Those from husband to wife, or from wife to husband, to the fifteenth penny. The Luctuosa Hereditas, the mournful succession of ascendents to descendents, to the twentieth penny only. Direct successions, or those of descendents to ascendents, pay no tax. The death of a father, to such of his children as live in the same house with him, is seldom attended with any increase, and frequently with a considerable diminution of revenue; by the loss of his industry, of his office, or of some life-rent estate, of which he may have been in possession. That tax would be cruel and oppressive which aggravated their loss by taking from them any part of his succession. It may, however, sometimes be otherwise with those children who, in the language of the Roman law, are said to be emancipated; in that of the Scotch law, to be forisfamiliated; that is, who have received their portion, have got families of their own, and are supported by funds separate and independent of

---

① See *Memoires concernant les Droits*, &c. tome i. p. 225.

第五篇 第一项和第二项的附录

生者到生者的不动产转移,也都经常同样地要征收印花税和登记税。

奥古斯都[1]向古罗马人民征收的二十便士取一的遗产税,就是对由生者到生者的财产转移征收的赋税。狄欧·卡修斯[2]关于这点曾做过详细地记述。他说,这个赋税是对所有因死亡而发生的继承、遗赠和捐赠征收的赋税,只有当受惠者是直系亲属或者穷人时才予免税。

对从死者到生者的转移征收二十取一的遗产税。

荷兰对继承权征收的赋税也是这种类型的赋税①。旁系亲属继承要被征税,税率按照关系的远近从5%—30%不等。对旁系亲属的遗赠,也征收同样的赋税。丈夫对妻子,或者妻子对丈夫的遗赠,税率为1/15。这种晚辈传给长辈的悲痛的继承,税率仅为1/20。直接继承或者长辈传给晚辈的继承不用缴税。父亲的去世,很少会给和他同住一起的子女们带来收入的增长,相反还往往会使收入减少很多。因为父亲去世了,他的劳动力就丧失了,他的官职就没有了,而他可能拥有的某种终身年金也就结束了。如果再取走这些子女继承财产的一部分,就会加剧他们的损失,那将是残忍的和难以忍受的。不过,按照罗马法中所说的解放了的子女,或者按照苏格兰法所说的分了家的子女,情况就有所不同了。因为他们分家时已经分到了他们应得财产的份额,有了他们自己的家庭,有了他们自己的财源,不再依赖于他们的父

荷兰的遗产税。

---

① 参见《欧洲法律和赋税的记录》,第1卷,第225页。
〔1〕 奥古斯都(Augustus),前63年~前14年,罗马帝国第一代皇帝。
〔2〕 狄欧·卡修斯(Dion Cassius),公元2世纪时的历史学家,著有《罗马史》。

— 1807 —

those of their father. Whatever part of his succession might come to such children, would be a real addition to their fortune, and might therefore, perhaps, without more inconveniency than what attends all duties of this kind, be liable to some tax.

<small>The feudal law taxed the transference of land,</small> The casualties of the feudal law were taxes upon the transference of land, both from the dead to the living, and from the living to the living. In ancient times they constituted in every part of Europe one of the principal branches of the revenue of the crown.

The heir of every immediate vassal of the crown paid a certain duty, generally a year's rent, upon receiving the investiture of the estate. If the heir was a minor, the whole rents of the estate, during <small>by wardships and reliefs,</small> the continuance of the minority, devolved to the superior without any other charge, besides the maintenance of the minor, and the payment of the widow's dower, when there happened to be a dowager upon the land. When the minor came to be of age, another tax, called Relief, was still due to the superior, which generally amounted likewise to a year's rent. A long minority, which in the present times so frequently disburdens a great estate of all its incumbrances, and restores the family to their ancient splendour, could in those times have no such effect. The waste, and not the disincumbrance of the estate, was the common effect of a long minority.

<small>and fines on alienation, which last still form a considerable branch of revenue in many countries.</small> By the feudal law the vassal could not alienate without the consent of his superior, who generally extorted a fine or composition for granting it. This fine, which was at first arbitrary, came in many countries to be regulated at a certain portion of the price of the land. In some countries, where the greater part of the other feudal customs have gone into disuse, this tax upon the alienation of land still continues to make a very considerable branch of the revenue of the sovereign. In the canton of Berne it is so high as a sixth part of the price of all noble fiefs; and a tenth part of that of all ignoble ones. [①] In the

---

① *Memoires concernant les Droits*, &c. tome i. p. 154.

## 第五篇 第一项和第二项的附录

亲了。无论他们父亲继承权的哪一部分分给了这些子女,对这些子女的财产来说都是一种实际的增加。所以,不像对其他继承权征税那样,对这种继承权征税不会带来什么更多的不便。

根据封建法律,对从死者到生者、从生者到生者的土地转移,都要征收赋税。在古代的欧洲,它们构成了各个地方皇室的主要收入之一。

皇室近臣的继承人要想获得地产的授权,必须支付一定的税额,通常为一年地租。如果继承人还未成年,在其未成年期间,这块地产的土地租金都归该国王所有,国王除了要抚养未成年人和支付寡妇应得的亡夫遗产(如果这块土地上正好有应享有亡夫遗产的寡妇的话),不用再支付任何其他费用。当继承人成年时,他还得对国王另外支付一种叫做继承权利金的赋税,这种赋税一般也是一年的地租。如果是现在,长时间的未成年期会使一大宗地产解除它所有的债务,而恢复其家族以前的辉煌;但在那个时代,长时间的未成年期却没有这样的功效,通常情况下未成年期长的结果不是债务的解除,而是土地的荒芜。

按照封建法律,不经国王的同意,其臣属不得转让土地。国王通常要勒索一笔罚金后才会同意。这笔罚金最初是任意索取的,后来在许多国家被规定为土地价格中的一定部分。在有些国家,尽管大部分其他的封建惯例已经废止了,但对于转让土地的赋税却仍然存在,是君主一项非常大的收入来源。在伯尔尼州,这项赋税税率非常高,对所有贵族的封地如果转让土地则征收土地价格 1/6 的赋税,而对平民则征收土地价格 1/10 的赋税①。

---

① 《欧洲法律与赋税的记录》,第 1 卷,第 154 页。

国民财富的性质与原理

canton of Lucerne the tax upon the sale of lands is not universal, and takes place only in certain districts. But if any person sells his land, in order to remove out of the territory, he pays ten per cent. upon the whole price of the sale. ① Taxes of the same kind upon the sale either of all lands, or of lands held by certain tenures, take place in many other countries, and make a more or less considerable branch of the revenue of the sovereign.

<small>These taxes on the sale of land may be levied by stamps or duties on registration.</small>   Such transactions may be taxed indirectly, by means either of stampduties, or of duties upon registration; and those duties either may or may not be proportioned to the value of the subject which is transferred.

<small>In Great Britain the duties are not proportioned to the value of the property.</small>   In Great Britain the stamp-duties are higher or lower, not so much according to the value of the property transferred (an eighteen penny or half crown stamp being sufficient upon a bond for the largest sum of money) as according to the nature of the deed. The highest do not exceed six pounds upon every sheet of paper, or skin of parchment; and these high duties fall chiefly upon grants from the crown, and upon certain law proceedings, without any regard to the value of the subject. There are in Great Britain no duties on the registration of deeds or writings, except the fees of the officers who keep the register; and these are seldom more than a reasonable recompence for their labour. The crown derives no revenue from them.

In Holland ② there are both stamp-duties and duties upon registration; which in some cases are, and in some are not proportioned to the value of the property transferred. All testaments must

---

① *Memoires concernant les Droits*, &c. tome i. p. 157.
② Ibid., pp. 223, 224, 225.

## 第五篇　第一项和第二项的附录

在卢塞恩州[1],并不是对所有的土地销售都征税,而是只限一定的地区。但如果一个人是为了搬出这个行政区域而变卖土地,那么就要支付全部销售收入 1/10 的赋税①。在许多其他国家,也有类似的对所有土地的出售征收赋税或者则对按一定条件保有的土地的出售征收赋税,这些税都或多或少构成了君主的一项重要收入。

这些交易可以按照印花税或登记税的方法来对其间接的征税。而这些赋税的税额可以与转让对象的价值成比例,也可以不与转让对象的价值成比例。

在大不列颠,印花税的高低与其说是按照转移财产的价值(最高金额的债券只需要 18 便士或者半克朗的印花税就可以了),不如说是按照契约的性质。最重的印花税种为每张纸或羊皮纸不超过 6 镑的印花税。这些高额的赋税主要是对国王的特许状和特定的法律手续征收的,而与转移对象的价值无关。在大不列颠,除了给保存登记簿的官员支付的手续费外,没有其他对契约或者文书的登记征收的赋税了。而且这个手续费很少超过对这些官员劳动的合理补偿的数额。君主没有从中得到任何收入。

荷兰既有印花税又有登记税②。有些场合这些赋税与转移财产的价值成比例,而在有些场合下则不与其价值成比例。所有

---

① 《欧洲法律与赋税的记录》,第 1 卷,第 157 页。
② 同上书,第 223、224、225 页。
[1] 卢塞恩市(Lucerne),瑞士中部的一座城市,位于群山环抱的月形状不规则的卢塞恩湖的北岸。这座城市是围绕一个 18 世纪建立的寺庙发展起来的。

— 1811 —

国民财富的性质与原理

In Holland some are proportioned and others not.

be written upon stamped paper of which the price is proportioned to the property disposed of, so that there are stamps which cost from three pence, or three stivers a sheet, to three hundred florins, equal to about twenty-seven pounds ten shillings of our money. If the stamp is of an inferior price to what the testator ought to have made use of, his succession is confiscated. This is over and above all their other taxes on succession. Except bills of exchange, and some other mercantile bills, all other deeds, bonds, and contracts, are subject to a stamp-duty. This duty, however, does not rise in proportion to the value of the subject. All sales of land and of houses, and all mortgages upon either, must be registered, and, upon registration, pay a duty to the state of two and a half per cent. upon the amount of the price or of the mortgage. This duty is extended to the sale of all ships and vessels of more than two tons burthen, whether decked or undecked. These, it seems, are considered as a sort of houses upon the water. The sale of moveables, when it is ordered by a court of justice, is subject to the like duty of two and a half per cent.

In France different sets of officers collect the stamp duties and the registration duties.

In France there are both stamp-duties and duties upon registration. The former are considered as a branch of the aides or excise, and in the provinces where those duties take place, are levied by the excise officers. The latter are considered as a branch of the domain of the crown, and are levied by a different set of officers.

Both stamps and registration duties are modern methods of taxation.

Those modes of taxation, by stamp-duties and by duties upon registration, are of very modern invention. In the course of little more than a century, however, stamp-duties have, in Europe, become almost universal, and duties upon registration extremely common. There is no art which one government sooner learns of another, than that of draining money from the pockets of the people.

Taxes upon the transference of property from the dead to the living, fall finally as well as immediately upon the person to whom the property is transferred. Taxes upon the sale of land fall altogether upon the seller. The seller is almost always under the necessity of selling, and must, therefore, take such a price as he can get. The buyer is scarce ever under the necessity of buying, and will, therefore, only give such a price as he likes. He considers what the land will cost

— 1812 —

第五篇  第一项和第二项的附录

的遗嘱都必须写在印花税纸上,印花税纸的价格与所处理的财产成比例。所以就有了不同价格的印花税纸,从每张 3 便士或 3 斯梯弗到每张 300 弗罗林(大约等于英国货币的 27 镑 10 先令)不等。如果立遗嘱的人使用的印花税纸价格低于它应该使用的印花税纸的价格,那么继承财产就会被没收。这项赋税是对继承权征收的其他赋税以外的赋税。除了汇票和一些其他商业票据外,所有其他的契约、债券和合同都要缴纳印花税。不过,这种赋税并不随着转移对象的价值的升高而成比例地升高。所有土地和房屋的出售,以及所有土地和房屋的抵押单据,都必须进行登记并且要给国家缴纳出售价格或者抵押品价格 2.5% 的赋税。这项赋税拓展到船舶的出售,无论是否有甲板,只要是出售超过两吨的船舶,都要征以赋税。这或许是把船舶看作了一种水上的房屋吧。按照法庭命令而出售的动产,同样也要征收 2.5% 的赋税。

在荷兰赋税与转移对象的价值有些成比例;有些不成比例。

　　法国也是既有印花税又有登记税。前者视为一种货物税,在实行这种赋税的州郡由货物税官员来征收这项赋税。后者则视为皇室统治的一种赋税,由不同的官员来征收。

在法国同员收印花税和登记税。

　　这些印花税和登记税的征税方法,都是最近才发明出来的。然而,在不到 100 年的时间里,印花税在欧洲已经几乎通用了,登记税也相当的普遍。一个政府向其他政府学习的技术中没有一种技术比从人民口袋中掏钱学得更快了。

印花税和登记税都是现代的征税方法;

　　对从死者到生者的财产转移所征收的赋税,最终也直接地落在了接受这些财产的人身上。对出售土地所征收的赋税完全都落在了卖者身上。卖者之所以出售土地,经常是因为他非卖不可,所以他必须接受他所能得到的价格。而买者很少是处于非买不可的境地,所以他只会给一个他愿意给的价格。他会把土地的

— 1813 —

him in tax and price together. The more he is obliged to pay in the way of tax, the less he will be disposed to give in the way of price. Such taxes, therefore, fall almost always upon a necessitous person, and must, therefore, be frequently very cruel and oppressive. Taxes upon the sale of new-built houses, where the building is sold without the ground, fall generally upon the buyer, because the builder must generally have his profit; otherwise he must give up the trade. If he advances the tax, therefore, the buyer must generally repay it to him. Taxes upon the sale of old houses, for the same reason as those upon the sale of land, fall generally upon the seller; whom in most cases either conveniency or necessity obliges to sell. The number of new-built houses that are annually brought to market, is more or less regulated by the demand. Unless the demand is such as to afford the builder his profit, after paying all expences, he will build no more houses. The number of old houses which happen at any time to come to market is regulated by accidents of which the greater part have no relation to the demand. Two or three great bankruptcies in a mercantile town, will bring many houses to sale, which must be sold for what can be got for them. Taxes upon the sale of ground rents fall altogether upon the seller; for the same reason as those upon the sale of land. Stamp-duties, and duties upon the registration of bonds and contracts for borrowed money, fall altogether upon the borrower, and, in fact, are always paid by him. Duties of the same kind upon law proceedings fall upon the suitors. They reduce to both the capital value of the subject in dispute. The more it costs to acquire any property, the less must be the neat value of it when acquired.

All taxes upon the transference of property of every kind, so far as they diminish the capital value of that property, tend to diminish the funds destined for the maintenance of productive labour. They are all more or less unthrifty taxes that increase the revenue of the sovereign, which seldom maintains any but unproductive labourers; at the expence of the capital of the people, which maintains none but productive.

# 第五篇 第一项和第二项的附录

价格和征收的赋税放在一起考虑费用。他不得不支付的赋税越多,他愿意支付的价格就越少。所以这种赋税,几乎总是落在了那些急需成交的人身上,因此也经常必然是残酷的、令人难以忍受的。对出售新建房屋所征收的赋税,如果只卖建筑物不卖地皮的话,通常会落在买者一方。因为建筑者一般必须获取他的利润,否则他就必然会放弃这个行业。因此,如果他垫付了赋税的话,一般来说买者都必须把这个赋税偿还给他。而对于出售旧房屋所征收的赋税,与对出售土地征收赋税的情况一样,通常会落在卖者身上。卖者之所以卖,许多情况下是由于方便或者他必须得卖。每年投放到市场上的新建房屋数量,或多或少地都受到需求的支配。除非这个需求在给建筑者支付所有的费用后还能给他提供利润,不然他就不会再建造房屋了。而对于任何时候投放到市场上的旧房屋数量,则是受偶然事件的支配,大部分与需求无关。如果一个商业城市里发生了两三件大破产的事件,就会有大量的房屋要出售,而且都会以能够得到的价格卖出。与对出售土地征收赋税的情况一样,对出售地皮租金所征收的赋税,就完全地落在了卖者身上。对债券和借款合同所征收的印花税和登记税全部地落在了借者一方,而且事实上也总是由他支付。同样地对诉讼手续征收的赋税落在了诉讼人身上。它减少了诉讼双方争讼对象的资本价值。为获得财产花费得越多,获得的净价值也必定会越少。

所有对各种财产转移征收的赋税,只要它们减少该财产的资本价值,就可能会导致减少用于维持生产性劳动的资本。君主的收入基本上都是用于维持非生产性劳动,而人民的资本则是用于维持生产性劳动。由于这些赋税都是以人民的资本作为代价来

| 国民财富的性质与原理

Even when proportioned to the value of the property they are unequal, because the frequency of transfer varies. They are certain, convenient and inexpensive.

Such taxes, even when they are proportioned to the value of the property transferred, are still unequal; the frequency of transference not being always equal in property of equal value. When they are not proportioned to this value, which is the case with the greater part of the stamp-duties, and duties of registration, they are still more so. They are in no respect arbitrary, but are or may be in all cases perfectly clear and certain. Though they sometimes fall upon the person who is not very able to pay; the time of payment is in most cases sufficiently convenient for him. When the payment becomes due, he must in most cases have the money to pay. They are levied at very little expence, and in general subject the contributors to no other inconveniency besides always the unavoidable one of paying the tax.

French stamp-duties on transfers are not much complained of, but the registration duties (or Contrôle) are said to be arbitrary and uncertain.

In France the stamp-duties are not much complained of. Those of registration, which they call the Contrôle, are. They give occasion, it is pretended, to much extortion in the officers of the farmers-general who collect the tax, which is in a great measure arbitrary and uncertain. In the greater part of the libels which have been written against the present system of finances in France, the abuses of the Contr le make a principal article. Uncertainty, however, does not seem to be necessarily inherent in the nature of such taxes. If the popular complaints are well founded, the abuse must arise, not so much from the nature of the tax, as from the want of precision and distinctness in the words of the edicts or laws which impose it.

The registration of mortgages, and in general of all rights upon immoveable property, as it gives great security both to creditors and purchasers, is extremely advantageous to the public. . That of the greater part of deeds of other kinds is frequently inconvenient and even

## 第五篇　第一项和第二项的附录

增加君主的收入，所以它们或多或少都是不经济的税种。

即便当这些赋税与转移的财产的价值成比例时，也还是不公平的，因为同样价值财产的转移次数却未必一定会相等。而如果不与转移财产的价值成比例时，大部分的印花税和登记税就是这样，就会更加的不平等了。不过，这种赋税从各个方面来讲都不是随意确定的，它们在所有的场合都是或者是非常清晰地确定的。尽管有时候它们会落在根本无力支付赋税的人身上，但支付的时间对于纳税人来说在很多情况下都是非常方便的。当到该缴纳赋税的时候，多数情况下他都是有钱来缴税的。这种赋税的征收费用很少，一般情况下纳税人除了必须缴税外，并没有其他的什么不便。

在法国，印花税并没有引起太多抱怨。但人们对于登记税却抱怨很多。据说登记税使得包收租税的人员有了机会大肆勒索，而且这种赋税在很大程度上又是任意的和不确定的。在大部分反对法国现行财政制度的小册子中[1]，登记税的滥用是一个主要的题目。不过，不确定性似乎不是这种赋税的内在本质。如果说这种普遍的抱怨是理由充分的话，那么这种滥用与其说是这种赋税的本性使然，不如说是因为征税法令或法律在用词上缺乏精确性和清晰性。

抵押单据和基本上所有不动产权利的登记，由于它可以给债权者和购买者双方提供很大的保障，所以对公众非常有利。而其他大部分契约的登记对于个人来说常常是不便的甚至是危险的，

---

[1] 此处的"Libels"，是用的它的古老的意思，相当于现代化的"Pamphlets"即小册子。参见默里的《牛津英文词典》中有关词目。

**Public registration of mortgages and all rights to immovable property is advantageous, but secret registers ought not to exist.**

dangerous to individuals, without any advantage to the public. All registers which, it is acknowledged, ought to be kept secret, ought certainly never to exist. The credit of individuals ought certainly never to depend upon so very slender a security as the probity and religion of the inferior officers of revenue. But where the fees of registration have been made a source of revenue to the sovereign, register offices have commonly been multiplied without end, both for the deeds which ought to be registered, and for those which ought not. In France there are several different sorts of secret registers. This abuse, though not perhaps a necessary, it must be acknowledged, is a very natural effect of such taxes.

**Many stamp-duties are duties on consumption.**

Such stamp-duties as those in England upon cards and dice, upon news-papers and periodical pamphlets, &c. are properly taxes upon consumption; the final payment falls upon the persons who use or consume such commodities. Such stamp-duties as those upon licences to retail ale, wine, and spirituous liquors, though intended, perhaps, to fall upon the profits of the retailers, are likewise finally paid by the consumers of those liquors. Such taxes, though called by the same name, and levied by the same officers and in the same manner with the stamp-duties above mentioned upon the transference of property, are however of a quite different nature, and fall upon quite different funds.

## Article III    Taxes Upon The Wages Of Labour

**A tax on wages must raise wages by rather more than the amount of the tax.**

The wages of the inferior classes of workmen, I have endeavoured to show in the first book, are every where necessarily regulated by two different circumstances; the demand for labour, and the ordinary or average price of provisions. The demand for labour, according as it happens to be either increasing, stationary, or declining; or to require an increasing, stationary, or declining population, regulates the subsistence of the labourer, and determines in what degree it shall be, either liberal, moderate, or scanty. The ordinary or average price of provisions determines the quantity of money which must be paid to the workman in order to enable him, one year with another, to purchase this liberal, moderate, or scanty subsistence. While the de-

## 第五篇　第一项和第二项的附录

对于公众来说也是毫无利益可言的。众所周知，所有应该保持秘密的登记簿根本就不应该存在。个人信用当然不能依赖于低级税收人员的正直和良心这种薄弱的保障。但由于登记费已经成为了君主的一种收入来源的场合，结果是登记机构普遍无休止地扩张，应该登记的契约要登记，不该登记的契约也要登记。法国有几种不同类型的秘密登记簿。这种登记簿的泛滥，尽管不一定是必然的结果，但我们得承认是这种赋税非常自然的结果。

<small>单所有权益但抵押和不动产权公记登记簿不存的密秘登记簿应在。</small>

在英格兰，对纸牌、骰子、新闻纸和定期刊物等的印花税完全是消费征收的赋税，这些赋税的最终支付落在了那些使用或消费这些消费品的人身上。而对零售淡色啤酒、葡萄酒和烈性酒营业执照征收的赋税，尽管或许是打算落在零售者的利润上，但同样地最终会落在这些消费者身上。尽管这些赋税和上面提到的对财产转移征收的印花税有着同样的名字，由同样的征税人员以同样的方法来征收，但性质却完全不同，它们最后落在了完全不同的资本上。

<small>许多印花税是对消费征税。</small>

## 第三项　劳动工资税

我在本书第一篇已经尽力阐述了，低级劳动者的工资在各个地方都必然受到两种不同情况的支配，即对劳动的需求和食物的一般价格或平均价格。对劳动的需求，根据它是增加的、停滞的还是减少的，或者说要求人口是增加、停滞，还是要求减少，支配着劳动者的生活资料，决定着这种生活资料的丰富、一般或者缺乏程度。食物的一般或平均价格，决定着必须支付给劳动者的货币数量以便使他们每年都能买到这些丰富的、一般的或者短缺的

<small>对工资征税收的赋税提高工资的幅度必然要高于税额。</small>

— 1819 —

mand for labour and the price of provisions, therefore, remain the same, a direct tax upon the wages of labour can have no other effect than to raise them somewhat higher than the tax. Let us suppose, for example, that in a particular place the demand for labour and the price of provisions were such, as to render ten shillings a week the ordinary wages of labour; and that a tax of one-fifth, or four shillings in the pound, was imposed upon wages. If the demand for labour and the price of provisions remained the same, it would still be necessary that the labourer should in that place earn such a subsistence as could be bought only for ten shillings a week, or that after paying the tax he should have ten shillings a week free wages. But in order to leave him such free wages after paying such a tax, the price of labour must in that place soon rise, not to twelve shillings a week only, but to twelve and sixpence; that is, in order to enable him to pay a tax of one-fifth, his wages must necessarily soon rise, not one-fifth part only, but one-fourth. Whatever was the proportion of the tax, the wages of labour must in all cases rise, not only in that proportion, but in a higher proportion. If the tax, for example, was one-tenth, the wages of labour must necessarily soon rise, not one-tenth part only, but one-eighth.

The rise in the wages of manufacturing labour would be advanced by the employers and paid by the consumers, and the rise in agricultural wages advanced by the farmers and paid by the landlords.

A direct tax upon the wages of labour, therefore, though the labourer might perhaps pay it out of his hand, could not properly be said to be even advanced by him; at least if the demand for labour and the average price of provisions remained the same after the tax as before it. In all such cases, not only the tax, but something more than the tax, would in reality be advanced by the person who immediately employed him. The final payment would in different cases fall upon different persons. The rise which such a tax might occasion in the wages of manufacturing labour would be advanced by the master manufacturer, who would both be entitled and obliged to charge it, with a profit, upon the price of his goods. The final payment of this rise of wages, therefore, together with the additional profit of the master manufacturer, would fall upon the consumer. The rise which such a tax might occasion in the wages of country labour would be advanced by the farmer, who, in order to maintain the same number of

第五篇　第一项和第二项的附录

生活资料。因此，当劳动需求和食物价格保持不变时，对劳动工资直接征税就只能会导致工资提高的幅度比税额略大。例如，我们假设有一个地方，劳动需求和食物的价格使得劳动的普通工资为 10 先令一周，并假设对工资征收的税率为 1/5，即每镑征收 4 先令。如果劳动需求和食物价格保持不变，那么该劳动者在该地仍然必须挣到每周 10 先令所能购买到的生活必需品，换言之，在支付了工资税后还应该有每周 10 先令的可自由支配的工资。但为了使征税后劳动者还有这样自由支配的工资，该地的劳动价格就必须很快提高，不仅仅是提高到 12 先令，而是要提高到 12 先令 6 便士。也就是说，为了能使他可以支付 1/5 的赋税，他的工资不是提高 1/5，而是必须要提高 1/4。无论税率如何，在所有的情况下，工资不但会按照这个税率提高，而且还会以高于税率的比例提高。例如，如果税率是 1/10，劳动工资肯定很快就会提高 1/8，而不是 1/10。

因此，尽管对劳动工资直接征收的赋税可能是从劳动者手中付出，但更确切地讲，这些赋税甚至还不能说是这些劳动者垫付的，至少在征税后劳动需求和食物的平均价格和征税前一样的情况下就是这样的。在所有这样的情况下，工资税和超过工资税的一些款项实际上都是由直接雇用他的人垫支的。在不同的情况下，这种赋税的最终支付会落在不同的人身上。这种赋税引起的制造业劳动工资的提高要由制造业主来垫付，他既有权利也不得不把将这个税额和利润加到货物价格上。这样，工资的提高和制造业主的最终利润的最终支付就落在了消费者身上。这种赋税引起的乡村劳动工资的提高将由农场主来垫付。农场主为了拥有和以前一样的劳动人数，将不得不投入更多的资本。为了收回

制造业工资的上涨由制造业主垫付而由消费者支付；农业工资的增加由农场主垫付而由地主支付。

labourers as before, would be obliged to employ a greater capital. In order to get back this greater capital, together with the ordinary profits of stock, it would be necessary that he should retain a larger portion, or what comes to the same thing, the price of a larger portion, of the produce of the land, and consequently that he should pay less rent to the landlord. The final payment of this rise of wages, therefore, would in this case fall upon the landlord, together with the additional profit of the farmer who had advanced it. In all cases a direct tax upon the wages of labour must, in the long-run, occasion both a greater reduction in the rent of land, and a greater rise in the price of manufactured goods, than would have followed from the proper assessment of a sum equal to the produce of the tax, partly upon the rent of land, and partly upon consumable commodities.

*The effect of the tax in raising wages is generally disguised by the fall in the demand for labour which it occasions.*

If direct taxes upon the wages of labour have not always occasioned a proportionable rise in those wages, it is because they have generally occasioned a considerable fall in the demand for labour. The declension of industry, the decrease of employment for the poor, the diminution of the annual produce of the land and labour of the country, have generally been the effects of such taxes. In consequence of them, however, the price of labour must always be higher than it otherwise would have been in the actual state of the demand; and this enhancement of price, together with the profit of those who advance it, must always be finally paid by the landlords and consumers.

*A tax on agricultural wages raises prices no more than one on farmers' profits.*

A tax upon the wages of country labour does not raise the price of the rude produce of land in proportion to the tax; for the same reason that a tax upon the farmer's profit does not raise that price in that proportion.

*Many countries have such taxes, e. g., France and Bohemia.*

Absurd and destructive as such taxes are, however, they take place in many countries. In France that part of the taille which is charged upon the industry of workmen and day-labourers in country villages, is properly a tax of this kind. Their wages are computed according to the common rate of the district in which they reside, and that they may be as little liable as possible to any over-charge, their yearly gains are estimated at no more than two hundred working days in the year. ① The tax of each individual is varied from year to year

---

① Memoires concernant les Droits, &c. tom. ii. p. 108.

## 第五篇 第一项和第二项的附录

这个更多的资本和资本的普通利润,他必须要保住较大部分的土地生产物也即保住较大部分土地生产物的价格,这样做的结果就是他少支付地主的地租。所以这种情况下,这种类型的劳动工资的提高和垫付这些工资的农场主的额外利润的最终支付就落在了地主身上。从长期来讲,所有对劳动工资直接征收的赋税,与部分地对地租征税、部分地对消费品征税但却有着和工资税相等收入的赋税相比,必然会使地租减少更多,制造品价格提高更大。

如果对劳动工资直接征税没有引起这些工资成比例的上升,这是因为它们通常引起了劳动需求的大幅下跌。产业的衰退、穷人就业的减少、年土地生产物和年全国劳动生产物的降低,一般来说都是这些赋税的结果。不过,由于这些赋税,劳动价格总是要高于在没有这些赋税时根据需求的实际状况所决定的劳动价格。而且这种价格的上涨连带垫支这部分价格的人的利润,最终总是要由地主和消费者来支付。

赋税所导致的工资的提高,一般都被它所引起的劳动需求的下跌所掩盖。

对乡村劳动工资征收的赋税,并不会导致土地天然产物的价格按照该赋税的比例提高,原因和对农场主利润征收的赋税不会按照赋税的比例提高价格一样。

对农业工资征税提高工资,不过农场主利润的资,会对农场主征税超农场主征高价格。

尽管这种赋税非常荒谬和有害,许多国家却都实行了这些赋税。在法国,对乡村劳动者和日工劳动征收的那部分的贡税就完全属于这种赋税。他们的工资是根据他们居住地区的普遍工资率来计算的,而且他们为了尽可能少承受额外负担,他们的年收入是按照不超过200天的工作日来估计的①。根据不同的情况每人应该缴纳的赋税也年年有所变化,这种不同的情况由州长制

许多国家都有这样的赋税,如法国和波希米亚。

---

① 《欧洲法律和赋税的记录》,第2卷,第108页。

according to different circumstances, of which the collector or the commissary, whom the intendant appoints to assist him, are the judges. In Bohemia, in consequence of the alteration in the system of finances which was begun in 1748, a very heavy tax is imposed upon the industry of artificers. They are divided into four classes. The highest class pay a hundred florins a year; which, at two-and-twentypence halfpenny a florin, amounts to 9 $l.$ 7 $s.$ 6 $d.$ The second class are taxed at seventy; the third at fifty; and the fourth, comprehending artificers in villages, and the lowest class of those in towns, at twenty-five florins. ①

A tax on the recompense of the liberal professions, etc., would also raise that recompense,

The recompence of ingenious artists and of men of liberal professions, I have endeavoured to show in the first book, necessarily keeps a certain proportion to the emoluments of inferior trades. A tax upon this recompence, therefore, could have no other effect than to raise it somewhat higher than in proportion to the tax. If it did not rise in this manner, the ingenious arts and the liberal professions, being no longer upon a level with other trades, would be so much deserted that they would soon return to that level.

but a tax on government offices would not raise salaries.

The emoluments of offices are not, like those of trades and professions, regulated by the free competition of the market, and do not, therefore, always bear a just proportion to what the nature of the employment requires. They are, perhaps, in most countries, higher than it requires; the persons who have the administration of government being generally disposed to reward both themselves and their immediate dependents rather more than enough. The emoluments of offices, therefore, can in most cases very well bear to be taxed. The persons, besides, who enjoy public offices, especially the more lucrative, are in all countries the objects of general envy; and a tax upon their emoluments, even though it should be somewhat higher than upon any other sort of revenue, is always a very popular tax. In England, for example, when by the land-tax every other sort of revenue was supposed to be assessed at four shillings in the pound, it was very popular to

---

① Id. tom. iii. [really i.] p. 87.

## 第五篇 第一项和第二项的附录

定协助自己的收税员或者委员来判定。在波希米亚,由于1748年开始的财政体系的改革,对手工业者的劳动征收了一种非常重的赋税。这些手工业者被分成了四个等级,最高的等级一年缴纳100弗罗林赋税,22.5便士等于1弗罗林,这样就达到9镑7先令6便士;第二个等级每年缴纳70弗罗林;第三个等级每年缴纳50弗罗林;第四个等级,包括乡村手工业劳动者和城市最低级等的手工业劳动者,他们每年缴纳25弗罗林①。

我在本书第一篇已经尽力阐述了,优秀的艺术家和自由职业者的报酬必然和下等职业的报酬保持一定的比例。所以对这种报酬征税除了会导致报酬提高的幅度略高于征税的比例外,没有其他的效果。如果报酬没有以这种方式提高,那么这些优秀的艺术和自由职业就不能够再和其他职业处于同样的水平,这样很多人就会放弃这些职业,从而不久就又使它们回到以前的水平。<sub>对自由职业的赋税也会提高该职业的报酬。</sub>

由于官员的报酬不像上述行业或者职业的报酬那样受到市场自由竞争的支配,所以并不总与这种职业性质所要求的报酬保持一个恰当的比例。在大多数国家,这种报酬或许都要高于该职业性质所要求的报酬。政府管理人员一般来说倾向于给他们自己和他们的直接下属以超过足够的报酬。所以在大多数情况下,官员的报酬都是很好的征税对象。而且担任公职的人,尤其担任油水较大部门公职的人,在所有的国家都是普遍嫉妒的对象。对他们的报酬征收的赋税,即便对他们的征税税率要略高于对其他收入的征税税率,也总是一种非常深得人心的税种。例如,在英格兰,当按照土地税法其他的各种收入的税率按说应该是每镑4<sub>但对官员征收赋税却不会提高薪酬。</sub>

---

① 《欧洲法律和赋税的记录》,第3卷,实际上是第1卷,第87页。

— 1825 —

lay a real tax of five shillings and sixpence in the pound upon the salaries of offices which exceeded a hundred pounds a year; the pensions of the younger branches of the royal family, the pay of the officers of the army and navy, and a few others less obnoxious to envy excepted. ① There are in England no other direct taxes upon the wages of labour.

## Article IV  Taxes Which, It Is Intended, Should Fall Indifferently Upon Every Different Species Of Revenue

<small>These are capitation taxes and taxes on consumable commodities.</small>   The taxes which, it is intended, should fall indifferently upon every different species of revenue, are capitation taxes, and taxes upon consumable commodities. These must be paid indifferently from whatever revenue the contributors may possess; from the rent of their land, from the profits of their stock, or from the wages of their labour.

### Capitation Taxes

<small>Capitation taxes ostensibly proportioned to revenue are altogether arbitrary.</small>  Capitation taxes, if it is attempted to proportion them to the fortune or revenue of each contributor, become altogether arbitrary. The state of a man's fortune varies from day to day, and without an inquisition more intolerable than any tax, and renewed at least once every

---

① [ Eds. 1 and 2 read 'a real tax of five shillings in the pound upon the salaries of offices which exceeded a hundred pounds a year; those of the judges and a few others less obnoxious to envy excepted. ' Under 31 Geo. II. , c. 22, a tax of Is. in the pound was imposed on all offices worth more than £ 100 a year, naval and military offices excepted. The judges were not excepted, but their salaries were raised soon afterwards. See Dowell, *History of Taxation and Taxes*, vol. ii. , pp. 135-136. The 6d. seems a mistake; the 5s. is arrived at by adding the 4s. land tax ( which was 'real' in the case of offices) and the Is. ]

先令时，对年薪超过百镑的官员征收的不动产税每镑征收5先令6便士（除皇室年轻成员的抚恤金、海军陆军军官的薪俸和少数其他不太受人羡慕的官职薪酬不征收这种赋税外）①，受到了大众的欢迎。在英格兰，没有其他的对劳动工资直接征税的赋税了。

## 第四项　打算无差异地落在各种收入上的赋税

这些赋税有人头税和消费品税。

目的在于无差异地落在各种收入上的赋税有人头税和消费品税。这些赋税必须是没有差异地用纳税人可能拥有的各种收入来支付，无论这些收入是来自土地地租、资本利润还是来自劳动工资。

### 人头税

名义上和收入成比例的人头税是完全武断的。

如果试图使人头税与每个纳税人的财富或收入都成比例，那么人头税就会变得完全武断了。一个人的财富状况每天都是不同的。如果没有比其他赋税更难以忍受的调查，而且每年不至少更新一次的话，那么征收这种赋税就只能够凭着臆断来定。所以

① 第1版和第2版中为“对年薪超过百镑的官员征收的不动产税为每镑征收5先令（除法官和少数其他不太受人羡慕的官职薪酬不征收这种赋税外）”。根据乔治二世三十年第22号法令，所有年薪超过百镑的官员每镑征税1先令，海军陆军军官除外。法官不排除在外，后来他们的薪酬很快就提高了。见道尔《课税和赋税史》第2卷，第135～136页。看来6便士是个错误，5先令是由4先令土地税（这对官员征税的情况是不动产税）加上这1先令构成的。

国民财富的性质与原理

year, can only be guessed at. His assessment, therefore, must in most eases depend upon the good or bad humour of his assessors, and must, therefore, be altogether arbitrary and uncertain.

If proportioned to rank they are unequal.
　　Capitation taxes, if they are proportioned not to the supposed fortune, but to the rank of each contributor, become altogether unequal; the degrees of fortune being frequently unequal in the same degree of rank.

In the first case they are always grievous and in the second they are intolerable unless they are light.
　　Such taxes, therefore, if it is attempted to render them equal, become altogether arbitrary and uncertain; and if it is attempted to render them certain and not arbitrary, become altogether unequal. Let the tax be light or heavy, uncertainty is always a great grievance. In a light tax a considerable degree of inequality may be supported; in a heavy one it is altogether intolerable.

In the poll taxes of William III. assessment was chiefly according to rank
　　In the different poll-taxes which took place in England during the reign of William III. ① the contributors were, the greater part of them, assessed according to the degree of their rank; as dukes, marquisses, earls, viscounts, barons, esquires, gentlemen, the eldest and youngest sons of peers, &c. All shopkeepers and tradesmen worth more than three hundred pounds, that is, the better sort of them, were subject to the same assessment; how great soever might be the difference in their fortunes. ② Their rank was more considered than their fortune. Several of those who in the first poll-tax were rated according to their supposed fortune, were afterwards rated according to their rank. Serjeants, attornies, and proctors at law, who in the first poll-tax were assessed at three shillings in the pound of their

---

① [ The first of these is under 1 W. and M. , sess. 1, c. 13. ]
② [ 1 W. and M. , sess. 2, c. 7, § 2. ]

## 第五篇  第一项和第二项的附录

大多数情况下,税额的评定只得依赖于估税人员的心情好坏,因此也就必然是完全武断的和不确定的。

如果人头税不与每个纳税人的推定财富成比例,而是与每个纳税人的身份成比例,那么人头税就会变得完全不公平了。原因在于同样身份的人他们的财富状况却往往不同。

所以,要想让这种赋税是公平的,就要变得完全武断和不确定;而要想让这种赋税是确定的、不武断的,就会变得完全的不公平。无论税负是重还是轻,不确定总会导致大量的不满。如果是较轻的税负,较大程度的不公平或许还可以忍受,而在赋税较重的情况下,不公平就是完全无法忍受的。

威廉三世统治时期,英格兰实行了不同的人头税①。大部分纳税人员的税额都是根据他们的身份来评估的,如公爵、侯爵、伯爵、子爵、男爵、士族、绅士以及贵族的长子和幼子等。对所有财产超过300镑的店主商人,即商贾中的境况较好者,都按照同样的评估征税,而不管他们之间财富可能存在很大的差异②。这种情况下,身份显得比财富数量更重要。最初有些人的人头税是按照他们的推定财富征税,后来改成了按照身份征税。高级律师、辩护律师、代诉人,最初对他们征收人头税就是按照他们的推定收入每镑征收3先令的赋税,后来改成了按他们绅士的身份征

---

① 这里面第一种人头税就是威廉和玛利一年第1次会议第13号法令。
② 威廉和玛利一年,第2次会议,第7号法令第2条。

supposed income, were afterwards assessed as gentlemen. ① In the assessment of a tax which was not very heavy, a considerable degree of inequality had been found less insupportable than any degree of uncertainty.

In France the assessment is by rank in the higher and by supposed fortune in the lower orders of people.

In the capitation which has been levied in France without any interruption since the beginning of the present century, the highest orders of people are rated according to their rank, by an invariable tariff; the lower orders of people, according to what is supposed to be their fortune, by an assessment which varies from year to year. The officers of the king's court, the judges and other officers in the superior courts of justice, the officers of the troops, &c. are assessed in the first manner. The inferior ranks of people in the provinces are assessed in the second. In France the great easily submit to a considerable degree of inequality in a tax which, so far as it affects them, is not a very heavy one; but could not brook the arbitrary assessment of an intendant. The inferior ranks of people must, in that country, suffer patiently the usage which their superiors think proper to give them.

The French tax is more rigorously exacted than the English taxes were.

In England the different poll-taxes never produced the sum which had been expected from them, or which, it was supposed, they might have produced, had they been exactly levied. In France the capitation always produces the sum expected from it. The mild government of England, when it assessed the different ranks of people to the polltax, contented itself with what that assessment happened to produce; and required no compensation for the loss which the state might

---

① [Under 1 W. and M. , c. 13, § 4, serjeants, attorneys and proctors, as well as certain other classes, were to pay 3ˢ. in the pound on their receipts. Under 1 W. and M. , sess. 2, c. 7, § 2, attorneys and proctors and others were to pay 20ˢ. in addition to the sums already charged. Under 2 W. and M. , sess. 1, c. a, § 5, serjeants-at-law were to pay £ 15, apparently in addition to the 3ˢ. in the pound. Under 3 W. and M. , c. 6, the poundage charge does not appear at all. The alterations were doubtless made in order to secure certainty, but purely in the interest of the government, which desired to be certain of getting a fixed amount. Under the Land Tax Act of 8 and 9 W. III. , e. 6, 5, serjeants, attorneys, proctors, etc. , are again charged to an income tax. ]

税①。估税时发现如果征收的赋税不太重的话,那么很大程度的不平等要比任何程度的不确定还更能为人所接受。

在法国,自本世纪初以来未曾间断的人头税,对于最上层人民是按照他们的身份以不变的税率征税。而对于最下层的人民则按照他们的推定财富来征税,每年评估的税额都有所不同。国王宫廷的官吏,高级法院的法官和其他官员、军队的士官等等,都是按照第一种方法来征税。而所有州郡的底层人民,则是按照第二种方法来征税。在法国,对于达官贵人来说,就这些赋税的影响而言只要对他们征收的赋税不是很重,他们比较容易接受一个相当不公平的赋税;但他们不能容忍的是州长武断的评估税额。在法国,下层人民只能忍耐接受他们的上级认为适合于他们的待遇。

> 法国,对较高等级的人他们按照们的身份估税;而对于较低的身人,则按照他们的财产估税。

在英格兰,各种人头税从来没有达到过他们预期的税收总额,也就是说从来没有征收到如果严格征收的话所可能征收到的税收总额。而法国的人头税却总是能够征收到他们所预期的税收总额。当温和的英格兰政府对各个阶层的人民征收人头税时,总是满足于评估时得到的税额;由于法律执行不严,不强迫缴纳

> 法国征收赋税要比英格兰赋税执行的严格。

---

① 根据威廉和玛利一年第13号法令第4条,高级律师、辩护律师、代诉人和一些其他的阶层,按照他们的收入每镑征收3先令的人头税。根据威廉和玛利第一年第7号法令第2条,辩护律师、代诉人和其他一些人除了每镑征收3先令的赋税外,还要另外征收20先令的赋税。根据威廉和玛利第1次会议第2号法令第5条,高级律师除了每镑征收3先令的赋税外,还要另外缴纳15镑。根据威廉和玛利三年第6号法令,没有提及每镑应该缴纳的赋税。这种改变毫无疑问是为了保证确定性,但这纯粹是为了政府的利益,它像得到一个确定的固定数额的税收。根据威廉三世八年、九年第6号法令第5条的土地税法令第8条,又对高级律师、辩护律师、代诉人等人员征收所得税。

sustain either by those who could not pay, or by those who would not pay (for there were many such), and who, by the indulgent execution of the law, were not forced to pay. The more severe government of France assesses upon each generality a certain sum, which the intendant must find as he can. If any province complains of being assessed too high, it may, in the assessment of next year, obtain an abatement proportioned to the over-charge of the year before. But it must pay in the mean time. The intendant, in order to be sure of finding the sum assessed upon his generality, was impowered to assess it in a larger sum, that the failure or inability of some of the contributors might be compensated by the over-charge of the rest; and till 1765, the fixation of this surplus assessment was left altogether to his discretion. In that year indeed the council assumed this power to itself. In the capitation of the provinces, it is observed by the perfectly well-informed author of the Memoirs upon the impositions in France, the proportion which falls upon the nobility, and upon those whose privileges exempt them from the taille, is the least considerable. The largest falls upon those subject to the taille, who are assessed to the capitation at so much a pound of what they pay to that other tax. ①

Capitation taxes on the lower orders of people are like taxes on wages.

Capitation taxes, so far as they are levied upon the lower ranks of people, are direct taxes upon the wages of labour, and are attended with all the inconveniencies of such taxes.

They are inexpensive and afford a sure revenue.

Capitation taxes are levied at little expence; and, where they are rigorously exacted, afford a very sure revenue to the state. It is upon this account that in countries where the ease, comfort, and security of the inferior ranks of people are little attended to, capitation taxes are very common. It is in general, however, but a small part of the public revenue, which, in a great empire, has ever been drawn from such taxes; and the greatest sum which they have ever afforded, might always have been found in some other way much more convenient to the people.

---

① [*Mémoires*, tom. ii. , p. 421. ]

## 第五篇　第一项和第二项的附录

赋税,这样就有很多不能缴纳的人或者不愿缴纳的人,由此而导致了国家遭受损失,但却也没有要求他们补偿这些损失。而法国政府则比较严厉,它给每个课税区评估了一个税收总额,该州州长必须竭尽全力去完成这个税额。如果有哪个州郡抱怨税负太重,那么在来年的税额评估时可以根据上一年多收的税额按比例给予一定的折扣,但本年度的税额却必须要完成。为了确保能完成本课税区评估的税额,州长有权把这个税额估计的大一点,这样有些纳税人的破产或者没有能力缴纳赋税而导致的税收减少就可以用剩余的人多缴纳的赋税来弥补。直到 1756 年,这种赋税总额的多余评估还是完全由州长一人决定。不过在这一年,枢密院把这种权力收归到了自己手中。根据消息相当灵通的法国赋税记录的作者的观察,各个州郡的人头税,落在贵族和那些享有特权可以免除贡税的人身上的比例最轻。人头税的大部分都落在了那些负担贡税的人身上,他们按照应该缴纳贡税的多少每镑征收一定的人头税①。

对底层人民征收的人头税,是对劳动工资直接征收的赋税,所以具有所有这种直接赋税的种种不便。

征收人头税的费用很少。在严格征收的地方,就可以给政府提供一项非常确定的收入。因此,在那些不是很看重低等人民的安逸、舒适和安全的国家,人头税非常普遍。不过对于一个大国来说,从这些赋税中得到的税收往往不过是公共收入的一小部分;而且这种赋税所提供过的最大金额,也总是可以用其他对人民更为便利的方法来征收到。

------

① 《欧洲法律和赋税的记录》,第 2 卷,第 421 页。

## Taxes Upon Consumable Commodities

<small>The impossibility of taxation according to revenue has given rise to taxation according to expenditure on consumable commodities,</small>   The impossibility of taxing the people, in proportion to their revenue, by any capitation, seems to have given occasion to the invention of taxes upon consumable commodities. The state not knowing how to tax, directly and proportionably, the revenue of its subjects, endeavours to tax it indirectly by taxing their expence, which, it is supposed, will in most cases be nearly in proportion to their revenue. Their expence is taxed by taxing the consumable commodities upon which it is laid out.

Consumable commodities are either necessaries or luxuries.

<small>either necessaries or luxuries, necessaries including all that creditable people of the lowest order cannot decently go without.</small>   By necessaries I understand, not only the commodities which are indispensably necessary for the support of life, but whatever the custom of the country renders it indecent for creditable people, even of the lowest order, to be without. A linen shirt, for example, is, strictly speaking, not a necessary of life. The Greeks and Romans lived, I suppose, very comfortably, though they had no linen. ① But in the present times, through the greater part of Europe, a creditable daylabourer would be ashamed to appear in public without a linen shirt, the want of which would be supposed to denote that disgraceful degree of poverty, which, it is presumed, no body can well fall into without extreme bad conduct. Custom, in the same manner, has rendered leather shoes a necessary of life in England. The poorest creditable person of either sex would be ashamed to appear in public without them. In Scotland, custom has rendered them a necessary of life to the lowest order of men; but not to the same order of women, who

---

① [Dr. John Arbuthnot, in his *Tables of Ancient Coins, Weights and Measures*, 2nd ed. , 1754, P. 142, says that linen was not used among the Romans, at least by men, till about the time of Alexander Severus. ]

## 消费品税

无论哪种人头税都不可能按照人民的收入成比例地来征税；这种不可能似乎导致了消费品税的发明。国家不知道怎样直接地、成比例地对人民的收入征税，它就试图间接地对他们的支出征税。在大多数情况下，这种支出都被认为和他们的收入基本上是保持着一定的比例。对他们的支出的对象即消费品征税，也就是对他们的支出征税了。

> 不能根据收入征税，就产生了根据消费品征收的赋税。

消费品或者是必需品，或者是奢侈品。

我对必需品的理解是，不仅包括那些维持生活所必不可少的商品，还包括那些根据该国家习俗最有信誉的人甚至是最底层的人缺了它都会感到不体面的商品。例如，麻布衬衫严格地讲不能算是生活的必需品。我想尽管希腊人、罗马人没有亚麻布，也生活得非常舒服[①]。但在现在的大部分欧洲地区，一个有信誉的员工如果没有穿麻布衬衫，都会羞于出现在大庭广众面前。没有麻布衬衫就意味着他穷到了丢脸的程度，而且一般都认为除非一个人行为极端差劲，不然不可能会那么贫穷。同样的，习俗也使得皮鞋成为英格兰生活的必需品。如果没有皮鞋，哪怕最穷的有信誉的男人或女人都羞于在大庭广众面前露脸。在苏格兰，对最下层阶级男人来说，习俗已经使得皮鞋成为生活的必需品，但对同阶层的女人却不然，她们即便光脚走路也没有什么不体面

> 消费品或者是必需品，或者是奢侈品。必需品包括最底层有信誉的人保持体面必不可少的东西。

---

[①] 约翰·阿巴斯诺特博士在他的《古代铸币、衡量和度量表》第2版，1754年，第142页中说，直到大约亚历山大·塞维鲁之前，罗马人都不使用亚麻布，至少男人不使用。

may, without any discredit, walk about bare-footed. In France, they are necessaries neither to men nor to women; the lowest rank of both sexes appearing there publicly, without any discredit, sometimes in wooden shoes, and sometimes bare-footed. Under necessaries therefore, I comprehend, not only those things which nature, but those things which the established rules of decency have rendered necessary to the lowest rank of people. All other things I call luxuries; without meaning by this appellation, to throw the smallest degree of reproach upon the temperate use of them. Beer and ale, for example, in Great Britain, and wine, even in the wine countries, I call luxuries. A man of any rank may, without any reproach, abstain totally from tasting such liquors. Nature does not render them necessary for the support of life; and custom nowhere renders it indecent to live without them.

<small>What raises the price of subsistence must raise wages.</small>　As the wages of labour are every where regulated, partly by the demand for it, and partly by the average price of the necessary articles of subsistence; whatever raises this average price must necessarily raise those wages, so that the labourer may still be able to purchase that quantity of those necessary articles which the state of the demand for labour, whether increasing, stationary, or declining, requires that he should have. A tax upon those articles necessarily raises their price somewhat higher than the amount of the tax, because the dealer who advances the tax, must generally get it back with a profit. Such a tax must, therefore, occasion a rise in the wages of labour proportionable to this rise of price.

<small>So that a tax on necessaries, like a tax on wages, raises wages.</small>　It is thus that a tax upon the necessaries of life, operates exactly in the same manner as a direct tax upon the wages of labour. The labourer, though he may pay it out of his hand, cannot, for any considerable time at least, be properly said even to advance it. It must always in the long-run be advanced to him by his immediate employer in the advanced rate of his wages. His employer, if he is a manufacturer, will charge upon the price of his goods this rise of wages, together with a profit; so that the final payment of the tax, together with

## 第五篇 第一项和第二项的附录

的。在法国,皮鞋对于男人女人来说都不是生活必需品。法国最底层的人们,他们有时在公众面前穿着木屐,有时光着脚板,这些也都无伤体面。所以我理解的必需品,不但包括那些天性使得它们成为最低阶层人民必需品的物品,也包括那些已经建立的关于体面的规则使得它们成为最低阶级人民必需品的物品。其他所有的东西我都称之为奢侈品。不过我这样的称谓,并不是包含对适度使用它们有丝毫的谴责。例如,英国的啤酒和淡色啤酒,甚至葡萄酒生产国的葡萄酒,我都称它们为奢侈品。任何阶层的人如果完全戒绝这些饮料都不会遭到任何谴责。因为天性没有使得这些饮料成为维持生活的必需品,而各地的习俗也没有使得它们成为缺之就有损体面的必需品。

由于各个地方的劳动工资,都是部分地受劳动需求支配,部分地受生活必需品的平均价格支配。所以,只要是提高平均价格就必然会提高劳动工资,使得劳动者仍然能购买到按照劳动的需求情况他所应该拥有的必需品数量,无论劳动需求是增加、停滞还是减少。对这些必需品征收赋税,必然会使它们的价格提高,而且使提高的幅度略高于那种税额,因为垫付这种赋税的商人,一般来说肯定要带上利润并收回这个垫付。所以,这种赋税必然会使得劳动工资随着这些必需品价格的上涨成比例地提高。

凡是提高生活资料价格的都会提高工资。

这样,对生活必需品征税就完全和对劳动工资直接征税效果一样。虽然是由劳动者手中付出这项税负,但至少从长期来说,他甚至连垫付也说不上。在长期当中,直接雇主必然会通过给他提高工资来把该劳动者垫付的赋税垫还给他。如果他的雇主是一个制造商,他必然会将提高的工资连同利润一起加到货物价格上,所以这种赋税连带其超出部分的最终的支付将落在消费者身

对品征税,对工资一样,因此对必需品征税,就像对工资征税一样,会提高工资。

— 1837 —

this over-charge, will fall upon the consumer. If his employer is a farmer, the final payment, together with a like over-charge, will fall upon the rent of the landlord.

<small>Taxes on luxuries even if consumed by the poor have no such effect,</small> It is otherwise with taxes upon what I call luxuries; even upon those of the poor. The rise in the price of the taxed commodities, will not necessarily occasion any rise in the wages of labour. A tax upon tobacco, for example, though a luxury of the poor as well as of the rich, will not raise wages. Though it is taxed in England at three times, and in France at fifteen times its original price, those high duties seem to have no effect upon the wages of labour. The same thing may be said of the taxes upon tea and sugar; which in England and Holland have become luxuries of the lowest ranks of people; and of those upon chocolate, which in Spain is said to have become so. The different taxes which in Great Britain have in the course of the present century been imposed upon spirituous liquors, are not supposed to have had any effect upon the wages of labour. The rise in the price of porter, occasioned by an additional tax of three shillings upon the barrel of strong beer, ① has not raised the wages of common labour in London. These were about eighteen pence and twenty-pence a day before the tax, and they are not more now.

<small>as they act like sumptuary laws, and so do not diminish the ability of the poor to bring up useful families.</small> The high price of such commodities does not necessarily diminish the ability of the inferior ranks of people to bring up families. Upon the sober and industrious poor, taxes upon such commodities act as sumptuary laws, and dispose them either to moderate, or to refrain altogether from the use of superfluities which they can no longer easily afford. Their ability to bring up families, in consequence of this forced frugality, instead of being diminished, is frequently, perhaps, increased by the tax. It is the sober and industrious poor who generally bring up the most numerous families, and who principally supply the demand for useful labour. All the poor indeed

---

① [1 Geo. Ⅲ, c. 7. ]

## 第五篇　第一项和第二项的附录

上。而如果雇主是农场主，那么这种赋税连带类似的超出部分，最终支付就会落在地主身上。

对我所说的奢侈品征税，即便是由穷人来消费情况都有所不同。被征税的消费品价格的升高，并不必然会引起劳动工资的提高。例如，尽管香烟是穷人和富人的奢侈品，但对烟草征税，却不会提高劳动工资。英格兰的烟草税价格已经是原先的 3 倍，法国的烟草税价格已经是原先的 15 倍，然而这么重的税负却没有影响劳动工资。同样的情况还有对茶和食糖征收的赋税，在英格兰和荷兰，茶和食糖已经成为最低阶层人民的奢侈品。对巧克力征收的赋税，在西班牙情况据说也是一样。对这些奢侈品征税，都和烟草税一样，不会影响劳动工资。在大不列颠，世纪以来对各种酒精饮料征收的赋税也没有人期望会对劳动工资产生什么影响。黑啤酒价格的上涨是由于高浓度啤酒每桶要征收 3 先令的附加税①，然而伦敦普通工人的工资却没有因此而提高。在征收这种赋税之前，他们每天的工资大概为 18 便士、20 便士，而现在他们的工资还是那样，并没有增加多少。

对奢侈品征税，即便是由穷人消费，都没有这种效果。

这些商品高昂的价格，不一定会减少下层人民抚养家庭的能力。对于节俭勤劳的穷人来说，对这些商品征税就好比是给他们颁布反对奢侈的法令一样，使得他们减少使用或完全不用那些他们原本就不易买得起的奢侈品。由于这种强制性节约的结果，他们抚养家庭的能力，不但不会减少，而且往往还会因为这种赋税有所增加。一般来说，正是这些节俭勤劳的穷人们抚养着大多数的家庭，主要满足着对有用劳动的需求。的确，并非所有

对奢侈品征收的赋税起着反奢侈法的作用，因此减少人对家庭的能力。

---

① 乔治三世一年第 7 号法令。

— 1839 —

国民财富的性质与原理

are not sober and industrious, and the dissolute and disorderly might continue to indulge themselves in the use of such commodities after this rise of price in the same manner as before; without regarding the distress which this indulgence might bring upon their families. Such disorderly persons, however, seldom rear up numerous families; their children generally perishing from neglect, mismanagement, and the scantiness or unwholesomeness of their food. If by the strength of their constitution they survive the hardships to which the bad conduct of their parents exposes them; yet the example of that bad conduct commonly corrupts their morals; so that, instead of being useful to society by their industry, they become public nuisances by their vices and disorders. Though the advanced price of the luxuries of the poor, therefore, might increase somewhat the distress of such disorderly families, and thereby diminish somewhat their ability to bring up children; it would not probably diminish much the useful population of the country.

<small>whereas a rise in the price of necessaries diminishes the ability of the poor to bring up useful families and supply the demand for labour.</small>

Any rise in the average price of necessaries, unless it is compensated by a proportionable rise in the wages of labour, must necessarily diminish more or less the ability of the poor to bring up numerous families, and consequently to supply the demand for useful labour; whatever may be the state of that demand, whether increasing, stationary, or declining; or such as requires an increasing, stationary, or declining population.

<small>Taxes on necessaries are contrary to the interest of the middle and superior ranks of people.</small>

Taxes upon luxuries have no tendency to raise the price of any other commodities except that of the commodities taxed. Taxes upon necessaries, by raising the wages of labour, necessarily tend to raise the price of all manufactures, and consequently to diminish the extent of their sale and consumption. Taxes upon luxuries are finally paid by the consumers of the commodities taxed, without any retribution. They fall indifferently upon every species of revenue, the wages of labour, the profits of stock, and the rent of land. Taxes upon necessaries, so far as they affect the labouring poor, are finally paid, partly by landlords in the diminished rent of their lands, and partly by rich

的穷人都是节俭勤劳的。对于那些肆意挥霍的、任性的人来说，即便是这些奢侈品的价格提高之后，他们还会一如既往地沉溺于这些奢侈品的享用，而不考虑这种放纵可能会给他们家庭带来的困苦。不过这种任性的人很少有能够抚养起来一个大家庭的，因为他们的孩子大都因为照料不周、管理不善及食物缺乏或不卫生而夭亡了。然而即便由于这些儿童身体健壮渡过了父母恶劣行径所带给他们的困苦难关，但父母恶劣行径的榜样作用通常也会腐蚀他们的品德。因此，这些儿童成人后不但不会通过他们的勤奋成为对社会有用的人，而且还会因为他们的恶行和目无法纪成为社会的败类。所以，尽管贫民奢侈品的价格提高了，可能会多少增加这种胡乱家庭的困苦，从而多少会缩减他们抚养子女的能力，但却不会大幅减少全国有用的人口。

而必需品价格的提高会降低穷人们抚养对社会有用的家庭的能力和减少满足劳动需求的能力。

任何必需品平均价格的提高，除非通过劳动工资也成比例地提高来予以弥补，不然肯定会或多或少地降低穷人们抚养大多数家庭的能力，从而减少满足有用劳动需求的能力。不管需求是增加、停滞还是减少，换句话也就是说要求人口数量是增加、停滞还是减少。

对必需品征收赋税不符合中层和上层人民的利益。

对奢侈品征税，除了会提高被征税的这种商品的价格外，不会提高任何其他商品的价格。对必需品征税，通过提高劳动工资，所以必然会提高所有制造品的价格，这样就会减少这些制造品的销售和消费。对奢侈品征收的赋税，最终由课税品的消费者来支付，而没有任何补偿。它们无差异地落在这些消费者的各种收入上，即土地地租、资本利润和劳动工资。而对必需品征收的赋税，就它们影响穷苦劳动者来说，这些赋税最终部分地由地主以减少地租的形式支付，部分地由富有的消费者（他们可能是地

consumers, whether landlords or others, in the advanced price of manufactured goods; and always with a considerable over-charge. The advanced price of such manufactures as are real necessaries of life, and are destined for the consumption of the poor, of coarse woollens, for example, must be compensated to the poor by a farther advancement of their wages. The middling and superior ranks of people, if they understood their own interest, ought always to oppose all taxes upon the necessaries of life, as well as all direct taxes upon the wages of labour. The final payment of both the one and the other falls altogether upon themselves, and always with a considerable overcharge. They fall heaviest upon the landlords, who always pay in a double capacity; in that of landlords, by the reduction of their rent; and in that of rich consumers, by the increase of their expence. The observation of Sir Matthew Decker, that certain taxes are, in the price of certain goods, sometimes repeated and accumulated four or five times, is perfectly just with regard to taxes upon the necessaries of life. In the price of leather, for example, you must pay, not only for the tax upon the leather of your own shoes, but for a part of that upon those of the shoe-maker and the tanner. You must pay too for the tax upon the salt, upon the soap, and upon the candles which those workmen consume while employed in your service, and for the tax upon the leather, which the salt-maker, the soap-maker, and the candle-maker consume while employed in their service. ①

In Great Britain, the principal taxes upon the necessaries of life are those upon the four commodities just now mentioned, salt, leather, soap, and candles.

Salt is a very ancient and a very universal subject of taxation. It was taxed among the Romans, and it is so at present in, I believe, every part of Europe. The quantity annually consumed by any individual is so small, and may be purchased so gradually, that nobody, it

---

① [Leather is Decker's example, *Essay on the Decline of the Foreign Trade*, 2nd ed. , 1750, pp. 29, 30. See also p. 10. ]

## 第五篇 第一项和第二项的附录

主也可能是其他人)通过购买提高了价格的制造品的形式来支付,而且他们往往还要支付一个相当大的额外数额。这些真正的生活必需品,而且就是为了让穷人消费的制造品,如粗毛制品等,它们价格的提高,必然要用工资的进一步提高来使这些穷人得到补偿。如果中层和上层人民了解他们自身利益所在,就应该总是反对所有对生活必需品征收的赋税,反对劳动工资直接征收的赋税。这两种赋税的最终支付完全都落在他们自己身上,而且还总是附加一个相当大的额外数额。尤税负最重的就是地主了,他们总是以双重身份来缴纳赋税:从作为地主的角度讲,他们要降低地租;从富有的消费者的角度讲,他们要增加他们的支出。马太·戴克尔先生关于对生活必需品征收的赋税的观察是相当公正的,有些商品的价格中有些赋税有时竟然会重复征收四五次。例如,在皮革的价格中,你不仅仅要支付你自己皮鞋的皮革的赋税,还要支付一个鞋匠和制革匠鞋子皮革的一部分赋税。而且,你还要支付这些工匠在为你服务期间所消费的盐、肥皂和蜡烛的赋税,以及制盐者、制肥皂者、制蜡烛者在他们工作时所消费的皮革的赋税①。

在大不列颠,对生活必需品征收的主要赋税就是刚才提到的四种商品即对盐、皮革、肥皂和蜡烛征收的赋税。

盐是一种非常古老也是非常普遍的征税对象。罗马就曾经对盐征收赋税,而且我相信在现在的欧洲所有地区,都有对盐征收的赋税。每个人盐的年消费量非常少,而且还可以一点一点

---

① 皮革是戴克尔所举的例子。《论对外贸易的衰落》,第 2 版,1750 年,第 29、30 页。还可以参看第 10 页。

seems to have been thought, could feel very sensibly even a pretty heavy tax upon it. It is in England taxed at three shillings and fourpence a bushel; about three times the original price of the commodity. In some other countries the tax is still higher. Leather is a real necessary of life. The use of linen renders soap such. In countries where the winter nights are long, candles are a necessary instrument of trade. Leather and soap are in Great Britain taxed at three halfpence a pound; candles at a penny; ① taxes which, upon the original price of leather, may amount to about eight or ten per cent. ; upon that of soap to about twenty or five and twenty per cent. ; and upon that of candles to about fourteen or fifteen per cent. ; taxes which, though lighter than that upon salt, are still very heavy. As all those four commodities are real necessaries of life, such heavy taxes upon them must increase somewhat the expence of the sober and industrious poor, and must consequently raise more or less the wages of their labour.

<sub>and also seaborne coal.</sub>　　In a country where the winters are so cold as in Great Britain, fuel is, during that season, in the strictest sense of the word, a necessary of life, not only for the purpose of dressing victuals, but for the comfortable subsistence of many different sorts of workmen who work within doors; and coals are the cheapest of all fuel. The price of fuel has so important an influence upon that of labour, that all over Great Britain manufactures have confined themselves principally to the coal countries; other parts of the country, on account of the high price of this necessary article, not being able to work so cheap. In some manufactures, besides, coal is a necessary instrument of trade; as in those of glass, iron, and all other metals. If a bounty could in any case be reasonable, it might perhaps be so upon the transportation of coals from those parts of the country in which they

---

① [See Dowell, *History of Taxation and Taxes*, 1884, vol. iv. , pp. 318, 322, 330. ]

的购买。所以即便盐税相当沉重,似乎人们对它也没有明显的感觉。在英格兰,盐税为每蒲式耳征收3先令4便士,大概是原价的3倍。在其他的一些国家,这种赋税还要更重。皮革是一种真正的必需品。亚麻布的使用,使得肥皂也成了生活必需品。在那些冬夜比较长的国家,蜡烛成了各个行业必要的工具。在大不列颠,皮革税和肥皂税都是每镑征收三便士半,蜡烛税是每镑征收一便士①。皮革税大约占了皮革原价的8%或10%;肥皂税大约占了肥皂原价的20%或25%;蜡烛税大约占了蜡烛原价的14%或15%。这些赋税比起盐税虽然较轻,但仍然是非常重的赋税。这四种商品都是真正的生活必需品,这么重的税负必然会或多或少地增加那些节俭勤劳的穷人们的费用,从而或多或少地提高他们的劳动工资。

在冬天像英国那样寒冷的国家里,在寒冷的季节,从燃料这个单词最严格的意义上讲,它是一种生活必需品,不仅仅烹调食物必不可少,而且要想给户内工作的许多劳动者提供舒适的生活也必不可少。在所有的燃料中,煤炭的价格最低。燃料价格对于劳动价格有着如此重要的影响,所以大不列颠所有的制造业主要都局限于产煤区。而在国内的其他地区,由于这种必需品高昂的价格,它们的生产成本就不会那么低。另外,有些像玻璃、铁和所有其他的金属工业这样的制造业,煤炭都是它们的必要生产手段。如果在某种情况下给予合理的津贴的话,那么就有可能将煤炭从富饶的产煤区运往煤炭稀缺区。然而,立法机构不但没有给

(还有海运煤炭。)

---

① 参见道尔《课税和赋税史》,1884年,第4卷,第318、322页。

abound, to those in which they are wanted. But the legislature, instead of a bounty, has imposed a tax of three shillings and threepence a ton upon coal carried coastways ;① which upon most sorts of coal is more than sixty per cent. of the original price at the coal-pit. Coals carried either by land or by inland navigation pay no duty. Where they are naturally cheap, they are consumed duty free; where they are naturally dear, they are loaded with a heavy duty.

<small>Such taxes at any rate bring in revenue, which is more than can be said of the regulations of the corn trade, etc., which produce equally bad effects.</small>
Such taxes, though they raise the price of subsistence, and consequently the wages of labour, yet they afford a considerable revenue to government, which it might not be easy to find in any other way. There may, therefore, be good reasons for continuing them. The bounty upon the exportation of corn, so far as it tends in the actual state of tillage to raise the price of that necessary article, produces all the like bad effects; and instead of affording any revenue, frequently occasions a very great expence to government. The high duties upon the importation of foreign corn, which in years of moderate plenty amount to a prohibition; and the absolute prohibition of the importation either of live cattle or of salt provisions, which takes place in the ordinary state of the law, and which, on account of the scarcity, is at present suspended for a limited time with regard to Ireland and the British plantations, have all the bad effects of taxes upon the necessaries of life, and produce no revenue to government. Nothing seems necessary for the repeal of such regulations, but to convince the public of the futility of that system in consequence of which they have been established.

<small>Much higher taxes on necessaries prevail in many other countries. There are taxes on bread,</small>
Taxes upon the necessaries of life are much higher in many other countries than in Great Britain. Duties upon flour and meal when ground at the mill, and upon bread when baked at the oven, take place in many countries. In Holland the money price of the bread consumed in towns is supposed to be doubled by means of such taxes. In lieu of a part of them, the people who live in

---

① [Saxby, *British Customs*, p. 307. 8 Ann. , c. 4; 9 Ann. , c. 6. ]

## 第五篇　第一项和第二项的附录

予津贴,反而还规定煤炭的沿海岸运输征收每吨 3 先令 3 便士的赋税①。对于大多数种类的煤炭来说,这已经是煤矿出产价格的 60% 以上了。对于通过陆运或者内陆河运来运输的煤炭,一律不用缴税。煤炭天然便宜的地方,煤炭的消费是免税的,而在煤炭天然昂贵的地方,却要负担重税。

尽管这些赋税会提高生活必需品的价格,从而提高了劳动价格,但它们却给政府提供了一项可能不容易从其他方法得到的相当大的收入。所以,有充足的理由继续征收这些赋税。由于谷物出口津贴在实际农耕状态下有提高谷物这种生活必需品价格的趋势,所以势必会产生上述所有类似的不良后果。而且它根本不给政府带来任何收入,常常还会给政府带来巨大的费用。在一般收成的情况下对进口外国谷物征收重税,实际上就等于禁止进口。在法律的正常情况下,是绝对禁止活牲畜及腌制食品进口的。现在由于这些物品缺乏,在爱尔兰和英国殖民在一定期限内暂时取消了这个禁令。所有这些规定都产生了对必需品征税的一切不良后果,而且没有给政府带来任何收入。要废止这些规定,看来没有必要采取什么手段,只需要让公众相信由这些规定所设立的制度没有用处就行了。

许多其他的国家对生活必需品征收的赋税要比大不列颠对必需品征收的赋税重得多。在许多国家,对正在磨坊研磨的面粉和粗粉、对正在火炉上烘烤的面包都征收赋税。在荷兰,由于这些赋税,据推测城镇里面包的价格翻了一倍。住在乡村的人们为

---

① 萨克斯贝:《不列颠关税》,第 307 页,安妮女王八年第 4 号法令,安妮女王九年第 6 号法令。

the country pay every year so much a head, according to the sort of bread they are supposed to consume. Those who consume wheaten bread, pay three guilders fifteen stivers; about six shillings and ninepence halfpenny. These, and some other taxes of the same kind, by raising the price of labour, are said to have ruined the greater part of the manufactures of Holland. Similar taxes, though not quite so heavy, take place in the Milanese, in the states of Genoa, in the dutchy of Modena, in the dutchies of Parma, Placentia, and Guastalla, and in the ecclesiastical state. A French author of some note has proposed to reform the finances of his country, by substituting in the room of the greater part of other taxes, this most ruinous of all taxes. There is nothing so absurd, says Cicero, which has not sometimes been asserted by some philosophers.

<small>and meat.</small>

Taxes upon butchers meat are still more common than those upon bread. It may indeed be doubted whether butchers meat is any where a necessary of life. Grain and other vegetables, with the help of milk, cheese, and butter, or oil, where butter is not to be had, it is known from experience, can, without any butchers meat, afford the most plentiful, the most wholesome, the most nourishing, and the most invigorating diet. Decency no where requires that any man should eat butchers meat, as it in most places requires that he should wear a linen shirt or a pair of leather shoes.

<small>A tax on a consumable commodity may be levied either periodically from the consumer or once for all from the dealer when the consumer acquires it.</small>

Consumable commodities, whether necessaries or luxuries, may be taxed in two different ways. The consumer may either pay an annual sum on account of his using or consuming goods of a certain kind; or the goods may be taxed while they remain in the hands of the deal-

了代替这种赋税的一部分,根据每个人可能消费的面包种类,每年缴纳一定的赋税。那些消费小麦面包的人,每人缴纳 3 盾 15 斯梯弗,大约为 6 先令 9 便士半。这些赋税,还有其他一些同样类型的赋税,由于提高了劳动价格,据说已经使荷兰大部分制造业破产了。尽管没有那么沉重,在米兰公国、热那亚各州、摩德纳公国、巴尔马、普拉逊蒂、瓜斯塔拉,甚至在教皇的领地,都征收了类似的赋税[1]。法国有位有点名气的作家就曾经提议改革财政体系,用这种最最破坏性的赋税去代替大部分的其他赋税。西塞罗说,哪怕是再荒谬的事情,有时也会有一些哲学家维护。

对家畜肉征收赋税要比对面包征收赋税还要普遍。当然,家畜肉是否在各个地方都是生活必需品值得怀疑。不过根据经验,即便没有家畜肉,如果有谷物和其他蔬菜,再加上牛奶、奶酪、黄油,如果没有黄油则用动植物油来代替,就可以做出最丰盛、最卫生、最营养、最使人精力充沛的食物。许多地方为了维持体面都要求应该穿着麻布衬衫或者皮鞋,但却没有一个地方要求必须吃家畜肉。和对肉类的赋税,

消费品,无论是必需品还是奢侈品,都可以以两种方法征税。一种是消费者为他使用或者消费的某种消费品每年支付一定数额的赋税,另一种是当商品还在商人手中而没有送到消费者手中对消费品征收的赋税可以向消费者定期征收,或在那人购买商品一次性地征收。

---

[1] 摩德纳(Modena),意大利北部,博洛尼亚西北偏西的一座城市。曾为古伊特鲁斯坦定居地(公元前 183 年之后)和罗马殖民地。摩德纳在公元 12 世纪成为自由市,并于 1280 年经历了强有力的伊斯特家族的统治。

巴尔马(Parma),意大利中北部一城市,位于米兰东南。由罗马人在公元前 183 年建成,于 12 世纪成为一个自由城,在 1545 年以后成为巴尔马公国和皮亚琴察公国的中心,该城于 1860 年成为撒丁尼亚王国的一部分并于 1861 年成了意大利的国土。

er, and before they are delivered to the consumer. The consumable goods which last a considerable time before they are consumed altogether, are most properly taxed in the one way. Those of which the consumption is either immediate or more speedy, in the other. The coach-tax and plate-tax are examples of the former method of imposing: the greater part of the other duties of excise and customs, of the latter.

<small>The first method is best when the commodity is durable.</small> A coach may, with good management, last ten or twelve years. It might be taxed, once for all, before it comes out of the hands of the coach-maker. But it is certainly more convenient for the buyer to pay four pounds a year for the privilege of keeping a coach, than to pay all at once forty or forty-eight pounds additional price to the coach-maker; or a sum equivalent to what the tax is likely to cost him during the time he uses the same coach. A service of plate, in the same manner, may last more than a century. It is certainly easier for the consumer to pay five shillings a year for every hundred ounces of plate, near one per cent. of the value, than to redeem this long annuity at five and twenty or thirty years purchase, which would enhance the price at least five and twenty or thirty per cent. The different taxes which affect houses are certainly more conveniently paid by moderate annual payments, than by a heavy tax of equal value upon the first building or sale of the house.

It was the well-known proposal of Sir Matthew Decker, that all commodities, even those of which the consumption is either immediate or very speedy, should be taxed in this manner; the dealer advancing nothing, but the consumer paying a certain annual sum for the licence to consume certain goods. ① The object of his scheme was to promote all the different branches of foreign trade, particularly the carrying trade, by taking away all duties upon importation and exportation, and thereby enabling the merchant to employ his whole capital and

---

① [ *Essay on the Causes of the Decline of the Foreign Trade*, 2nd ed. , 1750, pp. 78-163. ]

时,就对这个商品征收一定的赋税。对于那种在完全消耗掉以前可以使用相当长时间的消费品,最适合于采用第一种征税方法;而对那些可以立刻消费掉或者很快消费掉的商品,则适合于采用第二种征税方法。前者的征税方法的例子有马车税和金银器皿税,而其他大部分货物税和关税,就是后者征税方法的例子。

一辆马车如果管理得好,那么就可以用 10 年或 12 年。在它离开马车制造者手中之前,可以一次性地付清所有的赋税。但对于购买马车的人来说,为了获得拥有这辆马车的特权,与一次性给马车制造者支付 40 镑或 48 镑的额外价格,或一次性给马车制造者支付相当于他在使用同样的马车期间可能要缴纳的税额相比,购买者每年缴纳 4 镑的赋税肯定要更为方便一些。同样地,一件金银器皿可能会使用一个世纪以上的时间。对于消费者来说,每年每 100 盎司重量的器皿缴纳 5 先令的赋税,将近其价值的 1%,肯定要比一次性支付这项年金的 25 倍或 30 倍的税额要更为容易一些,因为在后种情况下,这件器皿的价格至少要提高 25% 或 30%。对房屋征收的各种赋税,每年支付一个较小数额的赋税肯定要比在房屋刚建成或者出售时一次性的支付相等价值的重税更为方便一些。

当商品是耐用品时,第一种方法更好。

马太·戴克尔先生有一个著名的提议,即所有的商品,甚至包括那些可以立即消费掉或者很快消费掉的商品,都应该按照消费者每年支付一定的年金以获得消费某种商品的许可证,而商人不用垫付任何税额的方法来征收赋税[①]。他这项计划的目的就在于废除所有对进出口征收的赋税,使商人的全部资本和全部信

---

① 《论对外贸易衰落的原因》,第 2 版,1750 年,第 78~163 页。

国民财富的性质与原理

Sir M. Decker proposes to adapt it also to other commodities by issuing annual licences to consume them, but this would be liable to greater objections than the second and usual method.

credit in the purchase of goods and the freight of ships, no part of either being diverted towards the advancing of taxes. The project, however, of taxing, in this manner, goods of immediate or speedy consumption, seems liable to the four following very important objections. First, the tax would be more unequal, or not so well proportioned to the expence and consumption of the different contributors, as in the way in which it is commonly imposed. The taxes upon ale, wine, and spirituous liquors, which are advanced by the dealers, are finally paid by the different consumers exactly in proportion to their respective consumption. But if the tax were to be paid by purchasing a licence to drink those liquors, the sober would, in proportion to his consumption, be taxed much more heavily than the drunken consumer. A family which exercised great hospitality would be taxed much more lightly than one who entertained fewer guests. Secondly, this mode of taxation, by paying for an annual, half-yearly, or quarterly licence to consume certain goods, would diminish very much one of the principal conveniences of taxes upon goods of speedy consumption; the piece-meal payment. In the price of three-pence halfpenny, which is at present paid for a pot of porter, the different taxes upon malt, hops, and beer, together with the extraordinary profit which the brewer charges for having advanced them, may perhaps amount to about three halfpence. If a workman can conveniently spare those three halfpence, he buys a pot of porter. If he cannot, he contents himself with a pint, and, as a penny saved is a penny got, he thus gains a farthing by his temperance. He pays the tax piece-meal, as he can afford to pay it, and when he can afford to pay it; and every act of payment is perfectly voluntary, and what he can avoid if he chuses to do so. Thirdly, such taxes would operate less as sumptuary laws. When the licence was once purchased, whether the purchaser drunk much or drunk little, his tax would be the same. Fourthly, if a workman were to pay all at once, by yearly, half-yearly or quarterly payments,

— 1852 —

## 第五篇　第一项和第二项的附录

用都能用于购买货物和船舶运输,而不用将他们资本的任何部分用来垫付赋税,从而促进对外贸易尤其是运输业的发展。然而,如果按照这个计划的方法对可以立即消费掉或者很快消费掉的商品征收赋税的话,看来会受到以下四种非常重要的反对意见。第一,这种征税方法与通常的征税方法相比更加不公平,或者说这种赋税不能较准确地与不同纳税人的费用和消费成比例。那些由商人垫支的淡色啤酒、葡萄酒和烈性酒的赋税,最终是由不同的消费者完全根据他们各自的消费量的比例进行支付。但如果这种赋税是以购买饮酒许可证的方式征收,那么节制不酗酒的人根据他的消费量的比例,就要比酗酒的人支付重得多的赋税;非常好客的家庭被征收的赋税就要比宾客少的家庭少支付很多赋税。第二,如果采用这种购买一年期、半年期或者季度许可证以消费某种商品的征税方法,将会大大缩减那种对很快消耗掉的商品征收的赋税的主要便利之一,即一件一件逐渐地纳税。目前一瓶黑啤酒的价钱为 3 便士半,其中对麦芽、酒花、啤酒征收的各种赋税和酿酒者为垫付这些赋税的超额利润共计大概能达到 1 便士半。如果一个劳动者可以方便地节省出 3 便士半,他就可以购买一瓶黑啤酒。如果他不能节省出来,他将不得不满足于一品脱的黑啤酒,这样他就节省了 1 便士,也就等于他获得了 1 便士,有这样的节制他就获得了一点钱。他一件一件地缴纳赋税,他愿付就付,何时能付就何时付,所有的支付行为都完全是自愿的,他如果想不付就可以不付。第三,这种赋税所起的反对奢侈的功能就减少了。一旦买到了许可证,无论这个购买者饮多还是饮少,所缴纳的赋税都是一样的。第四,如果要求一个劳动者一次性付清一年期、半年期或者季度的税额,这个税额等于目前各个时期

马太克尔先生提议,可以通过发放许可证的方法来征收他的其他商品赋税,但这种方法遭到了更多的反对。

a tax equal to what he at present pays, with little or no inconveniency, upon all the different pots and pints of porter which he drinks in any such period of time, the sum might frequently distress him very much. This mode of taxation, therefore, it seems evident, could never, without the most grievous oppression, produce a revenue nearly equal to what is derived from the present mode without any oppression. In several countries, however, commodities of an immediate or very speedy consumption are taxed in this manner. In Holland, people pay so much a head for a licence to drink tea. I have already mentioned a tax upon bread, which, so far as it is consumed in farm-houses and country villages, is there levied in the same manner.

<small>Excepting the four mentioned above, British excise duties fall chiefly on luxuries.</small>   The duties of excise are imposed chiefly upon goods of home produce destined for home consumption. They are imposed only upon a few sorts of goods of the most general use. There can never be any doubt either concerning the goods which are subject to those duties, or concerning the particular duty which each species of goods is subject to. They fall almost altogether upon what I call luxuries, excepting always the four duties above mentioned, upon salt, soap, leather, candles, and, perhaps, that upon green glass.

<small>Customs were originally regarded as taxes on merchants' profits,</small>   The duties of customs are much more ancient than those of excise. They seem to have been called customs, as denoting customary payments which had been in use from time immemorial. They appear to have been originally considered as taxes upon the profits of merchants. During the barbarous times of feudal anarchy, merchants, like all the other inhabitants of burghs, were considered as little better than emancipated bondmen, whose persons were despised, and whose gains were envied. The great nobility, who had consented that the king should tallage the profits of their own tenants, were not unwilling that he should tallage likewise those of an order of men whom it was much less their interest to protect. In those ignorant times, it was not understood, that the profits of merchants are a subject not taxable directly; or that the final payment of all such taxes must fall, with a considerable over-charge, upon the consumers.

The gains of alien merchants were looked upon more unfavourably

第五篇　第一项和第二项的附录

内他没有丝毫困难就可以支付的他所饮用的黑啤酒的赋税税额，这种一次性付清的方法常常就会给他带来很大的困难。所以看来很显然，如果采用这种征税方法，除非实行残酷的压迫手段，否则就不可能达到现在没有采用压迫的征税方法时所征收到的税收额。然而，在有些国家，对可以立即消费掉或者很快消费掉的商品就是以这种方式进行征税的。在荷兰，人们要想喝茶需要支付很多来购买饮茶许可证。前面我也提到了面包税，农舍和乡村消费的面包也，都是按照同样的方法征收赋税的。

货物税主要是对用于国内消费的国产商品征收的赋税。它只对用处最广的一些商品征收赋税。所以哪些商品应该征收这些赋税，每种商品应该征收怎样的赋税，都是一清二楚的。这些赋税，除了我上面提到的四种赋税即盐税、肥皂税、皮革税和蜡烛税(或许还加上玻璃税)外，其余几乎全部都落在了我所说的奢侈品上。

除了上面提到的四种赋税外，不列颠的货物税主要落在奢侈品上。

关税要远比货物税实行的早。这种赋税之所以称为关税(custom，有"习惯"之意)，就是表示这是一种自远古以来习惯性的支付。看来最初它被认为是对商人利润征收的赋税。在封建的野蛮混乱时期，商人也像城市里的其他居民一样，并不比解放了的农奴好多少，他们的人格被人轻蔑，他们的收入被人所嫉妒。那些大贵族们，既然已经同意国王向他们自己佃户的利润征收赋税，所以自然也不会不愿意国王对他们无意保护的阶层同样地征收赋税了。在那种愚昧的年代，他们不懂得是不能对商人的利润直接征税的，因为那样所有这些赋税的最终支付就会落在消费者身上，而且还要加上一个相当大的额外数额。

关税最初被认为是对商人征收的赋税。

外国商人的收入比英国商人的收入遭到了更多的嫉视。所

— 1855 —

| 国民财富的性质与原理

those of aliens being taxed more heavily. — than those of English merchants. It was natural, therefore, that those of the former should be taxed more heavily than those of the latter. This distinction between the duties upon aliens and those upon English merchants, which was begun from ignorance, has been continued from the spirit of monopoly, or in order to give our own merchants an advantage both in the home and in the foreign market.

So originally customs were imposed equally on all sorts of goods, and on exports as well as imports. — With this distinction, the ancient duties of customs were imposed equally upon all sorts of goods, necessaries as well as luxuries, goods exported as well as goods imported. Why should the dealers in one sort of goods, it seems to have been thought, be more favoured than those in another? or why should the merchant exporter be more favoured than the merchant importer?

The first was that on wool and leather, and the second tonnage (on wine) and poundage (on all other goods). Subsidies were additions to poundage. — The ancient customs were divided into three branches. The first, and perhaps the most ancient of all those duties, was that upon wool and leather. It seems to have been chiefly or altogether an exportation duty. When the woollen manufacture came to be established in England, lest the king should lose any part of his customs upon wool by the exportation of woollen cloths, a like duty was imposed upon them. The other two branches were, first, a duty upon wine, which, being imposed at so much a ton, was called a tonnage; and, secondly, a duty upon all other goods, which, being imposed at so much a pound of their supposed value, was called a poundage. In the forty-seventh year of Edward Ⅲ. a duty of sixpence in the pound was imposed upon all goods exported and imported, except wools, wool-fells, leather, and wines, which were subject to particular duties. In the fourteenth of Richard Ⅱ. this duty was raised to one shilling in the pound; but three years afterwards, it was again reduced to sixpence. It was raised to eight-pence in the second year of Henry Ⅳ.; and in the fourth year of the same prince, to one shilling. From this time to the ninth year of William Ⅲ. this duty continued at one shilling in the pound. The duties of tonnage and poundage were generally granted to the king by one and the same act of parliament, and were called the Subsidy of Tonnage and Poundage. The subsidy of poundage having continued for so long a time at one shilling in the pound, or at five per cent.; a subsidy came, in the language of the customs, to denote a general duty of this kind of five per cent. This subsidy, which is now called the Old Subsidy, still continues to be levied according to the book of

— 1856 —

## 第五篇 第一项和第二项的附录

以很自然地,前者被征收的赋税要比后者被征收的赋税更重。这种对外国商人和英国商人之间赋税的差别,最初源自于无知,垄断的精神又使其持续了下来,以便使我们自己的商人能够在国内市场和国外市场都拥有优势。

对外国人的利润征收较重的赋税。

除了这个差别外,古代的关税对所有的货物都平等地征税,不管它们是必需品还是奢侈品,是出口品还是进口品。当时的看法似乎是,为什么一种货物的商人要比另一种货物的商人享受更多的优惠呢?为什么出口商人要比进口商人享受更多的优惠呢?

最初的关税向所有种类的货物、出口货物和进口货物等地征收赋税。

古代的关税分为三部分。第一部分,或许可以说是所有关税中实行最早的关税,是对羊毛和皮革征收的关税。它似乎主要或者完全是出口税。当毛织品制造业在英格兰建立时,国王担心毛织品出口会让他失去对羊毛征收的部分关税,所以就对毛织品也征收了同样的赋税。另外两个部分,第一,是对葡萄酒征收的赋税,由于是每吨葡萄酒征收一定的赋税,所以称之为吨税;第二,对其他所有货物征收的赋税,由于是对货物的推定价值每磅征收一定的赋税,所以称之为磅税。爱德华三世四十七年,除了羊毛、羊皮、皮革及葡萄酒因征有特殊赋税外,其他所有的进出口商品都是每磅征收 6 便士的赋税。查理二世十四年,赋税每磅提到 1 先令,但在三年后又回到了每磅 6 便士。亨利四世二年,赋税提高到了 8 便士,在亨利四世四年,又回到每磅 1 先令。从这个时期起到威廉三世九年,这种赋税一直是每磅征收 1 先令。吨税和磅税根据同一个议会法律统统都拨给了国王,称为吨税补助税和磅税补助税。在一个很长的时期内,磅税补助税都是每磅征收 1 先令或 5% 的赋税。所以在关税用语中,补助税一般就是指这种 5% 的赋税。这种现在称之为旧补助税的补助税,至今仍在

rates established in the twelfth of Charles II. The method of ascertaining, by a book of rates, the value of goods subject to this duty, is said to be older than the time of James I. ① The new subsidy imposed by the ninth and tenth of William III. , ② was an additional five per cent. upon the greater part of goods. The one-third and the two-third subsidy ③ made up between them another five per cent. of which they were proportionable parts. The subsidy of 1747 ④ made a fourth five per cent. upon the greater part of goods; and that of 1759, ⑤ a fifth upon some particular sorts of goods. Besides those five subsidies, a great variety of other duties have occasionally been imposed upon particular sorts of goods, in order sometimes to relieve the exigencies of the state, and sometimes to regulate the trade of the country, according to the principles of the mercantile system.

<small>The prevalence of the principles of the mercantile system has led to the removal of nearly all the export duties,</small>
That system has come gradually more and more into fashion. The old subsidy was imposed indifferently upon exportation as well as importation. The four subsequent subsidies, as well as the other duties which have since been occasionally imposed upon particular sorts of goods, have, with a few exceptions, been laid altogether upon importation. The greater part of the ancient duties which had been imposed upon the exportation of the goods of home produce and manufacture, have either been lightened or taken away altogether. In most cases they have been taken away. Bounties have even been given upon the exportation of some of them. Drawbacks too, sometimes of the whole, and, in most cases, of a part of the duties which are paid upon the importation of foreign goods, have been granted upon their exportation. Only half the duties imposed by the

---

① [ Gilbert, *Treatise on the Court of Exchequer* 1758, p. 224, mentions a Book of Rates printed in 1586. Dowell, *History of Taxation and Taxes*, 1884, vol. i. , pp. 146, 165, places the beginning of the system soon after 1558. ]

② [ C. 23. ]

③ [ 2 and 3 Ann. c. 9; 3 and 4 Ann. , c. 5. ]

④ [ 21 Geo. II. , c. 2. ]

⑤ [ 32 Geo. II. , c. 10, on tobacco, linen, sugar and other grocery, except currants, East India goods ( except coffee and raw silk ), brandy and other spirits ( except colonial rum), and paper. ]

## 第五篇　第一项和第二项的附录

按照查理二世十二年制定的税率表来征收赋税。按照税率表审定应纳税货物价值的方法,据说在詹姆士一世之前就有了①。威廉三世九年、十年征收的新补助税,是对大部分货物额外征收了5%的赋税②。1/3 补助税及 2/3 补助税合起来就构成另一个5%③。1747 年对大部分货物征收的补助税是第四个 5%④。1759 年对一些特定货物征收的补助税是第五个 5%⑤。除了这五项补助税外,有时为了救国家之急需,有时为了根据重商主义体系的原则来调节国家贸易,还对一些特定货物征收了许多其他的赋税。

重商主义体系逐渐地越来越流行。旧补助税对出口货物和进口货物无差异地征收赋税。后来的四种补助税以及其他不定期地对一些特定货物征收的赋税,除了少数的一些赋税外,都完全地落在了进口的货物上。过去对国产品和制造品出口征收的赋税,大部分要么减轻了要么就完全取消了。多数情况下这些赋税都是取消了。甚至于还补贴一些货物的出口。对于进口的外国货物征收的赋税,当这些货物又出口时,有时会返还全部的赋税,大多数情况下返还其中一部分赋税。对于进口时征收的旧补

<small>重商主义体系的流行导致取消了几乎所有的出口税,</small>

---

① 吉尔伯特在《税务法庭论文集》,1758 年,第 224 页中提到在 1586 年印刷的《税率表》。道尔《课税和赋税史》1884 年,第 1 卷,第 146、165 页,说这种按照税率表审定应纳税货物价值的方法体系始于 1558 年后不久。

② 第 23 号法令。

③ 安妮女王二年、三年第 9 号法令,安妮女王三年、四年第 5 号法令。

④ 乔治二世二十一年第 2 号法令。

⑤ 乔治二世三十二年第 10 号法令,对烟草、亚麻布、糖和其他杂货(无核小葡萄干除外)、东印度货物(除咖啡和未加工的丝绸外)、白兰地和其他酒类(除殖民地甜酒)和纸类课征。

— 1859 —

old subsidy upon importation are drawn back upon exportation; but the whole of those imposed by the latter subsidies and other imposts are, upon the greater part of goods, drawn back in the same manner. This growing favour of exportation, and discouragement of importation, have suffered only a few exceptions, which chiefly concern the materials of some manufactures. These, our merchants and manufacturers are willing should come as cheap as possible to themselves, and as dear as possible to their rivals and competitors in other countries. Foreign materials are, upon this account, sometimes allowed to be imported duty free; Spanish wool, for example, flax, and raw linen yarn. The exportation of the materials of home produce, and of those which are the particular produce of our colonies, has sometimes been prohibited, and sometimes subjected to higher duties. The exportation of English wool has been prohibited. That of beaver skins, of beaver wool, and of gum Senega, has been subjected to higher duties; Great Britain, by the conquest of Canada and Senegal, having got almost the monopoly of those commodities.

<small>and has been unfavourable to the revenue of the state,</small> That the mercantile system has not been very favourable to the revenue of the great body of the people, to the annual produce of the land and labour of the country, I have endeavoured to shew in the fourth book of this Inquiry. It seems not to have been more favourable to the revenue of the sovereign; so far at least as that revenue depends upon the duties of customs.

<small>annihilating parts of it by prohibitions of importation,</small> In consequence of that system, the importation of several sorts of goods has been prohibited altogether. This prohibition has in some cases entirely prevented, and in others has very much diminished the importation of those commodities, by reducing the importers to the necessity of smuggling. It has entirely prevented the importation of foreign woollens; and it has very much diminished that of foreign silks and velvets. In both cases it has entirely annihilated the revenue of customs which might have been levied upon such importation.

<small>and reducing other parts by high duties.</small> The high duties which have been imposed upon the importation of many different sorts of foreign goods, in order to discourage their consumption in Great Britain, have in many cases served only to encourage smuggling; and in all cases have reduced the revenue of the customs below what more moderate duties would have afforded. The

## 第五篇 第一项和第二项的附录

助税在出口时只退还一半的税额;但以后的补助税和其他对大部分货物征收的赋税,在出口时会返还全部税额。这种越来越严重的优惠出口、限制进口的政策主要只对一些制造品原料才存在例外。我们的商人和制造业者都希望这些原材料尽可能的对自己便宜一些,尽可能的对其他国家的敌手和竞争对手昂贵一些。故此,有时允许外国原材料免税进口。例如,西班牙的羊毛、亚麻织品和粗制亚麻纱线。而对于国产品的原材料和殖民地特产原料的出口,则有时予以禁止,有时征以重税。比如,禁止英国羊毛的出口,对海狸皮、海狸毛和美远志树胶的出口征以较重的赋税。英国自从占领了加拿大和塞内加尔以后,就几乎垄断了这些商品。

重商主义体系对于大多数人民的收入、对于土地年产物和劳动年产物并不是十分有利,这点我在本书第四篇已经试图说明了。而对君主的收入也并不怎样的有利,至少对那些收入仰赖于关税的国家就是如此。〔对国家收入不利,〕

推行这种体系的结果,就是完全禁止了一些货物的进口。由于禁止在一些场合下会完全阻止这些货物的进口,在有些场合下会大幅减少这些货物的进口,所以进口商不得不通过走私来进口货物。外国毛织品的进口被完全阻止了,外国丝绸和天鹅绒的进口也大幅减少了。在这种情况下,本可以由这些货物的进口征得的关税税收都消失殆尽了。〔由于禁止进口,使部分国家收入没有了,〕

对许多种类的外国商品的进口征以重税,以阻止大不列颠消费这些商品的行为,在许多情况下只会鼓励走私。而在任何情况下,却都会减少关税税收,使其低于采用较轻的赋税时可能得到的收入数额。斯威夫特博士说,在关税的算术中,二加二不等于〔由于重税,减少了其他部分的国家收入。〕

国民财富的性质与原理

saying of Dr. Swift, that in the arithmetic of the customs two and two, instead of making four, make sometimes only one, ① holds perfectly true with regard to such heavy duties, which never could have been imposed, had not the mercantile system taught us, in many cases, to employ taxation as an instrument, not of revenue, but of monopoly.

<small>Bounties and drawbacks (great part of which is obtained by fraud) and expenses of management make a large deduction from the customs revenue.</small>

The bounties which are sometimes given upon the exportation of home produce and manufactures, and the drawbacks which are paid upon the re-exportation of the greater part of foreign goods, have given occasion to many frauds, and to a species of smuggling more destructive of the public revenue than any other. In order to obtain the bounty or drawback, the goods, it is well known, are sometimes shipped and sent to sea; but soon afterwards clandestinely relanded in some other part of the country. The defalcation of the revenue of customs occasioned by bounties and drawbacks, of which a great part are obtained fraudulently, is very great. The gross produce of the customs in the year which ended on the 5th of January 1755, amounted to 5,068,000$l$. The bounties which were paid out of this revenue, though in that year there was no bounty upon corn, amounted to 167,800$l$. The drawbacks which were paid upon debentures and certificates, to 2,156,800$l$. Bounties and drawbacks together, amounted to 2,324,600$l$. In consequence of these deductions the revenue of the customs amounted only to 2,743,400$l$. : from which, deducting 287,900$l$. for the expence of management in salaries and other incidents, the neat revenue of the customs for that year comes out to be 2,455,500$l$. The expence of management amounts in this manner to between five and six per cent. upon the gross revenue of the customs, and to something more than ten per cent. upon what remains of that revenue, after deducting what is paid away in bounties and drawbacks.

---

① [Swift attributes the saying to an unnamed commissioner of customs. ' I will tell you a secret, which I learned many years ago from the commissioners of the customs in London: they said when any commodity appeared to be taxed above a moderate rate, the consequence was to lessen that branch of the revenue by one-half; and one of these gentlemen pleasantly told me that the mistake of parliaments on such occasions was owing to an error of computing two and two make four; whereas in the business of laying impositions, two and two never made more than one; which happens by lessening the import and the strong temptation of running such goods as paid high duties, at least in this kingdom. ' Answer to a Paper Called a Memorial of the Poor Inhabitants, Tradesmen and Labourers of the Kingdom of Ireland' (in *Works*, ed. Scott, 2nd ed. , 1883, vol. vii. , pp. 165-166). The saying is quoted from Swift by Hume in his *Essay on the Balance of Trade*, and by Lord Kames in his *Sketches of the History of Man*, 1774, vol, i. , p. 474. ]

# 第五篇　第一项和第二项的附录

四,有时只等于一①。对于这样的重税来说,他的这段话是相当正确的。如果不是重商主义在多种场合下教导我们不要把课税作为收入手段,而要作为垄断手段,那么将永远不会采用这么重的赋税。

对国产品和制造品出口有时给予的补贴和对大部分外国货物再出口时返还的税额,引起了许多的欺诈行为,并且引起了对公共收入破坏性最强的某些走私。众所周知,为了得到这些津贴或退税,人们有时把货物装到船上送出海口。但随后不久就又从本国的其他地方秘密登陆。由津贴和退税所造成的关税收入缺口非常之大,其中大部分都是由于欺诈引起的。截至 1755 年 1 月 5 日,关税总收入达到 5068000 镑。尽管当年没有给谷物以补贴,从这收入中支出的津贴也达到 167800 镑。根据退税凭单和证明返还的退税金达到 2156800 镑。津贴和退税加起来就达到了 2324600 镑。由于这些减免项,关税收入就只有 2743400 镑了,从中再扣除薪俸和其他开支的管理费用 287900 镑。因此该年度关税纯收入只有 2455500 镑。这样,管理费用占了关税总收入的 5%—6% 之间,是扣除津贴和退税后剩余部分的 10% 以上。

津贴和退税(大部分从诈骗得到)以及管理费用使得关税收入大幅减少。

---

①　斯威夫特说这句话是一位不知姓名的关税委员说的。"我将告诉你一个秘密,这是我多年以前从伦敦的关税委员们那里听到的。他们说,当任何一种商品的税率高于一个适度的税率时,就会使这部分收入减少一半。其中一个绅士友善地告诉我,在这些场合国会之所以错是因为他们犯了二加二等于四的错误。而在征税这件事情上,二加二从来不会超过一。由于减少了进口,就吸引走私那些税负很重的货物,至少在这个王国是这样的。"对一篇称为"爱尔兰王国穷民、商人和劳工请愿书"的文章的答复(见《著作全集》,斯科特编,第二版,1883 年,第 7 卷,第 165、166 页)。休谟在他的《论贸易差额》中引用了斯威夫特的这句话;凯姆斯勋爵也同样在他的《人类历史纲要》(1774 年,第 1 卷,第 474 页)中引用了斯威夫特的这句话。

## 国民财富的性质与原理

<small>In the customs returns the imports are minimised and the exports exaggerated.</small>   Heavy duties being imposed upon almost all goods imported, our merchant importers smuggle as much, and make entry of as little as they can. Our merchant exporters, on the contrary, make entry of more than they export; sometimes out of vanity, and to pass for great dealers in goods which pay no duty; and sometimes to gain a bounty or a drawback. Our exports, in consequence of these different frauds, appear upon the customhouse books greatly to overbalance our imports; to the unspeakable comfort of those politicians who measure the national prosperity by what they call the balance of trade.

<small>The customs are very numerous and much less perspicuous and distinct than the excise duties.</small>   All goods imported, unless particularly exempted, and such exemptions are not very numerous, are liable to some duties of customs. If any goods are imported not mentioned in the book of rates, they are taxed at $4s. \ 9\frac{9}{20}d.$ for every twenty shillings value, ① according to the oath of the importer, that is, nearly at five subsidies, or five poundage duties. The book of rates is extremely comprehensive, and enumerates a great variety of articles, many of them little used, and therefore not well known. It is upon this account frequently uncertain under what article a particular sort of goods ought to be classed, and consequently what duty they ought to pay. Mistakes with regard to this sometimes ruin the customhouse officer, and frequently occasion much trouble, expence, and vexation to the importer. In point of perspicuity, precision, and distinctness, therefore, the duties of customs are much inferior to those of excise.

<small>They might with great advantage be confined to a few articles.</small>   In order that the greater part of the members of any society should contribute to the public revenue in proportion to their respective expence, it does not seem necessary that every single article of that expence should be taxed. The revenue, which is levied by the duties of excise, is supposed to fall as equally upon the contributors as that which is levied by the duties of customs; and the duties of excise are imposed upon a few articles only of the most general use and consumption. It has been the opinion of many people, that, by proper

---

① [Saxby, *British Customs*, p. 266.]

## 第五篇 第一项和第二项的附录

由于对几乎所有的进口货物都征以重税,所以我国的进口商人都尽可能地走私,而尽可能地少报关。而与之相反,我国的出口商人,有时为了虚荣心,装作可以免税的巨商,有时为了得到津贴或退税,他们报关的货物量总是要大于他们实际出口的货物量。由于这些不同种类的欺诈,从海关登记簿上看我国的出口远远地大于进口,这就给那些以所谓的贸易差额来衡量国家繁荣程度的政治家们带来了难以言表的鼓舞。

<sub>关于进口货物,海关告示最小了,货物夸大在报中口量化出口货物了。</sub>

所有进口的货物都征有一定的关税,只有一些特殊商品予以免税,而且这种免税的商品非常少。如果有的进口货物没有列入关税税率表中,那么就凭进口商的宣誓,对货物价值每20先令征收4先令9$\frac{9}{20}$便士的关税①,也就是将近前面说的五种补助税或五种磅税的关税。关税表中的品目非常宽泛,列举了种类繁多的商品,其中有很多都不常用,所以不为人所熟知。故此,经常无法确定某种特定类型的商品应该如何归类,进而也无法确定他们应该缴纳何种赋税。这些方面的差错有时会让关税官员出现失误,并常常给进口商带来很多的麻烦、花费和烦恼。所以,就明晰、精确和清楚来说,关税远远不及那些货物税。

<sub>税名相当多,货物税目繁,关税不如货物税明清晰、清楚。</sub>

为了使任何社会的大多数成员按照他们各自的支出,成比例地对公共收入做出贡献,似乎就没有必要对每件物品都征税了。国内货物税征取的收入跟关税征取的收入一样,都被认为同等地落在消费者身上;但是国内货物税仅仅对最广泛的用途和消费品征税。许多人都这样认为,通过适当的管理,关税同样地仅局限

<sub>他们局限于少数物品可能更处上好大。</sub>

---

① 萨克斯贝:《不列颠关税》,第266页。

management, the duties of customs might likewise, without any loss to the public revenue, and with great advantage to foreign trade, be confined to a few articles only.

*Foreign wines and brandies and East and West Indian products at present yield most of the customs revenue.* The foreign articles, of the most general use and consumption in Great Britain, seem at present to consist chiefly in foreign wines and brandies; in some of the productions of America and the West Indies, sugar, rum, tobacco, cocoanuts, &c. and in some of those of the East Indies, tea, coffee, china-ware, spiceries of all kinds, several sorts of piece-goods, &c. These different articles afford, perhaps, at present, the greater part of the revenue which is drawn from the duties of customs. The taxes which at present subsist upon foreign manufactures, if you except those upon the few contained in the foregoing enumeration, have the greater part of them been imposed for the purpose, not of revenue, but of monopoly, or to give our own merchants an advantage in the home market. By removing all prohibitions, and by subjecting all foreign manufactures to such moderate taxes, as it was found from experience afforded upon each article the greatest revenue to the public, our own workmen might still have a considerable advantage in the home market, and many articles, some of which at present afford no revenue to government, and others a very inconsiderable one, might afford a very great one.

*The yield of high duties is often lessened by smuggling or diminished consumption.* High taxes, sometimes by diminishing the consumption of the taxed commodities, and sometimes by encouraging smuggling, frequently afford a smaller revenue to government than what might be drawn from more moderate taxes.

*In the first case the only remedy is to lower the duty.* When the diminution of revenue is the effect of the diminution of consumption, there can be but one remedy, and that is the lowering of the tax.

*For smuggling the remedy is to lower the tax or increase the difficulty of smuggling.* When the diminution of the revenue is the effect of the encouragement given to smuggling, it may perhaps be remedied in two ways; either by diminishing the temptation to smuggle, or by increasing the difficulty of smuggling. The temptation to smuggle can be diminished only by the lowering of the tax; and the difficulty of smuggling can be increased only by establishing that system of administration which is most proper for preventing it.

*Excise laws are more embarrassing to the smuggler than the customs.* The excise laws, it appears, I believe, from experience, obstruct and embarrass the operations of the smuggler much more effectually than those of the customs. By introducing into the customs a system of administration as similar to that of the excise as the nature of the different duties will admit, the difficulty of smuggling might be very much increased. This alteration, it has been supposed by many people, might very easily be brought about.

## 第五篇 第一项和第二项的附录

于在少数的物品上,对公共税收没有任何影响,对对外贸易非常有利。

在英国用途最广泛的国外消费品目前似乎就是外国葡萄酒和白兰地了;美洲及西印度的产物,例如糖、酒、烟草、椰子等等,东印度的茶、咖啡、瓷器、各种香料及各种类纺织物等等。这些不同的物品可能当时可以支付从关税中收取的大部分收入。目前依靠国外制造业的税收,如果除去那部分包含在前述的列举的物品,为了这个目的而征收的大部分,不是为征税而课收的收入,而是为了垄断而征收的,或者说是为了给我们的商人在国内市场上一些优势。通过取消所有的禁令,并且对所有的国外制造业征收适中的税收,根据经验得出对外国产品征税能为国家提供最大的收入,我们自己的工人也许在国内市场上仍然有很大的优势,许多商品(其中一些目前不能给政府提供税收,有些提供很微不足道的一部分)很可能提供很大的收入。

<sup>国外的葡萄酒和白兰地以及西印度目前产品提供了关税的大部分收入。</sup>

<sup>重税的生产往往被走私或消费减少而抵消。</sup>

重税有时候会减少课税商品的消费,有时候会鼓励走私,相比税收更适中的税收来说,给政府提供的收入往往更少。

当收入的减少是由于消费减少的时候,只存在一种弥补措施,那就是降低税收。

<sup>在第一种情况下唯一的弥补措施是降低税收。</sup>

当税收减少是由于鼓励了走私的时候,可能就存在两种弥补措施;要么减少走私的诱惑,要么增加走私的难度。走私的诱惑仅仅可以通过降低税收来减少;走私的难度仅仅通过建立最合适的行政管理体制来增加。

<sup>对于走私,弥补的办法就是降低税收或是增加走私的难度。</sup>

我相信根据经验,货物法似乎比关税更有效地阻止了走私活动。在不同税收性质所允许的范围内,通过将行政管理体制引入关税,走私的难度将可能会大幅增加。许多人都认为这种改变是

<sup>货物税比关税更能阻止走私。</sup>

— 1867 —

## 国民财富的性质与原理

If customs were confined to a few articles, a system of excise supervision of stores could be instituted.

The importer of commodities liable to any duties of customs, it has been said, might at his option be allowed either to carry them to his own private warehouse, or to lodge them in a warehouse provided either at his own expence or at that of the public, but under the key of the customhouse officer, and never to be opened but in his presence. If the merchant carried them to his own private warehouse, the duties to be immediately paid, and never afterwards to be drawn back; and that warehouse to be at all times subject to the visit and examination of the customhouse officer, in order to ascertain how far the quantity contained in it corresponded with that for which the duty had been paid. If he carried them to the public warehouse, no duty to be paid till they were taken out for home consumption. If taken out for exportation, to be duty-free; proper security being always given that they should be so exported. The dealers in those particular commodities, either by wholesale or retail, to be at all times subject to the visit and examination of the customhouse officer; and to be obliged to justify by proper certificates the payment of the duty upon the whole quantity contained in their shops or warehouses. What are called the excise-duties upon rum imported are at present levied in this manner, and the same system of administration might perhaps be extended to all duties upon goods imported; provided always that those duties were, like the duties of excise, confined to a few sorts of goods of the most general use and consumption. If they were extended to almost all sorts of goods, as at present, public warehouses of sufficient extent could not easily be provided, and goods of a very delicate nature, or of which the preservation required much care and attention, could not safely be trusted by the merchant in any warehouse but his own.

Great simplification without loss of revenue would then be secured,

If by such a system of administration smuggling, to any considerable extent, could be prevented even under pretty high duties; and if every duty was occasionally either heightened or lowered according as it was most likely, either the one way or the other, to afford the greatest revenue to the state; taxation being always employed as an instrument of revenue and never of monopoly; it seems not improbable that a revenue, at least equal to the present neat revenue of the customs, might be drawn from duties upon the importation of only a few sorts of goods of the most general use and consumption; and that the duties of customs might thus be brought to the same degree of simplicity, certainty, and precision, as those of excise. What the revenue at present loses, by drawbacks upon the re-exportation of foreign goods which

## 第五篇 第一项和第二项的附录

轻而易举的。

已经说过担负关税的进口商自行决定,可能被允许将货物运进他们自己的仓库,或者将货物堆积在自己付费的或国家付费的仓库里,但是后者交由海关官员看管,他不在场时绝不能打开。如果商人将货物运进自己的仓库中,就必须马上支付关税,并且以后不可能被退还;为了确保仓库中的货物数量与所付关税的货物数量一致,仓库在任何时候都可以由海关官员参观检查。如果他们将货物运进公共仓库中,直到他将货物取出来供应国内消费的时候才交税。如果取出来是为了出口,也将免税;但是必须提供出口的保证。这些特殊商品的商人,或者是批发或者是零售,任何时候都可由海关官员访问及检查;并且一定要提供合适的证书来证明他们商店或仓库中的所有货物数量的税收。目前进口酒被征收的所谓的货物税就是按这种方式征收的,同样的行政管理体制可能被延伸到所有的进口商品上;只要这些关税像货物税一样,总是局限于一般用途和消费的几种商品。如果如同目前一样,这种赋税延伸到几乎所有的商品上,足够的公共仓库可能不容易被提供,而且非常易碎性质的商品,需要小心仔细保管的商品,除了在自己的仓库中,商人不放心放在其他任何的仓库中。

<sub_note>关于货物税的监管制度将被简化。如果关税限于少数商品,物品监管制度将被简化。</sub_note>

如果通过这种走私的管理体制,在很大程度上,相当高的关税也能阻止走私;如果每一种税收视情况时而降低时而提高,来给国家提供最大的收入;税收往往被用作一种收入的工具而不是垄断的工具;一种至少等同于目前关税净收入的收入,从少数几种一般用途和消费的进口商品上征收似乎也不是不合适的;因此关税可能跟货物税一样达到相同程度的简单、确定和正确。由于后来再次输入国内在国内消费的国外产品的再出口给予退税目

那么,可以确保没有任何损失的收入简化,

国民财富的性质与原理

are afterwards relanded and consumed at home, would under this system be saved altogether. If to this saving, which would alone be very considerable, were added the abolition of all bounties upon the exportation of home-produce; in all cases in which those bounties were not in reality drawbacks of some duties of excise which had before been advanced; it cannot well be doubted but that the neat revenue of customs might, after an alteration of this kind, be fully equal to what it had ever been before.

<small>while the trade and manufactures of the country would gain greatly.</small>  If by such a change of system the public revenue suffered no loss, the trade and manufactures of the country would certainly gain a very considerable advantage. The trade in the commodities not taxed, by far the greatest number, would be perfectly free, and might be carried on to and from all parts of the world with every possible advantage. Among those commodities would be comprehended all the necessaries of life, and all the materials of manufacture. So far as the free importation of the necessaries of life reduced their average money price in the home market, it would reduce the money price of labour, but without reducing in any respect its real recompence. The value of money is in proportion to the quantity of the necessaries of life which it will purchase. That of the necessaries of life is altogether independent of the quantity of money which can be had for them. The reduction in the money price of labour would necessarily be attended with a proportionable one in that of all home-manufactures, which would thereby gain some advantage in all foreign markets. The price of some manufactures would be reduced in a still greater proportion by the free importation of the raw materials. If raw silk could be imported from China and Indostan duty-free, the silk manufacturers in England could greatly undersell those of both France and Italy. There would be no occasion to prohibit the importation of foreign silks and velvets. The cheapness of their goods would secure to our own workmen, not only the possession of the home, but a very great command of the foreign market. Even the trade in the commodities taxed would be carried on with much more advantage than at present. If those commodities were delivered out of the public warehouse for foreign exportation, being in this case exempted from all taxes, the trade in them would be perfectly free. The carrying trade in all sorts of goods would under this system enjoy every possible advantage. If those commodities were

前所造成的损失,在这种体制下就会被全部保留下来。仅仅这种保留数目就会很大,如果再加上废除对所有的国内产品出口的津贴,实际上在任何情况下这些津贴都不是对预先所征货物税的一种退税,在这种改变之后,净关税收入可能完全等于改变之前的收入,这一点可能是毋庸置疑的。

如果这样的制度变化没有使公共收入遭受损失的话,一个国家的贸易和制造业肯定会获得相当的优势。最大多数的未课税的商品贸易,将会完全自由,并且可能在世界各地非常有利地运进运出。在这些商品中包含了所有的生活必需品以及制造业的所有原材料。只要生活必需品的自由进口降低了他们在国内市场上的平均价格,他就会减少劳动力的货币价格,但是不会在任何方面减少其真实的报酬。货币的价值和它即将购买的生活必需品数量成比例。生活必需品的价格完全独立于可以购买这些生活必需品的货币数量。劳动力货币价格的减少必将伴随着所有国内制造业价格的成比例下降,这样在所有国内市场上就可以获得一些优势。因为原材料的自由进口,某些制造业的价格将会以一个更大的比例降低。如果可以从中国和印度免税进口生丝,英格兰的丝织制造业者可能会以大大低于市价售出法国和意大利的丝织品。就不存在禁止国外丝织品和天鹅绒的必要了。本国商品的低廉的价格,不仅确保我国的工人可以占有国内市场,而且还可以对国外市场有较大的支配权。甚至课税商品的贸易将比当前更有利地进行。如果这些商品从公共仓库运出出口到国外,在这种情况下免除所有的税,他们的贸易将会是完全自由的。所有种类商品的运输贸易在这种制度下将享有一切可能得到的优势。如果这些商品运给国内消费,进口商到他有机会出售

然而一国的贸易和制造业将大大获利。

delivered out for home-consumption, the importer not being obliged to advance the tax till he had an opportunity of selling his goods, either to some dealer, or to some consumer, he could always afford to sell them cheaper than if he had been obliged to advance it at the moment of importation. Under the same taxes, the foreign trade of consumption even in the taxed commodities, might in this manner be carried on with much more advantage than it can at present.

<small>Sir Robert Walpole's excise scheme was something of this kind so far as wine and tobacco are concerned.</small>   It was the object of the famous excise scheme of Sir Robert Walpole to establish, with regard to wine and tobacco, a system not very unlike that which is here proposed. But though the bill which was then brought into parliament, comprehended those two commodities only; it was generally supposed to be meant as an introduction to a more extensive scheme of the same kind. Faction, combined with the interest of smuggling merchants, raised so violent, though so unjust, a clamour against that bill, that the minister thought proper to drop it; and from a dread of exciting a clamour of the same kind, none of his successors have dared to resume the project.

<small>The duties on foreign luxuries fall chiefly on the middle and upper ranks.</small>   The duties upon foreign luxuries imported for home-consumption, though they sometimes fall upon the poor, fall principally upon people of middling or more than middling fortune. Such are, for example, the duties upon foreign wines, upon coffee, chocolate, tea, sugar, &c.

<small>Those on the luxuries of home produce fall on people of all ranks.</small>   The duties upon the cheaper luxuries of home-produce destined for home-consumption, fall pretty equally upon people of all ranks in proportion to their respective expence. The poor pay the duties upon malt, hops, beer, and ale, upon their own consumption: The rich, upon both their own consumption and that of their servants.

The whole consumption of the inferior ranks of people, or of those below the middling rank, it must be observed, is in every country much greater, not only in quantity, but in value, than that of the middling and of those above the middling rank. The whole expence of the inferior is much greater than that of the superior ranks. In the first place, almost the whole capital of every country is annually distributed among the inferior ranks of people, as the wages of productive labour. Secondly, a great part of the revenue arising from both the rent of land and the profits of stock, is annually distributed among the same rank, in the wages and maintenance of menial servants, and

## 第五篇　第一项和第二项的附录

自己的商品时为止都没有义务提前交税，或者是为商人或者是为消费者，他总是能够比必须在进口之时就要提前交税的情况更便宜地出售自己的商品。在同样的税率下，国外课税消费品的贸易以这种方式被运输，可能比目前的更为有利。

罗伯特·沃尔波先生著名的货物税方案的目的，就葡萄酒和烟草而言，是要建立一种与这里提议非常相似的体制。尽管议案被递交议会审议，但仅仅包含了两种商品；一般而言大家认为这个议案即是更广泛同类方案的一个前奏。派系斗争，连同走私者的利益，引发了对这个议案的很多不公平的反对和暴力事件，所以首相认为最好是把它放弃掉。由于担心激起同样的反对呼声，他的继承者没有一个敢于重提这个计划。

> 罗伯特·沃尔波先生的货物税方案，就葡萄酒和烟草而言是类似的。

对国产用以满足国内消费的比较便宜的奢侈品的课税，尽管有时他们落在穷人的身上，但还是主要落在中产阶级或是中产阶级以上的人身上。例如国外葡萄酒、咖啡、可可、茶以及糖等等的关税。

> 国外奢侈品的关税要落在中产阶级以上的人的身上。

针对国内消费的国内生产的消费品的税收，根据各自的支出，完全平等地落在所有的阶层身上。穷人支付自身消费的麦芽、酒花、啤酒、麦酒的税；富者则支付自身及仆婢所消费的这些物品的税。

> 国内生产的消费品的税收要落在所有人的身上。

必须注意一点，在任何国家中，整个下层阶级人们的消费，或者中层阶级以下的人们更多一些，不仅仅是数量，而且价值上也比中产阶级和中产阶级以上的人们消费更多。下层阶级的人们整个支出要比上层阶级的人们要多得多。第一，几乎整个社会的所有资本每年都分配给下层阶级的人们，这是作为一种生产性的劳动。第二，每年也都分配在同样的阶层中，这是作为仆婢和其

—— 1873 ——

> Taxes on the consumption of the inferior ranks are much more productive than those on the consumption of he rich.

other unproductive labourers. Thirdly, some part of the profits of stock belongs to the same rank, as a revenue arising from the employment of their small capitals. The amount of the profits annually made by small shopkeepers, tradesmen, and retailers of all kinds, is every where very considerable, and makes a very considerable portion of the annual produce. Fourthly, and lastly, some part even of the rent of land belongs to the same rank; a considerable part to those who are somewhat below the middling rank, and a small part even to the lowest rank; common labourers sometimes possessing in property an acre or two of land. Though the expence of those inferior ranks of people, therefore, taking them individually, is very small, yet the whole mass of it, taking them collectively, amounts always to by much the largest portion of the whole expence of the society; what remains, of the annual produce of the land and labour of the country for the consumption of the superior ranks, being always much less, not only in quantity but in value. The taxes upon expence, therefore, which fall chiefly upon that of the superior ranks of people, upon the smaller portion of the annual produce, are likely to be much less productive than either those which fall indifferently upon the expence of all ranks, or even those which fall chiefly upon that of the inferior ranks; than either those which fall indifferently upon the whole annual produce, or those which fall chiefly upon the larger portion of it. The excise upon the materials and manufacture of home-made fermented and spirituous liquors is accordingly, of all the different taxes upon expence, by far the most productive; and this branch of the excise falls very much, perhaps principally, upon the expence of the common people. In the year which ended on the 5th of July 1775, the gross produce of this branch of the excise amounted to 3, 341, 837 $l.$ 9$s.$ 9 $d.$

> But such taxes must never be on the necessary consumption of the inferior ranks.

It must always be remembered, however, that it is the luxurious and not the necessary expence of the inferior ranks of people that ought ever to be taxed. The final payment of any tax upon their necessary expence would fall altogether upon the superior ranks of people; upon the smaller portion of the annual produce, and not upon the greater. Such a tax must in all cases either raise the wages of labour, or lessen the demand for it. It could not raise the wages of labour, without throwing the final payment of the tax upon the superior ranks of people. It could not lessen the demand for labour, without lessening the annual produce of the land and labour of the country, the fund from which all taxes must be finally paid. Whatever might be the state to which a tax of this kind reduced the demand for labour, it must always raise wages higher than they otherwise would be in that state; and the final payment of this enhancement of wages must in all cases fall upon the superior ranks of people.

第五篇　第一项和第二项的附录

他非生产性劳动者的工资及维持费。第三,资本获得利润的一部分属于这阶级,作为使用自己资本所得的收入。小商店店主、商人、各种零售商人每年挣得的利润额,到处都是非常之大,并在年收入中,占有一个极大的部分。第四,甚至土地地租中的一些部分也属于这一阶级;相当大的部分属于那些比中层阶级略低些的人所有,一小部分属于最下层阶级人民;因为普通劳动者有时也保有一两亩的土地。因此,尽管这些下层人们的支出,就他们个人而言非常少,然而就总体看,占社会总支出的最大部分;一国供上层阶级消费的土地和劳动的年产品中剩余的部分,不仅数量上而且价值上都总是少得多。因此,主要落在上层阶级人们身上,落在小部分年产物上的税提供的收入,比起那些同等地落在所有阶层人们身上,或者甚至主要落在下层人们身上的税,或者说同等地落在所有年产物上,主要落在大部分年产物上的税所提供的收入要小得多。所以,对国内生产的发酵酒和烈性酒的原料和制造业的货物税在所有各种货物税提供的收入中最多;这一部门的货物税大部分主要落在普通人的开支上。到1775年7月5日为止,这部门消费税的总收入累计3341837镑9先令9便士。<sub>下层阶级的消费税比富裕阶级的消费税更多。</sub>

不过必须记住,是对奢侈品征税而不是对下层阶级人们的必要消费品征税。所有必需品消费税的最后支付都全部落在上层阶级人们身上,落在年产品少部分而不是大部分上。在任何情况下,这样的税收要么提高劳动工资,要么减少劳动需求。如果没有将税收的最后支付落在上层阶级的身上,就不可能提高劳动工资。如果不减少一国土地和劳动的年产品,也就是所有赋税最后支付的来源,就不可能减少对劳动的需求。这种说收减少对劳动的需要,无论状态怎样,它都总是比没有处于这种状态将工资提<sub>但是这种赋税绝不是对下层阶级人们的必须消费品的课税。</sub>

| 国民财富的性质与原理

<small>Liquors brewed or distilled for private use are exempt from excise, though a composition must be paid for malting.</small>

    Fermented liquors brewed, and spirituous liquors distilled, not for sale, but for private use, are not in Great Britain liable to any duties of excise. This exemption, of which the object is to save private families from the odious visit and examination of the tax-gatherer, occasions the burden of those duties to fall frequently much lighter upon the rich than upon the poor. It is not, indeed, very common to distil for private use, though it is done sometimes. But in the country, many middling and almost all rich and great families brew their own beer. Their strong beer, therefore, costs them eight shillings a barrel less than it costs the common brewer, who must have his profit upon the tax, as well as upon all the other expence which he advances. Such families, therefore, must drink their beer at least nine or ten shillings a barrel cheaper than any liquor of the same quality can be drunk by the common people, to whom it is every where more convenient to buy their beer, by little and little, from the brewery or the alehouse. Malt, in the same manner, that is made for the use of a private family, is not liable to the visit or examination of the tax-gatherer; but in this case the family must compound at seven shillings and sixpence a head for the tax. Seven shillings and sixpence are equal to the excise upon ten bushels of malt; a quantity fully equal to what all the different members of any sober family, men, women, and children, are at an average likely to consume. But in rich and great families, where country hospitality is much practised, the malt liquors consumed by the members of the family make but a small part of the consumption of the house. Either on account of this composition, however, or for other reasons, it is not near so common to malt as to brew for private use. It is difficult to imagine any equitable reason why those who either brew or distil for private use, should not be subject to a composition of the same kind.

<small>It is said that a tax on malt smaller than the present taxes on malt, beer and ale taken together would bring in more revenue,</small>

    A greater revenue than what is at present drawn from all the heavy taxes upon malt, beer, and ale, might be raised, it has frequently been said, by a much lighter tax upon malt; the opportunities of defrauding the revenue being much greater in a brewery than in a malt-house; and those who brew for private use being exempted from all duties or composition for duties, which is not the case with those who malt for private use.

— 1876 —

第五篇　第一项和第二项的附录

得更高;这种工资提高的最后支付必须落在上层阶级人们身上。

　　不是为了出售,而只是为了自己消费的酿造的发酵饮料和蒸馏酒精饮料,在英国都没有交税的义务。这种豁免的目的是为了免去收税者对于私人家庭所作的讨厌的访问和检查,它使落在富人身上的税收负担往往比落在穷人身上的更轻。实际上,尽管有时很多家庭会自制蒸馏酒精饮料,但是还不是很普遍。但是在一国中,许多中产阶级和几乎所有的富人和大家庭自己酿造啤酒。因此,他们的烈酒比一般的酿造者每桶要少花费 8 先令,这些制造者从税收的利润以及从其他预付的费用上获得利润。因此比起普通家庭可以喝到的同样质量的饮料,这些家庭至少可以能够每桶便宜 9 先令或 10 先令的价格喝到,对于前者而言,在任何地方一点一点地从啤酒商或酒馆那里购买啤酒更方便。同样为私人家庭的使用而设置的麦芽税,也不一定要接受收税者的访问和检查。但是在这种情况下,家庭必须按每人 7 便士 6 先令的税收缴纳货物税。7 便士 6 先令等同于麦芽 10 蒲式耳的货物税;数量上完全等同于任何节俭家庭所有成员,包括男人、女人和小孩的可能的平均开支。但是在富裕的大家庭,那里的款宴比较多,家庭成员所消费的麦芽饮料仅仅构成家庭消费税的一小部分。然而,或许因为这个税,或许因为其他原因,供私人制造使用的麦芽不及自家酿造饮料那样通行。很难想象出一个公平的理由,为什么供私人制造使用的酿造或不被课征同一种税。

　　经常有这样的说法:目前来自麦芽、啤酒和麦酒等商品课征重税,可能对麦芽所征收的税要轻得多;瞒骗税收的机会在酿酒厂比在麦芽制造场要多得多;并且,那些自酿酒的消费者免去所有的税收,但是为自己消费而制造麦芽的人,却不能免税。

## 国民财富的性质与原理

<small>and figures are quoted to prove it.</small>   In the porter brewery of London, a quarter of malt is commonly brewed into more than two barrels and a half, sometimes into three barrels of porter. The different taxes upon malt amount to six shillings a quarter; those upon strong beer and ale to eight shillings a barrel. In the porter brewery, therefore, the different taxes upon malt, beer, and ale, amount to between twenty-six and thirty shillings upon the produce of a quarter of malt. In the country brewery for common country sale, a quarter of malt is seldom brewed into less than two barrels of strong and one barrel of small beer; frequently into two barrels and a half of strong beer. The different taxes upon small beer amount to one shilling and four-pence a barrel. In the country brewery, therefore, the different taxes upon malt, beer, and ale, seldom amount to less than twenty-three shillings and four-pence, frequently to twenty-six shillings, upon the produce of a quarter of malt. Taking the whole kingdom at an average, therefore, the whole amount of the duties upon malt, beer, and ale, cannot be estimated at less than twenty-four or twenty-five shillings upon the produce of a quarter of malt. But by taking off all the different duties upon beer and ale, and by tripling the malt-tax, or by raising it from six to eighteen shillings upon the quarter of malt, a greater revenue, it is said; might be raised by this single tax than what is at present drawn from all those heavier taxes.

$$\quad l. \quad s. \quad d.$$

In 1772, the old malt-tax produced. . . . .  722,023  11  11

The additional. . . . . . . .  356,776  7  $9\frac{3}{4}$

In 1773, the old tax produced. . . . . .  561,627  3  $7\frac{1}{2}$

The additional. . . . . . . .  278,650  15  $3\frac{3}{4}$

In 1774, the old tax produced. . . . .  624,614  17  $5\frac{3}{4}$

The additional. . . . . . . .  310,745  2  $8\frac{1}{2}$

In 1775, the old tax produced. . . . .  657,357  —  $8\frac{1}{4}$

## 第五篇　第一项和第二项的附录

在伦敦的黑啤酒酿造厂，一夸特麦芽通常被酿造成两升半，有时是三升的黑啤酒。麦芽所征收的各种税为每夸特 6 先令；黑啤酒和各种淡色啤酒为每桶 8 先令。因此，在黑麦酒酿造厂，麦芽、啤酒及谈色啤酒上的各种税，对麦芽每夸特的产品征收累计达 26 先令及至 30 先令的税收。在为普通乡村销售的黑啤酒，一夸特麦芽很少被酿造成少于强啤酒两桶以及淡啤酒一桶；经常被酿造成两桶半强啤酒的。不同的淡啤酒所征收的累计达每桶 1 先令 4 便士。因此，在乡村酿造厂，对麦芽、啤酒及淡色啤酒所征收的税，很少少于 23 先令 4 便士，经常是 26 先令。因此，就整个王国的平均计算，对麦芽、啤酒及淡色啤酒所征收的总税，估计不能少于 24 先令或 25 先令。但是，除去一切啤酒税、淡色啤酒税，而把麦芽税加大三倍，也就是说对麦芽每夸特的税由 6 先令提高至 18 先令，据说，仅仅是这单一税所得收入，都比由现在各种重税所得收入更多。

|  |  | 镑 | 先令 | 便士 |
|---|---|---|---|---|
| 1772 年 | 旧麦芽税收入⋯⋯⋯722923 | | 11 | 11 |
|  | 附加税⋯⋯⋯⋯⋯⋯356776 | | 7 | $9\frac{3}{4}$ |
| 1773 年 | 旧麦芽税收入⋯⋯⋯561627 | | 3 | $7\frac{1}{2}$ |
|  | 附加税⋯⋯⋯⋯⋯⋯278650 | | 15 | $3\frac{3}{4}$ |
| 1774 年 | 旧麦芽税收入⋯⋯⋯624614 | | 17 | $5\frac{1}{4}$ |
|  | 附加税⋯⋯⋯⋯⋯⋯310745 | | 2 | $8\frac{1}{2}$ |
| 1775 年 | 旧麦芽税收入⋯⋯⋯657357 | | – | $8\frac{1}{4}$ |

| | | | |
|---|---|---|---|
| The additional. . . . . . . | 323,785 | 12 | $6\frac{1}{4}$ |
| | 4) 3,835,580 | 12 | $-\frac{3}{4}$ |
| Average of these four years. . . . | 958.895 | 3 | $-\frac{3}{16}$ |
| In 1772, the country excise produced. . . . . | 1,243,128 | 5 | 3 |
| The London brewery. . . . . . | 408,260 | 7 | $2\frac{3}{4}$ |
| In 1773, the country excise . . . . . . . . | 1,245,808 | 3 | 3 |
| The London brewery. . . . . . . | 405,406 | 17 | $10\frac{1}{2}$ |
| In 1774, the country excise . . . . . . . | 1,246,373 | 14 | $5\frac{1}{2}$ |
| The London brewery. . . . . . . | 320,601 | 18 | $-\frac{1}{4}$ |
| In 1775, the country excise . . . . . . . | 1,214,583 | 6 | 1 |
| The London brewery. . . . . . . | 463,670 | 7 | $-\frac{1}{4}$ |
| | 4) 6,547,832 | 19 | $2\frac{1}{4}$ |
| Average of these four years. . . . . . | 1,636,958 | 4 | $9\frac{1}{2}$ |
| To which adding the average malt tax, or. . . | 958,895 | 3 | $-\frac{3}{16}$ |
| The whole amount of those different taxes comes out to be . . . . | 2,595,853 | 7 | $9\frac{11}{16}$ |

|  |  |  |  |  |  |
|---|---|---|---|---|---|
|  | 附加税…………………323785 | 12 | $6\frac{1}{4}$ |
|  | 合计………………… 3835580 | 12 | $-\frac{3}{4}$ |
|  | 4年的平均数……… 958895 | 3 | $-\frac{3}{16}$ |
| 1772年 | 地方国产税收入…… 1243128 | 5 | 3 |
|  | 伦敦酿造厂税额………408260 | 7 | $2\frac{3}{4}$ |
| 1773年 | 地方国产税收入…… 1245808 | 3 | 3 |
|  | 伦敦酿造厂税额…… 405406 | 17 | $10\frac{1}{2}$ |
| 1774年 | 地方国产税收入…… 1246373 | 14 | $5\frac{1}{2}$ |
|  | 伦敦酿造厂税额…… 320601 | 18 | $-\frac{1}{4}$ |
| 1775年 | 地方国产税收入…… 1214583 | 6 | 1 |
|  | 伦敦酿造厂税额…… 463670 | 7 | $-\frac{1}{4}$ |
|  | 合计………………… 6547832 | 19 | $2\frac{1}{4}$ |
|  | 4年的平均数……… 1636958 | 4 | $9\frac{1}{2}$ |
| 加入麦芽税平均数………… 958895 | | 3 | $-\frac{3}{16}$ |
| 两平均数的和…………… 2595853 | | 7 | $9\frac{11}{16}$ |

| 国民财富的性质与原理

But by tripling the malt tax, or by raising it form six to eighteen shillings upon the quarter of malt, that single tax would produce $\Big\}$ 2,876,685  9  $-\dfrac{9}{16}$

A sum which exceeds the foregoing by. . . . 280,832  1  2$\dfrac{14}{16}$

<small>Taxes on cyder and mum included in the old malt tax are counterbalanced by the 'country excise' duty on cyder, verjuice, vinegar and mead.</small>  Under the old malt tax, indeed, is comprehended a tax of four shillings upon the hogshead of cyder, and another of ten shillings upon the barrel of mum. In 1774, the tax upon cyder produced only 3083 $l.$ 6 $s.$ 8 $d.$ It probably fell somewhat short of its usual amount; all the different taxes upon cyder having, that year, produced less than ordinary. The tax upon mum, though much heavier, is still less productive, on account of the smaller consumption of that liquor. But to balance whatever may be the ordinary amount of those two taxes; there is comprehended under what is called The country excise, first, the old excise of six shillings and eight-pence upon the hogshead of cyder; secondly, a like tax of six shillings and eight-pence upon the hogshead of verjuice; thirdly, another of eight shillings and nine-pence upon the hogshead of vinegar; and, lastly, a fourth tax of eleven-pence upon the gallon of mead or metheglin: the produce of those different taxes will probably much more than counterbalance that of the duties imposed, by what is called The annual malt tax upon cyder and mum.

<small>If the malt tax were raised, it would be proper to reduce the excises on wines and spirits containing malt.</small>  Malt is consumed not only in the brewery of beer and ale, but in the manufacture of low wines and spirits. If the malt tax were to be raised to eighteen shillings upon the quarter, it might be necessary to make some abatement in the different excises which are imposed upon those particular sorts of low wines and spirits of which malt makes any part of the materials. In what are called Malt spirits, it makes commonly but a third part of the materials; the other two-thirds being either raw barley, or one-third barley and one-third wheat. In the distillery of malt spirits, both the opportunity and the temptation to smuggle, are much greater than either in a brewery or in a malthouse; the opportunity, on account of the smaller bulk and greater value of the commodity; and the temptation, on account of the superior height of the duties, which amount to 3$s.$ 10$\dfrac{2}{3}d.$ ① upon

---

① Though the duties directly imposed upon proof spirits amount only to 2s. 6d. per gallon, these added to the duties upon the low wines, from which they are distilled, amount to 3s. 10$\dfrac{2}{3}d.$ Both low wines and proof spirits are, to prevent frauds, now rated according to what they gauge in the wash. [ This note appears first in ed. 3; ed. 1 reads '2s. 6d. ' in the text instead of '3s. 10$\dfrac{2}{3}d.$ ']

三倍麦芽税,即麦芽税每夸特由 6 先令提高至 18 先令。此单一

税将产生以下的收入：⋯⋯⋯⋯⋯2,876,685　　9　　$-\dfrac{9}{16}$

对于前者的超过额⋯⋯⋯⋯　280,832　　1　　$2\dfrac{14}{16}$

实际上,这种旧的麦芽税中包含了苹果酒每半桶 4 先令的税和强烈啤酒每桶 10 先令的税。在 1774 年,苹果酒税收仅 3083 镑 6 先令 8 便士。这个税额可能比平常税额略微少一些,所有这些对苹果酒所课的税,这一年比平常收入要少。对强烈啤酒课税虽然课税很重,但因为这种酒的消费不大,所以收入更不如苹果酒税。但是,为弥补这两种税的在平常所有的数量,在所谓地方货物税中含有:第一,苹果酒每半桶 6 先令 8 便士的旧货物税;第二,酸果汁酒每半桶 6 先令 8 便士的旧货物税;第三,醋每桶 8 先令 9 便士的旧货物税;第四,蜂蜜酒每加仑 11 便士的旧货物税。这些不同的税收或许可以平衡所谓的苹果酒和强烈啤酒的年均麦芽税收,大概绰绰有余。

麦芽不但可以用来酿造啤酒和淡色啤酒,而且用以制造下等火酒和酒精。如果麦芽税被提高到每夸特 18 先令,那么减少加在那些以麦芽为原料的特殊种类的下等火酒和酒精上的不同货物税就是很必要的了。在所谓的麦芽通常只占原料的1/3,其他的2/3 或者全部是大麦,或者 1/3 是大麦,1/3 是小麦。在麦芽酒精的蒸馏所里面,走私的机会与诱惑,比在酿酒厂或麦芽制造场内要大得多;因为商品容量小价值大,所以走私的机会多;因为关税税率重,每加仑高达 3 先令 10 $\dfrac{2}{3}$ 便士①,所以走私诱惑力强

---

① 对标准强度的酒精征收的税虽然至每加仑 2 先令 6 便士,但加上对标准酒精从而蒸馏出来的下等酒精所课的税就有 3 先令 10 便士。为防止隐瞒,下等酒精和标准酒精均按发酵种原料的容积课税。本注首先见于第三版;第一版正义中为"2 先令 6 便士",而不是"3 先令 10 便士"。

the gallon of spirits. By increasing the duties upon malt, and reducing those upon the distillery, both the opportunities and the temptation to smuggle would be diminished, which might occasion a still further augmentation of revenue.

<small>but not so as to reduce the price of spirits.</small>   It has for some time past been the policy of Great Britain to discourage the consumption of spirituous liquors, on account of their supposed tendency to ruin the health and to corrupt the morals of the common people. According to this policy, the abatement of the taxes upon the distillery ought not to be so great as to reduce, in any respect, the price of those liquors. Spirituous liquors might remain as dear as ever; while at the same time the wholesome and invigorating liquors of beer and ale might be considerably reduced in their price. The people might thus be in part relieved from one of the burdens of which they at present complain the most; while at the same time the revenue might be considerably augmented.

<small>Dr. Davenant objects that the maltster's profits would be unfairly taxed, and the rent and profit of barley land reduced,</small>   The objections of Dr. Davenant to this alteration in the present system of excise duties, seem to be without foundation. Those objections are, that the tax, instead of dividing itself as at present pretty equally upon the profit of the maltster, upon that of the brewer, and upon that of the retailer, would, so far as it affected profit, fall altogether upon that of the maltster; that the maltster could not so easily get back the amount of the tax in the advanced price of his malt, as the brewer and retailer in the advanced price of their liquor; and that so heavy a tax upon malt might reduce the rent and profit of barley land. ①

---

① [ *Political and Commercial Works*, ed. Sir Charles Whitworth, 1771, vol. i. , pp. 222, 223. But Davenant does not confine the effect of the existing tax to the maltster, the brewer and the retailer. The tax, he says, which seems to be upon malt, does not lie all upon that commodity, as is vulgarly thought. For a great many different persons contribute to the payment of this duty, before it comes into the Exchequer. First, the landlord, because of the excise, is forced to let his barley land at a lower rate; and, upon the same score, the tenant must sell his barley at a less price; then the maltster bears his share, for because of the duty, he must abate something in the price of his malt, or keep it; in a proportion it likewise affects the hop merchant, the cooper, the collier, and all trades that have relation to the commodity. The retailers and brewers bear likewise a great share, whose gains of necessity will be less, because of that imposition; and, lastly, it comes heaviest of all upon the consumers. ' If the duty were put upon the maltster, it would be ' difficult for him to raise the price of a dear commodity a full $\frac{1}{3}$d at once; so that he must bear the greatest part of the burden himself, or throw it upon the farmer, by giving less for barley, which brings the tax directly upon the land of England. ' ]

增加对麦芽的关税,同时减少对蒸馏所收税,走私的机会和诱惑就可以减少,这样可以进一步增加国家收入。

英国不鼓励消费酒精饮料的政策已经过去一段时间了,因为酒精被认为有毁坏健康和损害人们道德的倾向。根据这一政策,蒸馏所被征收的税收不应该被这样大幅的减少,以便于不在任何方面降低这种酒精的价格。酒精饮料可能跟以往一样贵,然而与此同时,啤酒和淡色啤酒这类健康的、振奋精神的酒精饮料的价格可能大大降低。因此,人们也许能从日前抱怨的这种负担中部分地解脱放松出来,同时国家收入也可以大大增加。

<small>低饮料的价格却不这样,但酒精的价格是这样。</small>

戴夫南博士反对目前货物税体制的改变,这似乎没有任何根据。这些反对意见是这样的:这些税收不像现在的那样相当平等地对麦芽制造者、酿造者及零售业者征收,就其对利润的影响范围内,它将完全落在麦芽制造者身上;与酿造者及零售业者可以容易地收回预付的酒的价格不一样,麦芽制造者不容易将麦芽价格中的预付数量收回;并且对麦芽课以重税可能会减少大麦耕地的地租及利润①。

<small>戴夫南博士反对麦芽制造者利润公平征税,并对地租利润被减少。</small>

---

① 查理·怀特沃斯爵士编:《政治和商业著作》:1771 年,第一卷,第 222、223 页。但戴维南并不将现行课税的效果限于麦芽。他说,这种税"似乎是对麦芽征收的,并不像普通人所想的,完全落在这种商品身上。因为税收进入国库以前,许多人对它做出了贡献。第一是地主,由于这种税,他不得不按较低的地租出售他的土地;由于同一原因,佃户也必须按较低的价格出售他的大麦;然后是由麦芽制造者承担他的份额,因为由于这种税,他必须略微降低他的麦芽的价格;它也部分地影响酒花商、制桶匠、煤矿工以及与这种商品有关的一切行业。零售商和酿造商同样负担一个很大的份额,他们的收入必然要因课税而减少;最后,对消费者负担最重。"如果向麦芽制造者课税,"他很难将一切昂贵的商品的价格立即提高 1/3 便士,因此他必须自己承担税额的最大部分,或将其转嫁到农场主身上,对大麦少付价,这就使赋税直接落在英格兰的土地上"。

— 1885 —

# 国民财富的性质与原理

<small>but the change would make malt liquors cheaper, and so be likely to increase the consumption,</small> No tax can ever reduce, for any considerable time, the rate of profit in any particular trade, which must always keep its level with other trades in the neighbourhood. The present duties upon malt, beer, and ale, do not affect the profits of the dealers in those commodities, who all get back the tax with an additional profit, in the enhanced price of their goods. A tax indeed may render the goods upon which it is imposed so dear as to diminish the consumption of them. But the consumption of malt is in malt liquors; and a tax of eighteen shillings upon the quarter of malt could not well render those liquors dearer than the different taxes, amounting to twenty-four or twenty-five shillings, do at present. Those liquors, on the contrary, would probably become cheaper, and the consumption of them would be more likely to increase than to diminish.

<small>and the maltster could recover eighteen shillings as easily as the brewer at present recovers twenty-four or thirty and might be given longer credit.</small> It is not very easy to understand why it should be more difficult for the maltster to get back eighteen shillings in the advanced price of his malt, than it is at present for the brewer to get back twenty-four or twenty-five, sometimes thirty shillings, in that of his liquor. The maltster, indeed, instead of a tax of six shillings, would be obliged to advance one of eighteen shillings upon every quarter of malt. But the brewer is at present obliged to advance a tax of twenty-four or twenty-five, sometimes thirty shillings upon every quarter of malt which he brews. It could not be more inconvenient for the maltster to advance a lighter tax, than it is at present for the brewer to advance a heavier one. The maltster doth not always keep in his granaries a stock of malt which it will require a longer time to dispose of, than the stock of beer and ale which the brewer frequently keeps in his cellars. The former, therefore, may frequently get the returns of his money as soon as the latter. But whatever inconveniency might arise to the maltster from being obliged to advance a heavier tax, it could easily be remedied by granting him a few months longer credit than is at present commonly given to the brewer.

<small>The consumption of barley not being reduced, the rent and profit of barley land could not be reduced, as there is no monopoly.</small> Nothing could reduce the rent and profit of barley land which did not reduce the demand for barley. But a change of system, which reduced the duties upon a quarter of malt brewed into beer and ale from twenty-four and twenty-five shillings to eighteen shillings, would be more likely to increase than diminish that demand. The rent and profit

## 第五篇　第一项和第二项的附录

在相当长的时间里,税收不可能减少任何特殊行业的利润率,他必须与相邻地区的其他行业保持相同水平。目前麦芽税、啤酒税和淡色啤酒税不会影响这些商品商人的利润,他们可以通过增加他们商品的价格收回所有的税收以及增加的利润;实际上一种加在这些商品上的税如此之重以至于减少对他们的消费。但是麦芽的消费是在麦芽酒中,每夸特麦芽征收 18 先令的税收,不会使这种酒的价格高于课征于其他上面的税,目前是 24 先令或 25 先令。相反,这种酒可能变得更便宜,并且酒的消费更可能增加而不是减少。

但是这变化将使麦芽更便宜,并且能增加其消费。

不容易理解的是,比起啤酒制造者而言他能收回他的酒中预付的价格 24 或 25 先令,有时 30 先令,对于麦芽酒酿造者而言为什么收回麦芽中预付的价格非常困难?当然麦芽制造者有义务预付每夸特麦芽 18 先令的税,而不是 6 先令的税;但是酿酒者有义务为他酿酒所用的每夸特麦芽预付 24 先令或 25 先令,有时是 30 先令的税。比起目前酿酒者预付更重的税而言,麦芽制造者预付的税收更轻,这不可能更不方便。如果麦芽的处理时间比酿酒者在其仓库保存啤酒和淡色啤酒的时间更长一些的话,麦芽制造者就不会在他的仓库里总是存放麦芽。因此,前者收回他的资金,往往可与后者同样迅速。因为预付较重的税,麦芽制造者会感到的不便,这种情况很容易救济,只要给予他比现在给酿造者更长月份的时间来缴清税款就够了。

麦芽制造者可以像目前酿酒者获得时间信贷一样获得 18 先令,并且麦芽制造者像酿酒者获得 24 或 30 先令以及更长时间给予得先令。

如果不减少大麦的需求,没有什么可以减少大麦耕地的地租和利润。但是制度的改变,减少了每夸特麦芽的税率,酿制成啤酒和淡色啤酒的麦芽从 24 先令和 25 先令减少到 18 先令,将更有可能增加而不是减少需求。另外,麦芽耕地的地租和利润必须非

大麦的消费被减少,大麦种植土地的地租和利润不可能被减少,因为不存在垄断。

— 1887 —

of barley land, besides, must always be nearly equal to those of other equally fertile and equally well cultivated land. If they were less, some part of the barley land would soon be turned to some other purpose; and if they were greater, more land would soon be turned to the raising of barley. When the ordinary price of any particular produce of land is at what may be called a monopoly price, a tax upon it necessarily reduces the rent and profit of the land which grows it. A tax upon the produce of those precious vineyards, of which the wine falls so much short of the effectual demand, that its price is always above the natural proportion to that of the produce of other equally fertile and equally well cultivated land, would necessarily reduce the rent and profit of those vineyards. The price of the wines being already the highest that could be got for the quantity commonly sent to market, it could not be raised higher without diminishing that quantity; and the quantity could not be diminished without still greater loss, because the lands could not be turned to any other equally valuable produce. The whole weight of the tax, therefore, would fall upon the rent and profit; properly upon the rent of the vineyard. When it has been proposed to lay any new tax upon sugar, our sugar planters have frequently complained that the whole weight of such taxes fell, not upon the consumer, but upon the producer; they never having been able to raise the price of their sugar after the tax, higher than it was before. The price had, it seems, before the tax been a monopoly price; and the argument adduced to shew that sugar was an improper subject of taxation, demonstrated, perhaps, that it was a proper one; the gains of monopolists, whenever they can be come at, being certainly of all subjects the most proper. But the ordinary price of barley has never been a monopoly price; and the rent and profit of barley land have never been above their natural proportion to those of other equally fertile and equally well cultivated land. The different taxes which have been imposed upon malt, beer, and ale, have never lowered the price of barley; have never reduced the rent and profit of barley land. The price of malt to the brewer has constantly risen in proportion to the taxes imposed upon it; and those taxes, together with the different duties upon beer and ale, have constantly either raised the price, or what comes to the same thing, reduced the quality of those commodities to the consumer. The final payment of those taxes has fallen constantly upon the consumer, and not upon the producer.

常和那些肥沃程度相近、开垦很好的土地几乎相等。如果少一些的话,部分大麦耕地就会很快转为其他用途;如果更多一些的话,那么更多的土地就会很快转而种植大麦。如果土地的任何特殊产品的通常价格被称为垄断价格的话,对其征收的税收必定减少种植这些产物土地地租和利润。那些珍贵的葡萄园的税收,葡萄酒的实际需求减少以至于其价格总是高出其他肥沃程度近似、开垦很好的土地的价格的自然比例,必将减少这些葡萄园的地租和利润。葡萄酒的价格已经达到一般被送往市场的数量而获得的最高价格,如果不减少数量,价格不会被提高;如果没有更大的损失,价格也不会被减少,因为土地不可能被转化成为同样价值的产品。因此,所有税收的负担将完全落在地租和利润上;或许落在葡萄园上。当被认为对糖征收了新的税收的时候,我们的种植者经常抱怨这些税收的整个负担不是落在消费者身上,而是落在生产者身上;他们绝不能在税后提高糖的价格使其比以前的价格还高。这个价格在税前似乎是一个垄断价格;这个讨论引出糖不是一个合适的课税对象这样的证明,或许正好证明它是合适的课税对象;垄断者的得利,无论什么时候他们可以获得的时候,肯定是所有课税对象中最合适的。但是大麦的普通价格不是垄断价格;种植大麦的土地的地租和利润从来没有超过与其肥沃程度近似、同样被很好地开垦的土地的自然比例。对麦芽、啤酒、淡色啤酒所征收的各种税从来没有降低大麦的价格;从来没有降低大麦种植土地的地租和利润。麦芽的价格对于酿酒者来说总是在不断地与加在其上的税成比例增加;那些税与课征在啤酒和淡色啤酒上的税收一起,不断增加价格,或者降低这种商品的质量。这些税的支付最终落在消费者身上,而不是生产者身上。

国民财富的性质与原理

<small>The only sufferers would be those who brew for private use</small>   The only people likely to suffer by the change of system here proposed, are those who brew for their own private use. But the exemption, which this superior rank of people at present enjoy, from very heavy taxes which are paid by the poor labourer and artificer, is surely most unjust and unequal, and ought to be taken away, even though this change was never to take place. It has probably been the interest of this superior order of people, however, which has hitherto prevented a change of system that could not well fail both to increase the revenue and to relieve the people.

<small>Tolls on goods carried from place to place affect prices unequally.</small>   Besides such duties as those of customs and excise above-mentioned, there are several others which affect the price of goods more unequally and more indirectly. Of this kind are the duties which in French are called péages, which in old Saxon times were called Duties of Passage, and which seem to have been originally established for the same purpose as our turnpike tolls, or the tolls upon our canals and navigable rivers, for the maintenance of the road or of the navigation. Those duties, when applied to such purposes, are most properly imposed according to the bulk or weight of the goods. As they were originally local and provincial duties, applicable to local and provincial purposes, the administration of them was in most cases entrusted to the particular town, parish, or lordship, in which they were levied; such communities being in some way or other supposed to be accountable for the application. The sovereign, who is altogether unaccountable, has in many countries assumed to himself the administration of those duties; and though he has in most cases enhanced very much the duty, he has in many entirely neglected the application. If the turnpike tolls of Great Britain should ever become one of the resources of government, we may learn, by the example of many other nations, what would probably be the consequence. Such tolls are no doubt finally paid by the consumer; but the consumer is not taxed in proportion to his expence when he pays, not according to the value, but according to the bulk or weight of what he consumes. When such duties are imposed, not according to the bulk or weight, but according to the supposed value of the goods, they become properly a sort of inland customs or excises, which obstruct very much the most important of all branches of commerce, the interior commerce of the country.

## 第五篇 第一项和第二项的附录

由于这里的制度变更而可能受到伤害的唯一的人们是那些为自己私人使用酿酒的人。但是当前上层阶级所享受的贫穷劳动者和手工业者支付的重税豁免肯定是不公平的,应该被废除,尽管这种变革不会发生。然而,正是上层阶级人们的利益在此阻止了制度的改变,这种改变很可能会增加收入和减轻人们的痛苦。

> 唯一的受害者就是为私人用而酿造的人

除上述这些关税以及货物税之外,还存在其他几种更不公平更间接影响货物价格的税种。其中在法国的关税称为通行税,在古老的撒克逊时代被称为通行税。最原始的目的似乎跟我们的收费公路,或者对我们的运河和行航道征收的通行税相同,都是为了维持道路和航行。当这种赋税应用于这个目的的时候,这些关税大部分都根据货物的重量或容积来合理地征收。当这些税还是地方税和各省的税收的时候,适用于地方和各省的目的,这些税的管理在大多数情况下委托给特殊的城镇、教区或贵族来征收;这些社团被认为以这种或那种方式来对它们的使用负责。君主是完全不负责任的,在许多国家他们自己掌握了这种赋税的管理权;尽管在很多情况下,大幅提高税收,但在很多情况下却完全忽略了执行。如果英国的公路通行税变成了政府的一种收入来源的话,我们通过很多国家的例子可以知道可能的结果是什么。这样的通行税毫无疑问最终还是由消费者来承担;但是消费者并不是在其支付的时候按照支出的比例来交税的,不是根据价值,而是根据他所消费的货物的容量或者重量。当这样的税收不是根据重量或容积而是根据货物的推定价值来征收的时候,他们变成了内陆关税或货物税的一种,这种赋税阻碍了商业的所有重要部门,以及异国的国内贸易。

> 商品从一个地方到另一个地方通行的税均等影响货物价格。

| 国民财富的性质与原理

Some countries levy transit duties on foreign goods.

In some small states duties similar to those passage duties are imposed upon goods carried across the territory, either by land or by water, from one foreign country to another. These are in some countries called transit-duties. Some of the little Italian states, which are situated upon the Po, and the rivers which run into it, derive some revenue from duties of this kind, which are paid altogether by foreigners, and which, perhaps, are the only duties that one state can impose upon the subjects of another, without obstructing in any respect the industry or commerce of its own. The most important transit-duty in the world is that levied by the king of Denmark upon all merchant ships which pass through the Sound.

Taxes on luxuries do not reach absentees, but the fact that they are paid voluntarily recommends them.

Such taxes upon luxuries as the greater part of the duties of customs and excise, though they all fall indifferently upon every different species of revenue, and are paid finally, or without any retribution, by whoever consumes the commodities upon which they are imposed, yet they do not always fall equally or proportionably upon the revenue of every individual. As every man's humour regulates the degree of his consumption, every man contributes rather according to his humour than in proportion to his revenue; the profuse contribute more, the parsimonious less, than their proper proportion. During the minority of a man of great fortune, he contributes commonly very little, by his consumption, towards the support of that state from whose protection he derives a great revenue. Those who live in another country contribute nothing, by their consumption, towards the support of the government of that country, in which is situated the source of their revenue. If in this latter country there should be no land-tax, nor any considerable duty upon the transference either of moveable or of immoveable property, as is the case in Ireland, such absentees may derive a great revenue from the protection of a government to the support of which they do not contribute a single shilling. This inequality is likely to be greatest in a country of which the government is in some respects subordinate and dependent upon that of some other. The people who possess the most extensive property in the dependent, will in this case generally chuse to live in the governing country. Ireland is precisely in this situation, and we cannot therefore wonder that the proposal of a tax upon absentees should be so very popular in that

## 第五篇　第一项和第二项的附录

在许多小国中的类似于这种通行税的税收课征在那些通过一国领土的商品上,它们或者通过陆运或者通过水运,从一个国家到另一个国家。在一些国家,这种赋税被称为过境税。位于波河及各支流沿岸的意大利的一些小国,从这种赋税中获得一些利润,完全由外国人来支付,可能也是一个国家对另一国居民征收的唯一的税,并且没有阻碍自己国家的工商业的任何方面。丹麦国王征收了世界上最重要的过境税,他对通过波罗的海峡的所有商船征税。

一些国家对外国商品征收过境税。

像大部分关税及国产税那样对奢侈品征收的税,尽管它们完全没有差别地落在每个不同的收入种类上,最终还是会或者没有任何报偿地被消费这些商品的消费者支付,然而它们不会总是等同地或成比例地落在每个人的收入上。因为每个人的性格调节着他的消费程度,每个人是根据他的性格而不是他的成比例于他的收入来纳税的;浪费者比他们的应有比例要多,节约者要比他们的应有比例要少。在一个拥有巨大财富的人幼年时期,他通过消费的贡献通常很小,他从国家获得的支持收入很大。生活在其他国家的人没有通过消费做出贡献,但那个国家的支持是他们收入的来源所在。如果在后一种国家中不存在土地税,也不存在相当的动产或不动产的转移税,例如在爱尔兰,这种赋税的缺乏可以使不动产业主得到政府的很大保护,而无须贡献一先令。在某些方面从属于或依靠另一国政府的国家,这种不平等很可能是最大的。就某些方面说是隶属于或依赖于他国政府的国家最大。在附庸国拥有广大土地财产的人,一般情况下都会选择居住在统治国。爱尔兰恰好处于这种情况,因此对不动产业主课税的提议在该国非常受欢迎也就无足为奇了。可能要确定何种

对奢侈品课税的影响不在人们自己愿意付的事,但是支付这一实使有价值。

— 1893 —

country. It might, perhaps, be a little difficult to ascertain either what sort, or what degree of absence would subject a man to be taxed as an absentee, or at what precise time the tax should either begin or end. If you except, however, this very peculiar situation, any inequality in the contribution of individuals, which can arise from such taxes, is much more than compensated by the very circumstance which occasions that inequality; the circumstance that every man's contribution is altogether voluntary; it being altogether in his power either to consume or not to consume the commodity taxed. Where such taxes, therefore, are properly assessed and upon proper commodities, they are paid with less grumbling than any other. When they are advanced by the merchant or manufacturer, the consumer, who finally pays them, soon comes to confound them with the price of the commodities, and almost forgets that he pays any tax.

They are also certain

Such taxes are or may be perfectly certain, or may be assessed so as to leave no doubt concerning either what ought to be paid, or when it ought to be paid; concerning either the quantity or the time of payment. Whatever uncertainty there may sometimes be, either in the duties of customs in Great Britain, or in other duties of the same kind in other countries, it cannot arise from the nature of those duties, but from the inaccurate or unskilful manner in which the law that imposes them is expressed.

and payable at convenient times,

Taxes upon luxuries generally are, and always may be, paid piecemeal, or in proportion as the contributors have occasion to purchase the goods upon which they are imposed. In the time and mode of payment they are, or may be, of all taxes the most convenient. Upon the whole, such taxes, therefore, are, perhaps, as agreeable to the three first of the four general maxims concerning taxation, as any other. They offend in every respect against the fourth.

but take much more from the people than they yield to the state, since

Such taxes, in proportion to what they bring into the public treasury of the state, always take out or keep out of the pockets of the people more than almost any other taxes. They seem to do this in all the four different ways in which it is possible to do it.

First, the levying of such taxes, even when imposed in the most judicious manner, requires a great number of customhouse and excise officers, whose salaries and perquisites are a real tax

第五篇　第一项和第二项的附录

不在或多大程度不在时,一个人才能作为不动产业主受到课税,或者应当在什么时候开始或终止,这是有些困难。然而,除了这种非常特殊的情况,个人贡献中的由于这种赋税的而产生的任何不平等,更多的由产生这种不平等的环境来补偿;这种环境中每个人的交税都是自愿的;他完全有权利自己决定消费或者不消费这种课税商品。因此,如果这种赋税是适合地评定,对适合的商品课征,他们的支付比其他任何商品税的支付产生的抱怨都要少。当它们被商人或制造者预付时,最终支付的消费者将它和商品的价格混同起来,几乎忘记了他所支付的税金。

这种赋税是完全确定的,或可以是完全确定的,或者可以这样来评估,使得关于应该付多少或者什么时候支付,或者关于支付的数量和时间不留下丝毫疑点。在英国的关税中或者在其他国家同样的关税中,有时候发生什么不确定,它也不可能来自这些税收的性质,而是来自使用法律表达的方式中的不精确和不熟练。这种赋税也是确定的

奢侈品税一般或者可能总是零碎的,或者像纳税者购买他们支付税收的商品一样成比例的支付。他们支付的时间和方式是或许可能是所有税收中最方便的。因此,整体而言,这种赋税可能同其他任何税收一样,是符合关于税收四种原则种前三种的。最后第四个原则在每一个方面他们都与其他的相违背。在方便的时候支付,

这种赋税按照他们所带给国家公共财政国库的比例,总是比几乎其他任何的税从人民口袋中取出的多,或使人民得不到的多。他们似乎以四种可能的方式来造成这种总结。但是从人民那里取得的比他们交给国家的还要多,因为

第一,这种赋税的征收,即使是以最明智的方法来征收,也需要大量的海关和收税人员,他们的工资和奖金是真正对人民征收

## 国民财富的性质与原理

(1) the salaries and perquisites of customs and excise officers take a large proportion of what is collected;

upon the people, which brings nothing into the treasury of the state. This expence, however, it must be acknowledged, is more moderate in Great Britain than in most other countries. In the year which ended on the fifth of July 1775, the gross produce of the different duties, under the management of the commissioners of excise in England, amounted to 5,507,308 $l.$ 18 $s.$ 8 $\frac{1}{4}$ $d.$ which was levied at an expence of little more than five and a half per cent. From this gross produce, however, there must be deducted what was paid away in bounties and drawbacks upon the exportation of exciseable goods, which will reduce the neat produce below five millions. The levying of the salt duty, an excise duty, but under a different management, is much more expensive. The neat revenue of the customs does not amount to two millions and a half, which is levied at an expence of more than ten per cent. in the salaries of officers, and other incidents. But the perquisites of customhouse officers are every where much greater than their salaries; at some ports more than double or triple those salaries. If the salaries of officers, and other incidents, therefore, amount to more than ten per cent. upon the neat revenue of the customs; the whole expence of levying that revenue may amount, in salaries and perquisites together, to more than twenty or thirty per cent. The officers of excise receive few or no perquisites: and the administration of that branch of the revenue being of more recent establishment, is in general less corrupted than that of the customs, into which length of time has introduced and authorised many abuses. By charging upon malt the whole revenue which is at present levied by the different duties upon malt and malt liquors, a saving, it is supposed, of more than fifty thousand pounds might be made in the annual expence of the excise. By confining the duties of customs to a few sorts of goods, and by levying those duties according to the excise laws, a much greater saving might probably be made in the annual expence of the customs.

  Secondly, such taxes necessarily occasion some obstruction or discouragement to certain branches of industry. As they always raise the price of the commodity taxed, they so far discourage its consumption, and consequently its production. If it is a commodity of home growth or manufacture, less labour comes to be employed in raising and producing it. If it is a foreign commodity of which the tax increases in this manner the price, the commodities of the same kind which are made at home may thereby, indeed, gain some advantage in the

## 第五篇 第一项和第二项的附录

的一种税,并且不会给国库带来任何收入。然而必须承认,这种费用在英国比在其他任何国家都要更轻微一些。1775 年 7 月 5 日为止的那个年度,在英国货物税委员会的管理之下各种税收的总收入累计达 5507308 镑 18 先令 $8\frac{1}{4}$ 便士,这是以 5.5% 的费用征收的。不过,这种总收入中必须扣除支付在进口货物税上的奖金和退税,这将使其纯收入缩减到 500 万镑以下。盐税也是一种货物税,它的征收处于不同的管理下,要大得多。关税的纯收入不到 250 万镑;征收人员的工资以及其他事件的开支超过了 10% 以上。但是海关工作人员的奖金要比他们的工资高得多,在有的海关口岸超出工资的两倍甚至三倍。因此,如果工作人员的工资和其他事件的开支达到了海关净收入的 10% 还要多,征收这种赋税的整个费用,连同工作人员的奖金和工资一起可能到达 20% 或 30%。货物税的征收人员没有获得或很少获得奖金:因为这个收入部门的管理机构建立的时间较近,总的来说没有像海关那样腐败。时间不长所以还没有引进和允许产生许多弊害。倘若现在对麦芽税和麦芽酒税课征的所有税收的全部收入,被认为可以节约货物税年收入 50000 镑以上。如果海关税仅限于对少数几种商品课征,并且根据货物税法律征收这些税,可能将会有更多的海关年支出节约。(1) 关税和货物税的征收人员的奖金和工资占了所收税的很大比例;

第二,这样的税收必定对某些产业部门造成某种阻碍或抑制。由于他们总是提高课税产品的价格,因此会抑制商品的消费,随之抑制它的生产。如果这种商品是国内生产或制造,在生产和制造中所雇用的劳动力就少一些。如果它是国外产品,这样税收会使其价格提高,同类的国内产品因此在国内市场获得一些

(2) particular branches of industry are discouraged; home market, and a greater quantity of domestic industry may thereby be turned toward preparing them. But though this rise of price in a foreign commodity may encourage domestic industry in one particular branch, it necessarily discourages that industry in almost every other. The dearer the Birmingham manufacturer buys his foreign wine, the cheaper he necessarily sells that part of his hardware with which, or, what comes to the same thing, with the price of which he buys it. That part of his hardware, therefore, becomes of less value to him, and he has less encouragement to work at it. The dearer the consumers in one country pay for the surplus produce of another, the cheaper they necessarily sell that part of their own surplus produce with which, or, what comes to the same thing, with the price of which they buy it. That part of their own surplus produce becomes of less value to them, and they have less encouragement to increase its quantity. All taxes upon consumable commodities, therefore, tend to reduce the quantity of productive labour below what it otherwise would be, either in preparing the commodities taxed, if they are home commodities; or in preparing those with which they are purchased, if they are foreign commodities. Such taxes too always alter, more or less, the natural direction of national industry, and turn it into a channel always different from, and generally less advantageous than that in which it would have run of its own accord.

(3) smuggling is encouraged; Thirdly, the hope of evading such taxes by smuggling gives frequent occasion to forfeitures and other penalties, which entirely ruin the smuggler; a person who, though no doubt highly blameable for violating the laws of his country, is frequently incapable of violating those of natural justice, and would have been, in every respect, an excellent citizen, had not the laws of his country made that a crime which nature never meant to be so. In those corrupted governments where there is at least a general suspicion of much unnecessary expence, and great misapplication of the public revenue, the laws which guard it are little respected. Not many people are scrupulous about smuggling, when, without perjury, they can find any easy and safe opportunity of doing so. To pretend to have any scruple about buying smuggled goods, though a manifest encouragement to the violation of the revenue laws, and to the perjury which almost always attends it, would in most countries be regarded as one of those pedantic pieces of

## 第五篇  第一项和第二项的附录

优势,更多数量的国内产业因此可能转向生产这些产品。但是尽管外国商品价格的提高可能鼓励国内产业的某个部门,它必定会抑制几乎所有其他的产业。伯明翰制造业者所买外国葡萄酒越贵,他为买此葡萄酒而卖去的一部分金属器具或者一部分金属器具的价格就必然越便宜。因此,他的金属器皿那部分对他而言价值减少,他为之工作受到的鼓舞也就越少。一个国家消费者为另一种剩余产品支付得越多,他们出售用来购买它们的自己那部分剩余产品也就越便宜。他们自己的那部分剩余产品对他而言价值减少,他们增加生产的鼓励也就减少了。因此,消费产品的所有税收容易将生产性劳动的数量减少到自然会有的水平以下,如果是本国产品,影响的是课税商品;如果是外国产品,影响的是那些他们购买的商品。这些税收总是会改变一个国家产业的自然方向,使之转向另一个方向,这个方向一般和自己会采取的方向不同,并且也不是很有利。（2）尤其是产业的部门受到抑制;

第三,通过走私逃避这些税收的希望,常常招致财产的没收和其他的惩罚,这些可以完全毁灭掉一个走私者。一个人尽管违反国家法律毫无疑问地应该受到严厉惩罚,但他却常常无法违反自然法则的公证,对于自然法则不认为是犯罪的行为如果他所属国家的法律也没有定为犯罪,那么他在每一个方面来说都还是好公民。在那些腐败的政府中,至少存在大量不必要开支、滥用公共收入的现象,用来保障国家收入的法律很少受到尊重。当无须伪证就能找到很容易、很安全的走私机会时,对走私有所顾忌的人就不会太多了。假装对购买走私物品心存顾忌(尽管购买走私物品会鼓励人们去侵犯财政法规,也会鼓励几乎总是与走私相伴儿生的伪证),在大多数国家都被认为是伪善的一种表现,不会给（3）走私受到鼓励;

— 1899 —

hypocrisy which, instead of gaining credit with any body, serve only to expose the person who affects to practise them, to the suspicion of being a greater knave than most of his neighbours. By this indulgence of the public, the smuggler is often encouraged to continue a trade which he is thus taught to consider as in some measure innocent; and when the severity of the revenue laws is ready to fall upon him, he is frequently disposed to defend with violence, what he has been accustomed to regard as his just property. From being at first, perhaps, rather imprudent than criminal, he at last too often becomes one of the hardiest and most determined violators of the laws of society. By the ruin of the smuggler, his capital, which had before been employed in maintaining productive labour, is absorbed either in the revenue of the state or in that of the revenue-officer, and is employed in maintaining unproductive, to the diminution of the general capital of the society, and of the useful industry which it might otherwise have maintained.

and (4) vexation equivalent to expense is caused by the taxgatherers' examinations and visits.

Fourthly, such taxes, by subjecting at least the dealers in the taxed commodities to the frequent visits and odious examination of the tax-gatherers, expose them sometimes, no doubt, to some degree of oppression, and always to much trouble and vexation; and though vexation, as has already been said, is not strictly speaking expence, it is certainly equivalent to the expence at which every man would be willing to redeem himself from it. The laws of excise, though more effectual for the purpose for which they were instituted, are, in this respect, more vexatious than those of the customs. When a merchant has imported goods subject to certain duties of customs, when he has paid those duties, and lodged the goods in his warehouse, he is not in most cases liable to any further trouble or vexation from the customhouse officer. It is otherwise with goods subject to duties of excise. The dealers have no respite from the continual visits and examination of the excise officers. The duties of excise are, upon this account, more unpopular than those of the customs; and so are the officers who levy them. Those officers, it is pretended, though in general, perhaps, they do their duty fully as well as those of the customs; yet, as that duty obliges them to be frequently very troublesome to some of their neighbours, commonly contract a certain hardness of character which the others frequently have not. This observation, however, may very probably be the mere suggestion of fraudulent dealers, whose smuggling is either prevented or detected by their diligence.

## 第五篇 第一项和第二项的附录

任何人赢得荣誉,反而会让喜欢这样做的人比他的大部分邻居更像个骗子。受到公众这样的纵容,走私者往往被鼓励继续从事这样的贸易,他也被教导走私在某种程度上就是个无辜的行业。当税收法的严厉惩罚将要落在他头上时,他经常采用武力去捍卫他习惯地看作是自己正当财产的东西。可能从最开始,与其说是犯罪者,也许不如说是个粗心的家伙,最后往往变成一个最坚硬、最坚决的违反社会法律者。走私者破产,他以前用于维持生产性劳动的资本,要么被一国的财政收入吸收,要么被收税者吸收,用于维持非生产性劳动,这样就减少了社会的总资本,使本来可以维持的有用行业减少。

第四,这种赋税至少使经营课税商品的商人经常受到收税者的访问和烦人的检查,毫无疑问,有时候使他们受到某种程度的压力,并且总是遭受到很多麻烦和烦恼;正如前面说过的,虽然烦恼严格说来并不是支出,但它肯定等同于每个人愿意用来使自己免于这些烦恼的支出。货物税尽管对于制定的目的更加有效,但在这一方面比这些关税更麻烦。当一个商人进口了被课征某种关税的商品,当他支付了这些关税,并且将货物堆放在自己的仓库中,在大多数情况下他都不可能再遭受到海关人员的打扰和烦恼。被课征货物税的商品却不是如此。商人无法暂缓稽征人员不断的检查与访问。出于这个原因,货物税比这些关税更不受到欢迎;征收这些税的官员也是如此。据说那些官员尽管一般或许像海关的工作人员那样充分尽到自己的职责;然而,因为那些职责迫使他们不断麻烦他们的邻居,他们通常养成了其他人所没有的冷酷性格。不过,这种说法很可能仅仅是舞弊商人的看法罢了,因为他们的走私货物被货物税官员的勤勉所阻止或发现。

(4)税收者的检查和访问引起与支出相等的烦恼。

| 国民财富的性质与原理

<small>Great Britain suffers less than other countries from these inconveniencies.</small>    The inconveniencies, however, which are, perhaps, in some degree inseparable from taxes upon consumable commodities, fall as light upon the people of Great Britain as upon those of any other country of which the government is nearly as expensive. Our state is not perfect, and might be mended; but it is as good or better than that of most of our neighbours.

<small>Duties on commodities are sometimes repeated on each sale, as by the Spanish Alcavala,</small>    In consequence of the notion that duties upon consumable goods were taxes upon the profits of merchants, those duties have, in some countries, been repeated upon every successive sale of the goods. If the profits of the merchant importer or merchant manufacturer were taxed, equality seemed to require that those of all the middle buyers, who intervened between either of them and the consumer, should likewise be taxed. The famous Alcavala of Spain seems to have been established upon this principle. It was at first a tax of ten per cent. , afterwards of fourteen per cent. , and is at present of only six per cent. upon the sale of every sort of property, whether moveable or immoveable; and it is repeated every time the property is sold. ① The levying of this tax requires a multitude of revenue-officers sufficient to guard the transportation of goods, not only from one province to another, but from one shop to another. It subjects, not only the dealers in some sorts of goods, but those in all sorts, every farmer, every manufacturer, every merchant and shop-keeper, to the continual visits and examination of the tax-gatherers. Through the greater part of a country in which a tax of this kind is established, nothing can be produced for distant sale. The produce of every part of the country must be proportioned to the consumption of the neighbourhood. It is to the Alcavala, accordingly, that Ustaritz imputes the ruin of the manufactures of Spain. ② He might have imputed to it likewise the declension of agriculture, it being imposed not only upon manufatcures, but upon the rude produce of the land.

---

① Memoires concernant les Droits, &c. tom. i. p. 455. Uztariz, *Theory and Practice of Commerce and Maritime Affairs*, trans. by John Kippax, 1751, chap. 96, *ad init.* , vol ii. , p. 236. ]

② [ See the preceding note. Uztariz' opinion is quoted by Lord Kames, *Sketches of the History of Man*, 1774, vol. i. , p. 516. ]

## 第五篇 第一项和第二项的附录

不过,对消费品的课税和与此某种程度上不可分割的不便,落在英国人身上的负担和落在政费同样浩大的国家的民众身上的负担一样轻。我们的国家不是完美的,还是有待改善;但是比起我们的邻居来说,可能一样好或许还要更好。

> 英国比其他国家受到的不便要少一些。

由于有这样的概念:课征在消费品上的关税是对商人利润的征税,在一些国家,这种赋税被重复地对每一个商品的每一次出售都征收①。如果进口商和制造商的利润被征税,公平的做法应该是要求所有的介于他们中之一和消费者之一的中间商人也应该被征税。西班牙著名的消费税似乎就是建立在这个原则之上。这种赋税对每种财产的出售征收赋税,无论是动产还是不动产,在每一次出售的时候都重复征收,开始征收10%,后来征收14%,目前仅占6%。这种赋税的征收不仅需要大量的征税人员充分地监视货物由一个省到另一个省,而且需要监视货物由一个店铺转移到其他店铺。它不仅仅使某种商品的商人,而且使所有商品的商人,每一个农场主、每一个制造业者、每一个商人和店主,都受到稽征人的不断访问和检查。建立这种赋税的国家的大部分地区,就无法生产出供远距离销售的产品。一个国家每个地区的生产必须与相邻地区的消费成比例。因此,乌兹塔里茨将西班牙制造业的毁灭归因于这种消费税②。他本来还可以将农业的衰落同样归因于它,因为它不仅是对制造业征收,而且还对土地天然

> 税候一卖被征正是商品有时在每次买卖都重复征收,如西班牙的消费税。

---

① 《关于欧洲法律及赋税的纪录》,第1卷,第445页。还可以参见乌兹塔里茨:《商业和海事的理论与实践》,约翰·基帕克斯译,1751年,第96章,第2卷第236页。

② 参见上注。乌兹塔里茨的意见,由卡姆斯勋爵在《人类历史纲要》,1774年,第1卷,第516页中援引。

— 1903 —

国民财富的性质与原理

<small>and the 3 per cent. tax at Naples.</small>   In the kingdom of Naples there is a similar tax of three per cent. upon the value of all contracts, and consequently upon that of all contracts of sale. It is both lighter than the Spanish tax, and the greater part of towns and parishes are allowed to pay a composition in lieu of it. They levy this composition in what manner they please, generally in a way that gives no interruption to the interior commerce of the place. The Neapolitan tax, therefore, is not near so ruinous as the Spanish one.

<small>Great advantage is obtained by the uniformity of taxation in Great Britain.</small>   The uniform system of taxation, which, with a few exceptions of no great consequence, takes place in all the different parts of the united kingdom of Great Britain, leaves the interior commerce of the country, the inland and coasting trade, almost entirely free. The inland trade is almost perfectly free, and the greater part of goods may be carried from one end of the kingdom to the other, without requiring any permit or let-pass, without being subject to question, visit, or examination from the revenue officers. There are a few exceptions, but they are such as can give no interruption to any important branch of the inland commerce of the country. Goods carried coastwise, indeed, require certificates or coast cockets. If you except coals, however, the rest are almost all duty-free. This freedom of interior commerce, the effect of the uniformity of the system of taxation, is perhaps one of the principal causes of the prosperity of Great Britain; every great country being necessarily the best and most extensive market for the greater part of the productions of its own industry. If the same freedom, in consequence of the same uniformity, could be extended to Ireland and the plantations, both the grandeur of the state and the prosperity of every part of the empire, would probably be still greater than at present.

In France, the different revenue laws which take place in the different provinces, require a multitude of revenue-officers to surround, not only the frontiers of the kingdom, but those of almost each particular province, in order either to prevent the importation of certain goods, or to subject it to the payment of certain duties, to the no small interruption of the interior commerce of the country. Some provinces are allowed to compound for the gabelle or salt-tax. Others are exempted from it altogether. Some provinces are exempted from the

## 第五篇 第一项和第二项的附录

产物征收赋税。

在那不勒斯王国中存在类似的对所有合同价值征收 3% 的税,并且也向所有合同销售的价值征税。他们都比西班牙的税要轻,大部分城镇和教区都允许支付一种赔偿金来替代这种赋税。他们以他们自己喜欢的方式来征收,一般的方式是不用打扰当地的内地贸易。因此,那不勒斯的税不像西班牙的税那样具有毁坏性。<sub>在那不勒斯征收 3% 的税。</sub>

大不列颠联合王国统一了所有区域的税收制度,只有少数无关紧要的例外,使得一国的内部商业、内陆和海岸的贸易几乎完全自由。内陆贸易几乎是完全自由的,大部分的商品可以从一国的一端运输到另一个国家,不要求有任何的许可证或通行证,也没有受到任何的询问以及稽征人员的访问和检查。尽管也存在一些例外,但并不打扰一国内陆贸易的任何重要部门。实际上,沿海岸运输的货物需要证明书或海关通行证。然而如果将煤炭排除在外,其余的几乎都是免税的。这种国内贸易的自由是税收制度统一的结果,很可能也是英国繁荣的主要原因之一;每一个大国必定是自己大部分产品的最大最广阔的市场。如果由于同样的税制统一产生的同样的自由可以被扩大到爱尔兰和各个殖民地,这个国家的伟大和这个王国每一个部分的繁荣可能比目前的程度还要更大。<sub>英国获得了统一税制的最大好处。</sub>

在法国,不同的省份实行不同的税法,需要有大量的税收征收人员。他们不仅要驻扎在一国的边境,甚至连各省的边境都要驻扎。目的是为了防止某些商品的进口,或者对进口征收一定的关税,这样就使国内商业受到了不少的干扰。有的省份被允许用赔偿金来代替盐税;有的省份则完全免缴盐税。有的省份免缴烟

— 1905 —

国民财富的性质与原理

In France the diversity of taxes in different provinces occasions many hindrances to internal trade,

exclusive sale of tobacco, which the farmers-general enjoy through the greater part of the kingdom. The aids, which correspond to the excise in England, are very different in different provinces. Some provinces are exempted from them, and pay a composition or equivalent. In those in which they take place and are in farm, there are many local duties which do not extend beyond a particular town or district. The Traites, which correspond to our customs, divide the kingdom into three great parts; first, the provinces subject to the tarif of 1664, which are called the provinces of the five great farms, and under which are comprehended Picardy, Normandy, and the greater part of the interior provinces of the kingdom; secondly, the provinces subject to the tarif of 1667, which are called the provinces reckoned foreign, and under which are comprehended the greater part of the frontier provinces; and, thirdly, those provinces which are said to be treated as foreign, or which, because they are allowed a free commerce with foreign countries, are in their commerce with the other provinces of France subjected to the same duties as other foreign countries. These are Alsace, the three bishopricks of Metz, Toul, and Verdun, and the three cities of Dunkirk, Bayonne, and Marseilles. Both in the provinces of the five great farms (called so on account of an ancient division of the duties of customs into five great branches, each of which was originally the subject of a particular farm, though they are now all united into one), and in those which are said to be reckoned foreign, there are many local duties which do not extend beyond a particular town or district. There are some such even in the provinces which are said to be treated as foreign, particularly in the city of Marseilles. It is unnecessary to observe how much, both the restraints upon the interior commerce of the country, and the number of the revenue officers must be multiplied, in order to guard the frontiers of those different provinces and districts, which are subject to such different systems of taxation.

and the commerce in wine is subject to particular restraints.

Over and above the general restraints arising from this complicated system of revenue laws, the commerce of wine, after corn perhaps the most important production of France, is in the greater part of the provinces subject to particular restraints, arising from the favour which has been shewn to the vineyards of particular provinces and districts, above those of others. The provinces most famous for their wines, it will be found, I believe, are those in which the trade in that article is subject to the fewest restraints of this kind. The extensive market which such provinces enjoy, encourages good management both in the cultivation of their vineyards, and in the subsequent preparation of their wines.

第五篇 第一项和第二项的附录

草专卖税,王国的绝大部分地区的总包税人享有这样的待遇。但有些省份虽免缴烟草专卖税,却要缴纳赔偿金或等价物。实行这种赋税和包税的地方,还可能存在很多特殊的税收,这些税收仅限于某个城镇或地区之内。关税(Traites)与我们关税相应的税,将王国分为三大部分:第一,征收1664年关税的省份,被称为五大包税区的省份,包括皮卡第、诺曼底以及王国内陆省份的绝大部分;第二,征收1667年关税的省份,被称为外疆的各省,包括各省边境的大部分;第三,那些省份据说被当作外国的来对待,或者说因为允许与外国自由通商,他们和法国其他省份进行贸易时,被课征如同外国一样的关税。这些省份是阿尔萨斯、麦茨·图尔和凡尔登三个主教管区,以及敦刻尔克、贝允和马赛三个城市。在五大包税区各省(之所以被这样称呼,是因为古时关税区分为五大部门,其中的每一个部门都原本是特定的包税对象,尽管现在已经联合起来了)和被称为是外疆的各省,都存在许多地方税收,并且仅限于某个特定的城镇或地区。据说在被当作外国对待的各省也有一些这样的税收,尤其是在马赛市。没有必要评论对一国内部商业的限制有多大,以及需要多少税收征稽人员来保卫各省各地区的不同边境,他们实行不同关税制度。

<small>法国税收的多样性在不同的省份可能阻碍国内贸易。</small>

　　除了来自这种综合税收制度的一般约束之外,葡萄酒的贸易,是除了谷物之外法国最重要的产品,在各省的大部分地区都受到特别的限制,它产生于对特定省份和地区葡萄园的优惠政策。我相信将会发现,以葡萄酒最为出名的这些省份,在葡萄酒这种商品的贸易中受到的这种约束最小。这些省份占有的广泛的市场,既鼓励对葡萄园开垦的良好管理,也鼓励葡萄酒酿制上的良好管理。

<small>葡萄酒的贸易也受到特别的限制。</small>

国民财富的性质与原理

Milan and Parma are still more absurdly managed.
　　Such various and complicated revenue laws are not peculiar to France. The little dutchy of Milan is divided into six provinces, in each of which there is a different system of taxation with regard to several different sorts of consumable goods. The still smaller territories of the duke of Parma are divided into three or four, each of which has, in the same manner, a system of its own. Under such absurd management, nothing, but the great fertility of the soil and happiness of the climate, could preserve such countries from soon relapsing into the lowest state of poverty and barbarism.

The collection of taxes by government officers is much superior to letting the taxes to farm.
　　Taxes upon consumable commodities may either be levied by an administration of which the officers are appointed by government and are immediately accountable to government, of which the revenue must in this case vary from year to year, according to the occasional variations in the produce of the tax; or they may be let in farm for a rent certain, the farmer being allowed to appoint his own officers, who, though obliged to levy the tax in the manner directed by the law, are under his immediate inspection, and are immediately accountable to him. The best and most frugal way of levying a tax can never be by farm. Over and above what is necessary for paying the stipulated rent, the salaries of the officers, and the whole expence of administration, the farmer must always draw from the produce of the tax a a certain profit proportioned at least to the advance which he makes, to the risk which he runs, to the trouble which he is at, and to the knowledge and skill which it requires to manage so very complicated a concern. Government, by establishing an administration under their own immediate inspection, of the same kind with that which the farmer establishes, might at least save this profit, which is almost always exorbitant. To farm any considerable branch of the public revenue, requires either a great capital or a great credit; circumstances which would alone restrain the competition for such an undertaking to a very small number of people. Of the few who have this capital or credit, a still smaller number have the necessary knowledge or experience; another circumstance which restrains the competition still further. The very few, who are in condition to become competitors, find it more for their interest to combine together; to become copartners instead of competitors, and when the farm is set up to auction, to offer no rent, but what is much below the real value. In countries where the public revenues are in farm, the farmers are generally the most opulent people. Their wealth would alone excite the public indignation, and the vanity which almost always accompanies such upstart

## 第五篇 第一项和第二项的附录

这些不同的复杂的税法并非法国所特有。米兰这个小公国被划分为六个省份,对于不同的消费品,其中每个省份都有不同的税收体制。更小的帕马公国的领土被分为三个或四个省份,同样的,其中的每个省份都有自己的税收体制。在这种荒谬的管理之下,除了土壤十分肥沃,气候非常适宜,没有什么能够阻止这些国家沦入最贫穷、最野蛮的状态。

葡萄酒的贸易也受到特别的限制。

对消费品所课征的税收,一种是要么可能由行政机构来征收,其中的官员由政府任命或是直接对政府负责,每年的税收根据税收产品的变化也必定不同;另一种是他们可能被承包,承包者可以自行任命自己的官员,尽管他们的征税行为受到法律的约束,但却总是处于承包者的直接监督之下,并且直接对其负责。最好最经济的征税方法可能不是包税制度。除了必须支付规定的税收、官员的工资以及整个行政机构的开支之外,承包者必然总是要从税收中获取一定的利润,这部分利润跟他做的预付、承担的风险、他所遭遇的麻烦以及管理如此复杂的事情所需的知识和技能成比例。政府在自己的直接监督之下建立设有包税者的同样类型的行政机构,至少可以节省这部分超额利润。包收公共税收的任何巨大部门,既需要巨大资本,也需要巨大的信贷;单是这种情况就会将这种事业的竞争限制在少数人中。拥有这种资本和信贷的少数人中,具有必要知识或经验的人就为数更少了。另外一种情况进一步限制了竞争,有条件成为竞争者的少数人觉得为了他们共同的利益应该联合起来,成为合作者而不是竞争对手。当包税投标的时候,他们所出的标价远远低于真实价值。在公共税收承包的国家中,承包者们一般是最富有的人。仅仅他们的富裕就会激起公众的愤怒,而虚荣心又往往与这些暴发户紧紧

政府官员收税优于承包者包收税收。

fortunes, the foolish ostentation with which they commonly display that wealth, excites that indignation still more.

<sub>Farmers of taxes require sanguinary revenue laws.</sub>   The farmers of the public revenue never find the laws too severe, which punish any attempt to evade the payment of a tax. They have no bowels for the contributors, who are not their subjects, and whose universal bankruptcy, if it should happen the day after their farm is expired, would not much affect their interest. In the greatest exigencies of the state, when the anxiety of the sovereign for the exact payment of his revenue is necessarily the greatest, they seldom fail to complain that without laws more rigorous than those which actually take place, it will be impossible for them to pay even the usual rent. In those moments of public distress their demands cannot be disputed. The revenue laws, therefore, become gradually more and more severe. The most sanguinary are always to be found in countries where the greater part of the public revenue is in farm. The mildest, in countries where it is levied under the immediate inspection of the sovereign. Even a bad sovereign feels more compassion for his people than can ever be expected from the farmers of his revenue. He knows that the permanent grandeur of his family depends upon the prosperity of his people, and he will never knowingly ruin that prosperity for the sake of any momentary interest of his own. It is otherwise with the farmers of his revenue, whose grandeur may frequently be the effect of the ruin, and not of the prosperity of his people.

<sub>Taxation by monopolies let to farm is even worse.</sub>   A tax is sometimes, not only farmed for a certain rent, but the farmer has, besides, the monopoly of the commodity taxed. In France, the duties upon tobacco and salt are levied in this manner. In such cases the farmer, instead of one, levies two exorbitant profits upon the people; the profit of the farmer, and the still more exorbitant one of the monopolist. Tobacco being a luxury, every man is allowed to buy or not to buy as he chuses. But salt being a necessary, every man is obliged to buy of the farmer a certain quantity of it; because, if he did not buy this quantity of the farmer, he would, it is presumed, buy it of some smuggler. The taxes upon both commodities are exorbitant. The temptation to smuggle consequently is to many

第五篇　第一项和第二项的附录

相随,他们经常用一种愚昧的摆阔的形式来炫耀他们的财富,从而会更进一步激起公众的愤怒。

公共税收的承包者从来不会觉得惩罚企图逃税的法律太严厉。他们对于纳税人没有同情心,这些人不是他们的人民,并且如果纳税者在包收到期之后普遍出现破产的话,也不会影响到他们的利益。在一个国家处于紧要关头之时,君主最挂记的一定是自己税收的确切支付,此时这些包税者总是要抱怨,如果不采取目前执行的更严厉的法律,对他们来说甚至连正常的税收额他们都支付不起。在这种国家困难的紧要关头,他们的要求是不可能遭到反驳的。因此,税收法律逐渐变得越来越严厉。最残暴的税收总是出现于公共税收被承包的国家。最温和的税收总是出现在君主直接监督之下的税收国家。即使一个很坏的君主,比起税收承包者来说,对于子民都要更富同情心。他知道他的家族的永久辉煌依靠于他民众的繁荣,并且他绝不会为了自己眼前的利益而去毁坏其民众的繁荣。但是对承包者而言却相反,他们的辉煌经常来自于毁坏民众的繁荣,而不是来自于民众的繁荣。

<small>承包者的税收要求出台残暴的税收法律。</small>

税收有时候不仅以一定的税额包出,除此之外还会给予承包者对课税商品的垄断权。在法国,对烟草和盐征税就是按照这种方式来征收的。在这种情况下,承包者对人们索取的是两种而不是一种高额的利润:承包者的利润和垄断者的更加过度的利润。烟草是一种奢侈品,每个人都有权利来决定买与不买。但是盐是生活的必需品,每个人都必须从承包者那里购买一定数量的盐。因为,如果他不购买这一定数量的盐,一般来说就会认为他可能是从走私者那里购买这部分盐。在这两种商品上课征的税收都是高额的。因此很多人都抵挡不住走私的诱惑,然而在当时,法

<small>由承包者来征收的税收更加严厉。</small>

— 1911 —

国民财富的性质与原理

people irresistible, while at the same time the rigour of the law, and the vigilance of the farmer's officers, render the yielding to that temptation almost certainly ruinous. The smuggling of salt and tobacco sends every year several hundred people to the gallies, besides a very considerable number whom it sends to the gibbet. Those taxes levied in this manner yield a very considerable revenue to government. In 1767, the farm of tobacco was let for twenty-two millions five hundred and forty-one thousand two hundred and seventyeight livres a year. That of salt, for thirty-six millions four hundred and ninety-two thousand four hundred and four livres. The farm in both cases was to commence in 1768, and to last for six years. Those who consider the blood of the people as nothing in comparison with the revenue of the prince, may perhaps approve of this method of levying taxes. Similar taxes and monopolies of salt and tobacco have been established in many other countries; particularly in the Austrian and Prussian dominions, and in the greater part of the states of Italy.

In France the three branches of revenue which are levied by government officers are much more economical.

In France, the greater part of the actual revenue of the crown is derived from eight different sources; the taille, the capitation, the two vingtiemes, the gabelles, the aides, the traites, the domaine, and the farm of tobacco. The five last are, in the greater part of the provinces, under farm. The three first are every where levied by an administration under the immediate inspection and direction of government, and it is universally acknowledged that, in proportion to what they take out of the pockets of the people, they bring more into the treasury of the prince than the other five, of which the administration is much more wasteful and expensive.

The taille and capitations should be abolished, the vingtièmes increased, the taxes on commodities made uniform, and farming abolished.

The finances of France seem, in their present state, to admit of three very obvious reformations. First, by abolishing the taille and the capitation, and by encreasing the number of vingtiemes, so as to produce an additional revenue equal to the amount of those other taxes, the revenue of the crown might be preserved; the expence of collection might be much diminished; the vexation of the inferior ranks of people, which the taille and capitation occasion, might be entirely prevented; and the superior ranks might not be more burdened than the greater part of them are at present. The vingtieme, I have already observed, is a tax very nearly of the same kind with what is called the land-tax of England. The burden of the taille, it is acknowledged, falls finally upon the proprietors of land; and as the greater part of the capitation is assessed upon those who are subject to the taille at so much a pound of that other tax, the final payment of the greater part of it must likewise fall upon the same order of people. Though the number of the vingtiemes, therefore, was increased so as to produce an additional revenue equal to the amount of both those

— 1912 —

## 第五篇　第一项和第二项的附录

律的严厉以及承包者的警惕,使屈服于这种诱惑的人无疑会倾家荡产。盐和烟草的走私每年都使数百人坐牢,还有相当数量的人被送上绞刑台。以这种方式征收的税收,为政府提供了很大的收入。1767 年,烟草的包额为 22541278 里弗,盐的包额为 32492404 里弗。1768 年开始的这两种物品的包税,持续了 6 年。有些人认为,和君主的税收相比,人们的血汗根本不算什么,他们很可能都赞同这种收税的方法。很多国家都建立了类似的税收和对盐以及烟草的垄断。尤其是在奥地利和普鲁士领土内,以及在意大利很多城邦。

在法国,国王实际收入的大部分有八个不同的来源:贡税、人头税、二十取一的税、盐税、货物税、关税、官有财产及烟草包税。最后五项在很多省份都采用包征制。前面三项赋税,都是在政府的直接监督和控制之下由行政机构来征收的,普遍认为这三项是按照与从人们口袋中掏出来的钱成比例上缴国库的,他们上缴国库的数额要高于其他五种,而其他五种的管理更是浪费和奢靡。

<sub>法国政府的三个部门更加经济</sub>

现在法国的财政状态似乎可以进行三项非常明显的改革。首先,废除贡税和人头税,增加二十取一税,以便产生等同于其他税收数量的一个附加的税收,国王的税收就能得以保存;征税的开支应该大幅减少;贡税和人头税造成的下层人们的苦难可以完全废除;大部分上层人们的负担也不至于比现在更重。我在前面提及过的二十取一的税,与英格兰的所谓地租税非常相似。一般都认为贡税的负担最终落到土地所有者身上,并且人头税的大部分,仍按应纳贡税每镑若干的比率估征,它的大部分的最终支付必定还是落到同阶级人们的身上。因此,二十份取一的税的数量被增加,以便产生等同于这些税收的额外税收,但是上层阶

<sub>贡税和人头税应该被废除,二十取一税增加,对商品课征的税一来,包税被废除。</sub>

taxes, the superior ranks of people might not be more burdened than they are at present. Many individuals no doubt would, on account of the great inequalities with which the taille is commonly assessed upon the estates and tenants of different individuals. The interest and opposition of such favoured subjects are the obstacles most likely to prevent this or any other reformation of the same kind. Secondly, by rendering the gabelle, the aides, the traites, the taxes upon tobacco, all the different customs and excises, uniform in all the different parts of the kingdom, those taxes might be levied at much less expence, and the interior commerce of the kingdom might be rendered as free as that of England. Thirdly, and lastly, by subjecting all those taxes to an administration under the immediate inspection and direction of government, the exorbitant profits of the farmers general might be added to the revenue of the state. The opposition arising from the private interest of individuals, is likely to be as effectual for preventing the two last as the first mentioned scheme of reformation.

The French system is in every respect inferior to the British.

The French system of taxation seems, in every respect, inferior to the British. In Great Britain ten millions sterling are annually levied upon less than eight millions of people, without its being possible to say that any particular order is oppressed. From the collections of the Abb Expilly, [①] and the observations of the author of the Essay upon the legislation and commerce of corn, it appears probable, that France, including the provinces of Lorraine and Bar, contains about twentythree or twenty-four millions of people; three times the number perhaps contained in Great Britain. The soil and climate of France are better than those of Great Britain. The country has been much longer in a state of improvement and cultivation, and is, upon that account, better stocked with all those things which it requires a long time to raise up and accumulate, such as great towns, and convenient and well-built houses, both in town and country. With these advantages,

---

[①] [These estimates seem to have been quoted in England at the time, since the Continuation of Anderson's *Commerce*, under the year 1773, mentions 'the calculations of the Abbé D' Expilly published about this time in Paris.' which gave 8,661,381 births and 6,664,161 deaths as the number taking place in the nine years, 1754 to 1763, in France, inclusive of Lorraine and Bar. In his *Dictionnaire géographique, historique et politique des Gaulés et de la France*, tom. v. (1768), s. v. Population, Expilly estimated the population at 22,014,357. See Levasseur, *La Population francaise*, tom. i., 1889, pp. 215 and 216 note.
]

第五篇 第一项和第二项的附录

级的负担仍不至于加重。因为通常贡税对个人的地产和租户征税时会产生不平等,改革之后许多个人的负担肯定会增加。这些现在享有特惠权的利益者们,是最有可能阻止这种或其他同类改革的。其次,盐税、货物税、关税、烟草税,这些所有不同的税种在王国中被统一起来,征收这些税收的费用大大节省,王国内的贸易可能变得跟英格兰一样自由。再次,也是最后一点,在政府的直接监督和指挥之下把所有的这些税收交给一个行政机构去征收,包收的这部分高额利润可能被加入到国家利润中。来自私人利益的反对意见,也会阻止后两种改革计划的实现,就像阻止第一种改革计划的实现一样。

　　法国的课税制度在每一方面似乎都不如英国。在大不列颠对不到 800 万人每年征税 1000 万镑,不可能说有任何一个阶级受到压迫。据埃克斯皮利神父搜集的材料①和《谷物法与谷物贸易论》作者的观察,可能是这样的:法国包括洛林及巴尔在内,人口共约 2300 万乃至 2400 万,这可能是英国人口的三倍。法国的土壤及气候比英国的要好,这个国家的土地改良和开垦比较悠久。这样看来,凡是需要长时间来建造和积累的事物,法国都要比英国多,例如大都市以及城市和乡村的便利设施和建造良好的房屋。有了这些优势,在法国可以期望征收到 3000 万英镑的税

<sub>法国的制度在每个方面都不如英国。</sub>

---

① 这些估计是当时在英格兰所援引的,因为安德森的《商业》续编在 1773 年提到"大约在这个时候在巴黎刊行的埃克斯皮利神父的估计",在 1754~1763 年的九年中,法国(包括洛林和巴尔)出生人数为 8661381,死亡人数为 6664161。在他的《商卢鹤法国地利、历史和政治词典》,第 5 卷(1768 年)"人口"条目中,埃克斯皮利估计人口为 22014357。参见勒瓦瑟:《法国人口》,第 1 卷,1889 年,第 215 页和第 216 页注。

it might be expected that in France a revenue of thirty millions might be levied for the support of the state, with as little inconveniency as a revenue of ten millions is in Great Britain. In 1765 and 1766, the whole revenue paid into the treasury of France, according to the best, though, I acknowledge, very imperfect, accounts which I could get of it, usually run between 308 and 325 millions of livres; that is, it did not amount to fifteen millions sterling; not the half of what might have been expected, had the people contributed in the same proportion to their numbers as the people of Great Britain. The people of France, however, it is generally acknowledged, are much more oppressed by taxes than the people of Great Britain. France, however, is certainly the great empire in Europe which, after that of Great Britain, enjoys the mildest and most indulgent government.

<small>In Holland heavy taxes on necessaries have ruined manufactures.</small>  In Holland the heavy taxes upon the necessaries of life have ruined, it is said, their principal manufactures, and are likely to discourage gradually even their fisheries and their trade in ship-building. The taxes upon the necessaries of life are inconsiderable in Great Britain, and no manufacture has hitherto been ruined by them. The British taxes which bear hardest on manufactures are some duties upon the importation of raw materials, particularly upon that of raw silk. The revenue of the states general and of the different cities, however, is said to amount to more than five millions two hundred and fifty thousand pounds sterling; and as the inhabitants of the United Provinces cannot well be supposed to amount to more than a third part of those of Great Britain, they must, in proportion to their number, be much more heavily taxed.

<small>But perhaps Holland has done the best possible.</small>  After all the proper subjects of taxation have been exhausted, if the exigencies of the state still continue to require new taxes, they must be imposed upon improper ones. The taxes upon the necessaries of life, therefore, may be no impeachment of the wisdom of that republic, which, in order to acquire and to maintain its independency, has, in spite of its great frugality, been involved in such expensive wars as have obliged it to contract great debts. The singular countries of Holland and Zealand, besides, require a considerable expence even to preserve their existence, or to prevent their being swallowed up by the sea, which must have contributed to increase considerably the load of taxes in those two provinces. The republican form of government seems to be the principal support of the present grandeur of Holland. The owners of great capitals, the great mercantile families, have generally either some direct share, or some indirect influence, in the administration of that government. For the sake of the respect and authority which they derive from this situation, they are willing to live in a country where their capital, if they employ it themselves, will bring them less profit, and if they lend it to another, less inter-

收来支持国家,这跟在英国征收1000万英镑一样容易。根据我所能得到的最好但不完全的估计,法国的整个国家税收在1765年和1766年一般在3.08亿里弗到3.25亿里弗,不到1500万英镑,还不到期望值的一半,如果法国人民跟英国人民以同样比例纳税的话。然而一般认为,法国人民比英国人民所负担的税收要更多一些。因此法国肯定是欧洲的大国,除了英国,享受着最温和、最宽容的政府管理。

据说在荷兰课征在生活必需品上的重税已经毁坏了他们主要的制造业,甚至很可能正在逐渐阻碍他们的渔业和造船业贸易。课征在生活必需品上的税收在英国是微不足道的,因此也没有制造业被其损坏。英国制造业负担最重的税课征于原材料的进口,尤其是生丝进口税。荷兰中央政府和各城市的收入据说每年达525万镑以上,荷兰人口不超过英国居民的1/3,因此按人口比例交税,他们缴纳的赋税一定是重了。

荷兰对生活必需品的征税毁坏了他们的制造业。

在所有适合征税的课征对象都已经被征税之后,如果国家遇到紧急状态仍然需要新的税收,他们就必须对不适合征税的对象也课征税收。因此,对生活必需品征税,可能并不是因为荷兰政府的愚蠢无知,而是为了获得并保持独立。他们尽管已经非常节约,但还是卷入了昂贵的战争,不得不大举借债。荷兰和新西兰这些特殊的国家需要大量的开支,来维持自身的生存,或是防止他们被大海吞噬,这样肯定会大幅增加这两个地区的赋税。共和的政体似乎是荷兰现在辉煌伟大的主要支柱。大资本家、大商家,一般要么直接参加政府的行政管理,要么间接地影响政府的行政管理。他们为了从这种地位中得到的尊敬和权威,愿意居住在这样的国家:他们如果自己运用资本,会带来较少的利润;如果

但是荷兰或许已经做了可能最好的事情。

est; and where the very moderate revenue which they can draw from it will purchase less of the necessaries and conveniences of life than in any other part of Europe. The residence of such wealthy people necessarily keeps alive, in spite of all disadvantages, a certain degree of industry in the country. Any public calamity which should destroy the republican form of government, which should throw the whole administration into the hands of nobles and of soldiers, which should annihilate altogether the importance of those wealthy merchants, would soon render it disagreeable to them to live in a country where they were no longer likely to be much respected. They would remove both their residence and their capital to some other country, and the industry and commerce of Holland would soon follow the capitals which supported them.

把钱借给别人,利息会较低;他们从这个国家获得不多的收入进而也购买比欧洲其他国家要少的生活必需品和便利品。这些富裕阶层于此,必然会有种种不便,但必然会使国家的产业在某种程度上活跃起来。一旦有任何毁掉政府共和体制的国家灾难,摧毁了国家的共和制度,而将整个行政权力交到贵族和军人手中,这就会使得那些富商们的重要性完全消失,他们就不会再乐意继续在这个自己不为人所尊敬的国家居住下去了。他们会带着资本迁往其他国家,荷兰的工商业也将很快随着这些支持他们发展的资本迁移出去了。

# CHAPTER III
# Of Public Debts

When expensive luxuries are unknown, persons with large revenue are likely to hoard savings.

In that rude state of society which precedes the extension of commerce and the improvement of manufactures, when those expensive luxuries which commerce and manufactures can alone introduce, are altogether unknown, the person who possesses a large revenue, I have endeavoured to show in the third book of this Inquiry, can spend or enjoy that revenue in no other way than by maintaining nearly as many people as it can maintain. A large revenue may at all times be said to consist in the command of a large quantity of the necessaries of life. In that rude state of things it is commonly paid in a large quantity of those necessaries, in the materials of plain food and coarse clothing, in corn and cattle, in wool and raw hides. When neither commerce nor manufactures furnish any thing for which the owner can exchange the greater part of those materials which are over and above his own consumption, he can do nothing with the surplus but feed and clothe nearly as many people as it will feed and clothe. A hospitality in which there is no luxury, and a liberality in which there is no ostentation, occasion, in this situation of things, the principal expences of the rich and the great. But these, I have likewise endeavoured to show in the same book, are expences by which people are not very apt to ruin themselves. There is not, perhaps, any selfish pleasure so frivolous, of which the pursuit has not sometimes ruined even sensible men. A passion for cock-fighting has ruined many. But the instances, I believe, are not very numerous of people who have been ruined by a hospitality or liberality of this kind; though the hospitality of luxury and the liberality of ostentation have ruined many. Among our feudal ancestors, the long time during which estates used to continue in the same family, sufficiently demonstrates the general disposition of people to live within their income. Though the rustic hospitality, constantly exercised by the great land-holders, may not, to us in the

# 第三章 论公债

在商业扩张、制造业改良之前,社会处于原始状态,那时只有商业和制造业才可以产生昂贵的奢侈品这点还不为人所知,就像我在此书的第三篇中竭力阐述的,拥有大量财富的人除了维持他所能维持的人数之外,就别无他法来花费或享用这些财富了。在任何时候,一大笔收入可以说是由对大量生活必需品的支配权组成。在尚未开化的状态下,这种收入是用大量的生活必需品来支付的,例如平淡食物和粗糙衣服的原料、谷物和牲畜、羊毛和生皮。如果商业和制造业都不能为主人提供用来交换超过其消费的大部分剩余原料的物品时,他除了给尽可能多的人提供衣食之外,没有其他的方法处理这些剩余部分。富人和大人物的主要支出,也就是不奢侈的款待、不炫耀的慷慨。这些支出不易使人们毁灭,这些我在本书第三篇也尽力阐述过。但自私的享乐就不同了,这种追求即便微不足道,也可能会毁掉一个明智的人。例如斗鸡的狂热就毁灭过很多人。但是我相信,实际上被这样奢侈的款待和炫耀的慷慨所毁坏的实例并不是很多,尽管这样奢侈的款待和炫耀的慷慨曾经毁掉过许多人。在我们的封建祖先中,土地长期由同一个家庭所占有,这足以表明他们在生活上量入为出的一般特性。尽管大地主不断地提供乡村款待,对于当今的我们而

present times, seem consistent with that order, which we are apt to consider as inseparably connected with good economy, yet we must certainly allow them to have been at least so far frugal as not commonly to have spent their whole income. A part of their wool and raw hides they had generally an opportunity of selling for money. Some part of this money, perhaps, they spent in purchasing the few objects of vanity and luxury, with which the circumstances of the times could furnish them; but some part of it they seem commonly to have hoarded. They could not well indeed do any thing else but hoard whatever money they saved. To trade was disgraceful to a gentleman, and to lend money at interest, which at that time was considered as usury and prohibited by law, would have been still more so. In those times of violence and disorder, besides, it was convenient to have a hoard of money at hand, that in case they should be driven from their own home, they might have something of known value to carry with them to some place of safety. The same violence, which made it convenient to hoard, made it equally convenient to conceal the hoard. The frequency of treasuretrove, or of treasure found of which no owner was known, sufficiently demonstrates the frequency in those times both of hoarding and of concealing the hoard. Treasure-trove was then considered as an important branch of the revenue of the sovereign. All the treasure-trove of the kingdom would scarce perhaps in the present times make an important branch of the revenue of a private gentleman of a good estate.

So the ancient sovereigns of Europe amassed treasures.

The same disposition to save and to hoard prevailed in the sovereign, as well as in the subjects. Among nations to whom commerce and manufactures are little known, the sovereign, it has already been observed in the fourth book, is in a situation which naturally disposes him to the parsimony requisite for accumulation. In that situation the expence even of a sovereign cannot be directed by that vanity which delights in the gaudy finery of a court. The ignorance of the times affords but few of the trinkets in which that finery consists. Standing armies are not then necessary, so that the expence even of a sovereign, like that of any other great lord, can be employed in scarce any thing but bounty to his tenants, and hospitality to his retainers. But bounty and hospitality very seldom lead to extravagance; though vanity almost always does. All the ancient sovereigns of Europe accordingly, it has

言,这可能与我们认为的与良好节约不可分离的生活秩序不相符合,但我们必须承认,他们还是非常节省的,没有花完他们所有的收入。他们一般都有机会卖掉一部分羊毛和生皮来换回货币。他们可能用这部分货币来购买满足虚荣心的和奢侈的物品,当时的环境还是能够满足他们这种愿望的,但是他们更多的是把另一部分储存起来。实际上,很可能他们除了将所节省的钱存储起来之外,他们也不能用来作别的什么了。经商对于一个绅士来说是有失体面的,贷出去以获得利息在那时被认为是放高利贷,这是法律明文禁止的,因而这就更不体面了。而且,在那种暴力和混乱时代,把钱存在手边是一件很方便的事情。万一他们被逐出自己的居所,他们还能携带具有公认价值的东西逃往安全地带。暴乱同样地也使得存钱比较便利,使得隐藏这种匿藏物比较便利。地下宝藏的频繁发现或者发现的财富不知道主人是谁,充分表明了在那个年代存储和藏匿存储是常有的事情。地下宝藏在当时被认为是君主收入的一个重要部分。在今天,王国所有的地下宝藏恐怕也难以构成一个拥有巨大财富的绅士的主要收入部分。

　　就像民间流行的一样,节约与储藏的倾向也同样流行于君主之间。我在本书第四篇说过,在没有什么商业和制造业的国家,君主的处境也自然会使他为了积累而节约。在这种情况下,即使是君主也不能受虚荣心的控制,去喜欢一种华而不实的宫廷装饰。那个无知的时代,只能为这些华而不实的提供些装饰的小玩意儿。那时常备军是没有必要的,因此即使是君主的开支,也跟大地主一样,除了用于施舍给佃农和给予奴仆的款待之外,很少用作别用了。但是施舍和款待很少导致铺张浪费,而虚荣心却往往会导致铺张浪费。已经说过,因此,所有欧洲的古代君主都有

因此古代欧洲的君主积聚财物。

already been observed, had treasures. Every Tartar chief in the present times is said to have one.

<small>When luxuries are introduced, the sovereign's expenditure equals his revenue in time of peace,</small>  In a commercial country abounding with every sort of expensive luxury, the sovereign, in the same manner as almost all the great proprietors in his dominions, naturally spends a great part of his revenue in purchasing those luxuries. His own and the neighbouring countries supply him abundantly with all the costly trinkets which compose the splendid, but insignificant pageantry of a court. For the sake of an inferior pageantry of the same kind, his nobles dismiss their retainers, make their tenants independent, and become gradually themselves as insignificant as the greater part of the wealthy burghers in his dominions. The same frivolous passions, which influence their conduct, influence his. How can it be supposed that he should be the only rich man in his dominions who is insensible to pleasures of this kind? If he does not, what he is very likely to do, spend upon those pleasures so great a part of his revenue as to debilitate very much the defensive power of the state, it cannot well be expected that he should not spend upon them all that part of it which is over and above what is necessary for supporting that defensive power. His ordinary expence becomes equal to his ordinary revenue, and it is well if it does not frequently exceed it. The amassing of treasure can no longer be expected, and when extraordinary exigencies require extraordinary expences, he must necessarily call upon his subjects for an extraordinary aid. The present and the late king of Prussia are the only great princes of Europe, who, since the death of Henry IV. of France in 1610, are supposed to have amassed any considerable treasure. The parsimony which leads to accumulation has become almost as rare in republican as in monarchical governments. The Italian republics, the United Provinces of the Netherlands, are all in debt. The canton of Berne is the single republic in Europe which has amassed any considerable treasure. The other Swiss republics have not. The taste for some sort of pageantry, for splendid buildings, at least, and other public ornaments, frequently prevails as much in the apparently sober senate-house of a little republic, as in the dissipated court of the greatest king.

The want of parsimony in time of peace, imposes the necessity of contracting debt in time of war. When war comes, there is no money in the treasury but what is necessary for carrying on the

财宝,据说至今每一个鞑靼首领也还拥有财宝。

在一个充满各种昂贵奢侈品的商业国家里,君主跟他领土上所有的大地主一样,以同样的方式自然地花费他的大量财产来购买奢侈品。他自己的王国和邻国,给他提供丰富的昂贵的装点豪华的小玩意儿,构成了华而不实的宫廷壮观。为了同类的但低一级的浮华,贵族们解雇了他们的奴仆,让他们的佃农独立,使他们自己逐渐变得跟他们领土上的大部分富裕的市民一样无足轻重。贵族们追求无关紧要东西的行为,也同样影响着君主的行为。怎么能够对于认为他是在他领土上唯一的富人,这种快乐而无动于衷呢?如果他没有花费大部分钱财在这些享乐上(而实际上他很可能会这样做),以至于大大削弱国家的国防力量,那也不能指望他不花费掉超过支持这些国防力量的必须钱财的大部分用于享乐。他的日常开支跟他的收入持平,只要不是入不敷出就很好了。不能总是指望积聚财富,当突发事件要求额外支出的时候,他必定号召他所有的民众为这个突发事件出力。普鲁士现今的国王和已故的国王是欧洲唯一的大君主,自从1610年法国的亨利四世死后,他就被认为聚集了一笔可观的财富。为积累而节约的共和政府,几乎和君主政府一样也变得非常稀少了。意大利共和国、荷兰联邦都是负债的,伯尔尼是欧洲唯一积累了相当数目财富的共和国。其他的瑞士共和国都没有。就像那些最伟大国王放荡的宫廷一样,对于某些奢华或者至少富丽堂皇的建筑,以及其他公共装饰的追求,也经常在一些表面朴素的小共和国的参议院议会大厅很盛行。

在和平时期由于缺乏节俭,就被迫在战争时期举债。当战争来临的时候,国库中除了必要的日常建设开支之外再没有钱

国民财富的性质与原理

and in time of war he contracts debts.
ordinary expence of the peace establishment. In war an establishment of three or four times that expence becomes necessary for the defence of the state, and consequently a revenue three or four times greater than the peace revenue. Supposing that the sovereign should have, what he scarce ever has, the immediate means of augmenting his revenue in proportion to the augmentation of his expence, yet still the produce of the taxes, from which this increase of revenue must be drawn, will not begin to come into the treasury till perhaps ten or twelve months after they are imposed. But the moment in which war begins, or rather the moment in which it appears likely to begin, the army must be augmented, the fleet must be fitted out, the garrisoned towns must be put into a posture of defence; that army, that fleet, those garrisoned towns must be furnished with arms, ammunition, and provisions. An immediate and great expence must be incurred in that moment of immediate danger, which will not wait for the gradual and slow returns of the new taxes. In this exigency government can have no other resource but in borrowing.

The same causes which make borrowing necessary make it possible.
The same commercial state of society which, by the operation of moral causes, brings government in this manner into the necessity of borrowing, produces in the subjects both an ability and an inclination to lend. If it commonly brings along with it the necessity of borrowing, it likewise brings along with it the facility of doing so.

Merchants and manufacturers are able to lend,
A country abounding with merchants and manufacturers, necessarily abounds with a set of people through whose hands not only their own capitals, but the capitals of all those who either lend them money, or trust them with goods, pass as frequently, or more frequently, than the revenue of a private man, who, without trade or business, lives upon his income, passes through his hands. The revenue of such a man can regularly pass through his hands only once in a year. But the whole amount of the capital and credit of a merchant, who deals in a trade of which the returns are very quick, may sometimes pass through his hands two, three, or four times in a year. A country abounding with merchants and manufacturers, therefore, necessarily abounds with a set of people who have it at all times in their power to advance, if they chuse to do so, a very large sum of money to government. Hence the ability in the subjects of a commercial state to lend.

Commerce and manufactures can seldom flourish long in any state which does not enjoy a regular administration of justice, in which the people do not feel themselves secure in the possession of their property, in which the faith of contracts is not supported by law, and in which the authority of the state is not supposed to be regularly

了。在战争期间,为了国家防御而必须三倍四倍的建设,因而必须有多于平时三倍或四倍的收入。君主应该有方法来与其开支成比例地增加其收入,但他往往做不到这一点。课征的税收要等到它们被征收的 10—12 个月之后才能进入国库。但是在战争开始的时候,军队必须增加,舰队必须装备,设有驻军的城镇必须进入一个防御状态;军队、战舰以及那些被驻扎的城镇必须装备好武器、军火以及粮食。在那种紧急关头必须保障快速出现的巨大开支的供应,这是不会等待逐步缓慢的新税纳入国库的。在紧要关头,政府除了借债别无对策。

在战争时期他便借债。

同样的社会商业状态,由于道德所起的作用,使政府必须借债,在民众中既产生一种借债的能力又产生一种借债的倾向。如果这种社会的商业状态同时带来了借债的必要性,这样做也会带来借债的便利。

使借债成为一种必须的原因同样也使它变为可能。

一个工商业丰富的国家,必定有很多这样的人存在:经过他们之手的资本不仅有他的自有资本,还有所有借给他们的资本,或是将货物委托给他们的人的资本。对于那些没有贸易或商业而依靠他们的收入来生活的人,他们的收入每年通常仅仅经过他的手一次。而对于这些商人,资本却频繁地或更频繁地经过他们的手,他们经营的收入很快收回,其整个资本数量和信贷可能多次经过他们的手,一年两次、三次甚至四次。因此一个工商业很多的国家,必定有很多的人,他们如果愿意的话,总是可以预付给政府一大笔钱。因此,商业国家的民众有能力贷款。

商业和制造业可以贷款,

商业和制造业很少长期在这样一个国家繁荣:在那里没有正规的司法行政制度,人们感觉自己占有自己的财产不是很安全;在那里契约的诚信不受法律保护;在那里国家的权威不被认为会

and also willing. employed in enforcing the payment of debts from all those who are able to pay. Commerce and manufactures, in short, can seldom flourish in any state in which there is not a certain degree of confidence in the justice of government. The same confidence which disposes great merchants and manufacturers, upon ordinary occasions, to trust their property to the protection of a particular government; disposes them, upon extraordinary occasions, to trust that government with the use of their property. By lending money to government, they do not even for a moment diminish their ability to carry on their trade and manufactures. On the contrary, they commonly augment it. The necessities of the state render government upon most occasions willing to borrow upon terms extremely advantageous to the lender. The security which it grants to the original creditor, is made transferable to any other creditor, and, from the universal confidence in the justice of the state, generally sells in the market for more than was originally paid for it. The merchant or monied man makes money by lending money to government, and instead of diminishing, increases his trading capital. He generally considers it as a favour, therefore, when the administration admits him to a share in the first subscription for a new loan. Hence the inclination or willingness in the subjects of a commercial state to lend.

A government dispenses itself from saving if it knows it can borrow, whereas if there is no possibility of borrowing, it feels it must save. The government of such a state is very apt to repose itself upon this ability and willingness of its subjects to lend it their money on extraordinary occasions. It foresees the facility of borrowing, and therefore dispenses itself from the duty of saving.

In a rude state of society there are no great mercantile or manufacturing capitals. The individuals, who hoard whatever money they can save, and who conceal their hoard, do so from a distrust of the justice of government, from a fear that if it was known that they had a hoard, and where that hoard was to be found, they would quickly be plundered. In such a state of things few people would be able, and nobody would be willing, to lend their money to government on extraordinary exigencies. The sovereign feels that he must provide for such exigencies by saving, because he foresees the absolute impossibility of borrowing. This foresight increases still further his natural disposition to save.

The progress of the enormous debts which at present oppress,

经常用来强制有能力偿债的人必须偿债。总而言之,在一个对政府的公正没有一定信心程度的国家里,商业和制造业很少会繁荣。大商人和大制造业主在通常情况下将他们的财产委托给政府保护的信心,也会让在非常情况时,将他们的财产委托给政府使用。通过借钱给政府,他们甚至一分钟也不会减少他们的经营贸易能力和制造业能力。相反,他们通常还会扩大他们的商业和制造业。国家的紧急需求使政府在大多数情况下愿意以对贷款人极为有利的条件借款。政府提供给原贷款人的债券,可以转让给其他的贷款人,并且由于对政府普遍的信任,这些债券在市场上以高于最初价格的价格出售。商人或有钱人把钱借给政府,可以增加他的贸易资本,而不是减少贸易资本。因此,当行政机构允许他参加新债的首次发行时,他一般会认为这是一种优惠。这就是商业国家民众愿意或有倾向借款的原因。也愿意贷款。

这种国家的政府极其容易在非常时刻依靠民众的这种意愿和倾向来借款。它预见到借款的便利,因此自己就放弃了节省的责任。如果政府知道可以借到钱,他就会免去自己节省的责任,

在社会未开化的状态下不存在大商业资本,也不存在制造业资本。那些将自己节省的钱存储起来的个人,以及隐藏了自己存储的人,是出于对政府公正的不信任才这样做的。因为担心如果他们的存储被公之于众,并且存钱的地方被别人发现,那样他们将很快遭到抢劫。在这种状况下,很少有人,也没有人愿意在非常紧急的时刻给政府借款。君主发现他必须为这种紧急状况节省,因为他可以预见借钱是完全不可能的事情。这种远见也增强了他节约的自然倾向。如果不存在借钱的可能性,政府就觉得必须节约。然而能会必须节约。

巨额负债的增加进度相当一致,当前已经给欧洲所有的国家

| 国民财富的性质与原理

Nations have begun to borrow without special security and have afterwards mortgaged particular funds.
and will in the long-run probably ruin, all the great nations of Europe, has been pretty uniform. Nations, like private men, have generally begun to borrow upon what may be called personal credit, without assigning or mortgaging any particular fund for the payment of the debt; and when this resource has failed them, they have gone on to borrow upon assignments or mortgages of particular funds.

The unfunded debt of Great Britain is contracted in the first way.
What is called the unfunded debt of Great Britain, is contracted in the former of those two ways. It consists partly in a debt which bears, or is supposed to bear, no interest, and which resembles the debts that a private man contracts upon account; and partly in a debt which bears interest, and which resembles what a private man contracts upon his bill or promissory note. The debts which are due either for extraordinary services, or for services either not provided for, or not paid at the time when they are performed; part of the extraordinaries of the army, navy, and ordnance, the arrears of subsidies to foreign princes, those of seamen's wages, &c. usually constitute a debt of the first kind. Navy and Exchequer bills, which are issued sometimes in payment of a part of such debts and sometimes for other purposes, constitute a debt of the second kind; Exchequer bills bearing interest from the day on which they are issued, and navy bills six months after they are issued. The bank of England, either by voluntarily discounting those bills at their current value, or by agreeing with government for certain considerations to circulate Exchequer bills, that is, to receive them at par, paying the interest which happens to be due upon them, keeps up their value and facilitates their circulation, and thereby frequently enables government to contract a very large debt of this kind. In France, where there is no bank, the state bills (billets d'état ①) have sometimes sold at sixty and seventy per cent. discount. During the great re-coinage in King William's time, when the bank of England thought proper to put a stop to its usual transactions, Exchequer bills and tallies are said to have sold from twenty-five to sixty per cent. discount; ② owing partly, no doubt, to the supposed instability of the new government established by the Revolution, but partly too to the want of the support of the bank of England.

---

① [ See Examen , *des Reflexions politiques sur les Finances*. tom. i. , p. 225. ]

② [ James Postlethwayt, *History of the Public Revenue*, 1759, pp. 14, 15, mentions discounts of 25 and 55 per cent. The discount varied with the priority of the tallies and did not measure the national credit in general, but the probability of particular taxes bringing in enough to pay the amounts charged upon them. ]

带来压力,长期内这些债务可能还会毁灭这些国家。国家也像私人一样,一般开始的时候可以凭借所谓的个人信贷来借钱,不需要为债务的支付指派或抵押任何特殊资源,并且当这些办法借不到钱时,他们就不得不依靠这些殊资源的指派和抵押来借款。

> 国家开始借款的时候是没有特殊保证的,以后用特殊资源作抵押。

在英国所谓的无担保公债就是以这两种方式的前种方式借入的。它组成的一部分是没有利息或者被认为没有利息的债务,跟私人通过记账的借款类似;还有一部分是有利息的,跟私人通过汇票或期票的借款相似。对特殊服务所欠的款项;或者对尚未提供的服务或当时没有付款的服务所欠的债务;陆军海军以及军械方面的一部分债务;外国君主补助的欠债;海员的未付工资,通常构成第一种债务。有时为了支付部分债务或为了其他目的而发行的海军证券和财政部证券,通常构成第二种债务。财政部证券从发行之日起就担负利息;海军证券在发行一个月之后开始担负利息。英格兰银行,要么自动在当前的价值上贴现这些票据,要么同意政府以某种报酬条件流通财政部的债券,也就是以票面价值来接受证券,到期支付相应的利息,保持它们的价值,便利它们的流通,因此使政府能不断借到这种大额债务。在没有银行的法国①,国家的证券有时以60%、70%的折扣出售。在威廉国王时期经历了一次大的改制,英格兰银行认为应当中止与其正常的业务往来,据说财政部证券和符契以25%到60%的折扣出售②。毫无疑问,一部分原因是革命建立的新政府的不稳定性,

> 英国的无担保公债首先是以这种方式借到的。

---

① 参见杜弗内:《金融政策评论》,第1卷,第225页。
② 詹姆斯·波斯特思韦特:《公共收入史》,1759年,第14、15页提到25%和55%的折扣。但折扣随符契的次序优先而异,并不衡量国家的一般信用,但表明某一税种是否带来足够的收入去支付符契数额的可能性。

# 国民财富的性质与原理

<small>Mortgages of particular branches of revenue are either for a term of years, when money is said to be raised by anticipation or in perpetuity, when it is said to be raised by funding.</small>

When this resource is exhausted, and it becomes necessary, in order to raise money, to assign or mortgage some particular branch of the public revenue for the payment of the debt, government has upon different occasions done this in two different ways. Sometimes it has made this assignment or mortgage for a short period of time only, a year, or a few years, for example; and sometimes for perpetuity. In the one case, the fund was supposed sufficient to pay, within the limited time, both principal and interest of the money borrowed. In the other, it was supposed sufficient to pay the interest only, or a perpetual annuity equivalent to the interest, government being at liberty to redeem at any time this annuity, upon paying back the principal sum borrowed. When money was raised in the one way, it was said to be raised by anticipation; when in the other, by perpetual funding, or, more shortly, by funding.

<small>The annual land and malt taxes are always anticipated.</small>

In Great Britain the annual land and malt taxes are regularly anticipated every year, by virtue of a borrowing clause constantly inserted into the acts which impose them. The bank of England generally advances at an interest, which since the Revolution has varied from eight to three per cent. the sums for which those taxes are granted, and receives payment as their produce gradually comes in. If there is a deficiency, which there always is, it is provided for in the supplies of the ensuing year. The only considerable branch of the public revenue which yet remains unmortgaged is thus regularly spent before it comes in. Like an improvident spendthrift, whose pressing occasions will not allow him to wait for the regular payment of his revenue, the state is in the constant practice of borrowing of its own factors and agents, and of paying interest for the use of its own money.

<small>Under William III. and Anne anticipations gave rise to deficiencies.</small>

In the reign of king William, and during a great part of that of queen Anne, before we had become so familiar as we are now with the practice of perpetual funding, the greater part of the new taxes were imposed but for a short period of time (for four, five, six, or seven years only), and a great part of the grants of every year consisted in loans upon anticipations of the produce of those taxes. The produce being frequently insufficient for paying within the limited term the principal and interest of the money borrowed, deficiencies arose, to make good which it became necessary to prolong the term.

— 1932 —

另一部分原因是缺乏英格兰银行的支持。

当这种资源耗尽时,为了攒钱,指派和抵押某些特殊部门的公共收入来支付债务变得非常必要了,政府根据不同的情况通过两种方式来这样做。有时他们只是在很短的期限内进行这种指派和抵押,例如一年或是少数几年;有时是无限期的。在前一种情况下,资金在有限的期限内被认为是足以支付借入的本金和利息的。在另一种情况下,资金仅仅被认为足以支付利息,或者是等同于利息的永久年金,一旦归还了借进的本金数额,政府在任何时候都可以随意收回年金。当以前一方法来借钱时,被称为预支法;以后一方法借钱时,被称为永久付息法或简称为付息法。

抵押某一部分收入,时期为几年,被称为预支筹款;永久性的被称为付息筹款。

在英国,根据不断插入课税法令中的借款条款,政府预支了每年的土地税和麦芽税。英格兰银行一般先垫付并收取利息,自从大革命以来利息从 8% 变为 3%,在他们的税款逐步收到时才得到偿还的利息。如果不足(往往是不足的),则在下一年的盈余中被补充。公共收入中还没有抵押的唯一的重要部门,就这样在收入还没得到之前就已被消费了。就像一个浪费的挥霍者一样,他们的紧急情况不允许他等待规律的收入正常到来,这种状态经常出现在向自己的代理人和经理人借款时,为使用这种钱而支付利息。

每年的土地税和麦芽税一般都是预支的。

在威廉国王及安妮女王在位的大部分时期,永久付息的借款方法还不像现在一样为我们所熟悉,当时新税的大部分仅仅课征很短的时间(仅四年、五年、六年或七年),每年大部分的支出来自这些新税收入的预支借款。这些税收往往不足以在有限的时期内支付借入的本金以及利息,出现不足,于是延长课税期限去补足。

在威廉三世和安妮女王在位期间,预支导致不足。

— 1933 —

<small>and the term of the mortgage taxes was prolonged in 1697,</small>    In 1697, by the 8th of William III. c. 20. the deficiencies of several taxes were charged upon what was then called the first general mortgage or fund, consisting of a prolongation to the first of August, 1706, of several different taxes, which would have expired within a shorter term, and of which the produce was accumulated into one general fund. The deficiencies charged upon this prolonged term amounted to 5, 160, 459 $l.$ 14 $s.$ 9 $\frac{1}{4}d.$

<small>in 1701</small>    In 1701, those duties, with some others, were still further prolonged for the like purposes till the first of August, 1710, and were called the second general mortgage or fund. ① The deficiencies charged upon it amounted to 2, 055, 999 $l.$ 7 $s.$ 11 $\frac{1}{2}d.$

<small>in 1707,</small>    In 1707, those duties were still further prolonged, as a fund for new loans, to the first of August, 1712, and were called the third general mortgage or fund. The sum borrowed upon it was 983, 254 $l.$ 11 $s.$ 9 $\frac{1}{4}d.$

<small>in 1708.</small>    In 1708, those duties were all (except the old subsidy of tonnage and poundage, of which one moiety only was made a part of this fund, and a duty upon the importation of Scotch linen, which had been taken off by the articles of union) still further continued, as a fund for new loans, to the first of August, 1714, and were called the fourth general mortgage or fund. ② The sum borrowed upon it was 925, 176 $l.$ 9 $s.$ 2 $\frac{1}{4}d.$ ③

<small>in 1709,</small>    In 1709, those duties were all (except the old subsidy of tonnage and poundage, which was now left out of this fund altogether) still further continued for the same purpose to the first of August, 1716 and were called the fifth general mortgage or fund. ④ The sum borrowed upon it was 922, 029 $l.$ 6 $s.$ 0 $d.$

---

① [Postlethwayt, *op. cit.*, p. 40.]
② [*Ibid.*, p. 59.]
③ [*Ibid.*, pp. 63, 64.]
④ [*Ibid.*, p. 68.]

在 1697 年，根据威廉三世八年第 20 号法令，少数税额的不足由被称为第一次总抵押或基金来支付，将几种即将快要到期的不同的税延长到 1706 年 8 月 1 日，其收入累积为一个总基金。由这种延长期限支付的不足累计达 5160459 镑 14 先令 9 便士半。

在 1701 年，这些税以及其他一些税收因为同样的目的被进一步延长至 1710 年 8 月 1 日，这被称为第二次总基金或基金①。这次基金所负担的不足额累计达 2055999 镑 7 先令 11 便士半。

1707 年，这些税作为新的贷款又延长至 1712 年 8 月 1 日，这被称为第三次总抵押或基金。这笔借入的数量累计达 983254 镑 11 先令 9$\frac{1}{4}$ 便士。

1708 年，这些税（除去半额吨税、磅税这两种老的补助之外，一半被作为这种基金的一部分和苏格兰亚麻的进口税，这已经被联合条约剔出了）作为一种新的贷款再次被延长至 1714 年 8 月 1 日，被称为第四次总抵押或基金②。这笔借入的金额累计达 925176 镑 9 先令 2$\frac{1}{4}$ 便士③。

1709 年，这些税（除去吨税、磅税这两种旧补助之外，现在这些已经从这项基金中剥离出来）因同样的原因被延期到 1716 年 8 月 1 日征收，被称为第五次总抵押或基金④。这笔借入的金额累计达 922029 镑 6 先令。

---

① 波斯特思韦特：《公共收入史》，第 40 页。
② 同上书，第 59 页。
③ 同上书，第 63、64 页。
④ 同上书，第 68 页。

| 国民财富的性质与原理

<small>and in 1710.</small>　　In 1710, those duties were again prolonged to the first of August, 1720, and were called the sixth general mortgage or fund. ①

<small>In 1711 the taxes were continued for ever and made into a fund for paying the interest on £9,177,9668.</small>　　The sum borrowed upon it was 1,296,552*l*. 9*s*. 11$\frac{3}{4}$*d*.

　　In 1711, the same duties (which at this time were thus subject to four different anticipations), together with several others, were continued for ever, and made a fund for paying the interest of the capital of the South Sea company, which had that year advanced to government, for paying debts and making good deficiencies, the sum of 9,177,967*l*. 15 *s*. 4 *d*. ;② the greatest loan which at that time had ever been made.

<small>The only earlier taxes imposed in perpetuity to pay interest on debt were those for paying interest on the advances of the Bank and East India Company.</small>　　Before this period, the principal, so far as I have been able to observe, the only taxes which in order to pay the interest of a debt had been imposed for perpetuity, were those for paying the interest of the money which had been advanced to government by the Bank and East India Company, and of what it was expected would be advanced, but which was never advanced, by a projected land bank. The bank fund at this time amounted to 3,375,027 *l*. 17 *s*. 10$\frac{1}{2}$ *d*. for which was paid an annuity or interest of 206,501*l*. 13*s*. 5*d*. ③ The East India fund amounted to 3,200,000 *l*. for which was paid an annuity or interest of 160,000*l*. ;④ the bank fund being at six per cent., ⑤ the East India fund at five per cent. interest.

<small>In 1715 several taxes were accumulated into the Aggregate Fund.</small>　　In 1715, by the first of George I. c. 12. the different taxes which had been mortgaged for paying the bank annuity, together with several others which by this act were likewise rendered perpetual, were accumulated into one common fund called The Aggregate Fund,

---

　　① [Postlethwayt,*op. cit.*, p. 71.]
　　② [*Ibid.*, p. 311.]
　　③ [*Ibid.*, pp. 301-303.]
　　④ [*Ibid.*, pp. 319, 320.]
　　⑤ [The odd £ 4,000 of the £ 206,501 13s. 5d. was for expenses of management.]

— 1936 —

1710年，这些税再延长至1720年8月1日，被称为第六次总抵押或基金①。这笔借入的金额累计达1296552镑9先令11$\frac{3}{4}$便士。

1711年，同样的税（此时已需供应四种预支款项的本息）连同其他几种税，被永远征收，并且为支付南海公司的资金提供利息支付基金，这个公司已经预付给政府资金来支付债务，弥补税收不足②。这笔款项达9177967镑15先令4便士，为在当时做出的最大借款。

在此之前，据我所知，唯一的为了支付预付给政府的贷款利息而课征的赋税，就是为了支付由英格兰银行和东印度公司预付给政府的款项利息而征收的赋税。这项款项原本以为可以被计划中的土地银行预支，但是后来却没有被预支。此时银行基金累计达3375027镑17先令10便士半，并且支付年利息20650镑13先令5便士③。东印度公司的贷款为32万镑，为此支付的年金或利息是16万镑④；银行的贷款利息是6%⑤，东印度公司的贷款利息率为5%。

1715年，根据乔治一世一年的12号法令，那些抵押用来支付英格兰银行年息的各种赋税，以及其他也是由这项法令规定要永久征收的赋税，一起构成一个共同的基金，称为累积基金。它不

---

① 波斯特思韦特：《公共收入史》，第71页。
② 同上书，第311页。
③ 同上书，第301～303页。
④ 同上书，第319,320页。
⑤ 在206501镑13先令5便士的总数中，有4000镑用于管理支出。

which was charged, not only with the payments of the bank annuity, but with several other annuities and burdens of different kinds. This fund was afterwards augmented by the third of George I. c. 8. and by the fifth of George I. c. 3. and the different duties which were then added to it were likewise rendered perpetual.

<small>and in 1717 several others into the General Fund.</small> In 1717, by the third of George I. c. 7. several other taxes were rendered perpetual, and accumulated into another common fund, called The General Fund, for the payment of certain annuities, amounting in the whole to 724, 849 $l.$ 6 $s.$ 10 $\frac{1}{2}$ $d.$

<small>Thus most of the anticipated taxes were made into a fund for paying interest only.</small> In consequence of those different acts, the greater part of the taxes which before had been anticipated only for a short term of years, were rendered perpetual as a fund for paying, not the capital, but the interest only, of the money which had been borrowed upon them by different successive anticipations.

Had money never been raised but by anticipation, the course of a few years would have liberated the public revenue, without any other attention of government besides that of not overloading the fund by charging it with more debt than it could pay within the limited term, and of not anticipating a second time before the expiration of the first anticipation. But the greater part of European governments have been incapable of those attentions. They have frequently overloaded the fund even upon the first anticipation; and when this happened not to be the case, they have generally taken care to overload it, by anticipating a second and a third time before the expiration of the first anticipation. The fund becoming in this manner altogether insufficient for paying both principal and interest of the money borrowed upon it, it became necessary to charge it with the interest only, or a perpetual annuity equal to the interest, and such unprovident anticipations necessarily gave birth to the more ruinous practice of perpetual funding. But though this practice necessarily puts off the liberation of the public revenue from a fixed period to one so indefinite that it is not very likely ever to arrive; yet as a greater sum can in all cases be raised by this new practice than by the old one of anticipations, the former, when men have once become familiar with it, has in the great exigencies of the state been universally preferred to the latter. To

仅可以用来支付英格兰银行的年金，而且还可以用来支付其他年金和债务。后来，通过乔治一世三年第8号法令和乔治一世五年第3号法令，这项基金又进一步扩大了，并把附加在这项基金上的各种赋税也都同样地规定为永久性赋税了。

1717年，根据乔治一世三年第7号法令，又有其他几种赋税被规定为永久赋税，并构成了一个称为"普通基金"的共同基金。这项基金用来支付的一些年金，总额达到了724849镑6先令10便十半的年金。

1717年，几种其他的赋税构成了"普通基金"。

这些不同的法令，就使得以前大部分仅用来进行短期支付的赋税，都变成了永久性赋税。它们只是用来支付连续由预支办法所借入款项的利息，而不是支付其本金。

这样，大多数预支赋税变成了只用来支付利息的基金。

如果款项只用预支的办法去筹集，经过几年就会使公共收入摆脱债务，除了它在限定的期限内所能偿付的以外，只要它不再承担更多的债务，并在第一次预支得到清偿以前不再做第二次预支，政府就不必做任何其他的关注。但是大部分欧洲政府不可能做到这种关注。它们甚至在第一次预支时就使基金负担过重，如果不是这样的话，它们就在第一次预支得到清偿以前就进行第二次和第三次预支，故意使基金负担过重。这样，基金就不足以支付用它所借款项的本息，因此必须让它只支付利息或利息相等的永久年金，这种不顾未来的预支必然会产生更具破坏性的永久付息法。但是这种做法虽然必然会使公共收入摆脱债务从固定的时期变为不大可能到来的不确定性的未来，但是用这一新方法筹到的款项在所有场合必然会比用旧的预支方法更多，当人们一旦熟悉了新方法以后，在国家的重大紧急状况下，人们就普遍采用它而不用旧方法。解救当前的危急，总是与公共事务管理直接

永久年金一旦盛行起来，它比预支的办法更受欢迎。

| | |
|---|---|
| When once become famili- ar, per- petual funding is pre- ferred to ant- icipati- on. | relieve the present exigency is always the object which principally interests those immediately concerned in the administration of public affairs. The future liberation of the public revenue, they leave to the care of posterity. |

  During the reign of queen Anne, the market rate of interest had fallen from six to five per cent, and in the twelfth year of her reign five per cent. was declared to be the highest rate which could lawfully be taken for money borrowed upon private security. Soon after the greater part of the temporary taxes of Great Britain had been rendered perpetual, and distributed into the Aggregate, South Sea, and General Funds, the creditors of the public, like those of private persons, were induced to accept of five per cent. for the interest of their money, ① which occasioned a saving of one per cent. upon the capital of the greater part of the debts which had been thus funded for perpetuity, or of one-sixth of the greater part of the annuities which were paid out of the three great funds above mentioned. This saving left a considerable surplus in the produce of the different taxes which had been accumulated into those funds, over and above what was necessary for paying the annuities which were now charged upon them, and laid the foundation of what has since been called the Sinking Fund. In 1717, it amounted to 323, 434 *l.* 7 *s.* 7 $\frac{1}{2}$ *d.* ② In 1727, the interest of the greater part of the public debts was still further reduced to four per cent ;③ and in 1753 ④ and 1757, to three and a half and three per cent; which reductions still further augmented the sinking fund.

A fall in the market rate of interest led to a saving. which gave rise to the Sinking Fund.

A sinking fund facilitates the contraction of new debt.

  A sinking fund, though instituted for the payment of old, facilitates very much the contracting of new debts. It is a subsidiary fund always at hand to be mortgaged in aid of any other doubtful fund, upon which money is proposed to be raised in any exigency of the state. Whether the sinking fund of Great Britain has been more frequently applied to the one or to the other of those two purposes, will sufficiently appear by and by.

  Besides those two methods of borrowing, by anticipations and by

---

  ① [In 1717, under the provisions of 3 Geo. I., c. 7. *Postlethwayt, History of the Public Revenue*, pp. 120, 145. ]
  ② [Anderson, *Commerce*, A. D. 1717. ]
  ③ [Anderson, *Commerce*., A, D. 1727. ]
  ④ [This should be 1750. Anderson, *Commerce*, A. D. 1749. ]

有关人士主要感兴趣的目标。至于公共收入在未来如何摆脱债务,他们则留给后代人去关心。

在安妮女王统治期间,市场利息率从 6% 降至 5%;在她统治的第 12 年,宣布私人抵押借款可以收取的最高合法利息率为 5%。在大不列颠的大部分临时税收变成永久课征并在总基金、南海基金和一般基金之间分配以后不久,国家债权人也像私人的债权人一样,被说服接受 5% 的利息①,这样由短期转换为长期的大部分公债借款就产生了 1% 的节省,或者说由上述三大基金支付的年金节约了 1/6。这种节省使用作基金的各种税收在支付所担保的各项年金以后还有巨额剩余,为以后所称的"偿债基金"奠定了基础。1717 年,偿债基金为 323434 镑 7 先令 7.5 便士②。1727 年,大部分公债的利息进一步降至 4%③;1753 年④和 1757 年,又分别降至 3.5% 和 3%;利息降低进一步增加了偿债基金。

> 市场利息率的下降导致节省,从而产生偿债基金。

偿债基金虽然是为偿还旧债设立的,却非常有利于举借新债。它是一种补助基金,在国家的任何紧急时刻,可以随时用来弥补其他基金的不足进行借款。究竟大不列颠的偿债基金用在这两个目的方面哪一个较为频繁,慢慢就会十分明白。

> 偿债基金便于举借新债。

除了这两种借款方法即预支和永久付息以外,还有另外两种

---

① 1717 年,根据乔治一世三年 7 号法律的规定。波斯特思韦特:《公共收入史》,第 120、145 页。
② 安德森:《商业》,1717 年。
③ 安德森:《商业》,1727 年。
④ 应为 1750 年。安德森《商业》,1749 年。

国民财富的性质与原理

Money is also borrowed by terminable and life annuities.

Under William III. and Anne large sums were borrowed on annuities for terms of years.

perpetual funding, there are two other methods, which hold a sort of middle place between them. These are, that of borrowing upon annuities for terms of years, and that of borrowing upon annuities for lives.

During the reigns of king William and queen Anne, large sums were frequently borrowed upon annuities for terms of years, which were sometimes longer and sometimes shorter. In 1693, an act was passed for borrowing one million upon an annuity of fourteen per cent, ① *or of* 140, 000*l.* a year, for sixteen years. In 1691, an act was passed for borrowing a million upon annuities for lives, upon terms which in the present times would appear very advantageous. But the subscription was not filled up. In the following year ② the deficiency was made good by borrowing upon annuities for lives at fourteen per cent. , or at little more than seven years purchase. In 1695, the persons who had purchased those annuities were allowed to exchange them for others of ninety-six years, upon paying into the Exchequer sixty-three pounds in the hundred; that is, the difference between fourteen per cent. for life, and fourteen per cent. for ninety-six years, was sold for sixty-three pounds, or for four and a half years purchase. Such was the supposed instability of government, that even these terms procured few purchasers. In the reign of queen Anne, money was upon different occasions borrowed both upon annuities for lives, and upon annuities for terms of thirty-two, of eighty-nine, of ninety-eight, and of ninety-nine years. In 1719, the proprietors of the annuities for thirty-two years were induced to accept in lieu of them South Sea stock to the amount of eleven and a half years purchase of the annuities, together with an additional quantity of stock equal to the arrears which happened then to be due upon them. ③ In 1720, the greater part of the other annuities for terms of years both long and short were subscribed into the same fund. The long annuities at that time amounted to 666, 8 21 *l.* 8 *s.* 3 $\frac{1}{2}$ *d.* a year. ④ On the 5th of January, 1775, the remainder of them, or what was not subscribed at that time, amounted only to 136, 453 *l.* 12 *s.* 8 *d.*

During the two wars which begun in 1739 and in 1755, little money was borrowed either upon annuities for terms of years, or upon those for lives. An annuity for ninety-eight or ninety-

---

① [5 and 6W. and M. , c. 7. ]
② [4 W. and M. , c. 3. ]
③ [Anderson, *Commerce*, A. D. 1719. ]
④ [Anderson, *Commerce*, A. D. 1720. ]

借款方法,处于上述两种方法的中间地位。它们是定期年金借款法和终身年金借款法。 <sub>用定期年金法和终身年金法借款。</sub>

在威廉国王和安妮女王统治期间,常用定期年金借入巨额款项,有时期限会长一些,有时则短一些。1693 年,通过法案借入 100 万镑,年金为 40%①,即每年 140000 镑,定期 16 年。1691 年通过法案,借款 100 万镑,年金终身,其条件现在看起来是非常有利的。但没有足额认购。次年②,未认购数又用 14% 的终身年金借款去补足,七年多便可以收回本金。1695 年,允许购入上述年金的人换取 96 年期限的年金,其条件为向财政部 100 镑交入 63 镑,也就是说,终身年金 14% 与 96 年年金 14% 的差额以 63 镑售出,或者说四年半收回本金。由于政府地位不稳,甚至以这种条件也找不到买主。在安妮女王统治时期,在不同的情况以两种方法借款,或为终身年金,或为定期 32 年、89 年、98 年和 99 年的年金。1719 年,32 年年金的所有人被说服以其所有年金换取每股等于 11 年半年金的南海公司股票,当时年金应付未付余额也额外发给南海公司等价股票③。1720 年,大部分其他期限长短不一的年金也都归入同一基金。当时每年应付的长期年金共达 666821 镑 8 先令 3.5 便士④。1773 年 1 月 5 日,剩余的部分,即当时未认购足额的部分,只有 136453 镑 12 先令 8 便十。 <sub>在威廉国王和安妮女王统治期间,常用定期年金借入巨额款项。</sub>

在 1739 年和 1755 年开始的两次战争中,用定期年金或终身年金均不能借到款项。可是,1798 年或 1799 年的年金差不多像

---

① 威廉和玛利四年第 3 号法律。
② 威廉和玛利五年、六年第 7 号法律。
③ 安德森:《商业》,1719 年。
④ 安德森:《商业》,1720 年。

国民财富的性质与原理

<small>But little money was so borrowed in the wars of the middle of the eighteenth century, most people preferring a perpetual annuity,</small> nine years, however, is worth nearly as much money as a perpetuity, and should, therefore, one might think, be a fund for borrowing nearly as much. But those who, in order to make family settlements, and to provide for remote futurity, buy into the public stocks, would not care to purchase into one of which the value was continually diminishing; and such people make a very considerable proportion both of the proprietors and purchasers of stock. An annuity for a long term of years, therefore, though its intrinsic value may be very nearly the same with that of a perpetual annuity, will not find nearly the same number of purchasers. The subscribers to a new loan, who mean generally to sell their subscription as soon as possible, prefer greatly a perpetual annuity redeemable by parliament, to an irredeemable annuity for a long term of years of only equal amount. The value of the former may be supposed always the same, or very nearly the same; and it makes, therefore, a more convenient transferable stock than the latter.

<small>and annuities for terms and for lives were only given as premiums.</small> During the two last mentioned wars, annuities, either for terms of years or for lives, were seldom granted but as premiums to the subscribers to a new loan, over and above the redeemable annuity or interest upon the credit of which the loan was supposed to be made. They were granted, not as the proper fund upon which the money was borrowed; but as an additional encouragement to the lender.

Annuities for lives have occasionally been granted in two different ways; either upon separate lives, or upon lots of lives, which in French are called Tontines, from the name of their inventor. When <small>Tontines are preferred to annuities on separate lives, though they do not liberate the public revenue so quickly.</small> annuities are granted upon separate lives, the death of every individual annuitant disburthens the public revenue so far as it was affected by his annuity. When annuities are granted upon tontines, the liberation of the public revenue does not commence till the death of all the annuitants comprehended in one lot, which may sometimes consist of twenty or thirty persons, of whom the survivors succeed to the annuities of all those who die before them; the last survivor succeeding to the annuities of the whole lot. Upon the same revenue more money can always be raised by tontines than by annuities for separate lives. An annuity, with a right of survivorship, is really worth more than an equal annuity for a separate life, and from the confidence which every man naturally has in his own good fortune, the principle upon which is founded the success of all lotteries, such an annuity generally sells for something more than it is worth. In countries where it is usual for government to raise money by granting annuities, tontines are upon this account generally preferred to annuities for separate lives. The

终身年金一样值钱,因而人们可能认为,这些年金应当可以借入相同的款项。但是为家庭置备产业和为遥远未来预作打算而购买公债的人并不愿意购买价值不断下降的公债,而这部分人在认购人里占有很大的比例。因此,长期年金的内在价值虽然可能和永久年金的内在价值非常接近,可是不能找到和永久年金同样多的买主。新债认购人的用意是尽快抛售他们认购的公债,所以宁愿要可以由议会赎回的永久年金,而不要仅仅在数量相等而年限很长的、又不能赎回的年金。前者的价值可以认为总是相同或者几乎相同,因而是比后者更便于转让的资本。

但在18世纪中叶的战争中,用定期或终身年金借到的款项,大多数人永久年金。

在上述两次战争中,定期年金或终身年金都是作为一种给予新债购买者的奖金,此外还给予他们以应有的年金或利息。也就是说,它们不能作为所借款项的应付利息,而是作为对贷款人的一种额外鼓励。

年金终身年金为给定期和年金只作为奖予。

终身年金偶尔也用两种不同的方式给予:或者对个人终身给予,或是对一群人终身给予,后者在法文称为顿廷法(Tontines),它来自于发明人的名字。当年金对个人终身给予时,年金领取人死亡即解除了国家收入对他的负担。当年金按顿廷法给予时,国家收入的负担要等到这一群人全都死亡后才能解除,这一群人有时为20人或30人,生存者承继所有死亡者的年金,最后一人承继全部年金。用相同的收入做抵押,顿廷法总能比个人终身金法借到更多的款项。未死者有接受全部年金的权利,比由个人单独领取的年金更有价值,即使两者的数量相等,因为每个人自然都相信自己有好运气,这就是所有彩票成功的原理,因此这种年金售价高于其实际所值。在政府通常用给予年金去筹借款项的国家,因此一般采用顿廷法而不采用个人终身年金法。政府几乎总是

顿廷法优于终身年金法,人们要尽速接触公债务,他们非常乐意迅速地接触公债务的负担。

国民财富的性质与原理

expedient which will raise most money, is almost always preferred to that which is likely to bring about in the speediest manner the liberation of the public revenue.

<small>In France a much greater proportion of the whole debt is in life annuities than in England;</small>

In France a much greater proportion of the public debts consists in annuities for lives than in England. According to a memoir presented by the parliament of Bourdeaux to the king in 1764, the whole public debt of France is estimated at twenty-four hundred millions of livres; of which the capital for which annuities for lives had been granted, is supposed to amount to three hundred millions, the eighth part of the whole public debt. The annuities themselves are computed to amount to thirty millions a year, the fourth part of one hundred and twenty millions, the supposed interest of that whole debt. These estimations, I know very well, are not exact, but having been presented by so very respectable a body as approximations to the truth, they may, I apprehend, be considered as such. It is not the different degrees of anxiety in the two governments of France and England for the liberation of the public revenue, which occasions this difference in their respective modes of borrowing. It arises altogether from the different views and interests of the lenders.

<small>the difference is due to the fact that in England the lenders are merchants,</small>

In England, the seat of government being in the greatest mercantile city in the world, the merchants are generally the people who advance money to government. By advancing it they do not mean to diminish, but, on the contrary, to increase their mercantile capitals; and unless they expected to sell with some profit their share in the subscription for a new loan, they never would subscribe. But if by advancing their money they were to purchase, instead of perpetual annuities, annuities for lives only, whether their own or those of other people, they would not always be so likely to sell them with a profit. Annuities upon their own lives they would always sell with loss; because no man will give for an annuity upon the life of another, whose age and state of health are nearly the same with his own, the same price which he would give for one upon his own. An annuity upon the life of a third person, indeed, is, no doubt, of equal value to the buyer and the seller; but its real value begins to diminish from the moment it is granted, and continues to do so more and more as long as it subsists. It can never, therefore, make so convenient a transferable stock as a perpetual annuity, of which the real value may be supposed always the same, or very nearly the same.

In France the seat of government not being in a great mercantile city, merchants do not make so great a proportion of the people who advance money to government. The people concerned in

— 1946 —

宁愿采用能够募集更多钱的方法，而不采用以最迅速的方式解除公共收入债务负担的方法。

在法国，比在英格兰有更大部分的公债是用终身年金借入的。根据波尔多议会在 1764 年呈送国会的备忘录，法国全部公债估计为 24 亿里弗，其中以终身年金借入的为 3 亿里弗，占全部公债的 1/8。年金本身为每年 3000 万里弗，为 1.2 亿里弗的 1/4，这是全部公债的利息。我完全知道这种估计是不准确的，但是由于如此令人尊敬的团体认为它接近真实，我认为距离真实的程度总该不会太远。形成英格兰政府和法国政府借款方法不同的，不是它们对解除公共收入债务负担的渴望程度不同，而完全是由于贷款人的不同观点和利益。

在英格兰，政府位于世界最大的商业城市，向政府贷款的人一般是商人。通过贷款，他们不是想减少自己的商业资本，而是相反，他们想要增加自己的商业资本；除非他们期望从出售新债份额中得到利润，否则他们是不会认购的。但是如果他们付出货币所购到的不是永久年金，而只是他们自己或其他人的终身年金，他们并不总是可以从出售这些年金中得到利润。他们自己的终身年金在出售时总会受损失，因为在购买与自己年龄和健康状况接近的其他人的终身年金时，没有人会出比自己终身年金更高的价钱。当然，第三人的终身年金对买卖双方来说无疑价值是相等的，但它的实际价值在授予年金时刻就开始减少，在年金存续期间不断地越来越少。因此，它不可能像永久年金那样成为便于转让的资本，后者的价值被认为总是相同或几乎相同。

在法国，政府不是位于一个大的商业城市里，向政府贷款的人中商人并不占那么大的比例。与财政有关系的人，如总包税

> whereas in France they are persons engaged in the farming and collection of the taxes, who are chiefly bachelors.

the finances, the farmers general, the receivers of the taxes which are not in farm, the court bankers, &c. make the greater part of those who advance their money in all public exigencies. Such people are commonly men of mean birth, but of great wealth, and frequently of great pride. They are too proud to marry their equals, and women of quality disdain to marry them. They frequently resolve, therefore, to live bachelors, and having neither any families of their own, nor much regard for those of their relations, whom they are not always very fond of acknowledging, they desire only to live in splendour during their own time, and are not unwilling that their fortune should end with themselves. The number of rich people, besides, who are either averse to marry, or whose condition of life renders it either improper or inconvenient for them to do so, is much greater in France than in England. To such people, who have little or no care for posterity, nothing can be more convenient than to exchange their capital for a revenue, which is to last just as long, and no longer than they wish it to do.

> The system of perpetual funding prevents the people from feeling distinctly the burden of war.

The ordinary expence of the greater part of modern governments in time of peace being equal or nearly equal to their ordinary revenue, when war comes, they are both unwilling and unable to increase their revenue in proportion to the increase of their expence. They are unwilling, for fear of offending the people, who by so great and so sudden an increase of taxes, would soon be disgusted with the war; and they are unable, from not well knowing what taxes would be sufficient to produce the revenue wanted. The facility of borrowing delivers them from the embarrassment which this fear and inability would otherwise occasion. By means of borrowing they are enabled, with a very moderate increase of taxes, to raise, from year to year, money sufficient for carrying on the war, and by the practice of perpetual funding they are enabled, with the smallest possible increase of taxes, to raise annually the largest possible sum of money. In great empires the people who live in the capital, and in the provinces remote from the scene of action, feel, many of them, scarce any inconveniency from the war; but enjoy, at their ease, the amusement of reading in the newspapers the exploits of their own fleets and armies. To them this amusement compensates the small difference between the taxes which they pay on account of the war, and those which they had been accustomed to pay in time of peace. They are commonly dissatisfied with the return of peace, which puts an end to their amusement, and to a thousand visionary hopes of conquest and national glory, from a longer continuance of the war.

第五篇　第三章

人,未承包的税收征管员、宫廷银行家等等构成在国家处于紧急状态下向政府进行贷款的人的大多数。这种人出身寒贱,但常常拥有巨额财富,极为骄傲。他们傲慢得不肯和同等身份的人结婚,而高贵的女人又不屑和他们结婚。因此,他们常常决定独身,既没有自己的任何亲属,又不关心平日不愿与他们往来的其他亲戚的家属,他们只想自己一生过得快乐,不大在乎身后留有遗产。此外,不愿结婚或生活状况使他们不适于或不便于结婚的富人,在法国比在英格兰要多得多。对这种不大注意或根本不注意后代的人,不如将他们的资本交换为一种时间不长不短、恰如他们希望存在的长期收入。

在法国,贷款是包收的税收的主要承办人,他们从事或主管款而国,税收人们是独身者。

在和平时期,现代政府的大部分经常支出等于或将近等于它们的经常收入,一到战争发生,它们既不愿意也不能够按照支出增加的比例来增加它们的收入。它们之所以不愿意,是因为害怕触怒人民;由于税收巨大和猛然的增加,人民不久就会厌恶战争;它们之所以不能够,是因为它们并不清楚何种税收能足以提供所需要的收入。便利的借款方法给它们解除了这种害怕与不能两种情况所可能带来的困难。用借债的方法,它们只要稍稍增加税收,就能够逐年筹集到足以进行战争的经费;用永久付息的办法,它们只要尽可能地少增加税收,每年就能够筹集到最大可能数量的货币。在大帝国里,住在首都和远离战场的各个省份人民,许多人很少感觉到由于战争而带来的不便;而是自由自在地享受从报纸中读到的本国陆海军辉煌战功所带来的快乐。对他们来说,这种享乐补偿了他们因为战争所交纳的税收与在和平时期所习惯交纳的税收之间的差额。他们普遍对和平的恢复不满意,和平使他们再也得不到这种享乐,使他们对由于战争的长期继续所带

永久付息制度了明防止人民地感觉到战争负担的存在。

— 1949 —

| 国民财富的性质与原理

<small>Their burdens are not reduced on the conclusion of peace.</small>   The return of peace, indeed, seldom relieves them from the greater part of the taxes imposed during the war. These are mortgaged for the interest of the debt contracted in order to carry it on. If, over and above paying the interest of this debt, and defraying the ordinary expence of government, the old revenue, together with the new taxes, produce some surplus revenue, it may perhaps be converted into a sinking fund for paying off the debt. But, in the first place, this sinking fund, even supposing it should be applied to no other purpose, is generally altogether inadequate for paying, in the course of any period during which it can reasonably be expected that peace should continue, the whole debt contracted during the war; and, in the second place, this fund is almost always applied to other purposes.

<small>Any new taxes imposed are rarely sufficient to do more than pay the new interest. Sinking funds arise generally from reductions of interest.</small>   The new taxes were imposed for the sole purpose of paying the interest of the money borrowed upon them. If they produce more, it is generally something which was neither intended nor expected, and is therefore seldom very considerable. Sinking funds have generally arisen, not so much from any surplus of the taxes which was over and above what was necessary for paying the interest or annuity originally charged upon them, as from a subsequent reduction of that interest. That of Holland in 1655, and that of the ecclesiastical state in 1685, were both formed in this manner. ① Hence the usual insufficiency of such funds.

<small>and are constantly misapplied.</small>   During the most profound peace, various events occur which require an extraordinary expence, and government finds it always more convenient to defray this expence by misapplying the sinking fund than by imposing a new tax. Every new tax is immediately felt more or less by the people. It occasions always some murmur, and meets with some opposition. The more taxes may have been multiplied, the higher they may have been raised upon every different subject of taxation; the more loudly the people complain of every new tax, the more difficult it becomes too either to find out new subjects of taxation, or to raise much higher the taxes already imposed upon

---

① [Anderson, *Commerce*, mentions these reductions under their dates, and recalls them in reference to the British reduction in 1717.]

来的征服和国家光荣的无数虚幻的希望化为乌有。

的确,和平的恢复并不能使他们解除大部分战时课征的税收。这些税收已经被抵押,用来支付进行战争所举借公债的利息。如果在支付公债利息和政府的经常开支以后,旧的收入连同新税收一起产生了一些剩余收入,或许会转成偿债基金用来偿还债务。但是,第一,偿债基金即使不挪作其他用途,在可以合理地预期到和平会继续维持的时期内,一般也完全不足以偿付在战争时期所举借的全部债务;第二,这一基金几乎总是被挪作其他用途。

<sub>他们的负担不会因缔约结束而有所减少。</sub>

课征新税的目的只是为了支付用它们做担保所借款项的利息。如果它们提供了更多的收入,一般也既不是计划的也不是预期的,所以数目总是不大。一般偿债基金的产生,与其说是由于税收超过了应付利息或年金的剩余部分,不如说是由于这种利息在后来的降低所导致。1655年荷兰的偿债基金以及1685年教皇领地的偿债基金都是这样形成的①。所以这种基金常常不足以偿付债务。

<sub>开征了新税以外,很少有余。任何新开征的税除了支付利息,一般一般很少有余。偿债基金是由于利息降低而形成的,</sub>

在非常太平的时候,也有要求特别开支的各种事件,政府总是感觉到挪用偿债基金来应付这种开支比课征新税更加方便。每一年新税会被民众或多或少地立即感觉到,这样总是会引起一些低声的抱怨,遇到一些反对呼声。增加的税种越多,就每一种课税对象所课征的税收就越重;民众抱怨每一种新税收的声音越高,就越难找到新的课税对象,或只有大大提高已经课征的旧税

<sub>偿债基金经常被滥用。</sub>

---

① 安德森:《商业》,提到这两年利息的降低,并联系到1717年不列颠利息的降低。

the old. A momentary suspension of the payment of debt is not immediately felt by the people, and occasions neither murmur nor complaint. To borrow of the sinking fund is always an obvious and easy expedient for getting out of the present difficulty. The more the public debts may have been accumulated, the more necessary it may have become to study to reduce them, the more dangerous, the more ruinous it may be to misapply any part of the sinking fund; the less likely is the public debt to be reduced to any considerable degree, the more likely, the more certainly is the sinking fund to be misapplied towards defraying all the extraordinary expences which occur in time of peace. When a nation is already overburdened with taxes, nothing but the necessities of a new war, nothing but either the animosity of national vengeance, or the anxiety for national security, can induce the people to submit, with tolerable patience, to a new tax. Hence the usual misapplication of the sinking fund.

In Great Britain, from the time that we had first recourse to the ruinous expedient of perpetual funding, the reduction of the public debt in time of peace, has never borne any proportion to its accumulation in time of war. It was in the war which began in 1688, and was concluded by the treaty of Ryswick in 1697, that the foundation of the present enormous debt of Great Britain was first laid.

On the 31st of December 1697, the public debts of Great Britain, funded and unfunded, amounted to 21, 515, 742 $l.$ 13 $s.$ 8 $\frac{1}{2}$ $d.$ A great part of those debts had been contracted upon short anticipations, and some part upon annuities for lives; so that before the 31st of December 1701, in less than four years, there had partly been paid off, and partly reverted to the public, the sum of 5, 121, 041 $l.$ 12$s.$ 0 $\frac{3}{4}$$d.$; a greater reduction of the public debt than has ever since been brought about in so short a period of time. The remaining debt, therefore, amounted only to 16, 394, 701$l.$ 1 $s.$ 7 $\frac{1}{4}$$d.$

In the war which began in 1702, and which was concluded by the treaty of Utrecht, the public debts were still more accumulated. On the 31st of December 1714, they amounted to 53, 681, 076 $l.$ 5 $s.$ 6 $\frac{1}{12}$$d.$ The subscription into the South Sea fund of the short and long annuities increased the capital of the public debts, so that on the 31st of December 1722, it amounted to 55, 282, 978 $l.$ 1 $s.$ 3 $\frac{5}{6}$ $d.$ The reduction of the debt began in 1723, and went on so slowly that,

收水平。暂时停止还债不会被民众立即感觉到,不会引起小声和大声的抱怨。从偿债基金借支总是摆脱目前困难的最显而易见和最容易的办法。公债积累得越多,就越有必要去研究如何减少债务,挪用偿债基金的任何部分都会变得更危险、更具有毁灭性;而公债越不可能有大幅减少,就越有可能、更加肯定地会挪用偿债基金来支付和平时期产生的特别开支。当国家已经负担了过重的税收时,除了有必要进行一次新的战争以外,民众除了遇到进行民族复仇或事关国家安危的事情以外,没有什么能使他们再继续非常耐心地承担新税种了。因此偿债基金常常被滥用。

在大不列颠,从我们首次应用永久付息这种毁灭性的办法开始,和平时期减少的公债从来没有与战争时期积累的公债之间保持比例。正是在1688年开始,到1697年的里斯韦克条约结束战争为止,首次奠定了大不列颠目前巨额债务的基础。

不列颠债务起源于1688~1697年的战争,

1697年12月31日,大不列颠的公债,包括有基金的和没有基金的共达21515742镑13令8.5便士。其中大部分是用短期预支的方式借入的,一部分是用终身年金的方式借入的;因此,在1701年12月31日以前,在不到四年的时间部分地已经偿还,部分地回归于国库,共计减少5121041镑12先令3/4便士,后来公债的减少在如此短的时期内所减少的更大。因此,剩下的公债只有16394701镑1先令7便士又1/4便士。

战争留下了2150万镑的公债,1697~1701年减少了500万镑。

在1702年开始,在由乌特勒支条约结束的战争中,公债积累更多。1714年12月31日,共计达53681076镑5先令6便士又1/12便士。认购短期和长期年金的南海陆风基金增加了公债的本金,因此在1722年12月1日,共计达53681076镑1先令3便士又5/6便士。从1723年开始的公债减少进行得十分缓慢,在

从1702年至1722年公债增加了3900万镑,从1722年至1739年只减少830万镑。

on the 31st of December 1739, during seventeen years of profound peace, the whole sum paid off was no more than 8,328,354$l$. 17$s$. 11$\frac{3}{12}$$d$. the capital of the public debt at that time amounting to 46,954,623 $l$. 3$s$. 4$\frac{7}{12}$$d$.

<small>From 1739 to 1748 the increase was thirty-one and one-third millions.</small>　　The Spanish war, which began in 1739, and the French war which soon followed it, occasioned a further increase of the debt, which, on the 31st of December 1748, after the war had been concluded by the treaty of Aix la Chapelle, amounted to 78,293,313$l$. 1$s$. 10$\frac{3}{4}$$d$. The most profound peace of seventeen years continuance had taken no more than 8,328,354$l$. 17$s$. 11$\frac{3}{12}$$d$. from it. A war of less than nine years continuance added 31,338,689 $l$. 18 $s$. 6$\frac{1}{6}$$d$. to it. ①

<small>During the peace of 1748-55 the reduction was six millions, and the seven years' war added more than seventy-five.</small>　　During the administration of Mr. Pelham, the interest of the public debt was reduced, or at least measures were taken for reducing it, from four to three per cent. ; the sinking fund was increased, and some part of the public debt was paid off. In 1755, before the breaking out of the late war, the funded debt of Great Britain amounted to 72,289,673 $l$. ② On the 5th of January 1763, at the conclusion of the peace, the funded debt amounted to 122,603,336 $l$. 8 $s$. 2$\frac{1}{4}$$d$. ③ The unfunded debt has been stated at 13,927,589 $l$. 2 $s$. 2 $d$. But the expence occasioned by the war did not end with the conclusion of the peace; so that though, on the 5th of January 1764, the funded debt was increased (partly by a new loan, and partly by funding a part of

---

　　① See James Postlethwaite's *history of the public revenue.* [ Pp. 42,143-145,147,224,300. The reference covers the three paragraphs in the text above. ]

　　② [ *Present State of the Nation*, p. 28. ]

　　③ [ Anderson,*Commerce*,postscript *ad init.* ]

17 年的太平时期，到 1739 年 12 月 31 日，全部偿还的公债只有 8328354 镑 17 先令 11 便士又 3/12 便士，当时公债本金为 469546233 镑 3 先令 4 便士又 7/12 便士。

1739 年开始的西班牙战争，以及随后不久发生的法国战争，使公债进一步增加；到 1748 年 12 月 31 日，在战争由艾克斯拉·斯佩勒条约结束以后，共计达 78293313 镑 1 先令 10 便士又 1/4 便士。随后的 17 年太平盛世所减少的债务只有 8328354 镑 17 先令 11 便士又 3/12 便士。不到九年的连续战争增加公债 31338689 镑 18 先令 6 便士又 1/6 便士①。<sub>从1739年至1748年公债增加了3130万镑。</sub>

在佩勒姆先生当政期间，公债利息有所减少，或者至少是他采取了减少措施，利息从 4% 降至 3%；结果偿债基金有所增加，偿还了一部分公债。1755 年，在上次战争开始以前，大不列颠有基金的公债共 72289673 镑②。1763 年 1 月 5 日，和平条约缔结时，有基金的公债为 122603336 镑 8 先令 2 便士又 1/4 便士。没有基金的公债为 13927589 镑 2 先令 2 便士。但是由战争所造成的支出并没有随和平条约的缔结而终止③；因此，虽然在 1764 年 1 月 5 日有基金的公债增至（部分是由于借了新债，部分是由于将一部分无基金的公债转成有基金的公债）129586789 镑 10 先<sub>在1748年至1755年的和平时期里减少了600万镑公债，而七年战争又增加了7500万镑公债。</sub>

---

① 参见詹姆斯·波斯特思韦特：《公共财政史》，第 42、144～145、147、224、300 页。数字包括课文前三段所列。
② 《国家现状》，第 28 页。
③ 安德森：《商业》，后记。

the unfunded debt) to 129,586,789*l*. 10*s*. 134*d*. ① there still remained (according to the very well informed author of the Considerations on the trade and finances of Great Britain ②) an unfunded debt which was brought to account in that and the following year, of 9,975,017 *l*. 12*s*. 2$\frac{15}{44}$ *d*. In 1764, therefore, the public debt of Great Britain, funded and unfunded together, amounted, according to this author, to 139,561,807*l*. 2*s*. 4*d*. ③ The annuities for lives too, which had been granted as premiums to the subscribers to the new loans in 1757, estimated at fourteen years purchase, were valued at 472,500*l*; and the annuities for long terms of years, granted as premiums likewise, in 1761 and 1762, estimated at 27$\frac{1}{2}$ years purchase, were valued at 6,826,875 *l*. ④ During a peace of about seven years continuance, the prudent and truly patriot administration of Mr. Pelham, was not able to pay off an old debt of six millions. During a war of nearly the same continuance, a new debt of more than seventy-five millions was contracted.

<small>In the eleven years of peace before January 1775 the reduction was only ten and a half millions, and most of this was due to reductions of interest.</small>   On the 5th of January 1775, the funded debt of Great Britain amounted to 124,996,086*l*. 1 *s*. 6$\frac{1}{4}$ *d*. The unfunded, exclusive of a large civil list debt, to 4,150,236*l*. 3*s*. 11$\frac{7}{8}$ *d*. Both together, to 129,146,322 *l*. 5 *s*. 6 *d*. According to this account the whole debt paid off during eleven years profound peace amounted only to 10,415,474 *l*. 16*s*. 9$\frac{7}{8}$*d*. Even this small reduction of debt,

---

① [ The account is given in the Continuation of Anderson's *Commerce*, A. D. 1764, vol. iv. , p. 58, in ed. of 1801. The '$\frac{3}{4}$d. ' should be '$\frac{1}{4}$d. ' ]

② [ *Considerations on the Trade and Finances of this Kingdom and on the measures of administration with respect to those great national objects since the conclusion of the peace*, by Thomas Whately, 1766 (often ascribed to George Grenville), p. 22. ]

③ [ This is the amount obtained by adding the two items mentioned, and is the reading of ed. 1. Eds. 2-5 all read' £ 139,516,807 2s. 4d. , ' which is doubtless a misprint. The total is not given in *Considerations*. ]

④ [ *Considerations*, p. 4. ]

令 1 便士又 3/4 便士①,据《关于大不列颠贸易与财政的考察》②一书消息灵通的作者说,这一年和下一年仍然有无基金的公债 9975017 镑 12 先令 2 便士又 15/44 便士。因此,根据这位作者所述,1764 年大不列颠的公债,有基金和没有基金的共计达 139561807 镑 2 先令 4 便士③。1757 年对作为奖金给予新债认购人的终身年金,按相当于 14 年年金估计,共为 472500 镑;1761 年和 1762 年作为同一目的给予的长期年金,按相当于 27 年半年金估计为 600826875 镑④。在大约连续七年的和平时期中,帕勒姆先生的谨慎和的确爱国的政府仍没能还清 600 万镑旧债。在差不多时间一样长的战争中,又举借了 7500 万镑以上的新债。

1775 年 1 月 5 日,大不列颠有基金的公债共计达 124996086 镑 1 先令 6 便士又 1/4 便士。无基金的公债,不包括皇室的巨额债务在内,为 4250236 镑 3 先令 11 便士又 1/8 便士。两者合计为 129146322 镑 5 先令 6 便士。根据这种计算,11 年太平时期偿还的公债仅为 10415474 镑 16 先令 9 便士又 7/8 便士。然而,即使是这种小额还债,也不全是由国家经常收入的节约来偿还。有几

从 1775 年 1 月开始的 11 年平和期中,只减少了 1500 万镑的公债,这大部分是由于利息的降低。

---

① 数字见安德森:《商业》续编,1764 年,第 4 卷,第 58 页;1801 年版,3/4 便士。

② 托马斯·惠特利:《关于本国贸易与财政以及自从缔结和约以来有关这些巨大国家目标的行政措施的考虑》,1766 年(常常认为是乔治·格林维尔所写),第 22 页。

③ 这是将所提两项相加得出的总数,是第 1 版的数字。第 2 版至第 5 版均读为 139516807 镑 2 先令 4 便士,这无疑是印刷错误。《关于本国贸易与财政以及自从缔结和约以来有关这些巨大国家目标的行政措施的考虑》中无总数。

④ 《关于本国贸易与财政以及自从缔结和约以来有关这些巨大国家目标的行政措施的考虑》,第 4 页。

however, has not been all made from the savings out of the ordinary revenue of the state. Several extraneous sums, altogether independent of that ordinary revenue, have contributed towards it. Amongst these we may reckon an additional shilling in the pound land tax for three years; the two millions received from the East India company, as indemnification for their territorial acquisitions; and the one hundred and ten thousand pounds received from the bank for the renewal of their charter. To these must be added several other sums which, as they arose out of the late war, ought perhaps to be considered as deductions from the expences of it. The principal are,

|  | *l.* | *s.* | *d.* |
|---|---|---|---|
| The produce of French prizes . . . . | 690,449 | 18 | 9 |
| Composition for French prisoners . . . . | 670,000 | 0 | 0 |
| What has been received from the sale of the ceded islands | 95,500 | 0 | 0 |
| Total, | 1,455,949 | 18 | 9 |

If we add to this sum the balance of the earl of Chatham's and Mr. Calcraft's accounts, and other army savings of the same kind, together with what has been received from the bank, the East India company, and the additional shilling in the pound land tax; the whole must be a good deal more than five millions. The debt, therefore, which since the peace has been paid out of the savings from the ordinary revenue of the state, has not, one year with another, amounted to half a million a year. The sinking fund has, no doubt, been considerably augmented since the peace, by the debt which has been paid off, by the reduction of the redeemable four per cents. to three per cents, and by the annuities for lives which have fallen in, and, if peace were to continue, a million, perhaps, might now be annually spared out of it towards the discharge of the debt. Another million, accordingly, was paid in the course of last year; but, at the same time, a large civil list debt was left unpaid, and we are now involved in a new war which, in its progress, may prove as expensive as any of our former wars. ① The new debt which will probably be contracted

---

① It has proved more expensive than any of our former wars; and has involved us in an additional debt of more than one hundred millions. During a profound peace of eleven years, little more than ten millions of debt was paid; during a war of seven years, more than one bundred millions was contracted. [ This note appears first in ed. 3. ]

种与经常收入无关的特殊收入对此做出了贡献。其中我们可以算出有：每镑土地税附加 1 先令，共征收三年；作为他们取得新领土的赔款，从东印度公司收到的 200 万镑；从英格兰银行收到的 11 万镑，作为更新特殊许可证书的费用。此外还应加上几种款项的收入，它们是由最近战争产生的，或许应视为这次战争费用的扣除额。主要有：

|  | 镑 | 先令 | 便士 |
| --- | --- | --- | --- |
| 法国战利品收入 | 690449 | 18 | 9 |
| 法国俘虏赔偿金 | 670000 | 0 | 0 |
| 出售割让各岛所得的代价 | 95500 | 0 | 0 |
| 合计 | 1455949 | 18 | 9 |

如果在这个数目上再加上查塔姆伯爵和卡尔克拉夫特先生所估算的余额，加上其他同类军费的节余，再加上从英格兰银行、东印度公司和每镑土地税附加 1 先令所获得的款项，总数肯定会大大超过 500 万镑。可见，自从和平以来，由国家经常收入的节余所偿还的公债，平均说来，每年还没有达到 50 万镑。自从和平以来，由于一部分公债已经偿还、利率由 4% 降至 3% 导致要偿还利息的减少以及部分终身年金的满期，偿债基金已经得到大幅增加；如果和平能够继续下去，现在或许每年能从中拿出 100 万镑用来还债。因此，在去年就又偿还了 100 万镑；但是大笔皇室债务还没有还清，而我们现在又卷入了一场新的战争，随着战争的继续，费用可能和我们以前历次战争一样庞大①。在下次战役结

---

① 这次战争已证明比我们以前各次战争费用更加浩大，使国债增加 1 亿镑以上。在 11 年太平时期，只偿还了 1000 万镑；但是七年战争中，举债高达 1 亿镑以上。本注解首见于第 3 版。

before the end of the next campaign, may perhaps be nearly equal to all the old debt which has been paid off from the savings out of the ordinary revenue of the state. It would be altogether chimerical, therefore, to expect that the public debt should ever be completely discharged by any savings which are likely to be made from that ordinary revenue as it stands at present.

<small>The opinion that the national debt is an additional capital is altogether erroneous.</small> The public funds of the different indebted nations of Europe, particularly those of England, have by one author been represented as the accumulation of a great capital superadded to the other capital of the country, by means of which its trade is extended, its manufactures multiplied, and its lands cultivated and improved much beyond what they could have been by means of that other capital only. ① He does not consider that the capital which the first creditors of the public advanced to government, was, from the moment in which they advanced it, a certain portion of the annual produce turned away from serving in the function of a capital, to serve in that of a revenue; from maintaining productive labourers to maintain unproductive ones, and to be spent and wasted, generally in the course of the year, without even the hope of any future reproduction. In return for the capital which they advanced they obtained, indeed, an annuity in the public funds in most cases of more than equal value. This annuity, no doubt, replaced to them their capital, and enabled them to carry on their trade and business to the same or perhaps to a greater extent than before; that is, they were enabled either to borrow of other people a new capital upon the credit of this annuity, or by selling it to get from other people a new capital of their own, equal or superior to that which they had advanced to government. This new capital, however, which they in this manner either bought or borrowed of other people, must have existed in the country before, and must have been employed as all capitals are, in maintaining productive labour. When it came into the hands of those who had advanced their money to government, though it was in some respects a new capital to them, it was not so to the country; but was only a capital withdrawn from certain employments in order to be turned towards others. Though it replaced to them what they

---

① [ Garnier's note, *Recherches etc.* , tom. iv. , p. 501, is '*Pinto: Traité de la Circulation et du Crédit,* ' a work published in 1771 ('Amsterdam'), ' par l' auteur de l'essai sur le luxe, ' of which see esp. pp. 44, 45, 209-211. But an English essay of 1731 to the same effect is quoted by Melon, *Essai Politique sur le Commerce*, chap. xxiii. , ed. of 1761, p. 296. Cp. *Lectures*, p. 210. ]

束以前将要举借的新债，或许会将接近等于从国家经常收入节余所已经偿还的全部旧债。因此，期望从现有经常收入可能获得的节余去全部清偿公债，那完全是一种幻想而已。

有一位作者认为，欧洲各个负债国家的公债，尤其是英格兰的公债，是加在国家其他资本之上的一笔巨大资本的积累；通过它，国家的贸易得到扩张，制造业得以扩大，土地的耕种和改良也大大超过了单用其他资本可能达到的限度①。他没有考虑到：最初的债权人贷给政府的资本，从贷出的那一刻起，已经从起资本作用的一部分年产出变为起税收作用的一部分年产出，从维持生产性劳动者变为维持非生产性劳动者，一般情况下都是在一年之中花光和浪费了，甚至在未来没有进行再生产的希望。作为贷出资本的回报，他们诚然得到了一笔公债年金，在大多数情况下高于等量价值。这笔年金无疑地代替了他们的资本，使他们可以在和以前相同的范围内甚至在更大的范围内进行他们的贸易和经营，也就是说，他们能用这种年金做担保，向他人借入新的资本，或将其出售，从其他人那里借到一笔自己的新资本，等于或多于他们贷给政府的资本。可是，他们这样从其他人购得或借入的新资本一定是以前在国内就已经存在的，以前一定是像所有资本一样，用以维持生产劳动的。当它进入贷款给政府的那些人手中以后，虽然对他们来说它在某些方面是新资本，但对国家来说却不是新资本；它只是从某种用途中抽出转作其他用途的资本。虽然

<small>认为国债是一种额外资本的观点是完全错误的。</small>

---

① 加尼尔注：《研究》，第 4 卷，第 501 页为"平托：《信用流通论》"，1771 年，阿姆斯特丹，特别是第 44、45、209～211 页。但梅隆《商业政策论》，1761 年，第 23 章，第 296 页引证了另外一篇 1731 年英国论文，而本书下面第 879 页似乎提到了梅隆。比较《关于法律、警察、岁入及军备的演讲》，第 210 页。

had advanced to government, it did not replace it to the country. Had they not advanced this capital to government, there would have been in the country two capitals, two portions of the annual produce, instead of one, employed in maintaining productive labour.

*When necessary expenditure is met by taxes, it only diverts unproductive labour from one unproductive employment to another.*

When for defraying the expence of government a revenue is raised within the year from the produce of free or unmortgaged taxes, a certain portion of the revenue of private people is only turned away from maintaining one species of unproductive labour, towards maintaining another. Some part of what they pay in those taxes might no doubt have been accumulated into capital, and consequently employed in maintaining productive labour ; but the greater part would probably have been spent and consequently employed in maintaining unproductive labour. The public expence, however, when defrayed in this manner, no doubt hinders more or less the further accumulation of new capital; but it does not necessarily occasion the destruction of any actually existing capital.

*When it is met by borrowing, it diverts labour from productive to unproductive employment, and the only advantage is that people can continue to save more during the war,*

When the public expence is defrayed by funding, it is defrayed by the annual destruction of some capital which had before existed in the country; by the perversion of some portion of the annual produce which had before been destined for the maintenance of productive labour, towards that of unproductive labour. As in this case, however, the taxes are lighter than they would have been, had a revenue sufficient for defraying the same expence been raised within the year; the private revenue of individuals is necessarily less burdened, and consequently their ability to save and accumulate some part of that revenue into capital is a good deal less impaired. If the method of funding destroy more old capital, it at the same time hinders less the accumulation or acquisition of new capital, than that of defraying the public expence by a revenue raised within the year. Under the system of funding, the frugality and industry of private people can more easily repair the breaches which the waste and extravagance of government may occasionally make in the general capital of the society.

It is only during the continuance of war, however, that the system of funding has this advantage over the other system. Were the expence of war to be defrayed always by a revenue raised within the year, the taxes from which that extraordinary revenue was drawn would last no longer than the war. The ability of private people to accumulate, though less during the war, would have

它代替了贷款人借给国家的资本,却没有代替国家所丧失的资本。如果贷款人没有将资本贷给国家,国家就会有两个资本,两部分年产出,可以用来维持生产性劳动,而不只是一个资本和一部分年产出。

为了支付政府的费用,在一年中从自由的或没有被抵押的税收收入中筹集款项时,只是把一部分的私人收入从维持一种非生产性劳动转移到维持另一种非生产性劳动而已。他们所缴纳税款的一部分肯定会积累成为资本,用来维持生产性劳动,但大部分或许被花掉,只是用来维持非生产性劳动。可是,这种花销的公共支出肯定会或多或少阻碍新资本的积累,但不一定会破坏任何实际上已经存在的资本。

当公共支出用借债来支付,每年就会破坏一些国内已经存在的资本,即将以前用来维持生产性劳动的年产出转用于维持非生产性劳动。可是,在一年之中,由于在这种情况下筹集到了足够应付同一笔开支的收入,人民的税收负担比应有的负担要轻,所以个人的收入负担必然较小,因而他们将收入的一部分节省下来并积累成为资本的能力受到的损害较小。如果借债的方法比在一年之中筹集收入以应付公共开支的方法破坏了更多的旧资本,与此同时它也较少阻碍新资本的积累或获得。在借债制度下,私人的节俭和勤劳可以更容易地弥补政府的浪费和奢侈对社会总资本所形成的破坏。

然而,只有在战争持续期间,借债制度才对其他制度有这种好处。假如战争支出总是由一年内所筹集到的税收去支付,那么筹集其他收入的税收的时间就不会超过一年。私人积累的能力尽管在战时较小,但与在借债制度下相比,和平时期的积累能力

| 国民财富的性质与原理

which advantage disappears immediately peace is concluded. Under the other system, too, wars would be shorter and periods of peace longer.

been greater during the peace than under the system of funding. War would not necessarily have occasioned the destruction of any old capitals, and peace would have occasioned the accumulation of many more new. Wars would in general be more speedily concluded, and less wantonly undertaken. The people feeling, during the continuance of the war, the complete burden of it, would soon grow weary of it, and government, in order to humour them, would not be under the necessity of carrying it on longer than it was necessary to do so. The foresight of the heavy and unavoidable burdens of war would hinder the people from wantonly calling for it when there was no real or solid interest to fight for. The seasons during which the ability of private people to accumulate was somewhat impaired, would occur more rarely, and be of shorter continuance. Those on the contrary, during which that ability was in the highest vigour, would be of much longer duration than they can well be under the system of funding.

Moreover funding at length burdens the revenue so greatly that the ordinary peace expenditure exceeds that which would under the other system have been sufficient in war.

When funding, besides, has made a certain progress, the multiplication of taxes which it brings along with it sometimes impairs as much the ability of private people to accumulate even in time of peace, as the other system would in time of war. The peace revenue of Great Britain amounts at present to more than ten millions a year. If free and unmortgaged, it might be sufficient, with proper management and without contracting a shilling of new debt, to carry on the most vigorous war. The private revenue of the inhabitants of Great Britain is at present as much encumbered in time of peace, their ability to accumulate is as much impaired as it would have been in the time of the most expensive war, had the pernicious system of funding never been adopted.

The fact of part or the whole of the debt being held at home makes no difference.

In the payment of the interest of the public debt, it has been said, it is the right hand which pays the left. ① The money does not go out of the country. It is only a part of the revenue of one set of the inhabitants which is transferred to another; and the nation is not a farthing the poorer. This apology is founded altogether in the sophistry of the mercantile system, and after the long examination which I have already bestowed upon that system, it may perhaps be unnecessary to say any thing further about it. It supposes, besides, that the whole public debt is owing to the inhabitants of the country, which happens not to be true; the Dutch, as well as several other foreign nations, having a very considerable share in our public funds. But though the whole debt were owing to the inhabitants of the country, it would not upon that account be less pernicious.

---

① [Melon, *Essai politique sur le Commerce*, chap. xxiii. , ed. of 1761, p. 296. ]

还是要大一些。战争不一定会对任何旧的资本造成破坏,而和平则会造成更多新资本的积累。战争一般会更加迅速地结束,也不会那么盲目地随意进行下去。在战争持续期间,人民会感到它的全部负担,不久就会对战争表示厌倦;政府为了取悦人民,也就没有必要拖长战争,会尽快结束战争。没有真实或可靠的利益要争取时,预见到战争会带来沉重和不可避免的负担,人民不会轻易地同意进行战争。在私人积累能力略为受到损害的时期发生的机会要更少些,时间会更短些。反之,这种私人资本积累能力处于最活跃的时期比在借债制度下持续的时间要长久得多。

此外,债务一旦增加,即便是和平时期的某些时候,它所引起的税收增加给人民积累能力带来的损害,也与战时在其他制度下带来的损害一样大。大不列颠的平时税收已达每年 1000 万镑以上,如果任其自由和不做抵押,再加上适当管理以及不再举借一先令新债的情况下,也可能足以进行一场最激烈的战争。现在采用了这种有害的借债制度,在如今和平时期不列颠居民私人收入所承受的负担和积累能力所遭受到的损害,也会与耗资最大的战争时期收到的损害一样多。

有人说,在支付公债利息时,就是右手交给左手①。货币并没有走出国门。只是一部分居民的一部分收入转到了另一部分人手中而已;国家并没有减少一个法新。这种辩解完全是以重商主义的诡辩为基础,在我已经对这个学说进行详细考察之后,或许再没有必要对它说些什么。此外,它假定全部国债属于本国居民,它也并不一定事实就是如此。

---

① 梅隆:《商业政策论》,第 23 章,1761 年版,第 296 页。

国民财富的性质与原理

<sub>Land and capital,the two original sources of all revenue,are managed by landlords and owners of capital.</sub>
Land and capital stock are the two original sources of all revenue both private and public. Capital stock pays the wages of productive labour, whether employed in agriculture, manufactures, or commerce. The management of those two original sources of revenue belongs to two different sets of people; the proprietors of land, and the owners or employers of capital stock.

<sub>Taxation may diminish or destroy the landlord's ability to improve his land,</sub>
The proprietor of land is interested for the sake of his own revenue to keep his estate in as good condition as he can, by building and repairing his tenants houses, by making and maintaining the necessary drains and enclosures, and all those other expensive improvements which it properly belongs to the landlord to make and maintain. But by different land-taxes the revenue of the landlord may be so much diminished; and by different duties upon the necessaries and conveniences of life, that diminished revenue may be rendered of so little real value, that he may find himself altogether unable to make or maintain those expensive improvements. When the landlord, however, ceases to do his part, it is altogether impossible that the tenant should continue to do his. As the distress of the landlord increases, the agriculture of the country must necessarily decline.

<sub>and induce the owner of capital to remove it from the country.</sub>
When, by different taxes upon the necessaries and conveniences of life, the owners and employers of capital stock find, that whatever revenue they derive from it, will not, in a particular country, purchase the same quantity of those necessaries and conveniences which an equal revenue would in almost any other, they will be disposed to remove to some other. And when, in order to raise those taxes, all or the greater part of merchants and manufacturers, that is, all or the greater part of the employers of great capitals, come to be continually exposed to the mortifying and vexatious visits of the tax-gatherers, this disposition to remove will soon be changed into an actual removal. The industry of the country will necessarily fall with the removal of the capital which supported it, and the ruin of trade and manufactures will follow the declension of agriculture.

To transfer from the owners of those two great sources of revenue, land and capital stock, from the persons immediately interested in the good condition of every particular portion of land, and in the good management of every particular portion of capital stock, to another set of persons (the creditors of the public, who have no such particular interest), the greater part of the revenue arising from either, must, in the long-run, occasion both the neglect of land, and

土地和资本是全部私人收入和国家收入的两个原始来源。资本要支付生产性劳动的工资,无论是工业、农业还是商业领域中使用的生产性劳动。这两项原始收入来源的管理属于两类不同的人:土地所有人,资本所有者或使用者。

> 土地和资本这两个原始收入来源由地主和资本所有者管理。

土地所有人为了他自己的收入,通过建筑和维修佃户的房屋、建设和维修必要的沟渠和围墙以及其他应由地主做出和维持的耗资巨大开支的改良活动的方式,有兴趣力所能及地使土地状况保持良好。但是由于要课征各种土地税,地主的收入可能相应地减少;由于对生活必需品和便利品课征各种税,使那种已经减少了的收入变得真实价值如此之小,以致他发现自己不能进行或维持那种昂贵的改良活动。可是,当地主停做他应做的事情时,佃户也完全不可能继续做他们自己应做的事情。由于地主的困难增加,国家的农业必然衰落。

> 课税可能减少或摧毁改良土地的能力。

由于对生活必需品和便利品课税,资本所有者和使用者就发现,他们从资本获得的收入在某一国家不能买到等量收入在任何其他国家所能购买到的等量生活必需品和便利品时,他就会想要迁往某个其他国家。为了课征这种赋税,所有或大部分的商人和制造商,即所有或大部分的大资本所有者,不断受到收税人员的令人着辱和烦恼的问讯时,这种迁移的意向不久就会变成实际的行动。国家的产业必然会随着支持它的资本的迁移而衰落,在农业萧条之后,就是贸易和制造业的败落。

> 促使资本所有者将资本移往国外。

将土地和资本收入的大部分从这两个巨大收入来源的所有者,即从对土地的每一部分的良好状况保持和对资本的每一部分的良好管理直接感兴趣的人手中,移交给另一部分人(国家债权人,他们没有这种特殊的兴趣),在长时期内,必定造成土地的

## 国民财富的性质与原理

<small>The transference of the sources of revenue from the owners of particular portions of them to the creditors of the public must occasion neglect of land and waste or removal of capital.</small>

the waste or removal of capital stock. A creditor of the public has no doubt a general interest in the prosperity of the agriculture, manufactures, and commerce of the country; and consequently in the good condition of its lands, and in the good management of its capital stock. Should there be any general failure or declension in any of these things, the produce of the different taxes might no longer be sufficient to pay him the annuity or interest which is due to him. But a creditor of the public, considered merely as such, has no interest in the good condition of any particular portion of land, or in the good management of any particular portion of capital stock. As a creditor of the public he has no knowledge of any such particular portion. He has no inspection of it. He can have no care about it. Its ruin may in some cases be unknown to him, and cannot directly affect him.

<small>The practice of funding has always enfeebled states.</small>

The practice of funding has gradually enfeebled every state which has adopted it. The Italian republics seem to have begun it. Genoa and Venice, the only two remaining which can pretend to an independent existence, have both been enfeebled by it. Spain seems to have learned the practice from the Italian republics, and ( its taxes being probably less judicious than theirs) it has, in proportion to its natural strength, been still more enfeebled. The debts of Spain are of very old standing. It was deeply in debt before the end of the sixteenth century, about a hundred years before England owed a shilling. France, notwithstanding all its natural resources, languishes under an oppressive load of the same kind. The republic of the United Provinces is as much enfeebled by its debts as either Genoa or Venice. Is it likely that in Great Britain alone a practice, which has brought either weakness or desolation into every other country, should prove altogether innocent?

The system of taxation established in those different countries, it may be said, is inferior to that of England. I believe it is so. But it ought to be remembered, that when the wisest government has exhausted all the proper subjects of taxation, it must, in cases of urgent necessity, have recourse to improper ones. The wise republic of Holland has upon some occasions been obliged to

荒芜、资本的浪费或迁移。国家债权人对国家的农业、制造业和商业的繁荣,因而对它的土地的良好状况和对它的资本的良好管理无疑还是有些兴趣的。如果其中任何一类产业有正常的失败或衰落,各种税收收入就不再会足够支付他们的应收年金或利息。但是国家债权人,仅仅作为这种债权人来看,对任何特定部分土地的良好状况保持和任何特定部分资本的良好管理并不感兴趣。作为国家债权人,他并没有有关任何这种特定部分产业的知识。他对它没有进行监督。他也不可能去关心它。在某些情况下,它的败落并不为他所知,也不可能对他产生直接影响。

举债办法总是使每一个实行它的国家逐渐变得衰弱起来。意大利各个共和国似乎开始举债。热那亚和威尼斯是两个幸存的、可以称为独立存在的国家,均由于举债而受到削弱。西班牙似乎从意大利各个共和国学会了举债,而(它的税收制度还不如意大利各个共和国的税收制度那样合理)相对于它的天然实力而言,它受到了更大程度的削弱。西班牙的债务有长远的历史。它在 16 世纪末就已经债台高筑,比英格兰欠下一个先令大约要早 100 年。法国尽管拥有一切自然资源,也深受同样沉重的债务负担,变得衰弱无力。荷兰共和国也像热那亚和威尼斯一样,由于债务而变得同样衰弱。一种给每一个国家带来衰弱或毁灭的做法,难道单单在大不列颠就能够证明是完全无害了吗?

可以说,这些国家所建立的税收制度都比英格兰的税收制度要差。我相信事实是这样。但是必须记住的是,当最明智的政府对所有适宜的课税对象都征过税时,在紧急需要的情况下,也会对不适宜的课税对象进行征税。聪明的荷兰共和国在有些情况下,不得不课征一些与西班牙的大部分税收一样不方便的税收。

# 国民财富的性质与原理

The superiority of the British system of taxation will not enable Britain to support an unlimited burden.

have recourse to taxes as inconvenient as the greater part of those of Spain. Another war begun before any considerable liberation of the public revenue had been brought about, and growing in its progress as expensive as the last war, may, from irresistible necessity, render the British system of taxation as oppressive as that of Holland, or even as that of Spain. To the honour of our present system of taxation, indeed, it has hitherto given so little embarrassment to industry, that, during the course even of the most expensive wars, the frugality and good conduct of individuals seem to have been able, by saving and accumulation, to repair all the breaches which the waste and extravagance of government had made in the general capital of the society. At the conclusion of the late war, the most expensive that Great Britain ever waged, her agriculture was as flourishing, her manufacturers as numerous and as fully employed, and her commerce as extensive, as they had ever been before. The capital, therefore, which supported all those different branches of industry, must have been equal to what it had ever been before. Since the peace, agriculture has been still further improved, the rents of houses have risen in every town and village of the country, a proof of the increasing wealth and revenue of the people; and the annual amount of the greater part of the old taxes, of the principal branches of the excise and customs in particular, has been continually increasing, an equally clear proof of an increasing consumption, and consequently of an increasing produce, which could alone support that consumption. Great Britain seems to support with ease, a burden which, half a century ago, nobody believed her capable of supporting. Let us not, however, upon this account rashly conclude that she is capable of supporting any burden; nor even be too confident that she could support, without great distress, a burden a little greater than what has already been laid upon her.

Bankruptcy is always the end of great accumulation of debt

When national debts have once been accumulated to a certain degree, there is scarce, I believe, a single instance of their having been fairly and completely paid. The liberation of the public revenue, if it has ever been brought about at all, has always been brought about by a bankruptcy; sometimes by an avowed one, but always by a real one, though frequently by a pretended payment. ①

---

① [ *Histoire philosophique*, Amsterdam, 1773, tom. iv. , p. 274. ]

在公共收入的债务负担得到很大的解除以前,如果开始另一次战争,在进行中变得和上次战争一样耗费巨大,由于不可抗拒的必要性,不列颠的税收制度变得和荷兰的甚至和西班牙的税收制度一样使人民不堪重负。由于我国现行的税收制度比较优越,我国产业迄今为止受到的拘束很小,即使在最费钱的战争中,个人的节约和良好行为似乎能够通过节约和积累,弥补由于政府的浪费和奢侈对社会总资本所造成的一切破坏。在上次战争——大不列颠曾经从事的最费钱的战争结束时,它的农业也和战前一样繁荣,它的制造业和战前一样众多和一样的充分发达,它的商业和战前一样四通八达。可见,支持所有不同产业部门的资本必定和战前相等。自从和平以来,农业得到了进一步的改良,房屋租金在全国每一个城市和村庄均有所上升,这就证明了人民的财富和收入的增长;大部分旧税、特别是货物税和关税的主要部门的每年收入不断增长,同样证明了消费的增长,从而证明了生产的增长,只有生产工艺的增长才能支持消费的增长。大不列颠似乎很容易地支持了一种在半个世纪以前没有人相信它能够承受的负担。可是,我们不要因此就仓促地下结论,认为它能够支持任何负担。甚至也不要过分相信,它能毫不费力地承受比已经加在它身上的更重一些的负担。

当国债一旦积累到一定程度时,我相信它能够得到公正和彻底地清偿的实例很少。公共收入的解脱如果还有实现的可能,那也总是由破产所造成的;有时是通过坦白承认的破产,但总是通过实际的破产,尽管常常使用的是一种伪装的支付①。

① 《哲学史》,阿姆斯特丹,1773 年,第四卷,第 274 页。

## 国民财富的性质与原理

<small>Raising the coin has been the usual method of disguising bankruptcy though this expedient has much worse consequences than an open bankruptcy</small>  The raising of the denomination of the coin has been the most usual expedient by which a real public bankruptcy has been disguised under the appearance of a pretended payment. If a sixpence, for example, should either by act of parliament or royal proclamation be raised to the denomination of a shilling, and twenty sixpences to that of a pound sterling; the person who under the old denomination had borrowed twenty shillings, or near four ounces of silver, would, under the new, pay with twenty sixpences, or with something less than two ounces. A national debt of about a hundred and twenty-eight millions, nearly the capital of the funded and unfunded debt of Great Britain, might in this manner be paid with about sixty-four millions of our present money. It would indeed be a pretended payment only, and the creditors of the public would really be defrauded of ten shillings in the pound of what was due to them. The calamity too would extend much further than to the creditors of the public, and those of every private person would suffer a proportionable loss; and this without any advantage, but in most cases with a great additional loss, to the creditors of the public. If the creditors of the public indeed were generally much in debt to other people, they might in some measure compensate their loss by paying their creditors in the same coin in which the public had paid them. But in most countries the creditors of the public are, the greater part of them, wealthy people, who stand more in the relation of creditors than in that of debtors towards the rest of their fellow-citizens. A pretended payment of this kind, therefore, instead of alleviating, aggravates in most cases the loss of the creditors of the public; and without any advantage to the public, extends the calamity to a great number of other innocent people. It occasions a general and most pernicious subversion of the fortunes of private people; enriching in most cases the idle and profuse debtor at the expence of the industrious and frugal creditor, and transporting a great part of the national capital from the hands which were likely to increase and improve it, to those which are likely to dissipate and destroy it. When it becomes necessary for a state to declare itself bankrupt, in the same manner as when it becomes necessary for an individual to do so, a fair, open, and avowed bankruptcy is always the measure which is both least dishonourable to the debtor, and least hurtful to the creditor. The honour of a state is surely very poorly provided for, when, in order to cover the disgrace of a real bankruptcy, it has recourse to a juggling trick of this kind, so easily seen through, and at the same time so extremely pernicious.

## 第五篇　第三章

　　提高铸币面额是最常采用的手段,使用伪装支付的表象将实际的国家破产掩盖起来。例如,用议会法案或国王命令,宣布 1 枚 6 便士铸币的面额为 1 先令,20 枚 6 便士铸币等于 1 英镑,按旧面额借入 20 先令或将近 4 盎司白银的人,在新面额下,他只需偿还 20 枚 6 便士的铸币,或不到 2 盎司白银。大约 1.28 亿的国债,大约等于大不列颠拥有的有基金的和没有基金的全部债务的本金,这样就可以用大约 6400 万镑的现时货币去偿还。这诚然只是一种伪装的偿还,国家债权人实际上每镑应收款项就被骗去了 10 先令。灾难也会扩大到国家债权人以外,每一个私人的债权人也会遭到相应的损失,而这对国家债权人并无任何好处,在大多数情况下只有一个巨大的额外损失。国家付给他的铸币去偿付自己的债权人,从而在某种程度上弥补由国债所遭受的损失。但在大多数国家里,国家债权人大部分都是富人,他们对其余的同胞来说是债权人而不是债务人。因此,这种伪装的偿还方式在大多数情况下不是减轻而是加重国家债权人的损失;伪装的偿还还没有给国家带来任何好处,而是把灾难推广到其他大多数无辜的人民身上。它造成了私人财产总的和最有害的毁灭;在大多数情况下,使懒惰和奢侈浪费的债务人靠牺牲勤劳和节俭的债权人的利益而致富,将大部分的国家资本从可能增加和改善它的人手中转移到可能会浪费和毁灭它的人的手中。当国家有必要宣布自己破产时,也像私人必须这样做的时候一样,公平、公开和坦白承认的破产总是对债务人的名誉损害最小、对债权人损害也最小的方法。为了掩饰真实破产的耻辱,采取这种极容易被看破、同时又是极端有害的欺骗手法,对国家荣誉肯定也是最笨的保护策略。

〔提高铸币面额是掩饰公债破产的一种方法,虽然这种权宜之计比公开破产有更坏的后果。〕

— 1973 —

## 国民财富的性质与原理

<small>It has been adopted by many states, including ancient Rome,</small> Almost all states, however, ancient as well as modem, when reduced to this necessity, have, upon some occasions, played this very juggling trick. The Romans, at the end of the first Punic war, reduced the As, the coin or denomination by which they computed the value of all their other coins, from containing twelve ounces of copper to contain only two ounces: that is, they raised two ounces of copper to a denomination which had always before expressed the value of twelve ounces. The republic was, in this manner, enabled to pay the great debts which it had contracted with the sixth part of what it really owed. So sudden and so great a bankruptcy, we should in the present times be apt to imagine, must have occasioned a very violent popular clamour. It does not appear to have occasioned any. The law which enacted it was, like all other laws relating to the coin, introduced and carried through the assembly of the people by a tribune, and was probably a very popular law. In Rome, as in all the other ancient republics, the poor people were constantly in debt to the rich and the great, who, in order to secure their votes at the annual elections, used to lend them money at exorbitant interest, which, being never paid, soon accumulated into a sum too great either for the debtor to pay, or for any body else to pay for him. The debtor, for fear of a very severe execution, was obliged, without any further gratuity, to vote for the candidate whom the creditor recommended. In spite of all the laws against bribery and corruption, the bounty of the candidates, together with the occasional distributions of corn, which were ordered by the senate, were the principal funds from which, during the latter times of the Roman republic, the poorer citizens derived their subsistence. To deliver themselves from this subjection to their creditors, the poorer citizens were continually calling out either for an entire abolition of debts, or for what they called New Tables; that is, for a law which should entitle them to a complete acquittance, upon paying only a certain proportion of their accumulated debts. The law which reduced the coin of all denominations to a sixth part of its former value, as it enabled them to pay their debts with a sixth

可是,几乎所有的国家,古代和现代的,当落到有这种必要时,在某些情况下都玩弄了这种欺骗手段。罗马人在第一次布匿战争结束时,将阿斯(As)——他们用来计算所有其他货币价值的铸币或面额——从包含 12 盎司铜减到只包含 2 盎司铜,也就是说,他们用 2 盎司铜来表示过去总是代表 12 盎司铜价值的货币面额。共和国就使用这种方式,用它过去实际所欠债务的 1/6 的钱来偿还它原来所举借的巨额公债。现在我们可以想象,这样突然和这样规模巨大的破产,必然会引起一场激烈的群众喧闹;然而似乎它并没有引起任何喧闹。实施此事的法律也与所有其他有关铸币的法律一样,是由一个护民官提出并由人民议会通过的,并且或许是一项非常受欢迎的法律。在罗马,也像在所有其他古代共和国一样,穷人经常对富人和贵人负债;这些人为了在每年的选举中得到穷人的选票,常常以过高的利息向他们贷款,这些债务从来都没有偿还过,不久就积累成一笔巨大的数额,数额太大了,债务人无力偿还,也没有任何其他人能替他偿还。债务人畏惧非常严厉的处罚,在没有任何回报的情况下,不得不去投债权人所推荐的候选人的票。尽管所有禁止贿赂和收买的法律都有,候选人的乐善好施与偶尔由元老院命令分配的谷物一起,在罗马共和国后期都还是比较贫穷的公民获得生活资料的主要来源。为了使自己摆脱对债权人的这种屈服,较穷的公民不断要求完全取消债务,或通过他们所称的"新铜表法"[1]。也就是,只要偿还所积欠债务的一部分就算还清全部债务的法律。法律规定将所有铸

许多国家都采取这种办法,包括古代罗马在内。

---

[1] "新铜表法"(Nei Tables),因罗马旧有"十二铜表法"(Twlve Tabkea)而得名。

国民财富的性质与原理

part of what they really owed, was equivalent to the most advantageous new tables. In order to satisfy the people, the rich and the great were, upon several different occasions, obliged to consent to laws both for abolishing debts, and for introducing new tables; and they probably were induced to consent to this law, partly for the same reason, and partly that, by liberating the public revenue, they might restore vigour to that government of which they themselves had the principal direction. An operation of this kind would at once reduce a debt of a hundred and twenty eight millions to twenty-one millions three hundred and thirty-three thousand three hundred and thirty-three pounds six shillings and eight-pence. In the course of the second Punic war the As was still further reduced, first, from two ounces of copper to one ounce; and afterwards from one ounce to half an ounce; that is, to the twenty-fourth part of its original value. ① By combining the three Roman operations into one, a debt of a hundred and twenty-eight millions of our present money, might in this manner be reduced all at once to a debt of five millions three hundred and thirty-three thousand three hundred and thirty-three pounds six shillings and eight-pence. Even the enormous debt of Great Britain might in this manner soon be paid.

and has led to the universal reduction of the value of the coin.

By means of such expedients the coin of, I believe, all nations has been gradually reduced more and more below its original value, and the same nominal sum has been gradually brought to contain a smaller and a smaller quantity of silver.

Another expedient is to adulterate the coin,

Nations have sometimes, for the same purpose, adulterated the standard of their coin; that is, have mixed a greater quantity of alloy in it. If in the pound weight of our silver coin, for example, instead of eighteen penny-weight, according to the present standard, there was mixed eight ounces of alloy; a pound sterling, or twenty shillings of such coin, would be worth little more than six shillings and eight-pence of our present money. The quantity of silver contained in six shillings and eight-pence of our present money, would thus be raised very nearly to the denomination of a pound sterling. The adulteration of the standard has exactly the same effect with what the French call an augmentation, or a direct raising of the denomination of the coin.

---

① [This chapter of Roman history is based on a few sentences in Pliny, H. N. , lib. xxxiii. , cap. iii. Modern criticism has discovered the facts to be not nearly so simple as they are represented in the text. ]

— 1976 —

币的价值降到它原来价值的 1/6，使他们能够以所欠债务的 1/6 偿还全部债务，它等于就是最有利的新铜表法。为了满足人民，富人和贵人在几种不同的情况下不得不同意取消债务和实施新铜表法；他们部分地是出于同一理由的诱使才同意这项法律，部分地也是为了使国家收入摆脱债务，以便恢复政府的元气，他们自己就是这个政府的主要领导者。用这种办法，一项 1.28 亿镑的债务会立即就减为 21333333 镑 6 先令 8 便士。在第二次布匿战争中，阿斯的价值进一步贬值，首先，从含铜 2 盎司降至 1 盎司；后来从 1 盎司贬至 0.5 盎司；也就是说，降到原来价值的 1/24①；罗马的三次贬值如果合并成一次计算，那么像我国现币 1.28 亿镑的债务，就可以立即减为 5333333 镑 6 先令 8 便士。即使是大不列颠的巨额债务也可以这样立即被还清。

我相信，用这种办法，所有国家的铸币已经逐渐下降到远远低于其原来的价值的水平，同一面额的铸币所包含白银数量越来越少。导致铸币价值普遍降低。

为了相同的目的，各国有时在它们的铸币标准中掺假，也就是说，在铸币其中搀入了大量的合金。例如，每重一磅的我国银币，按现行标准只能掺入合金 18 英钱[1]，但现在却搀入 8 盎司合金。那么，一英镑或 20 先令这样的掺假货币就只等于我国现行货币的 6 先令 8 便士。我国现行货币 6 先令 8 便士中所包含的白银量，这样就被提高为接近一英镑的面值。货币标准的掺假和法另一种权宜之计就是铸币标准掺假，

---

① 这一章关于罗马的历史是根据普林尼《自然史》第 33 编第 3 章中的几句话。现代评论所发现的事实，不像本书中所说的那么简单。

[1] 英钱(penny-weight)，音译本尼威特，等于 1/20 盎司。

### 国民财富的性质与原理

but this is a treacherous fraud which occasions such indignation that it usually fails.

An augmentation, or a direct raising of the denomination of the coin, always is, and from its nature must be, an open and avowed operation. By means of it pieces of a smaller weight and bulk are called by the same name which had before been given to pieces of a greater weight and bulk. The adulteration of the standard, on the contrary, has generally been a concealed operation. By means of it pieces were issued from the mint of the same denominations, and, as nearly as could be contrived, of the same weight, bulk, and appearance, with pieces which had been current before of much greater value. When king John of France, ① in order to pay his debts, adulterated his coin, all the officers of his mint were sworn to secrecy. Both operations are unjust. But a simple augmentation is an injustice of open violence; whereas an adulteration is an injustice of treacherous fraud. This latter operation, therefore, as soon as it has been discovered, and it could never be concealed very long, has always excited much greater indignation than the former. The coin after any considerable augmentation has very seldom been brought back to its former weight; but after the greatest adulterations it has almost always been brought back to its former fineness. It has scarce ever happened that the fury and indignation of the people could otherwise be appeased.

It has been tried in England, Scotland and most other countries.

In the end of the reign of Henry VIII. and in the beginning of that of Edward VI. the English coin was not only raised in its denomination, but adulterated in its standard. The like frauds were practised in Scotland during the minority of James VI. They have occasionally been practised in most other countries.

For the paying off or reduction of the British debt a very considerable increase of revenue or diminution of expense is necessary.

That the public revenue of Great Britain can ever be completely liberated, or even that any considerable progress can ever be made towards that liberation, while the surplus of that revenue, or what is over and above defraying the annual expence of the peace establishment, is so very small, it seems altogether in vain to expect. That liberation, it is evident, can never be brought about without either some very considerable augmentation of the public revenue, or some equally considerable reduction of the public expence.

① Le Blanc, *Traité historique des Monnoyes de France*, 1792, *Essai politique sur le Commerce*, chap. xiii. , ed. of 1761, p. 177. ]

国人所说的铸币面额的增加或直接提高具有相同的效果。

铸币面额的增加或直接提高常常是公开和坦白承认的行为,按其性质来说也不得不是这样。通过使用这种办法,重量和体积较小的铸币现在使用以前用来称呼重量和体积较大的铸币的名称。反之,标准掺假的行为,则一般是秘密进行的行为。用这种办法,铸币工厂发行和以前同一面额的铸币,尽量使它的重量、体积和外貌与从前的价值较大的铸币相同。为了偿还债务,在法王约翰对他的铸币进行掺假时,要求所有铸币厂的官吏要宣誓保守秘密①。这两种做法都是不公正的。但是简单的提高面额是公开的不公正行为,而掺假则是阴险欺诈的不公正行为。因此,后者一经发现(它绝不可能长期不被发现),总是会比前者会激起更大的愤怒。大幅提高面额的铸币很少会恢复原来的重量,但在最大的掺假以后,铸币总是能恢复它原来的纯度。迄今为止还没有发现什么其他的方法能平息民众的义愤。

但是这种阴险狡诈的办法引起无法平息的愤怒。

格兰和苏格兰、英格兰大多数其他国家都做过铸币掺假的事情。

在亨利八世统治末期和爱德华六世统治初期,英格兰铸币不但面额有所提高,而且标准也有掺假。在詹姆斯六世的幼年时期,苏格兰也做过这种欺诈的事情。在大多数其他国家偶尔也这样做。

收入剩余或在支付和平建制的午度费用以后所剩的资金非常少,而想要大不列颠的国家收入能够完全摆脱债务或向这方面取得重大进步,似乎都是完全没有希望的。要不是国家收入有巨幅增长,或是国家支出有同样大幅地减少,这种摆脱显然是无法

清偿国债,收入须大幅增加或支出大幅减少。

———————

① 勒布朗克:《法国货币史》,1792 年和梅隆,《论商业政策》,第 13 章,1761 年版,第 177 页。

— 1979 —

## 国民财富的性质与原理

Alterations in taxation might increase the revenue considerably, but not sufficiently.

A more equal land tax, a more equal tax upon the rent of houses, and such alterations in the present system of customs and excise as those which have been mentioned in the foregoing chapter, might, perhaps, without increasing the burden of the greater part of the people, but only distributing the weight of it more equally upon the whole, produce a considerable augmentation of revenue. The most sanguine projector, however, could scarce flatter himself that any augmentation of this kind would be such as could give any reasonable hopes, either of liberating the public revenue altogether, or even of making such progress towards that liberation in time of peace, as either to prevent or to compensate the further accumulation of the public debt in the next war.

An extension of taxation to Ireland and the colonies would afford a larger increase.

By extending the British system of taxation to all the different provinces of the empire inhabited by people of either British or European extraction, a much greater augmentation of revenue might be expected. This, however, could scarce, perhaps, be done, consistently with the principles of the British constitution, without admitting into the British parliament, or if you will into the statesgeneral of the British empire, a fair and equal representation of all those different provinces, that of each province bearing the same proportion to the produce of its taxes, as the representation of Great Britain might bear to the produce of the taxes levied upon Great Britain. The private interest of many powerful individuals, the confirmed prejudices of great bodies of people seem, indeed, at present, to oppose to so great a change such obstacles as it may be very difficult, perhaps altogether impossible, to surmount. Without, however, pretending to determine whether such a union be practicable or impracticable, it may not, perhaps, be improper, in a speculative work of this kind, to consider how far the British system of taxation might be applicable to all the different provinces of the empire; what revenue might be expected from it if so applied, and in what manner a general union of this kind might be likely to affect the happiness and prosperity of the different provinces comprehended within it. Such a speculation can at worst be regarded but as a new Utopia, less amusing certainly, but not more useful and chimerical than the old one.

The land-tax, the stamp-duties, and the different duties of customs and excise, constitute the four principal branches of the British taxes.

做到的。

更加平等的土地税、更加平等的房租税,以及像上一章所提到的对现行关税和货物税制度的改革,或许可以在不增加大部分人民负担并让负担更平等地分配在全体人民身上的条件下增加国家收入。可是,最乐观的设计师也不能自我陶醉地认为,人们可以做出合理预期,在和平时期条件下,任何收入的增加能够使国家收入完全摆脱债务甚至向这方面取得重大进步,或在下一次战争中能够阻止或补偿国债的进一步积累。

> 税收制度改革大加收,但增加财政收入,还不够。

将不列颠的课税制度推广到帝国的所有地区,不论其居民为不列颠人或欧洲后裔人,可以期望收入大幅度增加。可是要做到这一点,根据不列颠宪法的原则,必须在不列颠议会中,或者在不列颠帝国总议会里使不同地区拥有公平和平等的代表权,每个地区的代表名额和它的税收收入所保持的比例,与大不列颠的代表名额和各大不列颠课征的税收收入保持的比例相同。许多有势力人物的私人利益和人民大众固执的偏见,的确在现在对这么重大的变革来说似乎是非常难于克服、或许是完全不可能克服的障碍。然而,假定不去考虑这种统一究竟是可行还是不可行,在这样一部理论性的著作中,或许还是可以考虑一下,不列颠的税收制度究竟可以在多大程度上适用于帝国的所有地区?这样的税收制度施行以后可以得到多大的收入?以及这种赋税制的普遍统一会怎样影响帝国各地区的幸福和繁荣?这种推测最坏的也不过被看作是一种新的乌托邦,肯定不是那么有趣,但可以肯定的是却绝不会比乌托邦更加无用、更加虚幻。

> 将不列颠的税收制度推广到各殖民地,爱尔兰和民会使收入有更大的增长。

不列颠税收由土地税、印花税、各种关税以及货物税四个主要部分构成。

国民财富的性质与原理

**The land-tax could well be extended to Ireland, America and the West Indies.**   Ireland is certainly as able, and our American and West Indian plantations more able to pay a land-tax than Great Britain. Where the landlord is subject neither to tithe nor poors rate, he must certainly be more able to pay such a tax, than where he is subject to both those other burdens. The tithe, where there is no modus, and where it is levied in kind, diminishes more what would otherwise be the rent of the landlord, than a land-tax which really amounted to five shillings in the pound. Such a tithe will be found in most cases to amount to more than a fourth part of the real rent of the land, or of what remains after replacing completely the capital of the farmer, together with his reasonable profit. If all moduses and all impropriations were taken away, the complete church tithe of Great Britain and Ireland could not well be estimated at less than six or seven millions. If there was no tithe either in Great Britain or Ireland, the landlords could afford to pay six or seven millions additional land-tax, without being more burdened than a very great part of them are at present. America pays no tithe, and could therefore very well afford to pay a land-tax. The lands in America and the West Indies, indeed, are in general not tenanted nor leased out to farmers. They could not therefore be assessed according to any rent-roll. But neither were the lands of Great Britain, in the 4th of William and Mary, assessed according to any rent-roll, but according to a very loose and inaccurate estimation. The lands in America might be assessed either in the same manner, or according to an equitable valuation in consequence of an accurate survey, like that which was lately made in the Milanese, and in the dominions of Austria, Prussia, and Sardinia.

**Stamp duties could easily be extended.**   Stamp-duties, it is evident, might be levied without any variation in all countries where the forms of law process, and the deeds by which property both real and personal is transferred, are the same or nearly the same.

The extension of the custom - house laws of Great Britain to Ireland and the plantations, provided it was accompanied, as in justice it ought to be, with an extension of the freedom of trade, would be in the highest degree advantageous to both. All the invidious restraints which at present oppress the trade of Ireland, the distinction between the enumerated and non-enumerated commodities of America, would be entirely at an end. The countries north of Cape Finisterre

爱尔兰肯定能够交纳土地税,我国的美洲和西印殖民地比大不列颠更能够缴纳土地税。地主不用缴纳什一税或济贫税的地方,相比于地主必须缴纳这两种税的地方,地主肯定更有能力来缴纳土地税。什一税,在不征收代金而必须以缴纳实物的地方,与实际缴纳土地税为每镑 5 先令来说,会更多地减少地主的地租。在大多数情况下,什一税达到土地真实地租或在完全付清农场主的资本和合理利润以后的地租的 1/4 以上。如果将所有的代金和移交俗人的教会收入除去以后,大不列颠和爱尔兰的全部教会什一税的收入估计在 600 万镑或 700 万镑以上。如果在大不列颠或北爱尔兰不征收什一税,地主就能够缴纳额外的 600 万镑或 700 万镑的土地税,其负担不比现在大部分人的负担更重。美洲不缴纳什一税,因此也完全能够缴纳土地税。当然,美洲和西印度的土地一般不是佃给佃户,也不是出租给农场主的。因此,这种土地不能按照地租登记簿去估计征税。但在威廉和玛利四年,对大不列颠土地征收的赋税也并未按照任何地租登记簿来估计征税,而是按照一种非常宽松和不准确的方法去估计征收的。美洲的土地可以按相同的方式去估计征收,或按准确测量的结果做出公正的评价,像最近在米兰公国以及在奥地利、普鲁士和萨的尼亚各国所做的那样。

<small>土地税能够推广到爱尔兰、美洲和西印度群岛。</small>

在所有法律诉讼形式与不动产和动产转移契约相同或大致相同的那些国家里,显然印花税可以不加更改地推行。

<small>印花税很容易得到推广。</small>

大不列颠的关税法推广到爱尔兰和各殖民地,只要伴有——从公正的角度来说就应当伴有——自由贸易的扩大,对两者都能带来最大的好处。现在压制爱尔兰贸易的一切招人怨恨的限制,美洲的列示商品和非列示商品的区别,均会完全被终止。菲尼斯特

The extension of the customs would be of great advantage to all, as it would be accompanied by an extension of free trade.

would be as open to every part of the produce of America, as those south of that Cape are to some parts of that produce at present. The trade between all the different parts of the British empire would, in consequence of this uniformity in the custom-house laws, be as free as the coasting trade of Great Britain is at present. The British empire would thus afford within itself an immense internal market for every part of the produce of all its different provinces. So great an extension of market would soon compensate both to Ireland and the plantations, all that they could suffer from the increase of the duties of customs.

Excise duties would require some variation,

The excise is the only part of the British system of taxation, which would require to be varied in any respect according as it was applied to the different provinces of the empire. It might be applied to Ireland without any variation; the produce and consumption of that kingdom being exactly of the same nature with those of Great Britain. In its application to America and the West Indies, of which the produce and consumption are so very different from those of Great Britain, some modification might be necessary, in the same manner as in its application to the cyder and beer counties of England.

as for example in the case of American beer.

A fermented liquor, for example, which is called beer, but which, as it is made of melasses, bears very little resemblance to our beer, makes a considerable part of the common drink of the people in America. This liquor, as it can be kept only for a few days, cannot, like our beer, be prepared and stored up for sale in great breweries; but every private family must brew it for their own use, in the same manner as they cook their victuals. But to subject every private family to the odious visits and examination of the tax-gatherers, in the same manner as we subject the keepers of alehouses and the brewers for public sale, would be altogether inconsistent with liberty. If for the sake of equality it was thought necessary to lay a tax upon this liquor, it might be taxed by taxing the material of which it is made, either at the place of manufacture, or, if the circumstances of the trade rendered such an excise improper, by laying a duty upon its importation into the colony in which it was to be consumed. Besides the duty of one penny a gallon imposed by the British parliament upon the importation of melasses into America; there is a provincial tax of this

雷角以北的各个国家会对美洲的一切产出开放自己的市场,就像该海角以南各国现在对美洲的一些产出开放自己的市场一样。由于关税法的这种统一,不列颠帝国所有不同地区之间的贸易,也会像现时大不列颠沿海贸易一样自由。这样,不列颠帝国就会在其领土以内为它所属地区的一切产出提供一个广大的国内市场。市场这么扩大起来,不久就会给爱尔兰和各殖民地补偿因关税增加而可能遭受到的损失。

在不列颠课税制度中,货物税是唯一需要根据它所适用于帝国不同地区的情况而在一些方面加以修改的税种。它在应用于爱尔兰时可能不需要作任何修正;实际上爱尔兰生产和消费与大不列颠的生产和消费性质完全相同。在它应用于美洲和群岛时,由于它们的生产和消费与大不列颠的生产和消费完全不同,所以必须做出某些修正,就像它应用于英格兰的苹果酒和啤酒消费时一样。

例如一种称为啤酒的发酵饮料是由糖蜜(melasses)制成的,它和我国的啤酒完全不同;它占美洲人民普通饮料的一大部分。这种饮料只能保存几天,不像我们的啤酒那样能够在大酿造厂制造和贮存待售,所以每个私人家庭必须自行酿造以供自己使用,就像烹调自己的食物那样。但是让每一个私人家庭接受税收人员讨厌的访问和调查,就像我们对麦酒店老板和以贩卖为目的的酿造厂商那样,那是完全违背自由的。如果出于平等的目的,认为必须对这种饮料课税的话,可以对它的制作原料课税或者在原料的制造地点课征;如果商业的具体情况不适于课征这样一种货物税,那么就在它输入殖民地以供消费时课税。除了不列颠议会对糖蜜输入美洲时课征的每加仑一便士的税收以外,在用其他

kind upon their importation into Massachusets Bay, in ships belonging to any other colony, of eight-pence the hogshead; and another upon their importation, from the northern colonies, into South Carolina, of five-pence the gallon. Or if neither of these methods was found convenient, each family might compound for its consumption of this liquor, either according to the number of persons of which it consisted, in the same manner as private families compound for the malttax in England; or according to the different ages and sexes of those persons, in the same manner as several different taxes are levied in Holland; or nearly as Sir Matthew Decker proposes that all taxes upon consumable commodities should be levied in England. This mode of taxation, it has already been observed, when applied to objects of a speedy consumption, is not a very convenient one. It might be adopted, however, in cases where no better could be done.

<small>Sugar, rum and tobacco could be made subject to excise.</small> Sugar, rum, and tobacco, are commodities which are no where necessaries of life, which are become objects of almost universal consumption, and which are therefore extremely proper subjects of taxation. If a union with the colonies were to take place, those commodities might be taxed either before they go out of the hands of the manufacturer or grower; or if this mode of taxation did not suit the circumstances of those persons, they might be deposited in public warehouses both at the place of manufacture, and at all the different ports of the empire to which they might afterwards be transported, to remain there, under the joint custody of the owner and the revenue officer, till such time as they should be delivered out either to the consumer, to the merchant retailer for home-consumption, or to the merchant exporter, the tax not to be advanced till such delivery. When delivered out for exportation, to go duty free; upon proper security being given that they should really be exported out of the empire. These are perhaps the principal commodities with regard to which a union with the colonies might require some considerable change in the present system of British taxation.

What might be the amount of the revenue which this system of taxation extended to all the different provinces of the empire might produce, it must, no doubt, be altogether impossible to ascertain with tolerable exactness. By means of this system there is annually levied in Great Britain, upon less than eight millions of people, more than

殖民地的船只把它输入马塞诸塞湾时,还课征一种地方税为每豪格海[1]八便士;另外还有一种地方税,在从北部各个殖民地输入南卡罗来纳时,每加仑课税五便士。如果这些方法都不方便,可以对每个家庭消费这种饮料课税,或是根据家庭人数,就像英格兰对私人家庭课征麦芽税那样;或是根据这里人的年龄和性别,像在荷兰课征几种不同的税收那样;要不然就像马修·德克尔爵士所得提议的在英格兰应当对消费品课征的所有各税那样征收。已经指出过,他的这种征税方式在应用于迅速消费的物品时不是很方便的方式。可是,在没有更好的办法时,也不妨采用。

食糖、甜酒和烟草在各处都不是生活必需品,但几乎已经变成是普遍的消费物品,因而是极其适宜的课税对象。假如与殖民地的合并能够实现,对这些商品的课税可以在它们离开制造商或种植人的手中以前征收;如果这种课税方式不适宜这些人的情况,他们可以将货物先存放在制造地或以后可能运往的帝国所有港口的公共仓库中,由所有人和税收人员共同管理;在将其交给消费者、交给国内消费零售商或交给出口商时,再进行课税。在这些商品出口时一律免税,但必须提供适当的担保,保证商品真正出口到帝国以外。这些商品或许是在和殖民地合并以后对现行的不列颠税收制度必须做出重大修改的主要商品。

对食糖、甜酒和烟草也可以课征货物税。

这样将税收制度推广到帝国的所有不同地区可以带来多少收入,肯定是不可能完全比较准确地加以确定。通过这种赋税制度的实行,在大不列颠不到 800 万人口中,每年课征的收入在

---

〔1〕 豪格海(hogshead),液量单位,英格兰等于 52.5 英加仑,美国等于 63 加仑。

国民财富的性质与原理

The increase of revenue thus obtained, if proportionate to the increased population taxed, would yield six millions and a quarter to be applied in reduction of debt, and this sum would of course be a growing one.

ten millions of revenue. Ireland contains more than two millions of people, and according to the accounts laid before the congress, ① the twelve associated provinces of America contain more than three. Those accounts, however, may have been exaggerated, in order, perhaps, either to encourage their own people, or to intimidate those of this country, and we shall suppose therefore that our North American and West Indian colonies taken together contain no more than three millions; or that the whole British empire, in Europe and America, contains no more than thirteen millions of inhabitants. If upon less than eight millions of inhabitants this system of taxation raises a revenue of more than ten millions sterling; it ought upon thirteen millions of inhabitants to raise a revenue of more than sixteen millions two hundred and fifty thousand pounds sterling. From this revenue, supposing that this system could produce it, must be deducted, the revenue usually raised in Ireland and the plantations for defraying the expence of their respective civil governments. The expence of the civil and military establishment of Ireland, together with the interest of the public debt, amounts, at a medium of the two years which ended March 1775, to something less than seven hundred and fifty thousand pounds a year. By a very exact account of the revenue of the principal colonies of America and the West Indies, it amounted, before the commencement of the present disturbances, to a hundred and forty-one thousand eight hundred pounds. In this account, however, the revenue of Maryland, of North Carolina, and of all our late acquisitions both upon the continent and in the islands, is omitted, which may perhaps make a difference of thirty or forty thousand pounds. For the sake of even numbers therefore, let us suppose that the revenue necessary for supporting the civil government of Ireland and the plantations, may amount to a million. There would remain consequently a revenue of fifteen millions two hundred and fifty thousand pounds, to be applied towards defraying the general expence of the empire, and towards paying the public debt. But if from the present revenue of Great Britain a million could in peaceable times be spared towards the payment of that debt, six millions two hundred and fifty thousand pounds could very well be spared from this improved revenue. This great sinking fund too might be augmented every year by the interest of the debt which had been discharged the year before, and might in this manner increase so very rapidly, as to be sufficient in a few years

---

① [Given in the Continuation of Anderson's *Commerce*, A. D. 1774, vol. iv. , p. 178, in ed. of 1801. ]

1000万镑以上。爱尔兰有200多万人口,再根据呈送美洲会议报告①,美洲12个加盟州有300多万人口。可是,这种报告可能有些夸大,或是为了鼓励他们自己的人民,或是为了恫吓这个国家的人民;因此我们假定我国北美洲和西印度殖民地的人口加在一起不超过300万人,或者说整个不列颠帝国在欧洲和美洲的居民不超过1300万人。如果说这种赋税制度在不到800万居民中能够征收到1000万镑以上的收入,那么,它在1300万居民中就当能征收到1625万镑以上的收入。从这项收入(假如这种制度能带来这项收入的话)中,应该扣除正常在爱尔兰和各个殖民地用来支付它们各自文官政府费用的收入。爱尔兰民事和军事建制的费用,加上公债利息,截止到1775年3月两年的平均数,约为每年75万镑。根据一项有关美洲和西印度主要殖民地收入的非常准确的计算,在这次骚乱开始以前,每年为141800镑。可是在这项计算中,马里兰、北卡罗来纳以及我国最近在大陆和各岛屿取得的领地收入都没有计算在内,其差额或许为3万或4万镑。因此,为了取得整数,让我们假定为支持爱尔兰和各个殖民地文官政府所必要的收入可能达100万镑。因此,还剩下1525万镑可以用来支付帝国的一般开支和偿还公债。如果在和平时期从大不列颠现在的收入能够节省100万镑用来偿还公债,那么从这种改进的收入中就可以节省出625万镑来偿还公债。由于前一年偿还公债而不用支付利息,这样一笔巨大的偿债基金可以每年有所增加,并且可能按这种方式增加十分迅速,在几年之内就足以清偿全部债务,从而完全恢复帝国的已经消沉和日趋虚弱的活力。

这样获得的收入增加,如果和人口的增加成比例,可提供625万镑来减债,而且这个数目自然会不断增长。

———————

① 安德森:《商业》续编,1774年,第4卷,第178页,1801年版。

to discharge the whole debt, and thus to restore completely the at present debilitated and languishing vigour of the empire. In the mean time the people might be relieved from some of the most burdensome taxes; from those which are imposed either upon the necessaries of life, or upon the materials of manufacture. The labouring poor would thus be enabled to live better, to work cheaper, and to send their goods cheaper to market. The cheapness of their goods would increase the demand for them, and consequently for the labour of those who produced them. This increase in the demand for labour, would both increase the numbers and improve the circumstances of the labouring poor. Their consumption would increase, and together with it the revenue arising from all those articles of their consumption upon which the taxes might be allowed to remain.

*Some necessary deductions from this estimate would be counterbalanced by additions resulting from a few simple alterations.* The revenue arising from this system of taxation, however, might not immediately increase in proportion to the number of people who were subjected to it. Great indulgence would for some time be due to those provinces of the empire which were thus subjected to burthens to which they had not before been accustomed, and even when the same taxes came to be levied every where as exactly as possible, they would not every where produce a revenue proportioned to the numbers of the people. In a poor country the consumption of the principal commodities subject to the duties of customs and excise is very small; and in a thinly inhabited country the opportunities of smuggling are very great. The consumption of malt liquors among the inferior ranks of people in Scotland is very small, and the excise upon malt, beer, and ale, produces less there than in England in proportion to the numbers of the people and the rate of the duties, which upon malt is different on account of a supposed difference of quality. In these particular branches of the excise, there is not, I apprehend, much more smuggling in the one country than in the other. The duties upon the distillery, and the greater part of the duties of customs, in proportion to the numbers of people in the respective countries, produce less in Scotland than in England, not only on account of the smaller consumption of the taxed commodities, but of the much greater facility of smuggling. In Ireland, the inferior ranks of people are still poorer than in Scotland, and many parts of the country are almost as thinly inhabited. In Ireland, therefore, the consumption of the taxed commodities might, in proportion to the number of the people, be still less than in Scotland, and the facility of smuggling nearly the same. In America and the

同时人民可以解除一些最沉重的税收负担,如对生活必需品和制造原料的课税。这样劳动穷人会生活得好一些,以较低廉的价格把他们所生产的产品运往市场。他们低廉的货物价格会增加对这种货物的需求,从而会增加对生产这种货物劳动的需求。对劳动需求的增加会增加贫民劳动的人数,从而改善他们的状况。他们的消费会增加,随之从对他们所消费的物品仍然课征的税收所产生的收入也会增加。

然而,从这种赋税制度产生的收入可能并不能立即按照纳税人数量的比例而有所增加。对于那些现有的税收负担比他们以前所习惯的负担有所加重的省份,帝国不得不在一段时间内给予它们以很大的宽容政策,而且即使税收在各地都尽可能相同程度严格地征收,那在每个地方也不会得到和人数成比例的税收收入。在一个贫穷的国家里,对应该缴纳关税和货物税的商品消费量很小;在居民稀少的国家里走私的机会非常大。在苏格兰的下层阶级人民中麦芽饮料的消费量则非常小;按照居民人数和税率(由于假设质量存在差别,麦芽税率在苏格兰有所不同)的比例来说,对麦芽、啤酒和淡色啤酒所征收的货物税带来的收入要少于英格兰。在货物税的这些特殊部门,我认为在苏格兰不会比在英格兰有更多的走私机会。对蒸馏的课税和大部分的关税,相对于两国的居民人数来说,在苏格兰产生的收入比在英格兰少,这不仅是因为课税商品的消费量较小所致,也是由于走私更加方便所导致。在爱尔兰,下层人民比在苏格兰更穷,国内许多地区几乎同样是居民稀少。因此在爱尔兰,课税商品的消费按人数比例来说可能比在苏格兰更少,而走私的便利则差不多相同。在美洲和西印度,即使是最低阶层的白人也比英格兰相同阶级的人状况要西印度群岛的最低等级的白人比英国同等级人的境况要好得多，他们对于常享用的各种奢侈品的消费可能也要多得多。确实，构成南方大陆殖民地和西印度群岛居民大部分的黑人，由于他们是处于奴隶状态，毫无疑问比苏格兰或爱尔兰的最穷苦的人境况要差。但是，我们不应当因此就认为他们比英国下层人民吃得要差，或者认为他们对可能课以中等税收的物品的消费比英国下层人民少。为了使他们好好干活，主人就应该使他们吃得好，身心健康，这符合主人的利益，同样主人也要让他干活的牲畜这样。因此，几乎到处的黑奴都有朗姆酒和糖蜜或云杉啤酒的定量配给，就像那些白人仆役一样；即使这些物品被课以中等的税收，这种配给大概也不会撤销。所以，就居民的人数来说，在美洲和西印度群岛课税商品的消费额将和大英帝国其他地区一样多。确实，走私的机会要多得多，因为美洲按国土面积来说，人口比苏格兰或爱尔兰都要稀薄得多。但是，如果把现在对麦芽和麦酒课征的各种捐税改为单独对麦芽课税，那么在这一消费税最重要的一个部门的走私机会差不多就全部被取消。如果关税不是几乎对所有进口商品征收，而只限于征收少数几种最普通用途和消费的商品，并对这些关税的征收适用于消费税法，那么走私机会虽然不会全部取消，也会大为减少。经过这两种看来很简单很容易的改革之后，关税和消费税就人口最稀薄省分的消费额之间的比率来说，所产生的收入就可能和现在按人口最稠密地区的消费额的比率所产生的收入一样多。

美洲人金银少。确实有人说过，美洲人没有金银货币，国内商业靠纸币流通，偶尔在他们手中出现的金银都作为他们从我们这里取得的商品的代价而全部送到大不列颠来了。但有人又说，没有金银，就不可能纳税。我们已经从他们手中得到了他们所拥有的全部金银。怎么可能从他们手中抽取他们所没有的东西呢？

更好,他们对自己通常爱好的各种奢侈品的消费或许要大得多。当然,占大陆南部和西印度殖民地居民大多数的黑人,由于处于奴隶状态,他们的状况比苏格兰或爱尔兰最穷的人还要差。可是,我们不能因此就认为,他们比英格兰的下层人民吃得更坏,所消费的轻税物品就更少。为了使他们工作得好,就要让他们吃好,让他们心情良好,就像这样的对待他的役畜一样的做法是合乎他的利益的。因此,黑人几乎到处都和白人一样,有甜酒、蜂蜜或针枞的供应;即使对这些东西课征轻税,这种供应或许也不会取消。可见,对课税商品的消费,按居民人数的比例计算,在美洲和西印度或许也和在不列颠帝国的任何地区一样大。走私的机会诚然会要大得多;美洲,按国土面积的比例来说,居民比苏格兰或爱尔兰要稀少得多。但是,如果现在把对麦芽和麦芽饮料所课征的各种税所得到的收入改为只对麦芽征收单一税来筹集,部门的货物税这一最重要的走私机会就会被完全杜绝。如果关税不是对几乎所有进口货物课征,而只是对少数几种最通用和消费最多的货物课征,如果关税也按照货物税法那样去课征,那么走私的机会虽然不会完全杜绝,也会大大减少。由于这两种显然是非常简单又非常容易的改革,从关税和货物税筹集到的收入,按消费的比例计算,在人口最稀少的地区或许也和现时在人口最稠密的地区一样多。

当然,有人说美洲人没有金币或银币;美洲的内部贸易是用一种纸币来进行,他们偶尔得到的金银全部送往大不列颠,用来交换他们从我们这里所购买得到的商品。又说,没有金银币就不可能纳税。我们已经得到了他们所拥有的全部金银。怎么可能从他们身上取得他们所没有的东西呢?

美洲人拥有的金银币很少。

# 国民财富的性质与原理

<small>but this is the effect of choice, not necessity.</small>  The present scarcity of gold and silver money in America is not the effect of the poverty of that country, or of the inability of the people there to purchase those metals. In a country where the wages of labour are so much higher, and the price of provisions so much lower than in England, the greater part of the people must surely have wherewithal to purchase a greater quantity, if it were either necessary or convenient for them to do so. The scarcity of those metals therefore, must be the effect of choice, and not of necessity.

It is for transacting either domestic or foreign business, that gold and silver money is either necessary or convenient.

<small>Paper is more convenient to the Americans for home trade,</small>  The domestic business of every country, it has been shewn in the second book of this Inquiry, may, at least in peaceable times, be transacted by means of a paper currency, with nearly the same degree of conveniency as by gold and silver money. It is convenient for the Americans, who could always employ with profit in the improvement of their lands a greater stock than they can easily get, to save as much as possible the expence of so costly an instrument of commerce as gold and silver, and rather to employ that part of their surplus produce which would be necessary for purchasing those metals, in purchasing the instruments of trade, the materials of clothing, several parts of household furniture, and the iron-work necessary for building and extending their settlements and plantations; in purchasing, not dead stock, but active and productive stock. The colony governments find it for their interest to supply the people with such a quantity of paper-money as is fully sufficient and generally more than sufficient for transacting their domestic business. Some of those governments, that of Pennsylvania particularly, derive a revenue from lending this paper-money to their subjects at an interest of so much per cent. Others, like that of Massachusett's Bay, advance upon extraordinary emergencies a papermoney of this kind for defraying the public expence, and afterwards, when it suits the conveniency of the colony,

现在美洲缺乏金银币并不是由于该国家贫穷的结果,即不是由于那里的人民没有能力购买这些金属。在一个工资比英格兰要高出许多而食品价格则比英格兰要低得多的国家里,大部分人民肯定会有财力购买更大数量的金银,如果他们需要或购买方便的话。因此,这种金属的稀少一定是他们自动选择的结果,而不是需要的结果。<sub>但这是选择的结果,而不是需要的结果。</sub>

正是为了进行国内贸易或对外贸易,使用金银货币才有必要或显得很方便。

每个国家的国内贸易,在本书第二篇已经指出过,至少在和平时期,可以用纸币进行,达到和用金银货币大致相同的便利程度。美洲人总是能运用比他们所能得到的更大资本去改良土地并从中获得利润,所以总是尽可能节省在金银这样昂贵的商业支付工具上的支出,而将必须用来购买这些金属的那一部分剩余产出用来购买生产工具、衣服原料、各种家庭用具以及为建筑和扩大他们开垦耕种所必需的五金器具,也就是说,不是用来购买死的资本,而是用来购买活的和生产性资本,对于他们来说这更为便利。各个殖民政府发现,向人民供应一定数量的纸币,纸币数量供应完全足够或者比进行国内贸易所需要的要略微多些,这样做是符合自己的利益的。有些政府,特别是宾夕法尼亚政府,以百分之几的利息率将纸币贷给人民,从中取得一项收入。其他的政府,如马萨诸塞政府,在特别紧急的情况下,用这种纸币来支付公共开支;以后在殖民地认为方便的时候,再根据它逐渐落价<sub>使用纸币进行国内贸易对美洲人更为方便,</sub>

redeem it at the depreciated value to which it gradually falls. In 1747① that colony paid, in this manner, the greater part of its public debts, with the tenth part of the money for which its bills had been granted. It suits the conveniency of the planters to save the expence of employing gold and silver money in their domestic transactions; and it suits the conveniency of the colony governments to supply them with a medium, which, though attended with some very considerable disadvantages, enables them to save that expence. The redundancy of paper-money necessarily banishes gold and silver from the domestic transactions of the colonies, for the same reason that it has banished those metals from the greater part of the domestic transactions in Scotland; and in both countries it is not the poverty, but the enterprizing and projecting spirit of the people, their desire of employing all the stock which they can get as active and productive stock, which has occasioned this redundancy of paper-money.

while for their exterternal trade they use as much gold and silver as is necessary.

In the exterior commerce which the different colonies carry on with Great Britain, gold and silver are more or less employed, exactly in proportion as they are more or less necessary. Where those metals are not necessary, they seldom appear. Where they are necessary, they are generally found.

In the trade between Great Britain and Virginia and Maryland tobacco is a more convenient currency than gold and silver.

In the commerce between Great Britain and the tobacco colonies, the British goods are generally advanced to the colonists at a pretty long credit, and are afterwards paid for in tobacco, rated at a certain price. It is more convenient for the colonists to pay in tobacco than in gold and silver. It would be more convenient for any merchant to pay for the goods which his correspondents had sold to him in some other sort of goods which he might happen to deal in, than in money. Such a merchant would have no occasion to keep any part of his stock by him unemployed, and in ready money, for answering occasional demands. He could have, at all times, a larger quantity of goods in his shop or warehouse, and he could deal to a greater extent. But it seldom happens to be convenient for all the correspondents of a merchant

---

① See Hutchinson's Hist. of Massachusett's Bay, vol. Ⅱ., page 436 & seq. ]

的情况,以贬低的价值将其赎回。1747 年①该殖民地政府以这种方式,用其所发行的纸币 1/10 的款项偿还它的大部分公债。对殖民者的方便是在他们的国内贸易中能够节省用于金银币的支出;对殖民政府的方便是向人民提供一种交易媒介物,尽管会带来很大的不方便,却可以节省用于金银上的开支。纸币过多势必将金银驱逐出国内交易领域,其理由和它在苏格兰将金银驱逐出大部分的国内贸易领域一样。在两国,不是贫穷,而是人民的创新和开拓精神,是他们将其能够得到的全部资本变成活的和生产的资本使用的愿望,才导致了纸币如此过多。

在各殖民地和大不列颠进行的外部贸易中,或多或少使用金银币,数量的多少与其使用的必要性大小完全成比例。在没有必要使用这些金属的地方,它们很少出现。在它们有必要存在的地方,通常可以找到它们。

<small>然而,在外部贸易中他们按是否有必要性来使用金银币。</small>

在大不列颠和盛产烟草的各个殖民地之间的贸易中,不列颠货物向殖民地进行赊销,通常时间相当长,然后殖民地再按照一定的价格用烟草向不列颠支付。对殖民者来说,用烟草支付比用金银币支付较为方便。对任何一个商人来说,用自己所经营的货物去支付与他进行生意往来客户所卖给他的货物,比用货币更为方便。这时的商人不必将自己资本的一部分保持不用,只作为现金去应付不时之需。他可以随时在他的店铺或仓库中保有更大数量的货物,在更大的范围内做生意。但是对一个商人的所有往来客户来说,接受这个商人所经营的货物并把货物作为自己卖给

<small>大不列颠与尼古丁马里兰之间的贸易中,烟草比金银币更为方便的支付工具。</small>

---

① 哈钦森:《马萨诸塞湾殖民地史》,第 2 版,1765～1768 年,第 2 卷,第 436 页及以下。

国民财富的性质与原理

to receive payment for the goods which they sell to him, in goods of some other kind which he happens to deal in. The British merchants who trade to Virginia and Maryland happen to be a particular set of correspondents, to whom it is more convenient to receive payment for the goods which they sell to those colonies in tobacco than in gold and silver. They expect to make a profit by the sale of the tobacco. They could make none by that of the gold and silver. Gold and silver, therefore, very seldom appear in the commerce between Great Britain and the tobacco colonies. Maryland and Virginia have as little occasion for those metals in their foreign as in their domestic commerce. They are said, accordingly, to have less gold and silver money than any other colonies in America. They are reckoned, however, as thriving, and consequently as rich, as any of their neighbours.

*The northern colonies generally find the gold and silver necessary to pay the balance on their trade with Great Britain.*

In the northern colonies, Pennsylvania, New York, New Jersey, the four governments of New England, &c. the value of their own produce which they export to Great Britain is not equal to that of the manufactures which they import for their own use, and for that of some of the other colonies to which they are the carriers. A balance, therefore, must be paid to the mother country in gold and silver, and this balance they generally find.

*The sugar colonies generally find the gold and silver necessary to pay the balance to Great Britain which arises from the sugar planters being absentees.*

In the sugar colonies the value of the produce annually exported to Great Britain is much greater than that of all the goods imported from thence. If the sugar and rum annually sent to the mother country were paid for in those colonies, Great Britain would be obliged to send out every year a very large balance in money, and the trade to the West Indies would, by a certain species of politicians, be considered as extremely disadvantageous. But it so happens, that many of the principal proprietors of the sugar plantations reside in Great Britain. Their rents are remitted to them in sugar and rum, the produce of their estates. The sugar and rum which the West India merchants purchase in those colonies upon their own account, are not equal in value to the goods which they annually sell there. A balance therefore must necessarily be paid to them in gold and silver, and this balance too is generally found.

The difficulty and irregularity of payment from the different colonies to Great Britain, have not been at all in proportion to the greatness or smallness of the balances which were respectively due from them. Payments have in general been more regular from the northern than from the tobacco colonies, though the former have generally paid a pretty large balance in money, while the

— 1998 —

他的货物的支付手段,不一定都常常会感到便利。不过与弗吉尼亚和马里兰做生意的不列颠商人恰好是这样一批往来客户;他们认为,接受烟草并把它作为他们售给这些殖民地货物的支付比接受金银币更为方便。他们期望从出售烟草中获得利润;而他们从支付的金银币中不能得到利润。因此,金银币在不列颠和烟草殖民地的贸易中很少出现。马里兰和弗吉尼亚在自己的国外贸易中也和在国内贸易中一样不需要有这些金属。因此,他们所有的金银币比任何其他美洲殖民地都要少。可是,它们被看作和任何相邻的殖民地一样繁荣,因而也一样富有。

在北部各殖民地,宾夕法尼亚、纽约、新泽西、新英格兰四个州等地,他们向大不列颠出口自己货物的价值并不等于他们从大不列颠进口供自己使用或运往其他殖民地货物的价值。因此,必须用金银币向母国支付贸易差额,他们一般都能找到这项金银。

<small>北部各殖民地一般必须有金银币,它们支付与不列颠之间的贸易差额。</small>

在盛产食糖的各个殖民地,每年出口到大不列颠的食糖价值比从殖民地进口的所有货物的价值要大得多。如果每年送往母国的食糖和甜酒都必须向这些殖民地支付,大不列颠就会不得不出口与差额相等的大量货币,从某一种政治家看来,对西印度贸易就是极端不利的。但许多主要食糖种植园主恰好都住在大不列颠。他们的地租是用他们地产的产出即食糖和甜酒支付给他们的。西印度商人在这些殖民地购买的食糖和甜酒的价值,不等于他们每年在这些殖民地出售货物的价值。因此,这个差额必须用金银币向殖民地支付,而这种金银也是常常能够找得到的。

<small>产糖殖民地一般找金银币,它们支付那些不在殖民地居住的植园主与大不列颠之间的贸易差额。</small>

各个殖民地偿付大不列颠货款的困难和规律性,根本不和它们各自所欠数额的大小成比例。一般说来,北部各个殖民地的支付比烟草殖民地更有规律,虽然前者一般使用货币支付相当大的

| 国民财富的性质与原理

Any difficulties have not been proportionate to the size of the balances due, and have arisen from unnecessary and excessive enterprise.

latter have either paid no balance, or a much smaller one. The difficulty of getting payment from our different sugar colonies has been greater or less in proportion, not so much to the extent of the balances respectively due from them, as to the quantity of uncultivated land which they contained; that is, to the greater or smaller temptation which the planters have been under of over-trading, or of undertaking the settlement and plantation of greater quantities of waste land than suited the extent of their capitals. The returns from the great island of Jamaica, where there is still much uncultivated land, have, upon this account, been in general more irregular and uncertain, than those from the smaller islands of Barbadoes, Antigua, and St. Christophers, which have for these many years been completely cultivated, and have, upon that account, afforded less field for the speculations of the planter. The new acquisitions of Grenada, Tobago, St. Vincents, and Dominica, have opened a new field for speculations of this kind; and the returns from those islands have of late been as irregular and uncertain as those from the great island of Jamaica.

It is not, therefore, the poverty of the colonies which occasions, in the greater part of them, the present scarcity of gold and silver money. Their great demand for active and productive stock makes it convenient for them to have as little dead stock as possible; and disposes them upon that account to content themselves with a cheaper, though less commodious instrument of commerce than gold and silver. They are thereby enabled to convert the value of that gold and silver into the instruments of trade, into the materials of clothing, into household furniture, and into the iron work necessary for building and extending their settlements and plantations. In those branches of business which cannot be transacted without gold and silver money, it appears, that they can always find the necessary quantity of those metals; and if they frequently do not find it, their failure is generally the effect, not of their necessary poverty, but of their unnecessary and excessive enterprize. It is not because they are poor that their payments are irregular and uncertain but because they are too eager to become excessively rich. Though all that part of the produce of the colony taxes, which was over and above what was necessary . for defraying the expence of their own civil and military establishments, were to be remitted to Great Britain in gold and silver, the colonies have abundantly wherewithal to purchase the requisite quantity of those metals. They

贸易差额,而后者则不支付差额或仅仅支付较小的差额。从各个食糖殖民地获得支付的困难,与其说是与各自所欠数额大小成比例,不如说是或多或少与它们各自的没有开垦土地的数量成比例;也就是说,与种植人所受到的贸易过度引诱大小成比例,或者与他们开垦和种植的荒地已经超过他们资本许可的范围有关。从牙买加这个大岛(这里现在仍然有许多没有开垦的土地)所收回的货款,因为这个缘故,比从较小的岛屿如巴巴多斯、安提瓜和圣克里斯托弗所收回的货款会更加不规律和不确定;后者在许多年来已经被完全开垦,因此给耕植人提供的投机机会较少。新近取得的格林纳达、多巴哥、圣文森特和多米尼加为这种投机开辟了新的天地;从这些岛屿收回的货款近来也和从牙买加大岛收回的货款同样不规则和不确定。

支付上产生的困难并不应与贸易差额大小成比例,

因此,就大部分殖民地来说,现在金银币的稀少并不在于贫困。他们对活的、生产资本的巨大需求,使得他们拥有尽可能少的死的资本更为方便,使它们对一种比金银较为低廉、使用起来却不那么合适的商业工具比较满意。结果它们就能将这种金银的价值变成生产工具、变成衣服原料、变成家庭用具、变成为建筑、扩大开垦和耕种所必要的铁器。在那些没有金银币就不能进行交易的业务部门,它们总是能找到必要数量的金银币;如果它们常常不能找到的话,它们的失败一般不是由于它们的必然贫困所造成的,而是它们的不必要和过度的经营所造成的。并不是因为它们穷,而是由于它们太急于过度的富有起来,才使得它们的支付是不规则和不确定的。虽然殖民地税收收入超过支付它们自己的民事和军事建制费用的剩余部分全部都以金银币的形式汇往大不列颠,殖民地还是有充足的财力购买必要数量的金银。

困难是由于不必要和过度的经营所产生的。

would in this case be obliged, indeed, to exchange a part of their surplus produce, with which they now purchase active and productive stock, for dead stock. In transacting their domestic business they would be obliged to employ a costly instead of a cheap instrument of commerce; and the expence of purchasing this costly instrument might damp somewhat the vivacity and ardour of their excessive enterprize in the improvement of land. It might not, however, be necessary to remit any part of the American revenue in gold and silver. It might be remitted in bills drawn upon and accepted by particular merchants or companies in Great Britain, to whom a part of the surplus produce of America had been consigned, who would pay into the treasury the American revenue in money, after having themselves received the value of it in goods; and the whole business might frequently be transacted without exporting a single ounce of gold or silver from America.

<small>It is justice that Ireland and America should contribute to the discharge of the British debt</small>

It is not contrary to justice that both Ireland and America should contribute towards the discharge of the public debt of Great Britain. That debt has been contracted in support of the government established by the Revolution, a government to which the protestants of Ireland owe, not only the whole authority which they at present enjoy in their own country, but every security which they possess for their liberty, their property, and their religion; a government to which several of the colonies of America owe their present charters, and consequently their present constitution, and to which all the colonies of America owe the liberty, security, and property which they have ever since enjoyed. That public debt has been contracted in the defence, not of Great Britain alone, but of all the different provinces of the empire; the immense debt contracted in the late war in particular, and a great part of that contracted in the war before, were both properly contracted in defence of America.

<small>Union would deliver Ireland from an oppressive aristocracy founded on religious and political prejudices.</small>

By a union with Great Britain, Ireland would gain, besides the freedom of trade, other advantages much more important, and which would much more than compensate any increase of taxes that might accompany that union. By the union with England, the middling and inferior ranks of people in Scotland gained a complete deliverance from the power of an aristocracy which had always before oppressed them. By an union with Great Britain, the greater part of the people of all ranks in Ireland would gain an equally complete deliverance from a much more oppressive aristocracy; an aristocracy not founded, like that of Scotland, in the natural and respectable

在这种情况下，它们尽管不得不将现在用来购买活的、生产性的资本的一部分剩余产出用来购买死的资本。在进行国内交易时它们不得不使用一种昂贵的而不是低廉的商业工具，购买这种昂贵工具的费用可能会稍稍抑制他们在改良土地的过度进取中的活力和热情。可是，可能不必要将美洲收入的任何部分用金银汇出。可以用对大不列颠商人或公司开出汇票并由他们承兑的方法汇款，先将美洲剩余产物的一部分委托给他们，他们在收到货物以后，就会用与其价值相等的货币向财政部交纳美洲的收入；全部业务的进行常常不必由美洲出口一盎司金银。

爱尔兰和美洲对大不列颠公债的清偿做出贡献，这是与公平正义相一致的。

爱尔兰和美洲对大不列颠公债的清偿做出贡献，这是与公平正义相一致的。这种公债是由于支持革命建立的政府而欠下的；正是由于这个政府，爱尔兰的新教徒现在不仅在自己国内享有全部权利，而且在自己的自由、自己的财产和自己的宗教的每一个方面都有保障；由于这个政府，美洲的一些殖民地得到了他们现在的特许证书，因而也就得到了他们的宪法；美洲的所有殖民地享有从来不曾有过的自由、安全和财产。这种公债的介入不仅是为了保卫大不列颠自己，而且也是为了保卫帝国的所有不同地区；尤其是最近战争中所借入的巨大债务，以及这次战争以前所借入的　大部分债务，可以说本来都是为了保卫美洲。

合并会使爱尔兰摆脱在宗教和政治偏见基础之上建立的压迫性贵族统治。

在和大不列颠合并以后，爱尔兰除了贸易自由之外，还会得到其他更重要的好处，足以补偿可能由于合并而使税负加重而有余。与英格兰合并以后，苏格兰的中、下层阶级的人民获得了完全摆脱了在过去总是使他们遭受贵族统治的压迫的权力。同大不列颠合并以后，爱尔兰所有阶层的人民也会获得一种从更具压迫性的贵族统治中得到的同样完全的解放；这种贵族统治不像苏

国民财富的性质与原理

distinctions of birth and fortune; but in the most odious of all distinctions, those of religious and political prejudices; distinctions which, more than any other, animate both the insolence of the oppressors and the hatred and indignation of the oppressed, and which commonly render the inhabitants of the same country more hostile to one another than those of different countries ever are. Without a union with Great Britain, the inhabitants of Ireland are not likely for many ages to consider themselves as one people.

The colonies would be delivered from rancorous factions which are likely to lead to bloodshed in case of separation from Great Britain.

No oppressive aristocracy has ever prevailed in the colonies. Even they, however, would, in point of happiness and tranquillity, gain considerably by a union with Great Britain. It would, at least, deliver them from those rancorous and virulent factions which are inseparable from small democracies, and which have so frequently divided the affections of their people, and disturbed the tranquillity of their governments, in their form so nearly democratical. In the case of a total separation from Great Britain, which, unless prevented by a union of this kind, seems very likely to take place, those factions would be ten times more virulent than ever. Before the commencement of the present disturbances, the coercive power of the mother-country had always been able to restrain those factions from breaking out into any thing worse than gross brutality and insult. If that coercive power were entirely taken away, they would probably soon break out into open violence and bloodshed. In all great countries which are united under one uniform government, the spirit of party commonly prevails less in the remote provinces than in the centre of the empire. The distance of those provinces from the capital, from the principal seat of the great scramble of faction and ambition, makes them enter less into the views of any of the contending parties, and renders them more indifferent and impartial spectators of the conduct of all. The spirit of party prevails less in Scotland than in England. In the case of a union it would probably prevail less in Ireland than in Scotland, and the colonies would probably soon enjoy a degree of concord and unanimity at present unknown in any part of the British empire. Both Ire-

格兰的那样,是建立在自然和受尊敬的出身和财富的差别的基础之上的,而是建立在所有差别中最可恶的一种即宗教和政治偏见的差别的基础之上的,这种差别比任何其他差别更能激起压迫者的粗暴无礼和被压迫者的憎恨和愤怒,一般会使得同一国家的居民比不同国家的居民更加彼此敌对。不与大不列颠合并,爱尔兰居民不可能在许多世纪中认为自己是同一国家的人民。

在美洲各个殖民地,从来没有盛行过压迫性的贵族统治。然而,即使是它们,从幸福和安定角度来说,也会从与大不列颠的合并中受益匪浅。这至少会使它们摆脱那种仇恨和恶毒的党派斗争,这种斗争是与那些小型的民主国家分不可开的,常常使它们人民的感情分裂,并扰乱它们政府(它们在形式上是接近民主的)的安定。在和大不列颠完全脱离时(如果不是通过这种合并的方式,否则似乎很有可能会发生脱离),这种党派斗争会变得比以前恶毒十倍以上。在现在的骚乱开始以前,母国的军事强制力量约束这种党派斗争,使之不致爆发成为比残忍和侮辱更加恶劣的事件。如果这种强制力量被完全取消,党派斗争或许不久就会爆发成公开的暴力行为和流血事件。在一个统一政府管辖之下联合起来的所有大国里,党派意识在边远省份比在帝国中心较少流行。这些省份与首都的距离、与发生党派和野心剧烈斗争的主要中心的距离,使它们较少卷入任何斗争党派的观点之中,使它们成为对所有各派的行为漠不关心和公正无私的袖手旁观者。党派意识在苏格兰就不像在英格兰那样流行。在合并以后,党派意识在爱尔兰或许就不像在苏格兰那样流行,而各个殖民地或许不久就会享受现时在不列颠帝国任何地区前所未闻的和谐和团结。当然,爱尔兰和各个殖民地的税收负担会比现在更重。可是,由

land and the colonies, indeed, would be subjected to heavier taxes than any which they at present pay. In consequence, however, of a diligent and faithful application of the public revenue towards the discharge of the national debt, the greater part of those taxes might not be of long continuance, and the public revenue of Great Britain might soon be reduced to what was necessary for maintaining a moderate peace establishment.

<small>East India with lighter taxes and less corrupt administration might yield an even larger addition of revenue.</small>

The territorial acquisitions of the East India company, the undoubted right of the crown, that is, of the state and people of Great Britain, might be rendered another source of revenue more abundant, perhaps, than all those already mentioned. Those countries are represented as more fertile, more extensive; and, in proportion to their extent, much richer and more populous than Great Britain. In order to draw a great revenue from them, it would not probably be necessary, to introduce any new system of taxation into countries which are already sufficiently and more than sufficiently taxed. It might, perhaps, be more proper to lighten, than to aggravate, the burden of those unfortunate countries, and to endeavour to draw a revenue from them, not by imposing new taxes, but by preventing the embezzlement and misapplication of the greater part of those which they already pay.

<small>If no such augmentation of revenue can be obtained Great Britain should reduce her expenses by ridding herself of the cost of the colonies in peace and war.</small>

If it should be found impracticable for Great Britain to draw any considerable augmentation of revenue from any of the resources above mentioned; the only resource which can remain to her is a diminution of her expence. In the mode of collecting, and in that of expending the public revenue; though in both there may be still room for improvement; Great Britain seems to be at least as economical as any of her neighbours. The military establishment which she maintains for her own defence in time of peace, is more moderate than that of any European state which can pretend to rival her either in wealth or in power. None of those articles, therefore, seem to admit of any considerable reduction of expence. The expence of the peace establishment of the colonies was, before the commencement of the present disturbances, very considerable, and is an expence which may, and if no revenue can be drawn from them, ought certainly to be saved altogether. This constant expence in time of peace, though very great, is insignificant in comparison with what the defence of the colonies has cost us in time of war. The last war, which was undertaken altogether on account of the colonies, cost Great Britain, it has already been observed, upwards of ninety millions. The Spanish war of 1739 was principally undertaken on their account; in which, and in the French war that was the consequence of it, Great Britain spent upwards of

于将公共收入勤勉地和踏实地用来偿还国债,大部分的税收不会长期课征下去,而大不列颠的公共收入不久就可能减少到一个为维持合适的和平建制所必需的水平。

东印度公司的领土取得,无疑的是属于国王的权利,也是属于大不列颠国家和人民的权利,这可能使另一种收入来源比所有上面已经提到的更为丰裕。这些国家被认为是更加肥沃、更加辽阔;按照它们的面积大小来说,可能比大不列颠更为富有和人口更加众多。为了从它们身上获取巨大的收入,不需要在课税已经充分或过分课税的国家再引入任何新的税收制度。大概更适当的办法,或许是减轻而不是加重这些遭受不幸的国家的税收负担,不是通过加征新税,而是通过防止大部分已经缴纳的税款被人中饱私囊和滥用的办法,去力图获得收入。

由于较轻的税收负担和较少的腐败管理,东印度可能提供相当大的税收增加额。

如果大不列颠不能够从任何上述资源中得到大幅增长的收入,那么给它留下的唯一办法是减少它的支出。在征收的方式上和公共收入的使用方式上,尽管似乎仍有改善的余地,但大不列颠至少似乎和它的任何邻国一样节约。它所维持的在和平时期保卫自己的军事建制,比在财富或力量方面可以和它匹敌的任何欧洲国家都要小。因此,在这些支出项目中似乎没有一种可以大幅削减。在这次骚乱开始以前,大不列颠对各个殖民地的和平时期的建制支出都很大,如果不能从它们身上获得收入的话,这种支出肯定应当完全取消。尽管这种和平时期的经常支出很大,但与我们在战争时期保卫殖民地的支出相比,都是微不足道的。上次战争完全是为了殖民地而进行的,上面已经提过,已经使大不列颠耗费 9000 万镑。在 1739 年的西班牙战争以及由它引起的法国战争中,大不列颠耗费了 4000 万镑,大部分应当公正地由各个

如果不能得到大幅的增加,大不列颠就应该通过取消在殖民地战争时期所花的支出的方式来减自己的开支。

— 2007 —

forty millions, a great part of which ought justly to be charged to the colonies. In those two wars the colonies cost Great Britain much more than double the sum which the national debt amounted to before the commencement of the first of them. Had it not been for those wars that debt might, and probably would by this time, have been completely paid; and had it not been for the colonies, the former of those wars might not, and the latter certainly would not have been undertaken. It was because the colonies were supposed to be provinces of the British empire, that this expence was laid out upon them. But countries which contribute neither revenue nor military force towards the support of the empire, cannot be considered as provinces. They may perhaps be considered as appendages, as a sort of splendid and showy equipage of the empire. But if the empire can no longer support the expence of keeping up this equipage, it ought certainly to lay it down; and if it cannot raise its revenue in proportion to its expence, it ought, at least, to accommodate its expence to its revenue. If the colonies, notwithstanding their refusal to submit to British taxes, are still to be considered as provinces of the British empire, their defence in some future war may cost Great Britain as great an expence as it ever has done in any former war. The rulers of Great Britain have, for more than a century past, amused the people with the imagination that they possessed a great empire on the west side of the Atlantic. This empire, however, has hitherto existed in imagination only. It has hitherto been, not an empire, but the project of an empire; not a gold mine, but the project of a gold mine; a project which has cost, which continues to cost, and which, if pursued in the same way as it has been hitherto, is likely to cost, immense expence, without being likely to bring any profit; for the effects of the monopoly of the colony trade, it has been shewn, are, to the great body of the people, mere loss instead of profit. It is surely now time that our rulers should either realize this golden dream, in which they have been indulging themselves, perhaps, as well as the people; or, that they should awake from it themselves, and endeavour to awaken the people. If the project cannot be completed, it ought to be given up. If any of the provinces of the British empire cannot be made to contribute towards the support of the whole empire, it is surely time that Great Britain

殖民地负担。在这两次战争中,大不列颠为殖民地花费的支出是前一次战争开始以前国债总额的两倍。如果不是由于这两次战争,那种国债到这个时候或许已经被完全还清;要不是为了殖民地,前一次战争可能不会进行,后一次战争肯定也不会进行。正是由于把各殖民地看作是不列颠帝国的省份,所以才为它们做了这项支出。但是,对维持帝国既没有贡献收入也没有贡献军力的那些国家,不可能被看作是帝国的省份,只能够看作是一个点缀,看作是帝国的一种华而不实的装饰物而已。但是如果帝国不再能应付维持这种装饰点缀的支出,它肯定应当将其放弃;如果它不能筹集到与其支出成比例的收入,它至少应当量入为出。如果殖民地依然拒绝向大不列颠纳税,却仍然被当作不列颠帝国的省份看待,在未来的防卫中,它们可能要使大不列颠负担和过去任何一次战争所负担的支出同样庞大。一个多世纪以来,大不列颠的统治者以在大西洋西岸拥有一个巨大帝国的想象来使人民感到快乐。可是,这个帝国迄今为止只存在于人们的想象之中。它迄今为止仍然不是一个帝国,而只是一个帝国的计划而已;不是一个金矿,而只是一个金矿的计划;这个计划已经耗费了巨额的开支,并继续在耗费巨额的开支,如果按迄今为止的方式继续实施下去,还可能要耗费巨大的开支,不可能有任何的利益;因为已经指出过,殖民地贸易垄断的结果,对人民大众只有损失而没有任何利益。现在肯定是到时候了,我们的统治者要么实现这个不仅是他们自己还有人民所一直沉迷的美梦,要么使自己从这个美梦中清醒过来,并力图使人民也清醒过来。如果计划不能完成,就应当将它放弃。如果不列颠帝国的任何省份不能对维持整个帝国做出贡献,大不列颠就应当免除自己在战争时期保卫这些省

should free herself from the expence of defending those provinces in time of war, and of supporting any part of their civil or military establishments in time of peace, and endeavour to accommodate her future views and designs to the real mediocrity of her circumstances.

份和在和平时期维持它们的民事或军事建制进行支出的义务,并力图使自己的未来观点和设计符合自己真实的平凡处境。

# APPENDIX

The two following Accounts are subjoined in order to illustrate and confirm what is said in the Fifth Chapter of the Fourth Book, concerning the Tonnage bounty to the White Herring Fishery. The Reader, I believe, may depend upon the accuracy of both Accounts.

*An Account of Busses fitted out in Scotland for Eleven Years, with the Number of Empty Barrels carried out, and the Number of Barrels of Herrings caught; also the Bounty at a Medium on each Barrel of Seasteeks, and on each Barrel when fully packed.*

| Years | Number of Busses | Empty Barrels carried out | Barrels of Herrings caught | Bounty paid on the Busses £. | s. | d. |
|---|---|---|---|---|---|---|
| 1771 | 29 | 5948 | 2832 | 2085 | 0 | 0 |
| 1772 | 168 | 41316 | 22237 | 11055 | 7 | 6 |
| 1773 | 190 | 42333 | 42055 | 12510 | 8 | 6 |
| 1774 | 248 | 59303 | 56365 | 16952 | 2 | 6 |
| 1775 | 275 | 69144 | 52879 | 19315 | 15 | 0 |
| 1776 | 294 | 76329 | 51863 | 21290 | 7 | 6 |
| 1777 | 240 | 62679 | 43313 | 17592 | 2 | 6 |
| 1778 | 220 | 56390 | 40958 | 16316 | 2 | 6 |
| 1779 | 206 | 55194 | 29367 | 15287 | 0 | 0 |
| 1780 | 181 | 48315 | 19885 | 13445 | 12 | 6 |
| 1781 | 135 | 33992 | 16593 | 9613 | 12 | 6 |
| Total, | 2186 | 550943 | 378347 | 155463 | 11 | 0 |

# 附　录

下面附录两个报告，用来说明和证实第四篇第五章有关白鲱渔业吨位奖金所阐述的内容。我相信读者可以信赖两个报告的正确性。

苏格兰11年中装备大渔船的报告，包括载出空桶数、捕获鲱鱼桶数，以及每桶海条平均奖金和每桶完全包装鲱鱼平均奖金。

| 年代 | 大渔船数 | 载出空桶数 | 捕获鲱鱼的桶数 | 付给每一个渔船的奖金 | | |
|---|---|---|---|---|---|---|
| | | | | 镑 | 先令 | 便士 |
| 1771 | 29 | 5948 | 2832 | 2085 | 0 | 0 |
| 1772 | 168 | 41316 | 22237 | 11055 | 7 | 6 |
| 1773 | 190 | 42333 | 42055 | 12510 | 8 | 6 |
| 1774 | 248 | 59303 | 56365 | 16952 | 2 | 6 |
| 1775 | 275 | 69144 | 52879 | 19315 | 15 | 0 |
| 1776 | 294 | 62679 | 43313 | 17592 | 2 | 6 |
| 1777 | 240 | 76329 | 51863 | 21290 | 7 | 6 |
| 1778 | 220 | 56390 | 40958 | 16316 | 2 | 6 |
| 1779 | 206 | 55194 | 29367 | 15287 | 0 | 0 |
| 1780 | 181 | 48315 | 19885 | 13445 | 12 | 6 |
| 1781 | 135 | 33992 | 16593 | 9613 | 12 | 6 |
| 共计 | 2186 | 550943 | 378347 | 155463 | 11 | 0 |

| | | |
|---|---|---|
| Seasteeks | 378347 | Bounty at a medium for each barrel of seasteeks, . . . . . £ . 0 8 2 $\frac{1}{4}$ |
| $\frac{1}{3}$ deducted | 126115 $\frac{2}{3}$ | But a barrel of seasteeks being only reckoned two-thirds of a barrel fully packed, one-third is deducted, which brings the bounty to . £ . 0 12 3 $\frac{3}{4}$ |
| Barrels full packed, | 252231 $\frac{1}{3}$ | |

Brought over—£ . 0 12 3 $\frac{3}{4}$

And if the herrings are exported, there is besides a premium of . . . . . . . . . . . . 0 2 8

So that the bounty paid by Government in money for each barrel, is . . . . . . . . . £ . 0 14 11 $\frac{3}{4}$

But if to this, the duty of the salt usually taken credit for as expended in curing each barrel, which at a medium is of foreign, one bushel and one-fourth of a bushel, at 10 s. a bushel, be added, viz. . . 0 12 6

The bounty on each barrel would amount to . £ . 1 7 5 $\frac{3}{4}$

If the herrings are cured with British salt, it will stand thus, viz. Bounty as before. . . . £ . 0 14 11 $\frac{3}{4}$

—but if to this bounty the duty on two bushels of Scots salt at 1 s. 6 d. per bushel, supposed to be the quantity at a medium used in curing each barrel is added, to wit, . . . . . . . . . . . . . . 0 3 0

The bounty on each barrel will amount to And,

£ . 0 17 11 $\frac{3}{4}$

When buss herrings are entered for home consumption in Scotland, and pay the shilling a barrel of duty, the bounty stands thus, to wit as before . £ . 0 12 3 $\frac{3}{4}$

From which the 1 s. a barrel is to be deducted. . 0 1 0

0 11 3 $\frac{3}{4}$

| | | | 镑 | 先令 | 便士 |
|---|---|---|---|---|---|
| 海条 378247 | 每桶海条的平均奖金 | | | | |
| | 但每桶海条仅仅计算了 2/3 桶完全包装鲱鱼，应该减去 1/3 桶 | | 0 | 8 | $2\frac{1}{4}$ |
| 扣减 1/3  126115 $\frac{2}{3}$ | 使奖金为 | | 0 | 12 | $3\frac{3}{4}$ |
| 完全包装的桶数 252231 $\frac{1}{3}$ | | | | | |
| 如果鲱鱼出口,另有奖金为 | | | 0 | 2 | 8 |
| 因此政府用货币支付给每桶的奖金为 | | | 0 | 14 | $11\frac{3}{4}$ |
| 但如加上腌制用的盐免税,每桶平均用外国盐 1.25 蒲式耳,每蒲式耳课税 10 先令 | | | 0 | 12 | 6 |
| 每桶奖金共计为 | | | 1 | 7 | $5\frac{3}{4}$ |
| 如果鲱鱼用不列颠盐腌制,奖金为 | | | 0 | 14 | $11\frac{3}{4}$ |
| 但如加上平均每桶用 2 蒲式耳苏格兰盐腌制免征的每蒲式耳 1 先令 6 便士的税 | | | 0 | 3 | 0 |
| 每桶奖金等于 | | | 0 | 17 | $11\frac{3}{4}$ |
| 当鲱鱼为供给苏格兰国内消费时,支付每桶 1 先令的税,奖金原来为 | | | 0 | 12 | $3\frac{3}{4}$ |
| 减每桶 1 先令 | | | 0 | 1 | 0 |
| | | | 0 | 11 | $3\frac{3}{4}$ |

But to that there is to be added again, the duty of the foreign salt used in curing a barrel of herrings, viz. . 　0　12　6

So that the premium allowed for each barrel of herrings entered for home consumption is. . 　£. 1　3　$9\frac{3}{4}$

If the herrings are cured with British salt, it will stand as follows, viz.

Bounty on each harrel brought in by the busses as above . . . . . . . . . . . £. 0　12　$3\frac{3}{4}$

From which deduct the 1 s. a barrel paid at the time they are entered for home consumption . . . . 　0　1　0

£. 0　11　$3\frac{3}{4}$

But if to the bounty the duty on two bushels of Scots salt at 1s. 6 d. per bushel, supposed to be the quantity at a medium used in curing each barrel, is added, to wit, . . . . . . . . . . . 　0　3　0

The premium for each barrel entered for home consumption will be . . . . . . . 　£. 0　14　$3\frac{3}{4}$

Though the loss of duties upon herrings exported cannot, perhaps, properly be considered as bounty; that upon herrings entered for home consumption certainly may.

An Account of the Quantity of Foreign Salt imported into Scotland, and of Scots Salt delivered Duty free, from the Works there for the Fishery, from the 5th of April 1771 to the 5th of April 1782, with a Medium of both for one Year.

| PERIOD. | Foreign Salt imported. Bushels. | Scots Salt delivered from the Works. Bushels. |
|---|---|---|
| From the 5th of April 1771, to the 5th of April 1782. | 936974 | 168226 |
| Medium for one Year | $85179\frac{5}{11}$ | $15293\frac{3}{11}$ |

It is to be observed that the Bushel of Foreign Salt weighs 84 lb. that oif British Salt 56 lb. only.

| | | | |
|---|---|---|---|
| 但仍须加上用外国盐每桶免征税 | 0 | 12 | 6 |
| 供国内消费的每桶鲱鱼的奖金为 | 1 | 3 | $9\frac{3}{4}$ |
| 如果鲱鱼用不列颠盐腌制 | 0 | 12 | $3\frac{3}{4}$ |
| 大渔船捕获鲱鱼每桶奖金 | 0 | 1 | 0 |
| 减去供应国内消费时每桶所付 1 先令 | 0 | 11 | $3\frac{3}{4}$ |
| 但如加上平均每桶用 2 蒲式耳苏格兰盐腌制免征的每蒲式耳 1 先令 6 便士的税 | 0 | 3 | 0 |
| 国内消费的每桶鲱鱼的奖金为 | 0 | 14 | $3\frac{3}{4}$ |

虽然出口鲱鱼的税收损失或许不能看作是奖金,但国内消费鲱鱼的税收损失则肯定可以看作是奖金。

从 1771 年 4 月 5 日至 1782 年 4 月 5 日苏格兰进口外国盐和从盐厂免税交付鲱渔业的苏格兰盐数量的报告。

| 时期 | 进口外国盐 | 从盐厂交付的苏格兰盐 |
|---|---|---|
| | 蒲式耳 | 蒲式耳 |
| 从 1771 年 4 月 5 日至 1782 年 4 月 5 日 | 936974 | 168226 |
| 各年平均 | $85179\frac{5}{11}$ | $15293\frac{11}{3}$ |

应注意的是,外国盐每蒲式耳重 84 磅,不列颠盐只重 56 磅。

# 译者后记

亚当·斯密(1723~1790)，出生于英国的苏格兰，青年时期就读于牛津大学，后在格拉斯哥大学任教，哲学教授。

亚当·斯密是古典政治经济学的集大成者，是伟大的资产阶级思想家，他探索了资本主义生产发展的规律，达到了他那个时代人类认识的高峰，对于资本主义的发展和人类社会的进步给予了极大的推动力。

研究经济学的人都熟悉亚当·斯密，而他的《国民财富的性质与原理》(又名《国富论》)更是经济学经典中的经典，人们一提起《国富论》，就会想到"看不见的手"(invisible hand)，认为"看不见的手"是斯密《国富论》的理论精髓。

斯密认为，每个人都应利用好自己的资本，使之产生最大的价值。从主观上讲，这个人并不想增进公共福利，更不知道他实际上增加了多少公共福利，他所追求的仅仅是个人的利益所得。但他这样做的时候，有一只看不见的手在引导着他去帮助实现增进社会福利的目标，而这种目标并非是他本意想追求的东西。通过追求个人利益，却无意识地增进了社会利益，其效果比真的想促进社会利益时所得到的效果要好。斯密之所以提出了这一论断，认为人们都有"利己心"，是"利己心"驱使着人们去获得最大利益,每个人都得到了利益,那么社会也就得到了,因为财富是所有国民对必需品和享用品的消费。这就是斯密"看不见的手"的实质。

《国富论》是斯密在结束了对法国的考察后于 1776 年完成的。当时英国正出于产业革命的前夜,18 世纪的启蒙运动正在抬头,要求推翻封建专制、进行理性主义反抗的呼声越来越高,平民阶级对中世纪的特权阶级、豪门贵族、大地主进行顽强的抵制和反抗。斯密对当时的社会现象进行了深刻的思考,深深地同情广大劳动人民的苦难状况。他认为社会的贫富差距和分配不公是由于经济活动中的不自由产生的,这种不自由是对中下等阶层而言,而官僚地主和行业主却享受着为所欲为的自由,他们束缚劳动人民从事经济活动的自由,限制劳动人民获得经济利益的权力,而他们自己却疯狂掠取劳动人民的劳动所得。在我们具体翻译过程中,可以知道他对欧洲各国的经济、社会、政治以及宗教状况的考察是十分必要的。这对我们从事经济学研究的人们是一个重要启示。

亚当·斯密还是劳动价值论的开创者,对后来马克思的劳动价值理论产生重大影响。他的劳动分工理论仍然是当前新兴古典政治经济学研究的课题。

他另一本著名《道德情操论》于 1759 年出版,早于《国富论》问世。自己在《道德情感论》第六版的说明中,也提出要写一系列的著作,说明法律和政治的一般原理,不仅涉及正义,而且涉及警察、国家、税收、军备以及其他任何成为法律对象的东西。因此,我们说,《国富论》研究的不仅是经济问题,更是经济活动中的道德和法律问题。我们不能孤立地把《国富论》仅仅看作一本经济学著作。

在翻译过程中,我们尽量把原文作者的本意和当今学术含义衔接起来,可能这个目标不容易达到,但我们已经尽我们最大的力量和潜能。我们在翻译中也参考了商务印书馆郭大力、王亚南前辈和陕西人民出版社杨敬年前辈的《国富论》译本,他们的译作各有特色,均对我们该版中译本产生了一定的积极作用和借鉴意义。在此我们表示衷心的感谢。

赵东旭

2006 年 12 月 15 日